CW01374045

The Chemical Brothers
Paused in Cosmic Reflection

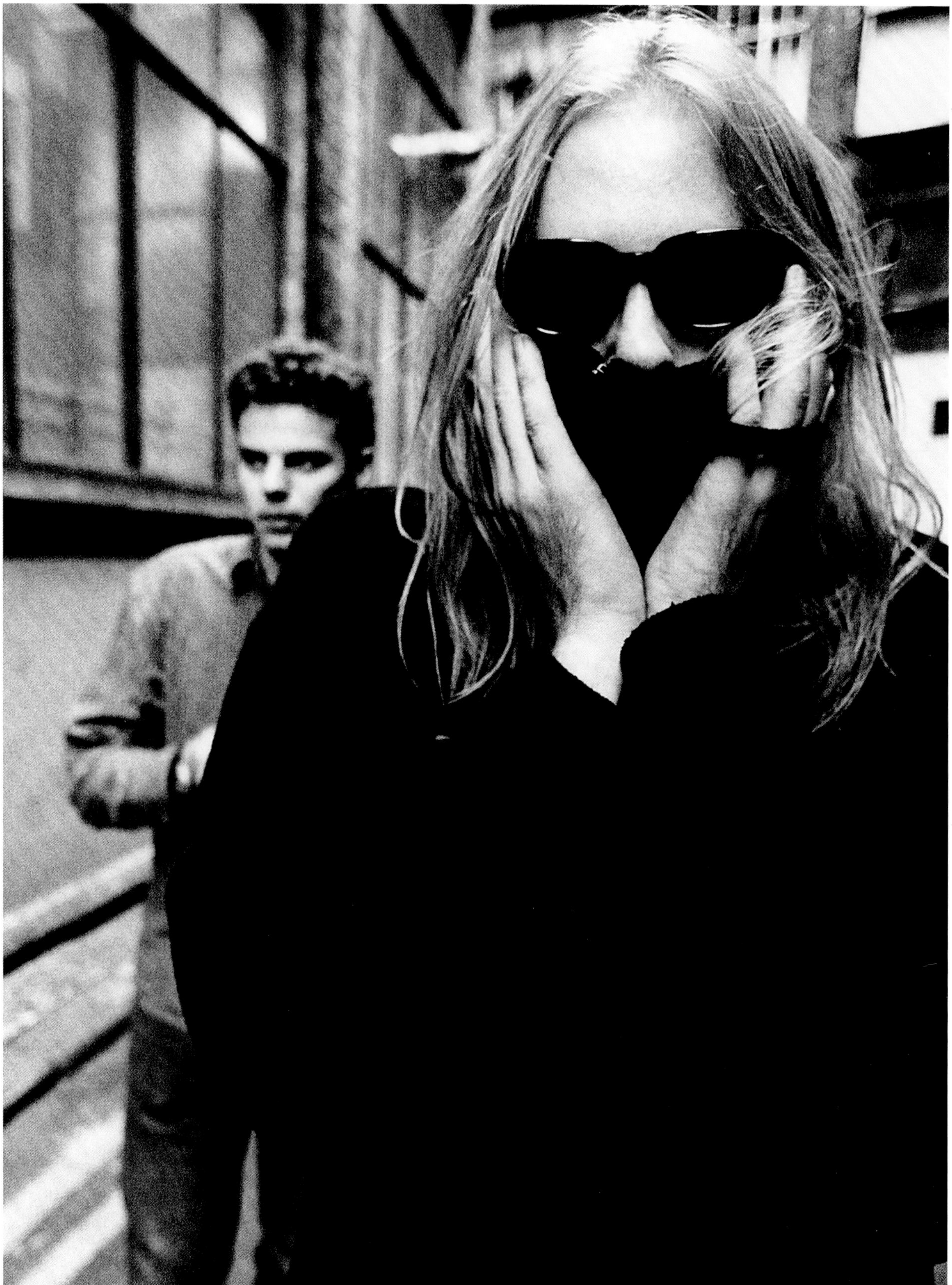

The Chemical Brothers

Paused in Cosmic Reflection
The Chemical Brothers with Robin Turner

WHITE RABBIT

*This book is dedicated to the memory of
Stuart 'Jammer' James, 1952–2015.
'Clear the dressing room please,
ladies and gentlemen . . .'*

First published in Great Britain in 2023 by White Rabbit,
an imprint of The Orion Publishing Group Ltd
Carmelite House, 50 Victoria Embankment
London EC4Y 0DZ

An Hachette UK Company

1 3 5 7 9 10 8 6 4 2

Copyright © Tom Rowlands, Ed Simons and Robin Turner 2023

The moral right of Tom Rowlands, Ed Simons and Robin Turner
to be identified jointly as the authors of this work has been asserted
in accordance with the Copyright, Designs and Patents Act of 1988.

All rights reserved. No part of this publication may be
reproduced, stored in a retrieval system, or transmitted
in any form or by any means, electronic, mechanical,
photocopying, recording, or otherwise, without the
prior permission of both the copyright owner and the
above publisher of this book.

A CIP catalogue record for this book is
available from the British Library.

ISBN (Hardback) 978 1 3996 0007 1
ISBN (eBook) 978 1 3996 0009 5
ISBN (Audio) 978 1 3996 0010 1

Front cover artwork by Kate Gibb
Band photograph by Khali Ackford
Origination by DL Imaging, UK
Printed in China by C&C Offset Printing Co. Ltd

MIX
Paper | Supporting
responsible forestry
FSC
www.fsc.org FSC® C104740

www.whiterabbitbooks.co.uk
www.orionbooks.co.uk

Contents

Another World: Entering Planet Dust	9
Where Do We Begin	17
Playground for a Wedgeless Firm: Manchester and Becoming The Dust Brothers	24
Song to the Siren	43
Life Is Sweet: DJing as The Dust Brothers	50
Live at Sabresonic Nightclub (and Other Stories)	59
Alive Alone	93
Setting Sun	104
It Doesn't Matter	117
Dig Your Own Hole	129
The Private Psychedelic Reel	140
Hey Boy Hey Girl	153
Surrender	163
Out of Control	173
Got Glint: DJing as The Chemical Brothers	191
Star Guitar	199
The Golden Path	207
Galvanize	215
The Salmon Dance	224
Further	231
Don't Think	247
Hanna	257
Wide Open	261
Got to Keep On	273
Eve of Destruction	281
We've Got to Try	291
No Geography	297
A Modern Midnight Conversation	305
For That Beautiful Feeling	311
UK Discography	325
Endnotes and Credits	330

Contributors

Adam Smith (one half of Vegetable Vision; Flat Nose George; video director: 'Galvanize'; film director: *Don't Think*; one half of Smith & Lyall)
Alex Nightingale (The Chemical Brothers' live agent)
Ailsa Robertson (The Chemical Brothers' video commissioner)
Aurora (vocal collaborator on *No Geography* album)
Beck Hansen (voice: 'Wide Open', 'Skipping Like a Stone')
Bernard Sumner (voice: 'Out of Control'; New Order; co-owner of The Haçienda)
Beth Orton (voice: 'Alive Alone', 'Where Do I Begin', 'The State We're In')
Chris York (long time Chemical Brothers promoter at SJM Concerts)
Dom & Nic (video directors: 'Setting Sun', 'Block Rockin' Beats', 'Hey Boy Hey Girl', 'The Test', 'Believe', 'Midnight Madness', 'The Salmon Dance', 'Wide Open', 'Free Yourself', 'Live Again')
Ed Simons (The Chemical Brothers)
Emma Warren (university friend; author)
Erol Alkan (DJ/producer)
Errol Kolosine (radio promotions, then general manager at Astralwerks, co-manager of The Chemical Brothers for the Americas)
Fatlip (voice: 'The Salmon Dance')
James Holroyd (university friend; The Chemical Brothers' tour DJ)
John Burgess (university friend; editor: *Jockey Slut*; promoter at Bugged Out!)
Jonathan Donahue (Mercury Rev; additional instrumentation: 'The Private Psychedelic Reel')
Justin Robertson (DJ/producer)
Kate Gibb (*Surrender, Come with Us, We Are the Night,* artwork artist)
Mia Hill (aka Whirlygirl, long-time Chemical Brothers fan)
Michael Brownstein (voice: 'No Geography'; author of *Let's Burn the Flags of All Nations*)
Michel Gondry (video director: 'Let Forever Be', 'Star Guitar', 'Go', 'Got to Keep On')
Nathan Thursting (aka Nathan Detroit, Glint promoter; DJ; The Chemical Brothers' DJ tour manager)
Ninian Doff (video director: 'We've Got to Try', 'Sometimes I Feel So Deserted')
Noel Gallagher (voice: 'Setting Sun', 'Let Forever Be')
Nick Dewey (The Chemical Brothers' manager)
Nick Dutfield (university friend)
Richard Young (photographer: '*Jesus' Amongst Fans, Olympia Music Festival, London, 1976*)
Robert Linney (The Chemical Brothers' manager)
Stephanie Dosen (voice: *Further*)
Steve Dub (aka Steve Jones aka Dubby, long-time studio engineer)
Steven Hall (founder: Junior Boy's Own)
Tim Burgess (voice: 'Life Is Sweet', 'The Boxer')
Tom Rowlands (The Chemical Brothers)
Vanessa Rowlands (club promotion/A&R at Deconstruction Records; Tom's wife)
Wayne Coyne (voice: 'The Golden Path')
WIZ (video director: 'Out of Control')

Paused in Cosmic Reflection   7

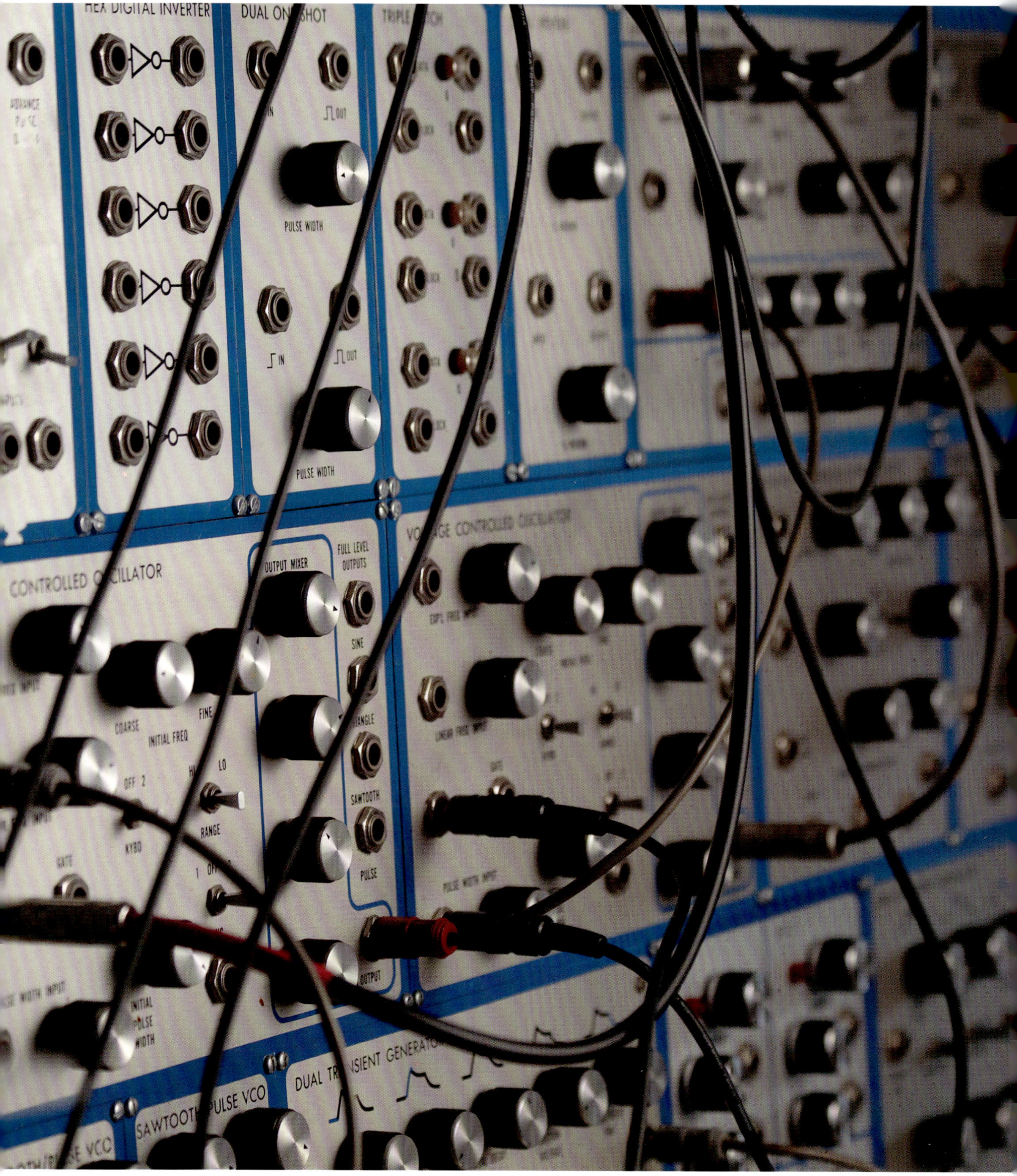
HEX DIGITAL INVERTER
PULSE WIDTH
PULSE WIDTH
OUTPUT MIXER
FULL LEVEL OUTPUTS
SINE
SAWTOOTH
PULSE
OUTPUT
COARSE
INITIAL FREQ
FINE
RANGE
GATE
KYBD
INITIAL PULSE WIDTH
SAWTOOTH
PULSE VCO

Another World: Entering Planet Dust

Somewhere in the south of England, almost as far south as you can go, there's a sacred space that's hidden from view.

It's not a public building and its location won't turn up on any map. You won't stumble across it if you veer off-path as a cycle lane disappears or your frantic dog pulls at its lead, driven half-wild by almost imperceptible sound drifting across woodland. This place was built to not be found.

But let's assume that this introduction was your invite and you're now standing outside a small outbuilding sat at the end of a gravel path, a path that offers the same kind of reassuring crunch that ground frost gives in deep winter.

The building is humble from the outside, as places of spiritual significance often are. Its outward appearance belies its internal workings. Creepers obscure bricks, a touch of condensation opaques the windows. And a soft, warm glow of electric light bleeds out, pulsing like a robot heartbeat.

Nothing outside points to what goes on inside. There's nothing to tell you that this is a private temple built with the express purpose of channelling higher powers. A lightning rod designed to capture mechanical magic.

Open the door, cross the threshold. Step into the heart of the machine.

The first thing you notice is that inside, the air is different. Electrically charged and almost tactile, it seems to visibly ripple, sound waves altering the atmosphere around you. It's like walking through kinetic energy.

There are two rooms, each with very limited floorspace. Where there should be walls, there are banks of synthesisers that climb one on top of the other, towering and arching above head height. Some are modern and glisten with a twenty-first-century sheen. Many are not; their vintage is unknown. Built in Japan, Germany, America, India, Britain, this is a veritable United Nations of analogue equipment. Each separate machine is loaded with untold stories from its previous life, flecked with specks of dust from long since forgotten histories.

Between the countless switches, knobs and dials, 10,000 lights alternate in red, green, blue, white and yellow. Each dances to its own internal rhythm. Tumbling across it all, a rainbow of rubber-coated copper wires dangles like vines across stark, clean silver. There are screens blinking information, levers and pulleys, dials, switches and flying faders and the occasional label. Dual voltage. Triple morphing. Time and triggers.

Although it may appear chaotic, this space has been carefully built to a masterplan, precision constructed by an unseen hand that has painstakingly positioned each separate piece in order to best capture oscillations from the sentient studio brain and net all the friction that happens right between the speakers. Each blinking light is a pulsar, each lead a synapse accurately placed to forge a connection between rational daytime ideas and the kind of spiralling madness that occurs after dark.

Maybe it's worth explaining what this place is.

Rowlands Audio Research is home to the steady heartbeat of The Chemical Brothers. Their music grows here, from formative ideas picked out on guitar or keyboard to final mixes that flow through the desk like jet planes roaring off the runway. Every song is birthed in these rooms before it lifts upwards to defy gravity or drills down towards the core of the earth in pursuit of deeper bass tones. Every alteration and pitch shift happens here, each tweak and mutation. This is where the echoes are born.

Although The Chemical Brothers' studio is set deep within the rolling green of the south coast, there is no sense that the bucolic surroundings affect the alchemy that goes on within its walls. The sounds that emanate from here – both the raw and the refined – are more synonymous with the city or even outer space than they are of a band getting it together in the country. They tap the deep nocturnal psychedelia of the dance floor, places where time stops, folding and bending reality as the music takes control. And they tap the small hours, those holy moments where a pinprick of light on the horizon becomes an overwhelming symbol of renewal and hope to a fragile mind.

I first met Tom Rowlands and Ed Simons in January 1994. They had walked into the office I'd just started working in. I was learning the ropes in the Heavenly press office, filling envelopes and hitting the phones selling everything from Essex techno to acid jazz to deep-fried Scottish rock 'n' roll. Really, we'd both just started there.

Although mainly known as a record label, Heavenly looked after the PR and management for plenty of out-of-house artists. Tom and Ed – then known as The Dust Brothers – had just joined the company's management roster, joining the already legendary Andrew Weatherall and then up-and-coming Belfast DJ David Holmes.

I knew a little about them, having bought their first single – 'Song to the Siren' – on a Junior Boy's Own 12-inch. Initially curious that it might be a release by the Paul's Boutique producers of the same name, I quickly became mesmerised by a full-force pile-driver of a record that was built around a heavy drum loop, a low throb of bass and a vocal loop that couldn't have been described in the song's title more aptly. It was the woozy sound of enchantment, giving off the distinct feeling that it might end up leaving you adrift on a dance floor before wrecking you against the speakers.

Stood in the corner of the office, it was impossible not to be struck by their look. Tom could have passed for a blond Ramone, hair plummeting straight down towards the floor; Ed was like an outtake from the *Check Your Head* cover brought to life, half-obscured under an oversized beanie. Every other sentence of his was punctuated by an infectious Muttley laugh. A cartoon blur of punk rock and hip hop channelling two generations of CBGBs; equal parts Grand Royal and Royal Trux. For a pair of up-and-coming DJs, they were pointedly unlike anyone else in their field.

Conversation led to invitation and later that week I found myself heading out to hear them DJ at The Job Club, a chaotic Friday night musical scramble at Gossips. Gossips was one of Soho's classic dive bars – a dingy claustrophobic basement with a ceiling low enough to do proper damage to your head if you elevated from the floor by more than a few inches. That fact would prove problematic during Tom and Ed's set.

Although they were playing the kind of early shift usually reserved for cleaners and bar staff, they had brought a crew of friends who were already at heroic, animalistic, end-of-the-night levels of inebriation. The foundation stones of Tom and Ed's set were low-slung grooves that built up into a degenerate, incessant funk. Thunderous basslines were received like anthems by their friends, who would each take it in turns to shin up the

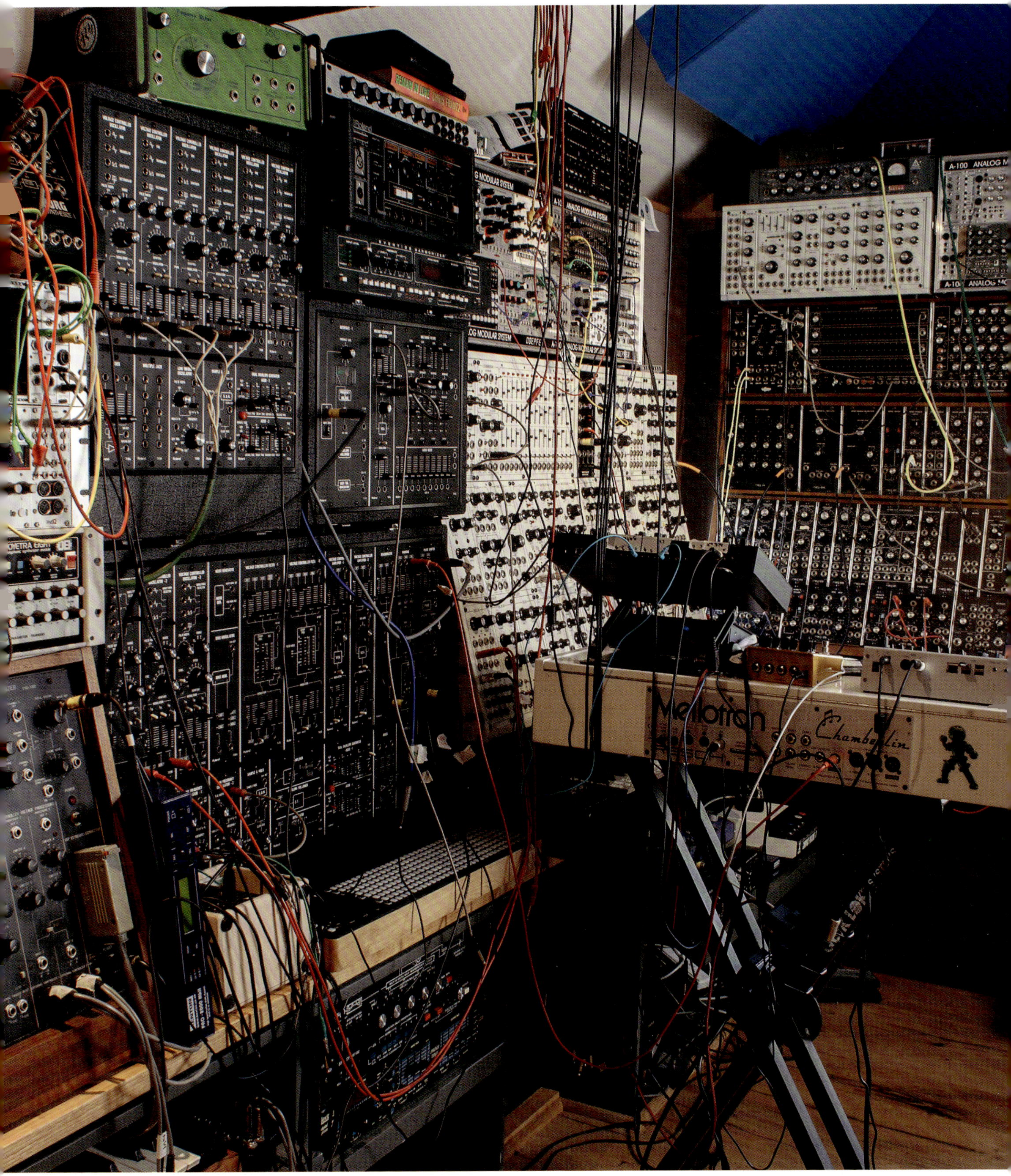
Mellotron

power surge of My Bloody Valentine and the constant chug that the bonus beats and instrumentals on side 2 of the latest US import 12-inches had. The results felt genuinely indestructible, like they were somehow reinforced to make them tougher than any other record around it, concrete slabs of brutalist sound pressed onto vinyl.

Back then, there were no banks of synthesisers with infinite blinking lights. There was a dual tape deck Hitachi stereo system in Tom's bedroom at his parents' house – a space called the Dust Bowl – where tracks were painstakingly bounced down to form pure, primal audio.

Although their DJ sets were taking place early doors or in the backrooms of big clubs while superstar DJs went through the motions on the main floor, The Dust Brothers sound was already in place. It had been defined by several years living in shared accommodation in Manchester. That city's clubs and record shops helped Tom and Ed to form their unified vision of what constituted their perfect club record. Initially, their own tracks were the jigsaw pieces that would fill perceived gaps in their DJ sets at their residency at the Naked Under Leather club night at the Old Steam Brewery on Oxford Road in Manchester's student district.

Within a year of me first meeting them, everything had changed. A chain of events was set off by a series of well-chosen remixes for like-minded artists (Primal Scream, Saint Etienne, The Charlatans and that Manic Street Preachers song about the quadriplegic war vet): two EPs that confidently laid the foundation stones for the future of the group; tentative steps into the global live arena; a headline DJ residency in the basement of a small London pub where many of those who'd inspired Tom and Ed in the first place queued up to play support to them and a necessary change of name. At the year's end, the music press knew who they were and major labels were forming a queue for their signatures.

When Tom and Ed's first album, *Exit Planet Dust*, was released in June 1995, I was naively pitching their vast sound to the UK press as 'The Prodigy meets Motörhead'. While there may have been a grain of truth in that primitive descriptor (it's quoted back as accurate in a front-cover piece for the first issue of *Muzik* magazine), it fails to take in any of the nuance in their music that was explored on that record.

Listen to *Exit Planet Dust* tracks 'One Too Many Mornings' – where time seems to warp and stretch like elastic – or 'Alive Alone' – where a young Beth Orton puts voice to the fragile, fragmented moment when you step out of a club into the bright morning light. There's a sound and a soul there that would give the record longevity and separate The Chemical Brothers from their contemporaries. Those tracks reflected and reframed aspects of the duo's musical upbringing (nodding to formative records on labels like 4AD, Creation, Studio One and Def Jam) and their desire and drive to fuse seemingly disparate elements together into beautiful new shapes. And they pointed to how the future would sound.

Years later, stood in the crowd at a sold-out Chemical Brothers show in Leeds – or London, Livorno or at the Latitude Festival, take your pick – there was a collective gasp as everyone around seemed to lose their breath for a second as a gorgeous, endless murmuration of digital birds arced out across the width of the stage. The soundtrack was a beatless version of 2015's 'Wide Open', where Beck Hansen sings of a love that's gradually slipping through his fingers. His voice floats above synths that swell and burst speaker stacks before diving off, hoping someone would catch them. Over in a dark corner, someone poured amyl nitrate over themselves and set a match to it, creating a moment of genuine pyrotechnic derangement. Back outside, the pubs hadn't yet kicked out.

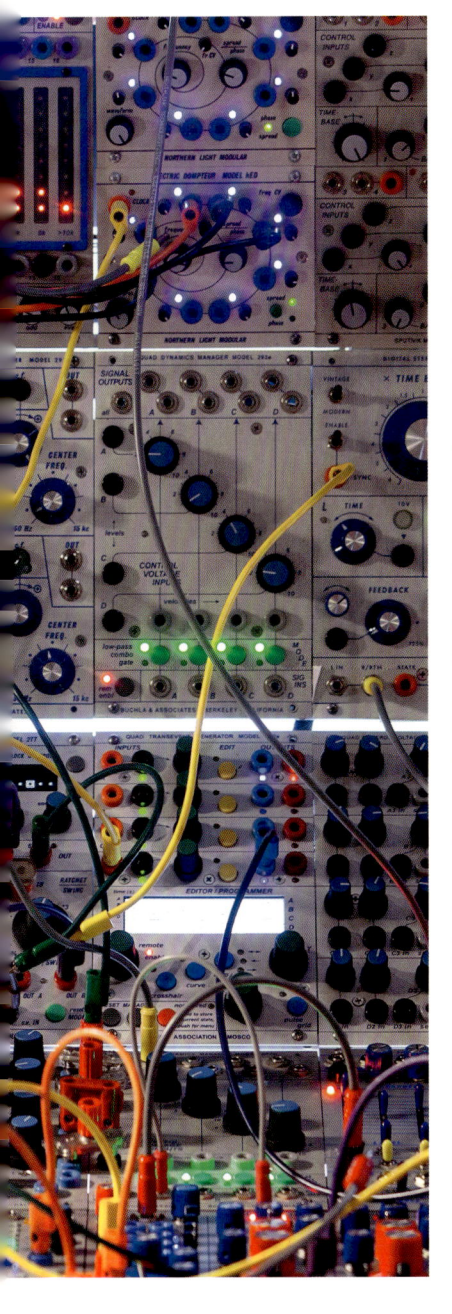

The world Tom and Ed created in that basement was pure, brilliant chaos. The dance floor was a maelstrom of intertwined bodies and the sound system rumbled along with motoring bass, hip-hop breaks, techno rhythm tracks and eventually Manic Street Preachers' 'La Tristesse Durera' – a song about a quadriplegic war veteran that hits the rare sweet spot between bracingly melancholic and ecstatic. Hearing it in this context, among Tom and Ed's community, it was a hands-in-the-air celebration that offered only unparalleled joy to a frenzied crowd. One night in a basement surrounded by maniacs made it very clear that The Dust Brothers weren't like anything else around.

Half a decade on from the Summer of Love, Britain's club culture had fractured. The unifying lysergic haze of acid house had dissipated, taking with it the egalitarian spirit it had inspired across clubland. In its place, multiple different pathways appeared, allowing tribes to separate. While house music was getting glammed up and elevating its core DJs to celebrity status, techno was becoming darker and harder.

The Dust Brothers created their own unique space in the gap that began to open up between those scenes. That debut – 'Song to the Siren' – and the handful of remixes they'd undertaken at that point weren't house or techno or rave, and they weren't rock or hip hop, yet they took aspects of each of those styles and forced them together into mini-symphonies where squalling electronics and dub basslines mixed with the gliding

Photos taken in Rowlands Audio Research, November 2022.

Paused in Cosmic Reflection 13

all around like solar flares. The emotional punch was almost overwhelming, coming after an hour when your senses have been through a spin cycle.

Those moments – those differences – are a large part of why the band are here, playing gigs at this scale three decades on, and why so many of their contemporaries have faded out. Whether cueing records in a basement club just below Wardour Street or manipulating pure electronic sound in a studio hidden in the English countryside, The Chemical Brothers' ambition has always been the same. It is to create a musical environment that overloads you and rewires your senses in the process.

Whether you're experiencing that all-round freakout while lost in the barrage of volume in a crowd as the earth shakes beneath your feet or alone, paused in cosmic reflection, in communion with the sound itself, is up to you. All routes are valid to get to the destination.

―――

Although The Chemical Brothers story is primarily that of Tom Rowlands and Ed Simons, it involves many more voices than just those of the two friends who work together under that name. It's a story that takes in musicians and madmen, visual designers and video directors, poets and promoters, DJs and dancers. It jumps from studio to stage, where gigs in sweatbox clubs quickly evolve into festival appearances (including an unprecedented six headline slots on one of the two main stages at Glastonbury) and packed-out arenas the world over. It involves meeting your heroes and harnessing the power of your peers. And it involves those music machines – strange instruments built by visionaries who may never have known that their creations would end up bending the minds of later generations on a nightly basis.

If we head back into the present, back inside Rowlands Audio Research, there's music being made. Let's not get in the way of this process; maybe this is a good time to explore the corners of the room. Everything has been kept; there's history in every box of old photographs and fliers, every well-worn record sleeve. The studio is part museum, part gallery space, a living history curated by the band as pieces are added and objects take root over time.

This book is a journey through that rich history. So, come with us.

SPECIAL LIVE P.A. featuring

A-TOM ~~ORBITAL~~

Featuring:
<u>Vinyl Masters:</u> Paul Saunders   James Murrey
<u>P.Zone:</u> Mark,   Nickey   &   Wayne
Tot "Marlow"   Quan
Queens   Simon Paul   Henerys
House Quake   &   Nostalgia
Warm up: Chris, Russel "Masters"

Sovereign Snooker Club
Totteridge Road
("Above Railway station")
High Wycombe, Bucks

Friday 30th March, 1990
9pm till 2 am
Arrive early

Admission £4.00 with this card

No re-admission
Enquiries on (0860) 240565

16   The Chemical Brothers

Where Do We Begin

Tom Rowlands was born on 11 January 1971 in Kingston upon Thames.

I used to religiously read the *NME* and *Melody Maker* when I was a teenager. So much music came to me through those papers. The late eighties were such a pivotal time for hip hop, and the way they wrote about the scene made a massive impression on me. One of the first big gigs I went to was Public Enemy at Hammersmith Odeon in 1987, which was a Def Jam showcase with Eric B. and LL Cool J. The Public Enemy track 'Miuzi Weighs a Ton' was seismic. I'd picked up a cheap drum machine by then and would try and copy their beats, the same with Eric B. & Rakim's *Paid in Full* album. When they came to London, I had to go. It was an incredible night, even though the tube carriage I was in on the way home got steamed.

The first bands I really loved were Madness and The Specials. They were huge when I was ten, eleven years old. There would be youth club discos where everyone did Nutty Boy dances. As that scene faded, early synth pop music took over and I became hooked on bands like Heaven 17, Alphaville and Depeche Mode. My next-door neighbour was a big Mode head and had a Roland SH101 keyboard that was an incredible, futuristic thing to play around on. Later, I went through a goth phase. The Sisters of Mercy's early EPs *Alice* and *Temple of Love* had such a strange, claustrophobic sound. I loved the relentlessness of how they programmed the drums. In their own ways, each of those genres made a huge impression on me – the sense of community at the discos and a fascination with music made by machines.

I grew up near Henley, just to the west of London. My parents (a director of photography dad and a mum who looked after me and my older brother, Huw) placed a lot of importance on learning music, and I had piano and guitar lessons from an early age. My guitar teacher had a big effect on me. He didn't care about scales; he just wanted me to be able to play things I liked. I'd come to our lessons with things I had heard on TV, things like the theme from *M*A*S*H*, 'The Windmills of Your Mind' and the James Bond theme. It was an amazingly effective approach from a cool primary school teacher.

By the time I was at secondary school, there were lots of people making music – lunchtime bands with some amazing musicians in. Indie music was big, though my real musical obsession was New Order. To this day, their *Everything's Gone Green* EP is probably my perfect record. I loved owning the 12-inch and saw it almost as a sacred object. Their music was so impactful. I loved how everybody in the band had such a clear, identifiable style that you could follow through the records.

Meanwhile, it was getting easier for people to get signed to a label or put their own records out. There was a lot going on in Reading, the nearest big town to Henley, and you'd see bands that would be at the forefront of what would eventually become known as the shoegaze scene. Those bands didn't feel that far removed from me and all of those lunchtime bands.

At school, I went through a series of bands, the last of which – Ariel – was with my best mates Matt Berry and Brendan Melck. We'd known each other for years and had managed to acquire a pretty diverse set of musical influences between us by then. I'd gravitated towards a lot of sample-based music, bands like Renegade Soundwave and The JAMs. I'd read about The JAMs in *NME* and had bought their *1987* album. I was fascinated by the samples and would try and find out where everything was from, even going so far as to write a letter to the band's King Boy D. He wrote back informing me of the existence of Dave Brubeck and Led Zeppelin – music I hadn't really investigated before. The JAMs opened me up to the idea that everything was a sample source. I'd go to Reading Library to withdraw my allotted five CDs a week, gradually working my way from A to Z. Renegade Soundwave occupied a similar territory to The JAMs, sampling music from *ITN News* on their 'Kray Twins' 12-inch, which they set to huge distorted drums. Those bands' influence remain a constant today.

Matt played bass and was really into bands like Cabaret Voltaire and the kind of cool, underground electronic music that would eventually become known as IDM [intelligent dance music]. He owned a 303 and a 606 – pretty incredible kit for a school band to be able to play around with – and he lived next to an abandoned mushroom farm where we could set up our equipment and rehearse for hours without annoying anyone. Brendan loved American storyteller songwriters like Jonathan Richman and Lou Reed. He was always a great force of energy and enthusiasm, a guitarist and a natural frontman. Through Brendan's older brother, the three of us had become obsessed with Kraftwerk. I remember going on school trips together and sharing Walkman headphones to listen to *Trans-Europe Express* on cassette.

In 1988, acid house hit the home counties. I got a front-seat view as a designated driver for Huw and his mates. They were really into going raving and used to get me to drive as I'd just passed my test. I was a very willing younger sibling. There were loads of mad clubs in places like Marlow and Maidenhead, which had a club called Valbonne.

As long as I drove them back and forth to clubs, Huw and friends would pay for me to get in. I can vividly remember hearing records at those nights, things like the original Pure Trance version of 'What Time Is Love' by The KLF, which was a properly brilliant, disorientating piece of music, E.S.P.'s 'It's You' and Bam Bam's 'Where's Your Child', a record so intoxicating and wild we still play it today. It was characterful, weird acid house music that felt powerful on the dance floor – but it was also so recognisable and identifiable it worked as a sort of twisted pop music. Hearing that at ear-splitting volume in a strobe-y, smoky club was unbelievable, a properly altering experience. On one of those nights, I stepped out of the club and was so hot and sweaty that I fainted the minute I hit the night air. I'd gone outside to wait for Huw and his gang and hit the floor immediately. When I came to, there were all these mangled ravers going, 'What's he had, what's he done?' and then my brother pulled me up saying, 'He's fine', before making me drive him home.

In the summer of 1989, I started going to big raves out on the outskirts of London, things like World Dance. Listening to people now, it would be easy to believe that everyone was out at those raves, but back then it was rare that you'd know people who'd gone. It was almost a secret society. You'd recognise signs, small signifiers in people, things like Kickers boots and Chipie T-shirts. You'd see someone and immediately think: 'They know.'

I'd been drawn to Manchester after I'd been taken to Hot – The Haçienda's Wednesday night acid house party – by friends. They were playing house music like T-Coy's 'Carino' and 'Voodoo Ray' by A Guy Called Gerald – music that was absolutely out of this world, and made by people from the city I was out clubbing in. My immediate reaction was, 'Wow, imagine being able to live in a city where you could go to this every week!' When I started university, I only met about four people who'd moved to the city with that in mind. You had arguably the epicentre of music in the world at that point just a bus ride up the road, yet the majority of people weren't really that bothered. They wanted the student union disco and 50p pints. It amazed me, and it meant that it was easy to build a friendship group from people who wanted the same collective experience, from people who'd been altered by rave culture and wanted to live right at the beating heart of it. Ed was one of the first people I met after moving to Manchester as we were on the same course. And one of the first things we bonded over was the fact that he'd been having the same experiences as me earlier that year in the exact same fields.

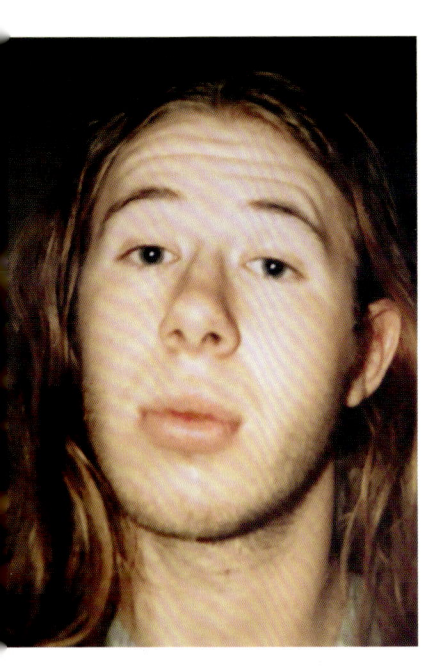

Growing up, the nearest great record shop was Record Basement in Reading. By the time I was seventeen, I had an Akai S1000 sampler and a Roland Juno 106 and was making music all the time in my bedroom. When I'd head into Record Basement to hear new music, I'd often take tapes of things I'd recorded at home. I've no idea where the confidence came from. I'd have given them to anyone who'd have listened back then.

After my first year as a student in Manchester, I went back home for the summer holidays and the guy who ran Record Basement – Phil Wells – told me he had an idea for a record and asked if I could put it together. He gave me an amazing sample from 'Cosmic Sea' by Mystic Moods Orchestra and asked me if I could take a loop from it and turn it into a track. Of course, I could do it for nothing. I went off and put it together. Phil really was the first person to go, 'Alright then, get on with it.' That push was massively motivational.

I took the finished thing back to Phil on cassette, and he pressed it up as a record and put it out under 'P.W. featuring Atom' on Law Records in 1990. It had a B-side by someone called Kim Strickland, who I never met. It just felt great to have an actual record with my name on. I even ended up doing a few PAs under the name Atom in clubs around Reading. The track was called 'Sea of Beats', which soon after became the first single release for Ariel. I'm pretty sure there's still about fifty copies in my mum and dad's garage.

Ed Simons was born in south London on 9 June 1970.

Speak & Spell by Depeche Mode came out when I was twelve years old. It was the first album I ever bought. I loved it as a pop record, and I loved the cleanness in its sound. I just followed chart music at that age really, and headed to WHSmith every Saturday with enough money to buy my two favourite 7-inch singles. Heaven 17 one week, Adam and the Ants the next.

Music only became a way of expressing some kind of identity to me when I became obsessed with The Smiths, adopting an image inspired by them that involved wearing long jumble sale overcoats, smoking cigarettes and being wistful in Belair Park in West Dulwich. I went to see them at Brixton Academy, maybe 1984 or '85. I was blown away – not so much by the music but by the crowd, which was so insane. I had never experienced anything as intense as that, everyone singing every word and rucking, which was the thing to do at that time.

Things changed massively for me around 1986 when I started going to The Mud Club. It was a night hosted by Philip Sallon, where DJs like Mark Moore played. I wouldn't have known who he was at the time, but he was making records as S'Xpress shortly afterwards. The night was at Busby's, which was below the Astoria on Charing Cross Road, and the soundtrack was party hip hop, electro and rare groove. There were big standout records like the first Public Enemy album (*Yo! Bum Rush the Show*) and they played lots of tracks with sirens on. It was pre-acid house and the look was very much American Classics, all old Levis and MA1 flight jackets. I wouldn't have known how to dress to get into a club – I was probably still in The Smiths-era jumble sale coat – but somehow I managed to drift in and hang around on the outside of what was going on.

In the summer of 1987, I had a friend whose older brother was pretty switched on to what I now know to have been the early acid and Balearic house scene. He was about four years older and he would tell us about crazy parties he was going to. We watched as he and his friends arrived in their back garden and spent a Saturday morning, then afternoon and then evening wigging out. I remember they would go from the Coldcut mix of Eric B. & Rakim to 'Last Night' by Kid 'n Play, and then someone would play Nu Shooz 'I Can't Wait' three times in a row, which people cheered ever more hysterically to when the bassline came in. Then this crew would sit in a circle communing to This Mortal Coil's 'Song to the Siren' or Santana's 'Samba Pa Ti'. There was an intensity to them from just being with each other and getting so much from whatever was coming out of the speaker. I can still remember watching this party and thinking I wanted that in my life: that union, that unselfconscious love of music, that togetherness in this strange community just happy to be there in that south London garden.

After finishing A Levels, a group of about twenty of us went to Ibiza for an end-of-school *Inbetweeners*-style holiday. Six people to a room in San Antonio, all having this wild time on our first holiday away from home. The same friend with the older brother who was already switched on to acid house heard that if you went to this boat club way down the beach beyond the Café del Mar, you could get tickets for Amnesia [nightclub]. Three of us formed a breakaway group and ended up on a night in Amnesia in the heyday of it all. It was something else. The whole thing had this very cool, young European playboy vibe, but the music was so different to anything I'd heard before. We were outside on the terrace, and as it started raining they played this Terence Trent D'Arby track 'Rain' that caught the mood perfectly. It was so unlike anything we'd experienced back home, a total escape.

Before university, I went away to Australia for a year where I worked making ice cream sundaes in a hotel by a beach. My social life was spent in the club underneath the hotel, drinking and dancing around to records by INXS and things like The Angels' 'Am I Ever Gonna See Your Face Again'. By the time I got back to Britain in the spring of 1989, south London had completely transformed. Everyone was going to raves every weekend, fashion had changed, music was different. There was a pub in Tulse Hill where you went to get tickets to Orbital raves. I'd be asking the same mates if they were up for going for a pint like we used to and they'd be poised by their cars, windows down, stereos blaring out Centreforce, the pirate rave station. Everyone was wearing the kit – ponytails, tracksuit bottoms, purple hooded tops. I'd been cut off from it all in Perth and had no concept of what was going on.

I wasn't against the idea of going to raves, but I must have been a bit scared of it. It was something entirely different and I couldn't quite process what was going on. Feeling

The Akai X7000 sampler was Tom's main instrument in the early days. The unwieldy power transformer was bought by his dad to convert US power for UK usage at Ariel gigs.

like I was missing out on something that my mates had all but become consumed with, I went to Camden Market and bought all these bootleg mixtapes, things like Carl Cox DJing at Sunrise. I'd go home after working my summer job and dance around my bedroom to these cassettes. That's how I first got into acid house music.

The first rave I went to was called Woodstock '89. Six of us packed into a car, leaving south London to find a party in a field somewhere miles away. All those tunes I'd heard coming out of car windows outside the local pub were suddenly coming out of a massive system, DJ ripping it up, MCs over the top. It was incredible, this was multicultural southeast England, everyone dancing together in a big field. It was like someone had turned a light on. The DJ would play a record like 'Let Me Love You for Tonight' by Kariya, and the wildness of the response was unbelievably powerful. After that, I went to outdoor raves every single weekend.

1989 was a crazy summer. Every week there was new music, classic records like 'Strings of Life' by Rhythim Is Rhythim, 'Grandpa's Party' by Monie Love and 'Salsa House' by Richie Rich. 'Give Me a Sign' by Index became the anthem for our little crew. Everyone used to have Centreforce on all the time. It was intoxicating. And there were Orbital raves every weekend. You'd head out to parties around 11 p.m. The location might change, and you'd find yourself chasing round trying to find the right place. And then when you got there, you'd hear it all crank up with a track like 'Your Love' by Frankie Knuckles. It was like nothing else in the world.

I loved it so much. It made sense of growing up in London. It was such an incredible time where people came together with a sense of wild abandonment; people from so many different backgrounds all dancing together. It made you feel like you were genuinely connected to where you'd grown up. It was so completely liberating at that exact point in British history where there had previously been such a grim greyness to everything. Suddenly there's this explosion of colour and people talking about harmony and friendliness. I still hope that in some way our gigs bring about a version of that sense of togetherness and optimism that that particular wave of music captured.

I went to university in Manchester with a load of school friends, but none of them were interested in the music scene that I'd become utterly obsessed with over the summer. I met Tom on one of my first days and he looked like a proper raver: green trousers, proper curtain bob haircut, Chevignon top. We started hanging out and I ended up at his room in the halls of residence. He had this stereo with big speakers – a briefcase of sound – and he put on a Tackhead record. I'd never heard them before. Listening to it, I thought, 'This is the stuff.' I think it was inevitable that we'd end up on the dance floor at The Haçienda together within a week or two, and so we did. The rest, as they say, is history.

Opposite: Original Ariel 12-inches of 'Sea of Beats', 'Rollercoaster' and 'T-Baby', which includes one of the first The Dust Brothers remixes.

Paused in Cosmic Reflection 23

Playground for a Wedgeless Firm: Manchester and Becoming The Dust Brothers

Ed Simons

We arrived in Manchester in the last few months of the Nude night at The Haçienda, back when Mike Pickering was DJing. It was a very colourful, very friendly night. Once you were on the dance floor, no one cared whether you were a student or not. It was a massive welcome to the city. The two of us experienced that together. It was such an important part of the DNA of The Chemical Brothers.

Parallel to getting into club music, New Order were a massive band for me. I don't think I consciously thought about New Order, or The Smiths, or Manchester United (who I'd supported since I was a kid) when I decided to go to Manchester for university. I think it was more moving from one city to another; it felt exciting to walk down the road out of Manchester Piccadilly train station into town. I didn't have any interest in not being in a city.

Bernard Sumner

We'd been touring in America extensively and then we went to Ibiza to record *Technique*. I was pretty much burnt out from partying too much, especially in America. We're teenagers at school, totally repressed, like most teenagers. Told we were shit and that the only thing worth living for was mathematics and English. Get a job as an accountant, become a draughtsman, are you any good at woodwork? Told what to do, stop having fun. Join the system, you'll be able to retire at sixty-five. We weren't very good at school – well, Stephen was, and Ian was – but when we found ourselves in a successful band, we were like dogs off the lead. We went wild on tour, a frenzy of hormones and exploratory investigative curiosity. We just went mad partying, as a lot of young bands do. We were given free rein and it all became a bit too much. I was physically and mentally burnt out and I needed a bit of time – a couple of years, a year and a half – back in Manchester to calm down and dry out.

So I came back just at the time that the whole acid house thing was kicking off. Out of the frying pan into the fire. This idea of a nice relaxing time watching *Antiques Roadshow*, recuperating, maybe getting the odd blood transfusion, was thrown out the window. We'd gone from America, which was wild, to Ibiza, which was wilder, to Manchester – much wilder. Went down to London a few times to clubs, obviously went to The Haçienda, and then lots and lots of parties after the club had closed for the night. Manchester was party central. There were mad bands around like Happy Mondays, The Stone Roses, a burgeoning Oasis. And I didn't relax or calm down, I just went extra mad in Manchester.

John Burgess (editor, *Jockey Slut*, *Disco Pogo*)

The first Friday after I moved to Manchester, my best mate from home invited me to go to The Haçienda. I really wanted to go on a Friday as that was a proper night, not a student one. I queued up with Tom and Ed and the crew they'd already formed in Manchester in their first week of university. Being outside The Haçienda was quite intimidating. The blacked-out window glass was moving in time to the 4/4 beat. I'd never been to a club like that before and didn't know how to dance. Tom told me to just bop about on my feet from side to side. So, my first Friday in Manchester, I was being taught how to dance by Tom in The Haçienda.

James Holroyd

I met Tom and Ed in 1989 when we were students. We'd moved up for the music scene as much as for the academia. I'd bump into them on Tuesday nights in the brand-new

Paused in Cosmic Reflection 25

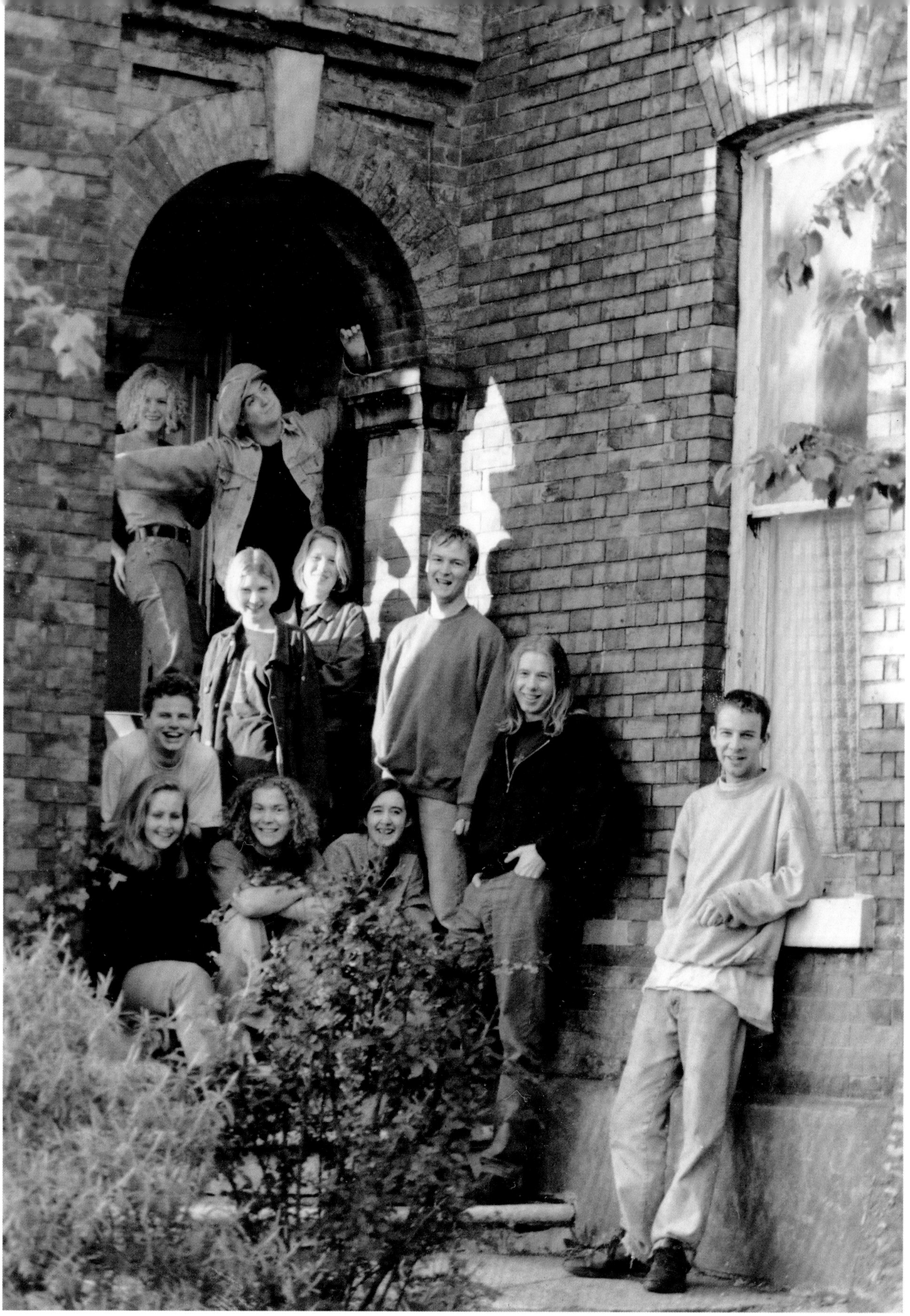

Opposite: The residents of 237 Dickenson Road, including Ed Simons (sat at the top of the steps), Tom Rowlands (second right) and Nick Dutfield (right).

Manchester Academy. Dave Booth was the DJ. He was ace and played to the indie kids and the ravers. I was on nodding and smiling terms with Tom and Ed a while. Our haircuts put us all in the rave corner.

The city had an almighty supply of mega-ness back then. Gigs, clubs and house parties round the clock 24/7. The music that inspired our move was suddenly close-up. Any night at The Haçienda could involve you dancing with your heroes: members of New Order, the Mondays, 808 State, A Certain Ratio.

The community was so tight, and still is. These heroes suddenly became normal people like all the other dancers on the floor. Normal people who did extraordinary things.

Ed Simons

There was a period when I was living at home where I graduated from buying ZX Spectrum games to spending every Saturday in record shops. I'd buy two 12-inches in the big HMV on Oxford Street. I'd take the whole day, getting the bus to central London and taking time to choose the right things. I dragged those records up to university with my little stereo and I ended up getting a regular DJ gig at the Owens Park BOP. It was a student night, not a club. I was a terrible DJ. There was a mic there, and I'd be shouting out to friends, 'I can see you getting down!' The most embarrassing MCing. I ended up getting sacked. We'd been playing Italian house and classics like 'Pump Up the Volume', but another guy had petitioned to take over. His first record was 'Dancing on the Ceiling' by Lionel Richie. The whole BOP went mad. I quickly realised I'd been on the wrong path.

John Burgess

Ed got us all to go to the BOP the weekend after he got sacked so we could give dirty looks to the replacement DJ.

Nick Dutfield

We were all studying history, so we met pretty soon after moving to the city. The people who arrived in Manchester in 1989 had applied to university just before the whole thing had kicked off. They weren't people who'd gone because it was the 'city of baggy'. That hadn't happened yet.

Tom was massively into hip hop. I remember going to his room in the halls of residence in first year and all of his record covers were guys in gaudy tracksuits, whereas mine were all miserable indie blokes in raincoats. I sat behind Ed in lectures early on and remember him having a Billabong T-shirt that must have been a relic from his year in Australia. I'd never seen those clothes in Britain before. He might have been their cultural stormtrooper.

Tom Rowlands

People used to call me, Ed and Nick the 'three blind mice'. Always walking round with our heads in the clouds.

Ed Simons

Tom was quiet but he loved going out. He was someone who wanted to get the very most out of life. We'd be out every night of the week, whether it was a gig or a club or something at the uni. We'd get back about two in the morning. At 7.30 a.m., I'd hear him getting up and going to the library. He could go out full pelt, then put the hours in studying. I would have been happier if he'd stayed in bed a bit more; it would have made me feel less guilty about doing that.

Emma Warren

Tom and Ed were at the centre of their own universe. I met them through one of their friends. When you become part of something that already exists, it takes a bit of time to work out what the dynamic is. But

Paused in Cosmic Reflection   27

Above: Tom and Nick.

Top right: Tom and Ed.

Bottom: Ed, Tom, Ness [Vanessa Rowlands] and Huw at Sugar Sweet in Belfast, 1994.

Bottom right: Nick.

Paused in Cosmic Reflection 29

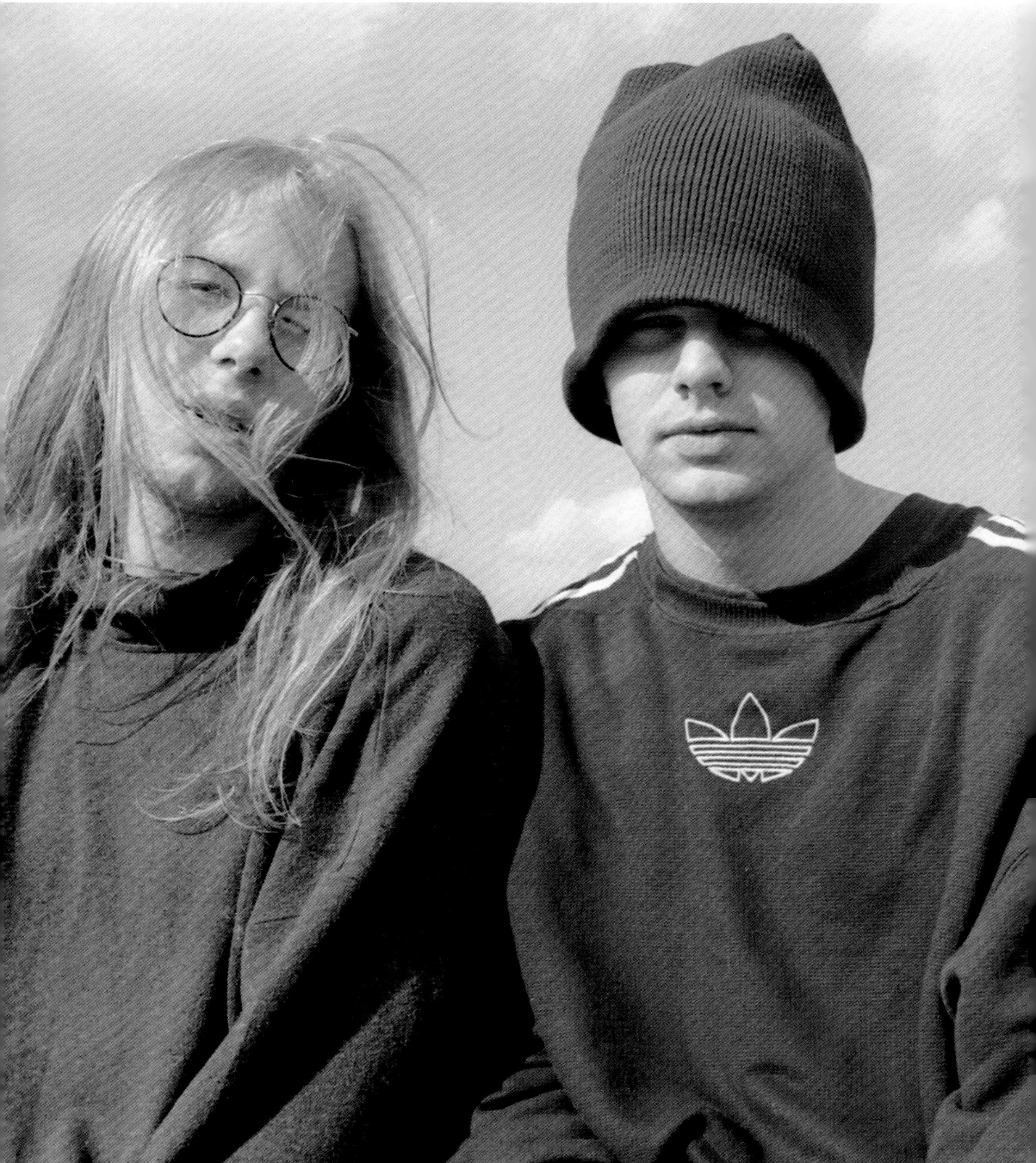

I could see Tom and Ed were on the dance floor all the time. They were scene-famous in Manchester. I recognised something in them similar to my experiences. They'd been to London clubs like I had. They didn't go to the same places, but they were Londoners doing a slightly more London-y version of clubbing in Manchester. There was lots happening up there at that time and the city was many, many different things at once. There were hardcore raves where everyone would be doing loads of speed, and then there were things where people from Cheshire would get really dressed up to go to The Haçienda. I'd see them at specific things like Most Excellent and certain nights at The Haçienda.

Ed Simons

As well as going to clubs, Tom and I started buying records together. You had to earn your stripes in Eastern Bloc [record shop], or just be prepared to buy whatever mad record had been put in front of you.

Tom Rowlands

As students, we were limited as to what records we could get hold of. One of the places where we would pick things up was Eastern Bloc. Justin Robertson was key to us getting a foot in the door. He must have seen kindred spirits in two students from the south of England. His kindness was so important to us building up confidence and building a record collection that would start to define us early on. Justin was a beacon. He'd grown up in a village near where I was from, had been a student in the city and had ended up properly integrated into the club scene. A lot of cities have a division between locals and students, where the two camps don't really mix at all. Back then, it didn't feel like there was any difference. We'd go into the shop having been to his club nights, thinking he might have seen us there and might sell us good records.

Eastern Bloc was an intimidating shop back then. We were used to shops with the same kind of atmosphere in London. If you didn't have an idea of what sort of thing you wanted when you went in, you'd get pretty short shrift. There would be a line of kids at the counter with their Walkmans and tapes recorded from Shelley's nightclub in Stoke going, 'What's this fookin' track with a big saxophone on it mate?' And the response was always along the lines of 'Fook off, don't bring that in here.' We'd wait patiently while all that went on.

Justin Robertson

Tom and Ed used to hang around in Eastern Bloc where I worked at the start of the nineties. I'd been a student a few years before so recognised a couple of fellow travellers. They quickly became really integral to the club I ran – Most Excellent – and we'd hang out afterwards back at various people's houses, listening to records, talking about music and doing all the other things that go on at that time in the morning. We must have been quite close as Ed would call me up at home about things. I'd have notes by the phone saying, 'Ed called'.

Ed Simons

Richard Moonboots was another big inspiration behind the counter in Eastern Bloc. It's strange to think that now, the entire history of recorded music is available for anyone to play, as well as every new track. Back then, we didn't have walls and walls of vinyl, we had what we had and we improvised between some of the old records we'd bought as teenagers and new records we were buying or being given by Moonboots at Eastern Bloc. He was important in shaping what we played. There was a quality threshold in the records we were getting off him. Later on, some of those tracks might have been reissued or people found a way to get hold of them after hearing them in our sets, but there was a time when only we had them.

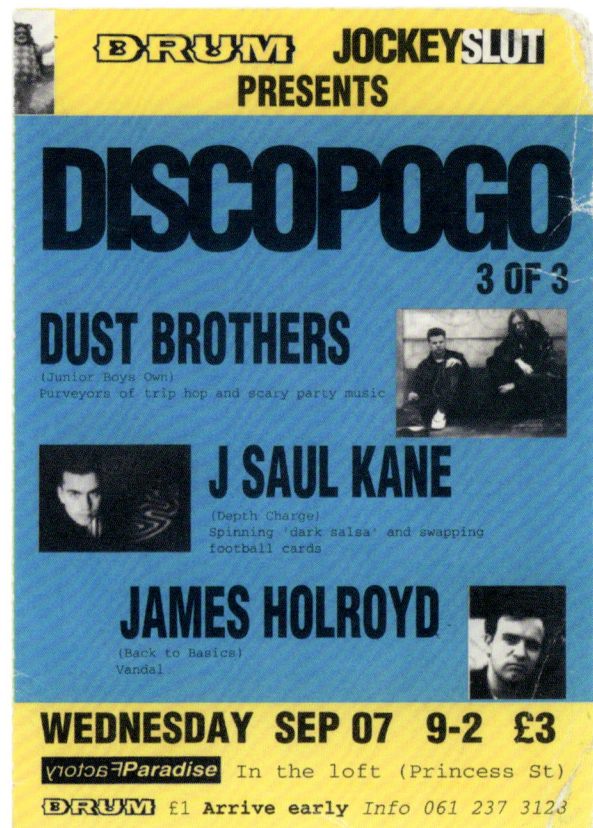

Tom Rowlands

The currency of records was high back then. I remember getting one record from Moonboots and it had the master sleeve that had all the ordering details on it: all the information you needed when it came to restocking the record. He gave it to me and said, 'No one else'll be getting that now.' He'd give you records where he'd already stickered over the labels so you couldn't see who it was by. There was a real generosity of spirit back then and an excitement on our side to go there and have this world open right up. That shop really was the heart of dance music in the north. Arguably of the whole country.

When Eastern Bloc's label F.R.O. (Fuck Right Off) put out Ariel's version of 'Sea of Beats' in our second year of university, things went to the next level. John and Mike and Andy E. who ran the shop were big characters in the city – you'd see them at The Haçienda, they were friends with Justin. Getting acceptance from those people felt exciting.

James Holroyd

Everyone you knew was having house parties and putting on DJ nights. Sometimes those parties were just a crew of mates; some of them turned into something else. 237 Dickenson Road is an address that will chime with a few people from that time.

Nick Dutfield

In the second year, we all moved into a house share at 237 Dickenson Road. 237 wasn't a massive party house. When Justin did a remix of an Ariel track, he called it the '237 Turbo Nutters' remix. That's how he would have referred to us. But I always felt we weren't really living up to the extreme nuttiness that that title implies. There was a girl called Pauline who was one of the eight people who lived at Dickenson Road. She was part of the Freedom to Party rave crew who all used to go to Angels in Burnley. We were Balearic, so we were a bit snooty about them. One night we'd gone to see Justin DJ at Konspiracy and got back home to find Pauline had organised a party in the

EXCLUSIVE A REAL CHAMPION BILL PRESENTING **DRUM & JOCKEY SLUT** HEAVYWEIGHT ENTERTAINMENT * * * * * * * *

DRINKING CLUB

FEATURING [All Guaranteed And Confirmed] LATE NITE SUPPING DRUM £1

DUST BROTHERS
* Trip Hop Heroes Return to Spiritual Home Turf *

FROM BRITAINS TOP POP GROUP
SAINT ETIENNE:
BOB STANLEY & PETE WIGGS
* On the Wheels of Steel *

LIVE! EARL BRUTUS
* Glam Art Terrorists from the Ef's Cool Icerink Label *

SATURDAY **JUNE 18** JOSHUA BROOKS 9 – 2 £3
* Opposite Paradise Factory *   * Arrive Early *

basement that went on for hours and hours. Tom, Ed and myself were just spectators, watching our house get taken over by ravers off their tits. The whole place was shaking. We ended up hiding in Tom's room. It's probably because of that party that Bernard ended up knocking on the door.

Ed Simons

We were at home watching *Blind Date* on a Saturday night when the doorbell rang. It was Bernard Sumner, thinking there was a party on. I think he'd been day walking, he looked pretty sozzled. He asked, 'Has the party started yet?' Nick came in nervously saying, 'Bernard from New Order is at the door.' We all tried to get a look at him. When we told him there wasn't a party on, he shouted 'Fuck you, you wurzels.' He wandered off, really pissed off, and we tried to follow him down the road.

Bernard Sumner

The Haçienda used to finish at 2 a.m. Back then we had James Anderton as chief of police – God's cop himself. He wanted everything shut by 10 p.m. so the police could all go home, but things were open til 2 a.m. It was really just me going to the club at that point; I used to hang around with the Mondays. You didn't really see other members of New Order there – not by the time acid house hit.

One night, I was out with some friends who were a bit scally-ish and a few Happy Mondays. We were trying to find a party, which we always used to do every time we were out. Sometimes we'd go up to Gooch Close, which was a very dodgy place to go to, but always at the end of the night I'd get a bag of booze and ask where the party was. Someone had a piece of paper with an address of some place in Didsbury or somewhere.

Bag of booze, scally mates in tow, a couple of Mondays or their mates, we went to the address and banged on the door. The door slowly opened about six inches and this eyeball peered out. When the person saw me, the door opened a bit wider, and I saw this guy with long hair – must have been Tom – and he took a look at me and my mates. I thought it was a look of disgust, but it must have been a look of recognition. I thought, 'Why is he looking at me like that?' I said, 'Is this where the party is? I can hear music!' and he replied, 'There's no party here.' I decided that he didn't like the look of me, or the look of my friends, because of the way he was looking at me. I was pretty off it, I think I said to him, 'Well fuck off then, you wurzel bastard.' I never knew until years later that it was Tom and Ed, because Ed appeared behind him. I just thought they were snotty students and they didn't like us. I think there were about eighteen of us.

Ed suddenly put his head over Tom's shoulders and said, 'You're not coming in here dressed like that.' And Tom said, 'No trainers.' They should have let us in, they'd have had loads of fun and made new contacts in the Manchester area. I could have introduced them to the city's criminal underworld.

Nick Dutfield

As a historian I can deal with the fact that different witnesses have different accounts. I remember when Bernard turned up, I answered the door to him. As he was leaving, I said, 'Take this, it's my lucky bottle of amyl.' He said, 'Haven't you got any money?' It was the greatest moment of my life.

Tom Rowlands

By our third year we'd been handed the keys to the kingdom, in that we could go downstairs in Eastern Bloc to where the

Far right: DJ, club promoter and Most Excellent record selecter Justin Robertson, who Tom and Ed met while at university in Manchester.

34   **The Chemical Brothers**

records first came in. Apart from the people who worked behind the counter, we were often the first people hearing new records.

They had a brilliant Robin Hood mentality in there. You'd get a stack of records, give them twenty quid and they'd give you a tenner back. Off you went with fifty quid's worth of records. Can't have been great for the shop but it was definitely very helpful to us when we were starting out DJing with very little money between us. We were in the magic circle, as it were. We hadn't been there for a long time; we were just two wurzels standing at the counter, as Bernard Sumner would have said.

Nick Dutfield

I'd talk to Ed about music and he was really intrigued by the way it could affect people. He'd recall being at a family party where there was a DJ, and he marvelled at the power that that person had over a crowd of people, that they had this supreme power to affect people's moods. He was always convinced that it was less about the latest tunes and the hippest mixes and more about how you made people feel in the moment.

Paused in Cosmic Reflection

Justin Robertson

Ariel were zeitgeisty in the early nineties, in that they combined guitar music with electronics. Most Excellent had a Balearic, eclectic approach to music, and they fitted perfectly. They became a sort of in-house band for the club, playing our parties and club nights. I remixed 'Sea of Beats' before going on to co-produce a couple of tracks with them before they signed to Deconstruction.

When I went into the studio with Tom it became apparent quite quickly that he not only knew his way around, but that he knew a hell of a lot more than I did about how it all worked. As we stripped back the band's recordings, it became obvious to me that the little bleeps and whirrs and odd psychedelic noises were what really made the records, the bits that would end up being glossed over or buried when tracks were produced properly.

John Burgess

Some people had T-shirts with the Ariel logo, which were really hard to get hold of. *The Face* and *i-D* each wrote about them as being the coolest T-shirt in Manchester.

Emma Warren

You'd see Tom on the dance floor and you'd see him playing in clubs with Ariel. In our small universe, Tom was the one who'd made a record. You couldn't say that about many people. Records were things that other people made, not the people you were on the dance floor with.

John Burgess

Tom and Ed and their crew were the ace faces at Most Excellent. It was a small scene, and they were front and centre of things. I remember going shopping for tambourines and maracas with Ross Mackenzie, who was the promoter of the night. He'd hand them out to Tom and Ed's crew, who would be in the middle of the floor with all of this percussion, making sure the party went off. The Brickhouse only held about 150 people. If you've got five or six people going nuts in the middle of the floor, and Tom's about six foot seven, they're going to stand out.

Tom Rowlands

We'd go out to Justin's nights and Nick would be in the middle of the dance floor, setting himself alight with amyl nitrate. There would be fire in the middle of the dance floor. Perfectly normal night out.

Nick Dutfield

It was exciting to meet someone who was actually doing something in a band, who was putting records out. I'd gone to university with an acoustic guitar and had pretensions of being something. Knowing someone who'd made records was genuinely exciting. When you'd go to the Dry Bar with Tom, there would be all these people who'd nod at him. And I think that was because they knew he was in a band and there was an unspoken thing that you might end up in a band together one day, like The Fall.

Vanessa Rowlands (née Rand, Deconstruction Records)

I was doing club promotions at Deconstruction in the early nineties. It was a tiny office back then. I remember Mike Pickering bringing in 'Sea of Beats' by Ariel. We signed them for a single off the back of that and we instantly bonded. I was going up to Manchester all the time with work, so we hung out loads. Tom and I started going out shortly after.

James Holroyd

The music landscape was so good. You couldn't not be at the counter of Eastern

Bloc jostling for the piles of daily imports and trying to snap up the things you'd heard the night before.

Justin Robertson

It was pretty obvious from first meeting Tom and Ed that they'd form a team and end up making their own music together. The Dust Brothers was the perfect combination of Tom's sonic wizardry and vision, and Ed's appreciation and connoisseurship of music, his rigorous good taste. Their music combined those two dynamics, while also absorbing the sounds around them in clubs and in records they bought, to make them their own. They were always interested in music where hip-hop beats met acid house sounds. They just happened to take it as far as it could possibly go when they made music themselves.

Ed Simons

The first time we DJed together was at a wedding of a couple we used to go clubbing with. Naked Under Leather came soon after.

Emma Warren

I was friendly with Phil South and Alex Kohler who started Naked Under Leather. They were music heads with really interesting record collections who were coming from a completely different place to Tom and Ed. They had their own unique taste and feel. Everyone had grown up on the same dance floors but everyone had found their own influences.

Tom and Ed looked totally natural stood behind the decks at the first Naked Under Leather. It looked good. They looked like they were having a good time playing the best possible records to their universe, building the energy levels up as high as they could take them. And the energy levels were high. It was a good club night.

John Burgess

Naked Under Leather was in the Old Steam Brewery. It was Phil and Alex's night, and Tom and Ed were the residents. The venue was always a bit sticky and a bit wet, like the cellar of a pub. That place only held eighty, maybe a hundred people. That's where they mastered the art of playing all those instrumental B-sides that were beat-y and bass-y and had sirens on them.

Ed Simons

We did Naked Under Leather probably five times a year. We'd really just go and throw the records on and that had a big effect. We'd play that big MC5 speech (the intro to 'Ramblin' Rose'), and 'Foodwinefood' by Ariel was a really big record there. It was really wild, and it felt democratic. Lots of different tribes all going crazy. Andy Weatherall played there once. After an hour or so of playing, he had his shirt off, loving it.

Vanessa Rowlands

The first time I heard Tom and Ed play was at Naked Under Leather. It's a bit hazy, but it was absolutely brilliant and it properly kicked off. It was like a family event, a gang of twenty or more mates meeting up for a party. It was super exciting and we all went back to their house afterwards, which stank.

When Tom and Ed DJed on New Year's Eve 1992, our group of mates spent the whole time they were playing trying to rugby tackle each other on the dance floor. Nick tackled me and I ended up breaking my ankle. I spent the rest of the night dancing on it. I somehow managed to drive back to London the next day, crying in agony.

John Burgess

I was the editor of the student magazine at the polytechnic. My friend Paul Benney and

Above: DJing in Nottingham.

I had always talked about doing a fanzine in those hours after the clubs had finished and you were round at someone's house chatting. *Why don't we do a T-shirt, why don't we do a fanzine . . .* It came out of that. Andy Weatherall used to talk about that period being very creative, because clubs closed early and people didn't want to go to bed so lots of ideas formed before the sun came up. We were able to start *Jockey Slut* because I had access to all the tools to make it. I did the first interview with Tom and Ed as The Dust Brothers in the second issue on the day after the last Naked Under Leather, which Weatherall played at. They quickly became a kind of in-house band for us.

Tom Rowlands

There wasn't a grand plan when we chose the name 'The Dust Brothers'. It just sounded cool and exotic. We loved what they [the original Dust Brothers] did, loved their productions. I suppose it's the ultimate thing in sampling, pinching another artist's name: 'We'll take the drum beat and we'll take the name too.' It does seem quite mad in hindsight. The idea that anyone might have thought that the version of us playing in a pub in Fallowfield in 1992 might be the actual Dust Brothers was pretty far-fetched. I don't think anyone was turning up to the Old Steam Brewery student union bar expecting to hear Mike Simpson and John King from Los Angeles. Looking back, it was a pretty ridiculous thing to do.

Robert Linney

I'd been working behind a desk at Heavenly Recordings for a few years, witnessing various madmen roll in throughout the day. I co-managed Andrew Weatherall with the wonderful Jeff Barrett, who ran the label. We'd flirted with the idea of signing Andrew's band Sabres of Paradise to a major label, and had met with London Records and Deconstruction. They were both key labels in British electronic music at that time. We went back and forth between those companies and got to know the people who worked there. One time I was at Deconstruction, Vanessa, who worked there, said, 'Would you meet with my boyfriend?'

We met in the Ship Inn on Wardour Street, which was Heavenly's local. I recognised Tom from Junior Boy's Own parties. Ariel was coming to an end and The Dust Brothers were just starting to get talked about. Him and Ed were interested in management, so we agreed to give it a go. You never know how things are going to turn out in music, but there was clearly something different – and special – in what Tom and Ed were doing.

Quickly afterwards, Deconstruction got interested in signing The Dust Brothers. On hearing that, several major labels followed suit immediately. It quickly went a wee bit crazy. Not so much in financial terms – it was decent money, but it wasn't Gay Dad money. They were still a pretty left-field electronic act. Virgin got 'Leave Home' into the Top 20 in the UK Singles Chart and *Exit Planet Dust* reached the Top 10, but I think if you'd have told the people in 1995 that the band would go on to sell 15 million albums over the next thirty years, six of which would go to Number 1 in the UK, you'd have blown their minds. What Tom and Ed were doing was new and the territory was uncharted. No one knew what the longevity or the appeal of electronic music would be back then.

Emma Warren

I remember sitting at home listening to Radio 1 and hearing a pop quiz question: 'Who are Ed Simons and Tom Rowlands?' That was the point where I realised they were famous. When they changed their name, we thought it was hilarious that they'd had a letter from the actual Dust Brothers. It was a drama. What were they going to change the name to? People get attached very quickly to names, and The Dust Brothers was a wicked name. But it was someone else's and they couldn't continue with it.

Robert Linney

Those early years were pretty surreal. We had one major label fly us to New York for three days, where they put us up in the trendiest hotel and took us out to Robert De Niro's restaurant. Then I got woken up at night by a fax coming through with a cease-and-desist letter from the Dust Brothers, who wanted their name back.

Nick Dutfield

One of the things that's never really taken into account – and it's a reason why The

Paused in Cosmic Reflection 39

Dust Brothers or The Chemical Brothers are underrated – is that, in 1992, if you'd have asked anyone in the industry what you needed to do to make it, they'd have said you needed songs and a singer. The Dust Brothers ignored that and made their own path. To then go on to have Number 1 albums and singles without following any of that advice isn't anything anyone's done before or since. I'm not sure people recognise how revolutionary that is. In a way, the decision Tom made to go in a different direction to the one he'd followed with Ariel is really testament to how shrewd he is. He had all of that and turned away and went in a completely different direction.

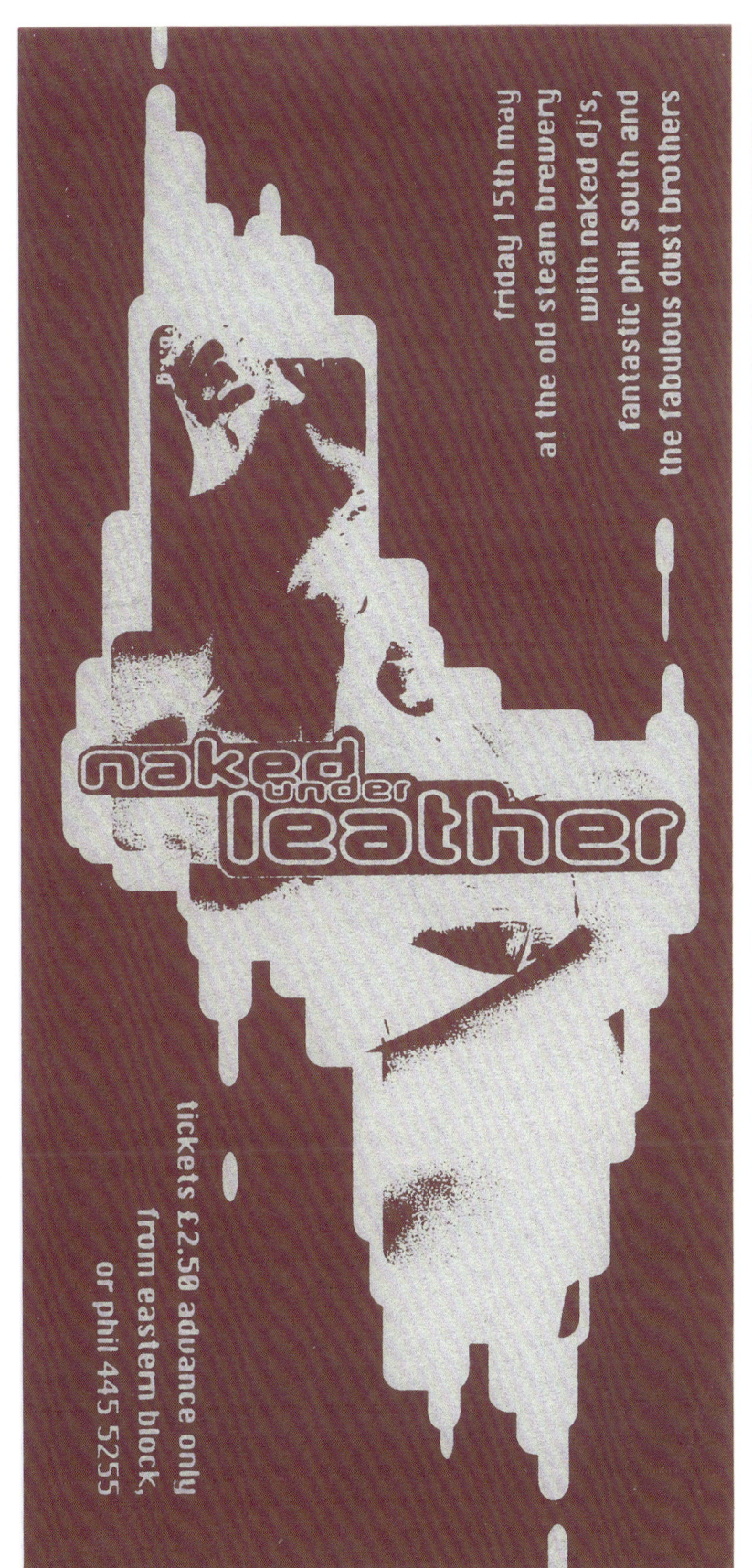

naked under leather

friday 15th may
at the old steam brewery
with naked dj's,
fantastic phil south and
the fabulous dust brothers

tickets £2.50 advance only
from eastern block,
or phil 445 5255

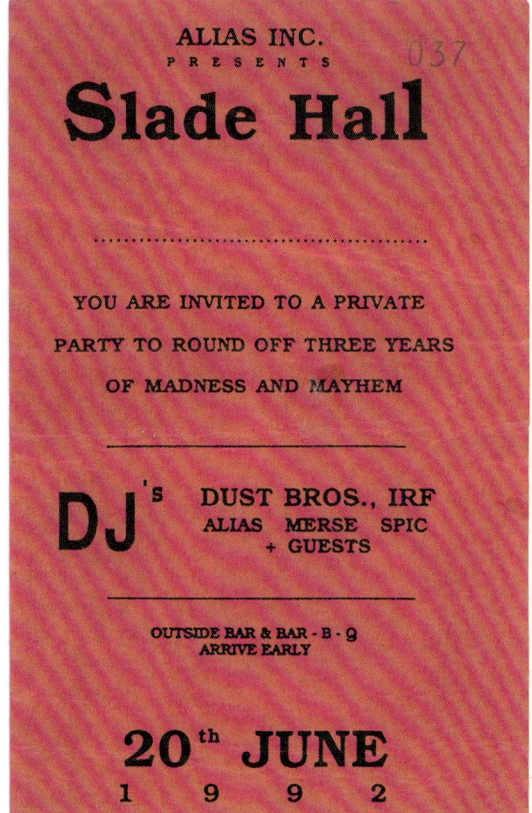

ALIAS INC.
PRESENTS

Slade Hall

037

....

YOU ARE INVITED TO A PRIVATE
PARTY TO ROUND OFF THREE YEARS
OF MADNESS AND MAYHEM

———

DJ's DUST BROS., IRF
ALIAS MERSE SPIC
+ GUESTS

———

OUTSIDE BAR & BAR-B-Q
ARRIVE EARLY

20th JUNE
1 9 9 2

Paused in Cosmic Reflection 41

song to the siren
45 rpm
THIS SIDE ONLY

Song to the Siren

A steady, lo-fidelity 111 bpm, 'Song to the Siren' might be slower than you remember but it's all the more powerful for it. Like a crack of thunder, a punch to the gut or a drill aimed straight at your skull, 'Song to the Siren' is debut single as manifesto, a blueprint for a vision of the future.

First released on a one-sided green label 12-inch in 1992, 'Song to the Siren' was unlike anything else around. Three decades later, it still stands alone, perfectly capturing the spirit of a punk-rock dance floor, where an otherworldly, hypnotic voice wrecks unsuspecting souls on the speaker stacks. All that from the duo that Andrew Weatherall would christen the masters of chunk rock (an apt descriptor at that point in their career, but one that sadly didn't stick around for long).

The Dust Brothers' self-pressed run of 12-inches quickly sold out before being picked up by the Junior Boy's Own label in the spring of 1993. Andrew Weatherall remixed the track in the early days of his Sabres of Paradise guise.

Tom: 'Song to the Siren' was very much just us on our own. It's a product of a really different age. The track was mixed on the Hitachi hi-fi system I had in my old bedroom back at my parents' house. It had a record player and two cassette decks that you could record from one to the other, and it had an input which meant you could play an external source straight in and record it. So you could record drums on it, then play the drums on one tape and record another layer on top. Each time you added a layer, the audio degraded slightly. People pay a lot of money to achieve that kind of sound today. It took ages to make. I'd been playing around with the idea in my bedroom for a long time. In fact, all of those early tracks took a long time. Both 'Song to the Siren' and 'Chemical Beats' were probably made over the space of a year from start to finish.

Ed: 'Song to the Siren' was a way of the two of us expressing ourselves musically. Ariel had become more song based than they'd been when they started out. They had a proper label who needed singles. 'Song to the Siren' was us doing something just for the fun of it. There wasn't really any more ambition other than to see what it could do for us that summer. Maybe it would be a calling card and would help us get a few more DJ gigs. There wasn't any higher aspiration at that point. We'd literally just left university and I was living back at home with my mum. If we could have a fun summer and get some DJ gigs as the two of us, that would have been a result.

Tom: The ambition with the track was to create the thing – the sound – that our DJ sets were lacking. That's always the ambition with making music, to this day. Back then we were always searching out the second track on the instrumental B-side of hip hop imports and there weren't ever enough records like that to keep us going. We were really into things like 'In Dub' by Renegade Soundwave and bands like Meat Beat Manifesto, records that had a slow heaviness to them. I've always loved those records that stop the night for a moment, records that stop you in your tracks and change the direction of everything. I think it's one of the reasons why there's longevity to 'Song to the Siren'. It's never really fitted seamlessly into other things. To this day, it has that same effect in the live set. It feels like everything is pitching down.

Ed: Andy Weatherall, Justin Robertson and Darren Emerson each used to play the track a lot. You'd notice it in their sets because clubs were soundtracked by fast techno at that point. It sounded odd. It was an end-of-the-night record at Sabresonics; you'd hear the record that preceded it being pitched down and the siren coming in. And it got played a lot at The Drum Club. We used to religiously go to The Drum Club; it was a brilliant night that took place in the Sound Shaft behind Heaven. Darren played there all the time. He was quite a technical DJ back then; he could cut up records and play them as if they were hip-hop tracks, cutting between two copies, which was incredible to hear.

That original green label pressing of 'Song to the Siren' sounds genuinely awesome. It's so loud. It has terrible BBC Micro computer artwork that I did with a mate from school. We called the label Diamond Records which might have been after a college nickname I had (Eddie Diamond). The 12-inch was one-sided and we printed up 900 copies ourselves which we obviously needed to sell.

The marketing on it was a very basic hustle. I used to ring up record shops and say, 'I'm coming into town. I heard Andy Weatherall playing the other day. There was this record with a big siren on it and a fuck-off beat', because it so obviously is the record with the siren and that beat. And then I'd go to the shop later on with a box of twenty and say, 'I've got this record that Andy Weatherall's been playing out a lot, big siren thing.' And shops would buy it, because they'd had the Siren Bloke on the phone earlier that day. I'd do a bowl around central London shops, call in the morning and visit in the afternoon. Flying in Kensington Market bought loads. The 12-inch had my mum's phone number on there. I'd get home and she'd have taken a message. 'A lovely man called Darren Emerson rang. He'd like you to call him back, he left his number.'

Tom: Technically, the record was really helped by whoever mastered it; apologies for having forgotten who did that job. It had just been recorded at home straight onto a cassette with no compression, none of the things you'd have in a studio to make it sound good. It was just recorded live straight onto a cassette.

With Ariel we'd recorded in proper studios, and we'd worked with people like Hugo Nicholson and Charles Webster in Nottingham. Deconstruction were very plugged into 'dance world', so you'd end up in posh studios working with people who'd made lots of big records. It was educational and informative, in that it sharpened thoughts about what I wanted to do, as opposed to what a record company were telling me I should be doing. Playing a track like 'Song to the Siren' out, even if it was fifty of your mates going crazy, it felt like you were doing the right thing for the right reasons. So what if some people in shops said, 'It's too slow.' It didn't bother me; it's still one of my favourite things we've done.

Ed: 'We had this mad Siren Bloke on the phone going on about Weatherall, but we think it's too slow.'

Tom: Andy Weatherall playing the record was such a big thing for us as people – as fans – and for the record.

Ed: We owe such a lot to Andy Weatherall. There were labels that tried to sign 'Song to the Siren' but we kept running up against the same thing. Tom was already in a signed band. I wasn't going to sign a record deal on my own. It wasn't really what I wanted to do. When Boy's Own [JBO] came along through Andy, that felt exciting and doable. We had a meeting with Andy, which was a really cool moment. I'd been summoned into the back room of a club. Tom wasn't there for some reason. I said we'd sign to JBO if he remixed it. That was all that mattered back then. We used to follow it round, trying to be there for the moment Andy would play the record in his sets.

Tom: 'Fucking hell, not those two again.'

Ed: We definitely heard it at Sabresonics. Then we tried to repeat that moment in different cities wherever he was playing. We went to Nottingham and to Back2Basics in Leeds. Tom had a big Ford Sierra estate in those days that we'd pile into.

Tom: The bloke who sold it to me said, 'Good for ram-raiding, that one.' *I'll obviously bear that in mind, good sir*. Probably would have been a very good car for Siren Bloke. I remember we were once in a club that got ram-raided. The Wiggly Worm in Manchester, probably on a night when Justin was DJing. A proper Northern Soul name, that. You couldn't physically get out of the club because there was a car wedged into the doorway. 'Best stay down there lads, bit of bother at the door.'

Justin Robertson

When Ed came in with the first 12-inch copies of 'Song to the Siren', it just made total sense. Obviously, it was fucking amazing, but it wasn't a surprise that the two of them would make music that complete and visionary. All of the records we were listening to back at people's houses after clubs, all of the records they were painstakingly sourcing in the shop, records they'd told me about, it didn't surprise me that they'd made that genius record. Of course they made that record. And although you could hear bits and pieces of other things in there – Depth Charge, Renegade Soundwave, hip-hop instrumentals – it didn't sound like anything else around. Absolutely new, untameable, it's all intent. It sounded like nothing else around and it blew everything else to bits. I always used to open my sets with it, which was a good and a bad decision as everything that followed it sounded crap by comparison. It got people's attention but nothing afterwards sounded anything like as good.

When I played, I'd tend to slow things down at the end of the set to play things like One Dove, records that felt very euphoric. 'Song to the Siren' goes in the other direction. It takes that old-school, downtempo Balearic shuffle and turbocharges it with the kind of sound that you'd have heard in the techno end of the set, combining them all together, channelling things from the past to make something utterly new. It's almost like an entire night out condensed into a song.

The interesting thing about that time was it wasn't year zero for dance music, as acid house had already happened. Electronic music was breaking out of being just about house. People came to the dance music scene from lots of different places, be it soul boys, disco heads, people into shoegaze or industrial music or rock music, and the things that people would end up listening to at afterparties – dub or Cocteau Twins, This Mortal Coil, records that work when the sun is coming up. 'Song to the Siren' channels all of those kinds of influences and experiments on them, using them to make new things. I guess that was the spirit of the time. As a track, it's so much more than a siren and a breakbeat. It's alchemy, really. Magic.

Steven Hall (Junior Boy's Own)

We were in a deal with London Records and the contractual period was close to being up. We'd just put out the One Dove album and we were having real trouble as London just didn't want to release anything that we wanted to do. I came up with the idea of starting a new label – Junior Boy's Own – as a way of putting out things we liked because we were stagnating. London were going to drop us, which we didn't know but probably suspected, and Andy [Weatherall] was thinking of leaving the setup too.

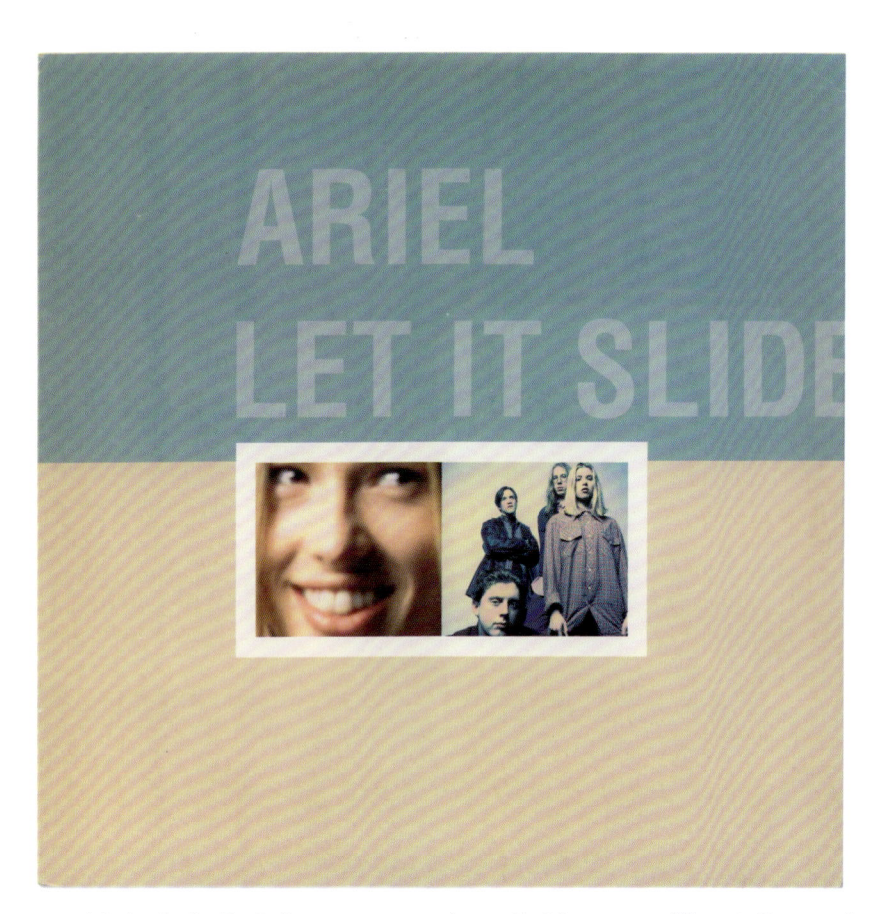

But there was still an obligation to take any records that we wanted to release on Junior Boy's Own into London. We had to get them to pass on them before we could put them out. But that part was easy because they just weren't interested in any of it. I'd taken Underworld in, Fire Island, X-Press 2. Pete Tong and Tracy Bennett, who were our points of contact there, knocked them all back. And I took The Dust Brothers. They were completely uninterested, which gave us the opportunity to release it on Junior.

The original 12-inch of 'Song to the Siren' had been pressed up by CT Records, who were friends of ours who had an office next to Boy's Own in Ladbroke Grove. Although I got a copy from them, I first heard it through Andy. He told me he'd met them, that they'd been going to lots of his shows, and they were part of Justin Robertson's Most Excellent/Spice crew in Manchester. They'd given him the track that he'd been playing. He loved it but knew that it was very different. Because it was slow. To me, it felt something like 'Radio Babylon' by Meat Beat Manifesto, which was a big record at the time. Andy said if we signed it, he'd do a remix, which was what Ed and Tom wanted. I got in contact with them and signed the record for something like 500 quid. No options, just as a one-off single with remixes by Andy. I'm not sure Ed and Tom knew the difference between the London Records setup and Junior or whether they cared. I think they were just happy to have a wider release for the single.

We were releasing through a network of dance music distributors. It wasn't even indie distribution, like Rough Trade or anyone like that. Our records wouldn't have got in the *NME* indie charts then because dance distribution was a cottage industry outside of the indie charts, and it was almost the Wild West. You could release records and they wouldn't be noticed in a wider world, or by the people that were bothered about sampling. You could play fast and loose with the whole thing. We'd expect to sell a certain amount of records within the scene we were in, and we didn't expect them to do much outside of that world. And everyone was doing sample-based

The Ever So Cool Hot Naked Ten

Selectah 'Wede Man' (Moonroof)
Dust Brothers 'Song to the Siren' (Junior Boys Own)
Ariel 'Let it Slide (hitting the bottle mix)' (Deconstruction)
Ultra Violet Catastrophy Trip Harder (Switched)
Hector ZaZou I'll Strangle You (Cramped)
Man Know Who 'I Think I Wanna Rock' (Nu-Groove)
Flowered Up 'It's On' (Heavenly)
RSW 'Black Eye Boy' (Mute)
LLCoolJ 'Mama Said Knock You Out' (Def Jam)
Beastie Boys 'Jimmy James' (Capitol)

records in that world but they weren't going to bother the BPI chart machine because dance shops didn't have the BPI machines. We were completely outside of the record industry.

We'd have initially pressed around 5,000 copies of 'Song to the Siren'. That was our benchmark on things. People bought our stuff on the label alone; people were collecting our records even back then. A decent chunk would have gone on export. In the end, it sold a lot more – more like 20,000 over time. You'd sell out what was out there then press up more copies. Five hundred, two thousand. There wasn't any issue with getting records pressed like there is now. Pressing plants could turn things round in days.

Things were mixed up then. It was the last vestiges of the Balearic years, but a lot of DJs we'd normally send records to didn't really get the track. It was hard and it was slow. But it was popular with the kind of people who were fans of Andy, at the point when he started to become what people think of him now.

Initially, I don't think Ed and Tom had much more ambition for the track other than to get Andy Weatherall to remix it and have it out on a proper label. They were young, enthusiastic kids who just wanted to put music out, which we could do for them. In time, things changed as they started getting asked to remix lots of rock 'n' roll bands, and their name started appearing on records by bands they'd grown up with. There was a sense that they might be a bit different to everything else.

Previous page: The Dust Brothers' 'top ten', which accompanied their first ever interview in Jockey Slut *Issue 2, March 1993.*

Below: DJ and Producer Andrew Weatherall.

Opposite: The first four The Dust Brothers releases

Paused in Cosmic Reflection 49

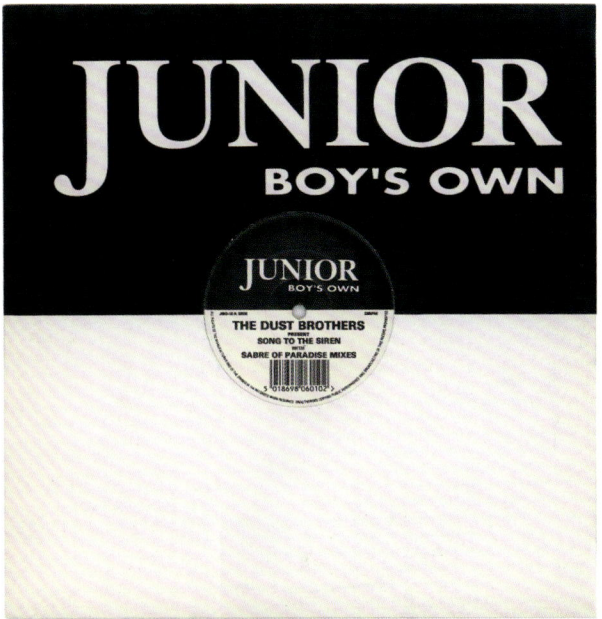

Life Is Sweet: DJing as The Dust Brothers

The Dust Brothers might have been born in a student house share at 237 Dickenson Road, Manchester, but they grew up behind record decks. The music they played in those formative years was unique. While other DJs trying to make themselves known might have scrabbled round for upfront promos and import 12-inches, The Dust Brothers took what they could grab from supportive friends at Eastern Bloc, along with records they'd bought as teenagers and the rejects that had made their way to the £1 box. That combination in the right hands – their hands – seemed to create a tractor beam that would draw people into the middle of the floor for an unholy, ecstatic tumult, time after time.

Ed Simons

I remember reading a DJ saying, 'I don't understand DJ duos, it's a one-man job.' That didn't make sense to me at all. When we started out, it was the two of us doing what we did, together. That was the only way it really made any sense.

Tom Rowlands

Right from the start we had a very specific kind of record in mind that we wanted in our DJ sets. A massive drum beat and an almost industrial-sounding rhythm. I loved noisy music, I loved ethereal-sounding indie music and I loved heavy dub basslines. There were a lot of contemporary records had that sound, records by people like Renegade Soundwave, Meat Beat Manifesto and Depth Charge.

There was something different about what we were doing. It was influenced by someone like Andy Weatherall. We knew the breadth of music he liked and played, and we tried to find records that fitted into that wider world. It was connected to that. I was really into Tackhead and the kind of noisy music that was somewhere between dub, hip hop and industrial music. I loved those huge Keith LeBlanc drum breaks.

Our early recordings and remixes were us trying to hit the same sweet spots as records by those artists in order to make music to fit in our DJ sets.

Ed Simons

We didn't have tons and tons of records. We were students, on student money. We had to make things work. I remember when we got 'Wede Man' [by Selectah], it immediately felt like the perfect Naked Under Leather record. The tempo, the sampled guitar, the words.

We'd look for things in the bargain bin of Vinyl Exchange. We would always be drawn to the second track on the B-side of a 12-inch, those heavy instrumental tracks, bonus beats. That was usually the version that worked for us. In the early days we used to play an 808 State remix of 'Owner of a Lonely Heart' by Yes. It's a brilliant record that takes a snatch of guitar and some of the drum fills from the original, but really it's its own thing: one of those building tracks that help lift the energy in the room. It has that great churning build. That would have been a pound in the bargain basement. 808 State's Graham Massey was such a huge part of electronic music going overground in this country in the late eighties but a lot of his background is in psychedelic guitar music. No one else seemed to have picked up on it.

Another track we used to play a lot from one of the *Pay It All Back* compilations. It was a Mark Stewart track called 'These Things Happen'. It's really sinister. We liked records that had an acid line that weren't technically acid house. In the early nineties, we were nineteen, twenty years old and Britain was really bleak. At the time I think we were quite unconscious of that. We weren't

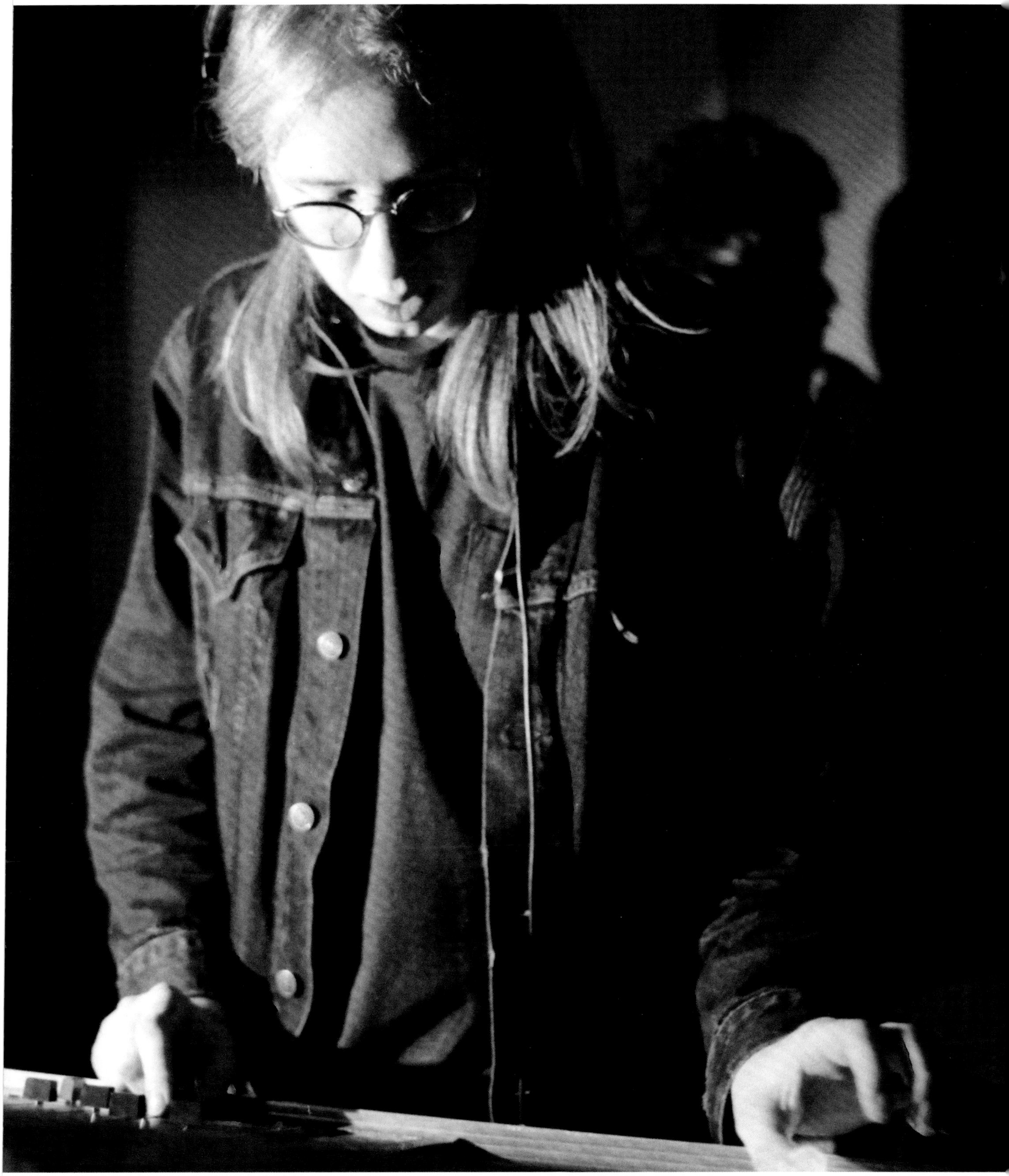

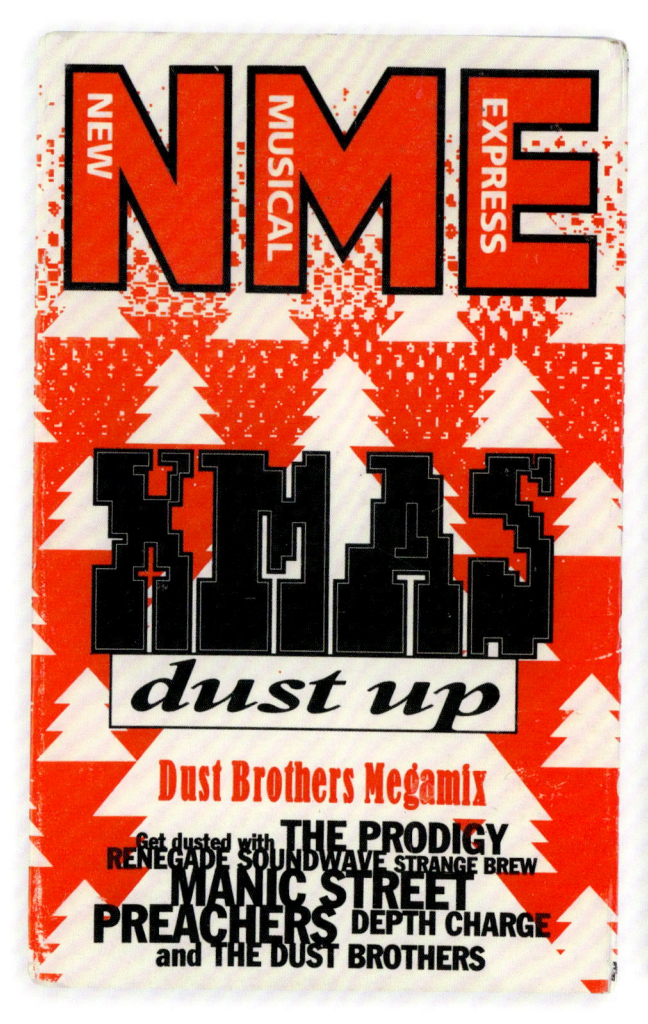

the eighties and when we were playing it in the nineties. And they still do now.

Tim Burgess

I first met Tom and Ed at the first Heavenly Sunday Social. I went up to say hello because they'd done a really great remix of The Charlatans track 'Patrol'. That first night was so incredible that I started going down there every week. As someone who used to go to The Haçienda, I felt the Social was the best thing that happened in clubs since The Haç. I've never been to anything since anywhere in the world that's matched the feeling of those nights, all of which were soundtracked by The Dust Brothers. They'd be playing Beastie Boys and Barry White in the same set and all these other acid records that I didn't know but I wanted to know.

Pretty soon they asked me to sing on a track on the album they were making. They sent me two tracks – both of which I knew because they were playing them as part of their sets. One was 'In Dust We Trust', the other one was called 'Delik'. As an instrumental, 'Delik' must have been played nine or ten times out of the thirteen weeks their residency was on. Having heard it down there, I felt connected to it. I knew I could write something that would work with the music.

Ed Simons

Things snowballed very quickly at the Social. I arrived early at The Albany on maybe the third week, before it got really busy after the fourth week. They were piping some music into the upstairs bar as people were coming in and paying to go downstairs. I was listening and one after another, there was each of our big records. I hadn't had a drink, was getting ready to DJ thinking, 'They've played that . . . and that . . . and that . . . what the fuck.' Someone was playing our whole set. I didn't know who the DJ was, but they'd bought all of the records from our set. It was bad. Then it dawned on me that the bar was playing a tape of our set from the previous

The free The Dust Brothers mix cassette given away with NME, *December 1994.*

Opposite: Flyers from the first four weeks of the Heavenly Sunday Social and the Job Club.

54 **The Chemical Brothers**

the Heavenly Sunday social
at The Albany, nr. Great Portland St. Tube
every Sunday in August (7, 14, 21, 28)
resident DJ's The Dust Brothers

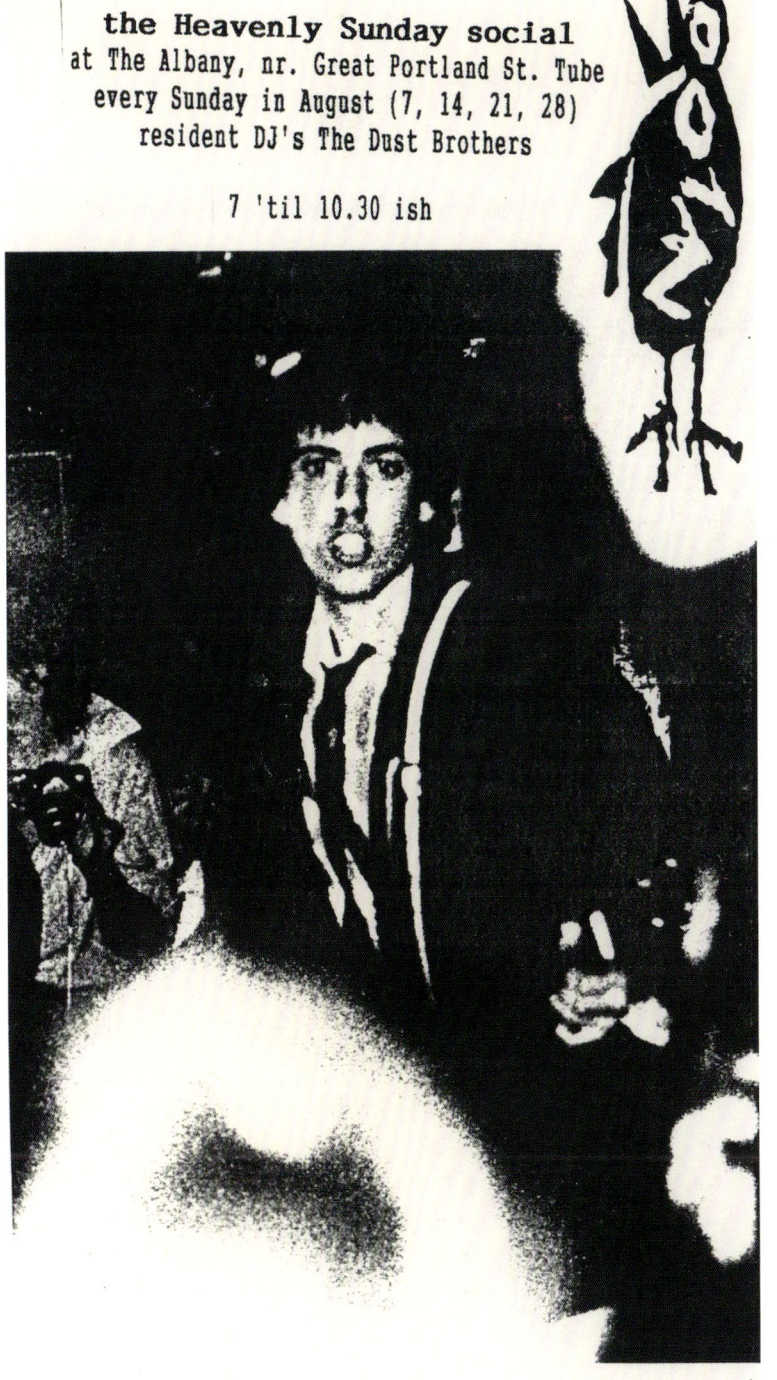

7 'til 10.30 ish

August's Heavenly Heroes & guests
Paolo Hewitt, Saint Etienne, Gareth Sweeney, Kris Needs
playing what comes naturally
£3 in, get in early
HVN 44

£6

10.00pm-3.30am!
every friday!

the job club

"hi, we run the job club. every Friday night we hear the same thing-laughing, great music and the clink of glasses. why not shuffle down for a drink, a chat and a dance. anyway, that's enough about us-here's our disk jockeys for july!"

2nd justin robertson/the dust bros./angela
9th nick james/john nelson
16th ralph lawson(back to basics)/john beach
23rd darren emerson/the dust bros.
30th dean thatcher/sean rolfe
plus residents reckless, fearless & owain

gossips,
meard street,
soho w1

runner-up in the Job Club Club of the Year Award

week. In my mind, I was convinced that someone had already stolen everything we were doing.

Around the time the Social was running, there were a few occasions where we got invited to play at other clubs. Those records just didn't work in the same way, without the same crowd, in that room. We had to quickly adapt the way we played away from that dance floor. We weren't technically the greatest DJs, but we spent a long time trying to find a way to make those records work together. Other people starting to promote nights meant there were other places to go and play. It wasn't so alien. The only thing I bristle at is that the shorthand for the music we were making was 'big beat'. That term became synonymous with lads, with being unsophisticated. It was a way of dismissing what was quite innovative about the music we were making. We weren't really part of any scene. We were always striving to make and play exciting, mind-altering psychedelic music.

Paused in Cosmic Reflection

The Chemical Brothers

Paused in Cosmic Reflection 57

GOOD MORNING LOYAL (AND NOT SO LOYAL)
SABRESONIC ASSAULT SQUAD MEMBERS....
LOOK AT THE QUALITY OF THIS LINE UP!

18th MARCH : FROM GOD'S OWN COUNTRY IT'S JOHNNY MOY AND PERFORMING LIVE IT'S THE MASTERS OF CHUNK ROCK, THE DUST BROTHERS.

25th MARCH : PULL ON YA HARD HATS AND TIE YA FLAPS DOWN IT'S TONY SAPIANO and SPICELAB LIVE.

1st APRIL : 'PURE' AT SABRESONIC: EDINBURGH'S FINEST TAKE OVER THE CONTROLS, TWITCH, BRAINSTORM, and EGE BAM YASI.

8th APRIL : LAURENT GARNIER 5 HOUR SESSION.

15th APRIL : SABRESONIC WELCOMES BOB JONES, YES PUNTERS THE BOB JONES OPENS HIS SURGERY!

22nd APRIL : IT'S 4 A.M. FINISHING AND A RETURN VISIT FROM THE MIGHTY RITCHIE HAWTIN, AND A LIVE PERFORMANCE FROM NEURO PROJECT.....

P.S. REGULAR ASSAULT SQUAD WILL BE FAMILIAR WITH A CERTAIN PAUL WELLER TRACK THAT'S RARER THAN ROCKING HORSE SHIT.... WELL NOT ANY MORE, IT'S OUT ON THE 28th MARCH FEATURED ON 'THE HUNG UP E.P.' (GO DISCS RECORDS)

P.P.S. "NEVER TRUST A HIPPY WITH A LANYER!"

A.W.

Live at Sabresonic Nightclub (and Other Stories)

The Dust Brothers' first gig was at Andrew Weatherall's club night Sabresonic, which took place at Happy Jax on Crucifix Lane, London SE1 on 18 March 1994. The band started working with Vegetable Vision (Adam Smith and Noah Clark) after the show.

Tom Rowlands

I knew immediately that we shouldn't try to DJ at Sabresonic. The other people playing on the night were real DJs. We didn't see ourselves like that. I always felt like I was coming from the perspective of a musician; playing live felt more natural. As much as we loved DJing, we felt more confident going into that environment as a live act.

Ariel had been a good education when it came to The Dust Brothers shows, mainly because I learnt how not to do things. Those Ariel shows were incredibly stressful. We'd turn up to great clubs like Venus in Nottingham, which would be packed full of people on a night out. A few hours later, you're on a makeshift stage trying to tune a Rickenbacker guitar that's feeding back endlessly while attempting to add live vocals over the top of temperamental electronics. We'd play our own songs and then move on to covers that we'd played at school as a band. There was something truly Balearic about it, and we always thought that the people in the kind of clubs that played that music would really get into it. But they didn't. We'd run live sequencers, there would be things coming off a DAT and it would be so sweaty it would invariably fall apart. Then, after you've played for twenty minutes, you're left trying to pack up gear that's drenched in sweat while a full-on club night is firing all around you.

The fact was that people didn't want what we were doing at their clubs. They wanted to hear the DJ playing. They didn't want something that came along and broke up the night. And that informed us how The Dust Brothers shows would be. They needed to be part of the night, not an add on.

Ed Simons

Andy Weatherall wanted us to play Sabresonic in some way. We knew the club as we'd already been a few times. The music was hard. A lot of techno. We didn't feel up to it as DJs, so we very quickly put together a live set that was eighteen minutes long. I'm still quite obsessed with the length of our original live show. I sometimes think that eighteen minutes was the perfect length for a live show. Leave the crowd wanting more. A lot more.

Tom Rowlands

Andy Weatherall and Dublin DJ Johnny Moy were on before us. When we turned up, they pointed us towards the stage. We refused to play on it. I still think back to the youthfulness of that: 'We're not doing that, it's ridiculous.' We set up above the toilets at the back of the venue, carrying our gear up ladders. Everyone was facing the wrong way when we came on. We felt like we were standing firm on a principle, saying that we're not going on stage as the main attraction or the turn for the night.

With hindsight, I think if I was running a club and someone turned up and said, 'We're the band booked to play but we're not getting on the stage you've got set up', I'd have told them to do one. But, as in so many other ways, Andy Weatherall was different and obviously thought, 'Why not?' Their whole ethos was brilliant. I'm pretty sure there aren't many other clubs that would have been so accommodating of having to run audio lines to the back of the venue where the toilets are when there was a perfectly good stage at the front of the room. And all for a

Top: Adam Smith

Top right: Noah Clark and projectors with customised 'strobe' wheels.

Below: Vegetable Vision projector beams.

band with two 12-inches out. But it made total sense to us. The fact the request was accommodated was a testament to the spirit of the club and the times we were in. And that strength of will definitely helped propel us.

Ed Simons

There were a few electronic bands playing live in the early nineties. We'd gone to see Kraftwerk when we were at university in 1991 and Tom had been in Ariel, so we knew it was something that could happen, but initially we just DJed. We got offered to do Sabresonic very early on; we'd only done a handful of remixes and *Fourteenth Century Sky* was just out. From the very start, we knew we didn't want to be in the spotlight on stage. We decided that we wanted to have visuals projected right on top of us. And lots of strobes. That ethos has been the same for every gig we've played in the thirty-odd years since. And it's always been with Adam, who is such a massive part of how we present ourselves.

Adam Smith

We always used to say Vegetable Vision was a state of mind, not a plate of food.

The original Vegetable Vision family was me, Marcus [Lyall], Joe Wright [director] and Noah Clark. We started doing visuals at parties in the late eighties. We used to do visuals at Sabresonic once a month. If you were down there setting up in the day, someone would be knocking out bootleg Ralph Lauren shirts. The club would drip with damp – it was the kind of place you'd always catch a cold – and there was a permanent low-level fog outside. The names of the streets were all Dickensian: Crucifix Lane, Vinegar Yard. I had a conversation with Ed where he said they were thinking about going out live and asked if we'd be interested in doing visuals. He'd seen what we did at Sabresonic and at gigs by The Sandals, who they had recently remixed.

Weatherall was a real champion of Noah and I. We didn't realise what it meant to get the Weatherall stamp of approval. We would get asked to do visuals at clubs all over the country and I'd just think it was because we were the best, but the reality was that it was down to Andy talking us up.

I can remember first hearing The Dust Brothers' music on a 12-inch that came out on Junior Boy's Own ('Song to the Siren'). There was something incredibly fresh about the sound of the record, at a point where a lot of dance music felt quite bloated. Acid house was quite a way in the distance already. Their record felt raw and vital and energetic; it was rough around the edges and it made you want to dance.

Ed asked if we wanted to do visuals for their live shows. At that point, they weren't entirely sure about putting themselves on stage. I think they thought of themselves as backroom boys, as it were. If you think about it, there was a time when electronic producers were scorned for going out live. Kraftwerk had always done it, but the vast amount of this generation of artists hadn't made the move. Having the visual thing there was very important.

We were up for it straight away. As you get older you have a tendency to overthink things, but back then it was much more, 'Right, love that music, let's do it.' Sometimes the best work is the stuff that the least thought has gone into, things that are immediate reactions.

Chris York (promoter, SJM Concerts)

The first Dust Brothers gig I put on was at the Astoria, supporting Underworld in

Paused in Cosmic Reflection 61

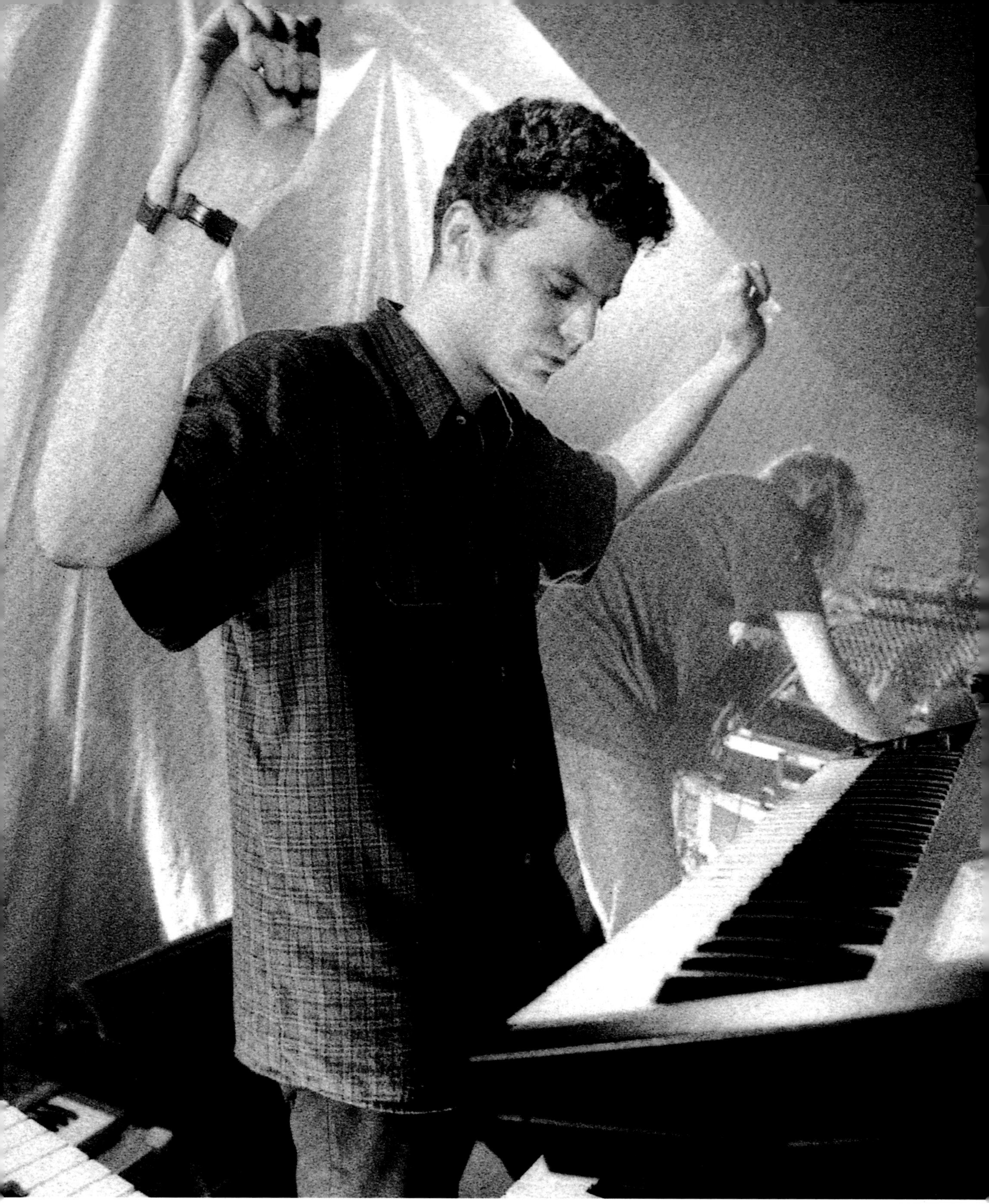

October 1994. There hadn't been that many good electronic acts playing live at the turn of the nineties; the domestic scene was very underground. The guys who ran the Megadog events are really underrated in the development of live electronic music in the UK. They gave a platform to lots of acts that weren't that commercially successful, at a time when mainstream promoters wouldn't touch them. When I started working at SJM, I found myself in a position to put those kinds of bands on. Tom and Ed were very connected with Manchester and I was based up there with SJM, so I put a lot of time into trying to make things work.

Alex Nightingale (The Chemical Brothers' live agent)

I first got involved with Tom and Ed after spending a lot of Sunday nights down The Albany. I was working with Primal Scream and I got Tom and Ed to DJ on a Christmas tour the year *Give Out But Don't Give Up* came out. Throb and Martin Duffy took a shine to them; they always looked out for them in the midst of a lot of chaos. I always remember Tom and Ed being really polite, asking about catering and the like. Really nice guys. I started booking their shows the following year.

James Holroyd

Two friends of mine – Jonno and Paul – started a fanzine called *Jockey Slut*. Soon after, they started a club night called Bugged Out! for the growing community around the magazine. I was resident DJ there. The club was pretty special from the off, full of hungry music heads. Tom and Ed and their new out-there productions got them on the front cover of the mag and a live show at Bugged Out! It was psychedelic and beat-y, an absolutely fresh amalgamation of sound and vision. Adam and Noah were up scaffold towers with 16mm film loops around their necks. I warmed up with some very slow and moody music that I saw as relevant. I like to think of it as a pressure cooker with a captive audience. The main event is coming, vibe headroom is the key. My memory is blurry, but it may have even been that night that Tom and Ed said they were doing a little tour and asked if I fancied coming along. That little tour has been going on ever since with pretty much the same ethos. Eternal love to them.

Some of my first gig experiences with them were at the kind of venues and clubs that it would never have crossed my mind I'd be playing at. I remember being stood looking at DJs in The Haç in '87, '88, thinking, 'This place is ace, imagine being the DJ.' Six years later, I'm warming up in the same booth, working a 90 bpm pressure cooker. My god it felt good!

Tom Rowlands

At early Dust Brothers gigs, I'd take an Akai MPC3000 sequencer/sampler, a Juno 106 and a few other bits and pieces. Some of the songs we'd play off the Akai sequencer, and then when we were reloading we'd have bits on the DAT player or a multitrack and we'd mix between the two. It's interesting listening to recordings of our early gigs, where you can hear the bits we're mixing out of tracks and into drum machines. That was a safety net, because you didn't want everything to collapse in front of a room full of people, but the setup meant we could go off on a techno tangent if the mood took us. The setup was very much like DJing between an 8-track digital recorder and some sequencers. In many ways, it was a less fancy version of what we do now.

We used floppy discs at the time, so you'd have to load things up while something else was playing. We'd have an ADAT (an 8-track DAT) and a mixer. We didn't have enough money to have two systems running. That was a big thing we learnt early on when working in the studio with Dubby. He showed us all these techniques – how you make dub mixes of things, with delays feeding back into each other. All those experiences fed in.

For me, it was so exciting to hear those kinds of sounds on a big PA system Really raw, old synthesisers having mad wig-outs through a massive sound system is an exciting thing to hear, even more so if you're playing it. There's a CAT synthesiser that we still use in the live setup that has these really brutal nasty frequencies and harmonics in it. Hearing that playing loud was incredibly inspiring. I always remembered Kevin Shields talking about hearing things at insane volumes – it reveals different bits within the music that you can't otherwise pick up. It's true – but could explain why he also suffers from tinnitus.

Adam Smith

In those days a lot of people doing visuals were using early video projectors and showing fractal patterns. We were using slide projectors, sixteen-millimetre film projectors. It would create this woozy sensation. The imagery was very graphic and very bold, which it needed to be to cut through and be bright enough, because the projectors weren't that strong.

Once we started working with Tom and Ed, we made a decision that the visuals would all be black and white. I don't think there was a conversation about that; we didn't analyse things back then, we just did it.

Ed Simons

Our live shows were initially propelled by the fact that we're not natural performers. We just wanted blinding lights and visuals from the get-go. Done properly, visuals hugely intensify the experience of the music. Blinding lights definitely fulfilled a similar role to the sirens on the records.

When *Exit Planet Dust* came out, we started thinking about how to put on a proper live show. We used to play a lot in tents in European festivals. Those gigs were a real learning curve, in that they provided a way to get our music across to a broad section of people. Early on, we were playing at rock festivals. We wouldn't necessarily be in a dance tent as there probably wouldn't have been much of a dance tent back then. Within a few years, we were playing at the end of the night on the main stage, sometimes kind of quasi-headlining above another band. We'd use samples from other people's records in our sets, things like 'Eight Miles High' by The Byrds or 'Temptation' by New Order. Perhaps that was our way of making our music digestible to what was primarily a rock audience.

Robert Linney

Some of their earliest gigs were supporting The Prodigy. They played with them at the Astoria and Blackpool Empress Ballroom. A few months later, The Chemical Brothers played the Astoria themselves. Keith Flint from The Prodigy joined them on stage for the encore, and promptly kicked the power cable out while dancing.

Adam Smith

Vegetable Vision was a bit like being in a band. Touring, arriving in a different city every day. It was exciting and we were all having a lot of fun. And we were really tight, like Ed and Tom. We were best mates, meshed into each other's lives both personally and with work. It meant that touring was like two old couples going on holiday together. It meant if you weren't getting on with your other half, you could sit and bitch with someone from the other couple.

Previous page: Playing at The Haçienda, June 1995.

Opposite: Sugar Sweet in Belfast, 1994.

Paused in Cosmic Reflection 65

66   **The Chemical Brothers**

Paused in Cosmic Reflection 67

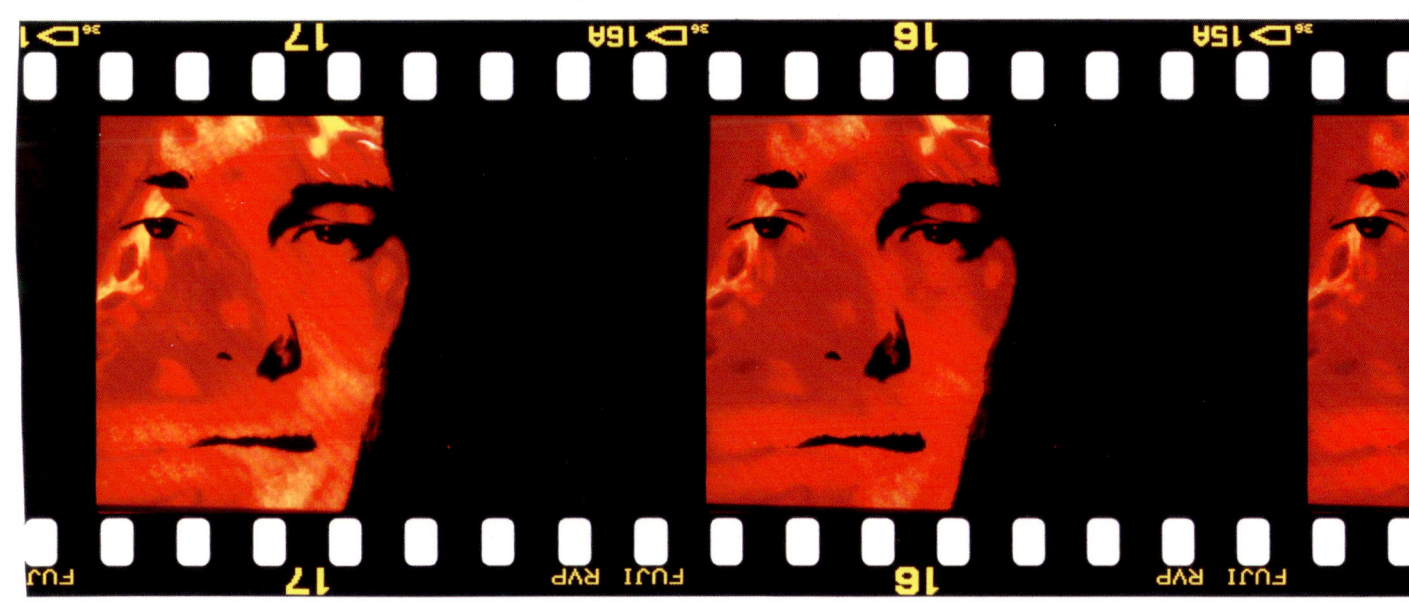

Tom Rowlands

We quickly realised that Adam and Noah were similarly bloody-minded. Their purity of vision could be frustrating at times, but it worked. I remember at Glastonbury they had to use cinema projectors. They'd be setting up with these massive projectors and people would ask, 'Why are you doing it like this?' Like us, they had these rules of engagement and it had to be that way. We were still touring with all these old synthesisers that would go out of tune or sometimes just die completely, and that was definitely mirrored on the visual side of things, where Noah would have built something out of a Hornby railway set to do some mad strobing effect. They had things made out of stuff they'd found in army surplus stores or bought off old guys they'd somehow met.

They'd accumulate all this vintage equipment and then add more to it as the years went on. And then you'd find yourself on the main stage at Glastonbury, with everyone else having a much slicker operation than you. You've got this setup with all this stuff added on, like a house built in the twelfth century that's got all these bits stuck to it, but there's no way you'd ever have designed it that way.

Adam and Noah were a brilliant combination of people to work with. There was always a lot of excitement on tour with those two, they were quite big characters. The circus has rolled into town. They were both giant and angry and lovely. You'd get to the venue and there would invariably be some massive falling out already. It was a good gang of people to go round the world with.

Adam Smith

We used to pick a lot of equipment up off the Ministry of Defence. They had no use for AV equipment as video had taken over, so they were getting rid of all that kind of technology. Our contact there would sort us out everything – projectors, lenses – and he'd always demand cash, which we didn't really think anything of at the time. We also had a yellow transit van that used to belong to British Telecom.

Tom Rowlands

I don't really know how the transition between club shows and festival shows happened. One minute you're playing above the toilets at the back of Sabresonic and the next you're headlining the Pyramid Stage at Glastonbury.

Previous page: Early visuals for The Chemical Brothers' shows by Vegetable Vision.

Left: Adam, Tom and Noah.

Opposite: Adam and Noah editing 16mm film loops.

[The Chemical Brothers supported Oasis at Knebworth on Saturday, 10 August 1996.]

Alex Nightingale

I'd been working with them a while and I got a call to say Noel Gallagher was cherry-picking the bill for some upcoming shows at Knebworth. The Oasis agent asked if The Chemical Brothers would support. Any other band on the planet would have said yes. These were going to be the biggest live shows in British music history. But the offer was so low. Obviously support bands get paid two and six, but this wasn't even covering the cost of a van from London. I was a bit nonplussed. The gig was in daylight, and there was no money in it. So I went to run it past Tom and Ed. I was told the show was non-negotiable, had to be done. Unbeknownst to me, they'd recorded 'Setting Sun' with Noel, and this was a relationship that they wanted to solidify.

Fast-forward to the day. An interesting crowd. When I get to a show, I always like to have a wander around to see how it's set up, so I went looking for a merch stall. I ended up at the one furthest from the stage. It's the only show in my life where I've seen band-branded binoculars. I hovered on buying a pair, then thought it might look a bit naff turning up backstage with a pair of limited-edition Oasis binoculars. They're probably worth a fortune now.

The band were very nervous before the gig. The size of the crowd is something I don't think any of us will ever forget, even when they were on relatively early. The show itself was thirty minutes long and they were sandwiched between The Bootleg Beatles and Ocean Colour Scene. It was tough to go out there in daylight. However many banks of strobes you've got going off, they don't really have a great deal of effect at that time of the day. The response was OK, but I don't think it'll go down as one of their all-time live gig experiences. Job done, and the lesson learnt was that dusk slots don't really work, daylight slots really don't work. Avoid at all costs.

Adam Smith

As things got bigger and the band started playing outdoor stages at festivals, we were limited by lenses and how much distance they could cover. We'd send faxes to the promoter of the festival demanding that the scaffold tower had to be a maximum of

70   **The Chemical Brothers**

Paused in Cosmic Reflection 71

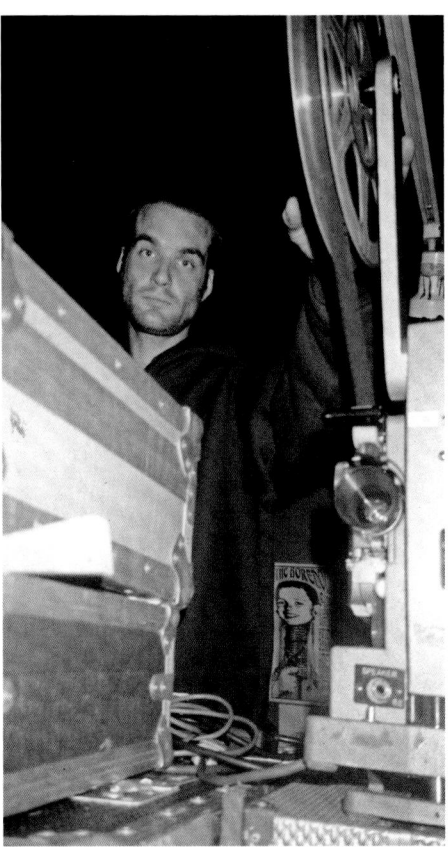

Previous page centre:
USA tour, 1997.

Previous page bottom right:
(L–R) Crippsy, Ed, Noah, Cozy and Tom.

Left: Early visuals by Flat Nose George.

Top centre: (L–R) Robert Linney (manager), Adam Smith, Alex Nightingale (live agent).

twenty-seven metres away from the front of house. If it was further than that, our lenses couldn't fill the screens. We turned up at Glastonbury in 1997 to set up and the tower was further back. It was one of the muddy years, and we arrived telling them, 'We're going to have to move the scaffold tower.' They said, 'We can't do that, the festival's in full swing', and we replied, 'We can't do a show if it's back here.' The same thing happened in France. 'We can't move the tower.' 'You go and tell the band they can't play then.' I'd send these faxes that had absolute instructions about the distance. They ended up shifting it in the pouring rain. I'm not sure we were much help.

Eventually we had to upgrade the slide projectors to Xenon ones that were these huge beasts. They were Kodak slide projectors mounted on this massive casing with a huge Xenon bulb and a huge fan to cool them. We used to lug these things up a scaffold tower. Sometimes we'd have to erect the scaffold tower ourselves. You're supposed to have side supports, which we never bothered with. We used to have people up there with us as it was the best place to watch a gig from, it became a bit of a party. I shudder to think how unsafe it all was.

Alex Nightingale

21 June 1999. Midsummer's day and a national holiday in France known as the Fête de la Musique. There are gigs in every venue, in the streets, everywhere. The Chemical Brothers were booked to play La Cigale, which is the best venue in Paris. A really beautiful old ballroom. When we got there, we realised the curfew was at 10 p.m. 'Why are we playing on a national holiday at half eight?' Because there's a club on after. 'Why aren't we playing the club night rather than an early evening gig?' I couldn't argue with any of it, so I bid them adieu and went away thinking I'd made a big mistake.

The gig was incredible, beyond anything anyone could have expected. Audiences in Paris can sometimes be quite hard to win over; this was bedlam. The sound was mind-blowing. When it finished, sunlight was still streaming down Le Pigalle, people everywhere, joyous like a festival. And Tom and Ed loved it. When everything seems stacked against you, you can end up having a gig that you know you'll remember for the rest of your life.

Ed Simons

We always wanted to play Glastonbury and put on a good show. There was a real wave of people loving dance music at festivals, which Glastonbury seemed to capture better than anywhere else. When Orbital headlined there, it just sounded right. The whole idea of buzzing on the leylines, the energy that's flowing through that place, the open skies. Electronic music just sounds really good in that context.

We didn't headline the Other Stage the first time we played Glastonbury in 1997; that honour went to Kula Shaker. It was quite a hard year weather-wise, but when we headlined the Pyramid Stage in 2000, it was one of those really bright early summer evenings. There's something indescribable about how the sun drops over the whole festival, where everyone experiences the beauty of nature together. You come on just as it's dusk. Because you're really in nature and the whole thing is a primal experience, it shapes the way audiences react.

And then the gig, and that massive, massive crowd. We had maybe three screens behind us and some back projection. It felt very state of art. The visuals were synced to the music, but the syncing was done by hand with Adam and Noah feeding reels of film into projectors, stopping and starting. All done very much on the fly.

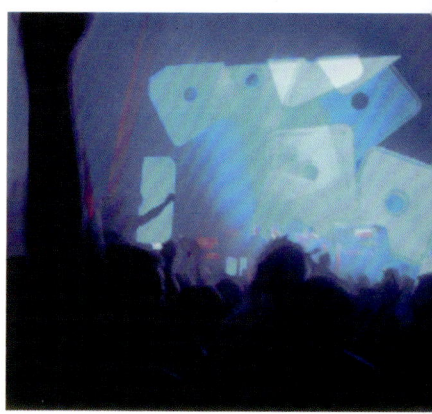

Paused in Cosmic Reflection 73

74   **The Chemical Brothers**

There's something so special about the crowd at Glastonbury. It's obviously changed over the years, but one constant is that you always know they're staying put. They are present. They want to have a good time, they're getting together with friends away from home, collectively creating this third space. It's about communing. And I think that's what our music has always been about. People at festivals come to see us but they come to see each other as well, to share a transcendent experience. Everything we do coincides with what Glastonbury does. It's about surrendering to something magical, almost indescribable really. It's not just dance music, but it brings in that energy. It's a perfect environment. The sense of getting it together in the countryside, away from the urban centres, is a beautiful thing.

People go on about the weather at Glastonbury, but I think the weather systems can really help alter the atmosphere. We played in 2007 and I remember driving down. We were playing on the Sunday night, and I'd stayed home while all my friends were there. It was a big show as it was one of the first times we were using the LED screens. And the weather was terrible. As I was driving down, I kept getting texts from mates saying, 'I'm sorry, I'm heading home, I can't do any more, I'm too old for this.' As I drove into the site, the crew were trying to work out how they were going to get everything on stage; it was being blasted with rain and wind. We were up against The Who on the main stage. We had no idea how the hell the show was going to take place, let alone go down. There was a despondency, but a stoic feeling that the show must go on. And when we got on stage, there was this incredible, palpable determination from the crowd that seemed to say, 'This is the end of this Glastonbury. We're here, we're drenched, we're cold and we are going to fucking have it.' It was one of the most intense atmospheres, from such a generous crowd.

We've become associated with Glastonbury, and a big part of that is down to the television coverage. Since 2007, whenever we've been televised, Adam and Marcus will go in and help direct the transmission, using the visuals in a different way so they feel integrated into the broadcast. You know it's worked when social media erupts with people sat at home saying, 'Currently having my mind blown by The Chemical Brothers'. I don't love being filmed but Glastonbury is the one time when I think there are people at home who are having their own communal experience.

[The Chemical Brothers headlined the Pyramid Stage at Glastonbury in 2000, the last year before the festival erected a security fence. Their crowd was said to have been one of the biggest the festival had ever seen. They headlined the Other Stage in 2004, 2007, 2011, 2015 and 2019.]

Adam Smith

The evolution of the live show happened as the stages got bigger. Instead of one screen, we'd use three screens. We'd bring in lights to augment the visuals. We went through some real characters in terms of lighting designers. It was often a battle with them: visuals used to get sneered at because it was all about the lights; their lights would invariably be a lot brighter than our projectors. It would start off as a relationship where they'd be eager to get involved and it would end in a fight where we're demanding they get the lights off the visuals. We've now got this right, with the lights facing into the audience and becoming part of the visual show. It used to be a very frustrating show for a lighting designer to work on because we had such a clear idea of how it all should look.

We went from a one-screen show with three or four projectors to a three-screen show with multiple projectors. We weren't projecting onto old sheets, we were using fastfold screens that were traditionally used for posh AV conferences. It was quite punk rock. Noah was brilliantly technical and made these devices to strobe the slides in time with the music. His dad had run an AV company when he was a kid, so he'd grown up around the machines we were using. The whole operation was so incongruous. We would rent these machines and screens from very strait-laced AV companies that were used to doing presentations at hotels on Park Lane. Then we would put them up in filthy venues where sweat would drip from the ceilings, so we'd have to clean them off before returning them so we could get the deposit back.

In the early days, it was more of an experimental approach. Let's see what we've got and try to make it all work together. We'd get the set and break it down into sections and then visualise each section. When we started using three screens we needed to sequence hundreds of slides for the show. So Noah built this incredible huge lightbox and we would stay up all night matching images to the music.

[Adam and Noah split up as Vegetable Vision in 2000. Adam continued working with the band, first as Flat Nose George, then in partnership with original Vegetable Vision collaborator Marcus Lyall (Smith & Lyall).]

Mia Hill (aka Whirlygirl)

The first time I saw The Chemical Brothers live, a light switched on in my brain. They were set to play a new festival called Coachella. I was a new mom, navigating my new role on this planet. I'd taken a hiatus from all things self-indulgent. It felt like forever since I'd been to a concert, let alone a club or rave, but I had this compulsion to experience how The Chemical Brothers' music translated in a live setting. I suppose part of that compulsion to see them, especially in a festival setting, had to do with making up for lost time knowing I missed their tour stops earlier that year, and missed them a few years earlier when they played at Organic.

The day they played was glorious, a blistering, hot affair situated on tidily manicured, wide-open polo fields under the California desert sun. My husband and I spent the hottest parts of the afternoon chasing down whatever shady spots we could find. After what felt like forever, the opening 'thud thud thud' of 'Hey Boy Hey Girl' rippled across the field, vibrating through my shoes and working its way up my spine, making every hair stand on end. The song swelled and I was compelled to inch a bit closer. But I held firm a bit further back, just past the soundboard, with breathing space to move and a good view to take in whatever visual delights were in store. I turned around and saw some people skipping (not running, but literally skipping) toward the human throng and closer to the stage.

Up on stage I could barely make out the two people behind the madness as they worked their wizardry with their arsenal of gear. The bursts of lights and flashing visuals reminded me of those old warehouse raves, with their continuous reels of movie clips and animations projected on the walls – only

NEW SET | not thousand of colours

1. LEAVE HOME — B+W MOKE, PLANES, GUNS, COPS ETC.
2. MUSIC RESPONSE — FIGURES (VARIOUS) SINGLE # MULTIPLE.
3. B.R.B — BUILDINGS, BRICKS, IDENTIKIT # ALLEYWAYS
4. SIREN. — COLOUR SPARKLER)
5. 3 LITTLE BIRDYS / JABBA — *) — NUMBERS (from R.1)
6. HEY BOY, HEY GIRL. — LYRICS, DOORWAYS, EQUATIONS.
7. DOESN'T MATTER — B+W ROBOT, GREY ROBOT + MULTI ROBOTS.
8. OUT OF CONTROL. — HANDS, TEXTURES # PINEWOODS.
9. SLOWDOWN B-BEAT, GOT GLINT. BLUE, EYES # BLUE SPLASH.
10. SUNSHINE UNDERGROUND. SUNSET # FACES
11. UNDER THE INFLUENCE. — B+W PATTERNS # SPARKLER!
12. SETTING SUN. — FLAMES # FIREPLACES.
13. CHEM BEATS — BEST OF KNEB CHEM BEATS.
14. FLASHBACK — G+Y # G+Y HEADLIGHTS.
15. P.P.R — STAINED GLASS, CLOWNS + EYES.

TOUR * ORGANISE EDIT + TRANSPORT OF TAPES.
  * SET LIST.   * PETERSON
  * 4 WAYS   * PACK (5 days camera)
  *

78 The Chemical Brothers

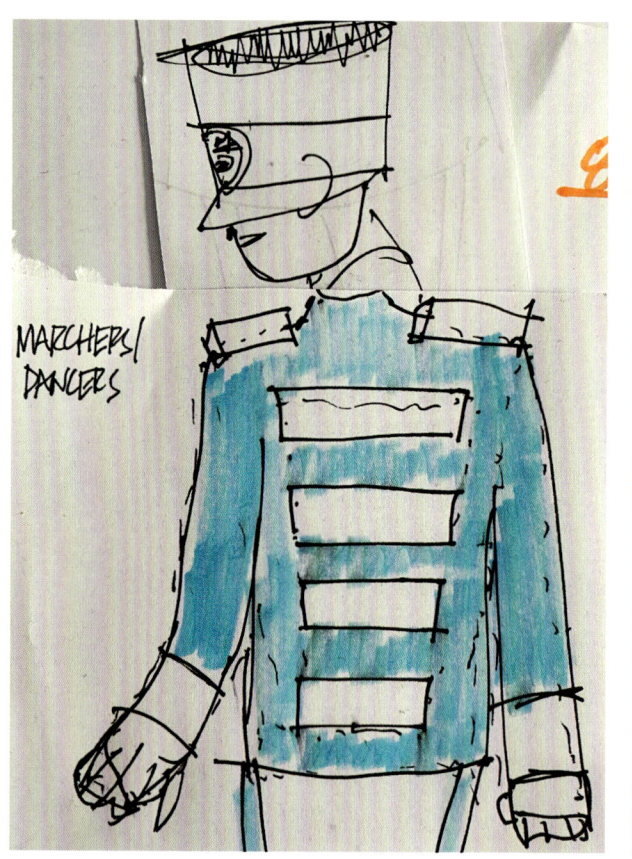

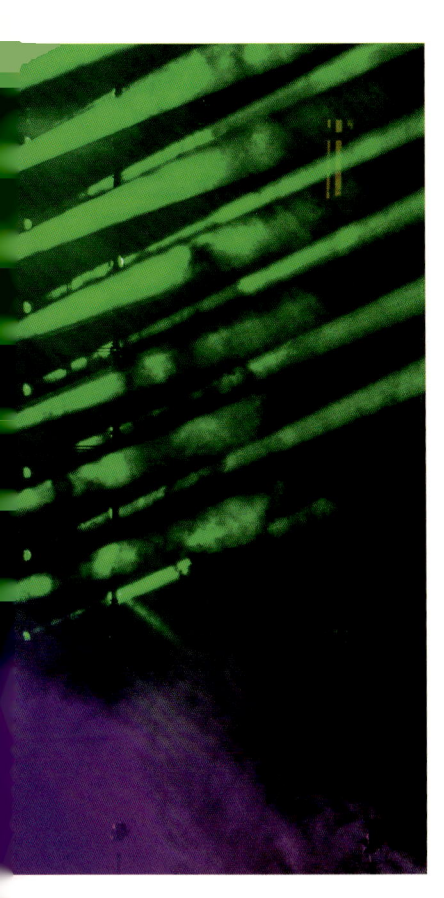

Previous page right: Visuals set list for Smith and Lyall.

Bottom left: Adam Smith and Marcus Lyall.

Right: No Reason tour visuals and sketches.

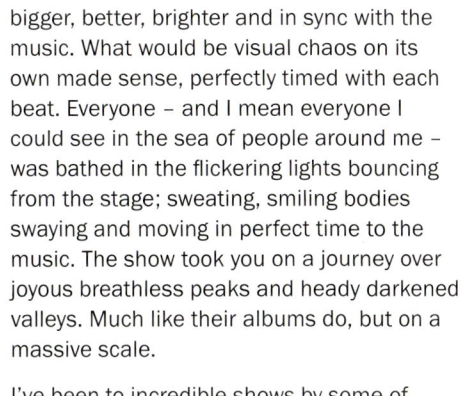

bigger, better, brighter and in sync with the music. What would be visual chaos on its own made sense, perfectly timed with each beat. Everyone – and I mean everyone I could see in the sea of people around me – was bathed in the flickering lights bouncing from the stage; sweating, smiling bodies swaying and moving in perfect time to the music. The show took you on a journey over joyous breathless peaks and heady darkened valleys. Much like their albums do, but on a massive scale.

I've been to incredible shows by some of my other favourites over the years, but this experience really moved me. It opened my eyes and ears to the emotions made real by two people working their machines and making all this magical beautiful swirling noise. Then just like that – it was over far too soon – and 'The Sunshine Underground' brought the show to a close in all its epic, twinkling glory. Seeing people react to the show – bodies moving in time; hands held high; the odd person having a wide-eyed moment while fixating on a pulsating visual; the laughter, joy, that feeling of sweet exhaustion afterward and seeing others with the same expressions on their faces. It felt primal, communal and so beautiful.

At The Chemical Brothers shows, I absolutely feel like I'm part of an extended family. So much so, that after that first show I saw, I had to find 'my tribe'. This meant getting out of my comfort zone and into internet land, where I joined the mailing list and got a lot more than I bargained for (or at least my inbox did – the mailing list was a never-ending hive of activity). Once the mailing list dispersed, I meandered to the Chems message board and found even more like-minds to geek out with. Some fans are casual and some are hardcore, travelling the world to experience the band live. It is always special to be enjoying a show with people in the Chemical community – including the time I brought my son along for his first Chemical Brothers show. Some fans I've met because of The Chemical Brothers are so dear they're like family. They brighten my doorstep and my personal life. The Chemical Brothers' fans are some of the kindest, most generous souls I've had the pleasure of knowing. There are no better people than them to experience a show with. Love Is All, indeed.

James Holroyd

Over the years, the gigs have gone big and the production is massive. I still approach it with the original idea I had all those years ago: there is a build of energy at a gig that you have to try and ride. It's always different, but after hundreds of gigs I'm prepared for most scenarios. A Saturday night in Manchester or Brixton is gonna go bang, but there have been some tricky ones over the years. We were due to be playing in Bologna to 10,000 very up-for-it Italians. A customs problem had held up the PA at the border and the show was gonna have to be cancelled – but the stuff eventually got through, meaning it would arrive while the gig was supposed to be on. Waiting for it to arrive left me playing to thousands of baying Italians for five and a half hours. I've no idea how I managed on eighty records. I remember playing both sides of a single by The Fall. When the PA arrived, every movement of the installation was applauded like a song. The first forklift came in and the barriers got breached. The crew were working like mad to build it. The intensity and appreciation of their efforts led to a celebratory riot when the band finally got on – firecrackers, the lot.

Paused in Cosmic Reflection

Chris York

The Chemical Brothers at Brixton Academy was a rite of passage for so many people from the late nineties onwards. It was almost a joke. 'Are we doing Brixton again?' But it usually was the right answer once an extensive and sometimes futile wild goose chase had taken us all round every other crap venue in London. There was one year where we did five nights at Brixton Academy. No one did five nights there. And they were some of the best shows I'd ever seen The Chemical Brothers do. They can deliver a level of intensity at any size of venue, be it Brixton, the O2 or in a festival field. Or a club. There's no let-up in the energy from start to finish.

Ed Simons

Our live show has never been formulaic. It's dance music and it expresses something, and it isn't mannered. There's weird noises and a rhythm that you can dance to, but it's untutored. It's music that heads straight to a heart level, almost bypassing logic. Things that we might have been criticised for, where music might be described as 'bombastic' . . . there's nothing wrong with being bombastic or powerful. A good gig hopefully taps into something that people maybe aren't aware they're holding at that moment. And the very nature of what we do is implicit permission for people to lose control, a permission for a sort of wildness to enter the audience and the air above that. The music does that, the visuals do that, hopefully me and Tom do that. I think our interaction, the fact that we're so obviously into the music, generates a connection and an energy. Bringing that wildness of expression to a festival or a gig venue, maybe that's what generations of people have picked up on in our live shows.

At a great show, there's a crackle of electricity in the air and a sense of perpetual motion in the crowd. It's an unsaid thing on stage between me and Tom. You feel it though, you know things are going well. It's a sense of magic in the air. You catch the odd person's facial expression and you can see they're entirely lost in the music. In the pauses in between tracks, the volume rises and you can feel a real hysteria taking over. That's when you know things are working.

Tom Rowlands

When we play live now, it's with the same aim as when we first started playing. We've always wanted people to be overwhelmed.

Opposite: The four-metre robots George and Mildred, designed by Smith and Lyall.

Above: Behind the projection screens.

Next page: Visuals at the 02 Arena in London, November 2019.

We want people to feel like it's too much. We were trying to do that at Sabresonic and we're still trying to do it now. And there's no communication with the audience other than through the music. Not talking has always been a core belief. Neither Ed nor I ever wanted to be that person instructing you to have a good time. We want you to join us on the ride, but we're not telling you what to do or when to react. It's got to be of your own volition. You're joining us because of the sheer force of what's happening around you.

James Holroyd

Warming up for The Chemical Brothers is about creating a backdrop for what's to come. After I've played, there's a moment when I leave the stage and get into the wings in complete darkness, and then the intro music begins. It casts a spell on the crowd. When the band come on and the crowd erupts, it's something that never ceases to thrill me. If the job's done good, I grab a beer and I stand there wondering how it must feel to be in the band.

Ed Simons

I think 'Chemical Beats' is the essence of what we do live. It feels like our anthem, a track that we'll never not play live. It's not the track with the fancy visuals or the stunning colours. We play it with the oscilloscope visuals: green lights and lasers. If a gig hasn't connected, 'Chemical Beats' can often turn things on its head. You look at the audience, and that track is way older than half the people in the crowd. But there's something about the universality of 'Chemical Beats', the repetition of the big beat, the wildness of the metallic acid riff. I think it's one of those records that people don't need to have heard before to be moved by it. You're not relying on a sense of familiarity, there's something about the music that primally connects. The way we present that track is a very archetypal acid house experience – the green light, the green lasers, the riff that just won't stop. I'm not saying it's just that track, but there's something about moments like that that transcend a kind of promotional roundabout. People come to see bands to hear the hits – we have those moments, where people want to hear 'Galvanize' or 'Hey Boy Hey Girl' – but I think with 'Chemical Beats', people are picking up on something much more elemental. Something that's being viscerally expressed and responded to.

Adam Smith

When I stopped working with Noah, I started to think about using the visuals to vocalise samples in the songs. Technology was changing, it was becoming much easier to sync things perfectly. The first time I did this was with my dad made up as a clown voicing the words, 'You are all my children now.'

From there, I began working with dancers and physical performers. It's become a huge part of the show. Working with the actor Mark Monero was a huge influence on how things turned out.

Ed and Tom have faith in our ideas and understand the value of investing in the visuals. Our visuals for the live shows have featured an amazing cast of actors over the years. People like Romola Garai, Benedict Wong and Akram Khan have all appeared. The late, great Marcello Magni – one of the best physical theatre actors in the world – was amazing to work with. Those collaborators are essential to it all, each person adds their own bit of magic.

LED screens were a game changer for The Chemical Brothers' gigs. Finally, this was something that was brighter than the lights we'd been competing with for years. You feel an LED, in that it's a light pushing out to you, as opposed to a light that's being projected.

These days there are 9,000 cues in the show. Most live shows will have around 2,000. The detail and precision in there is crazy. Getting lights to lock with animations has been a real achievement – a character on the screen raises their arm and a light moves in their hand. The great thing about the LED screens is that you can shine light through them, so you can have the lights and visuals being completely interactive. We're lucky that we found Paul Normandale and JC, lighting engineers who understood exactly what it is Marcus and I want to do.

Paused in Cosmic Reflection 83

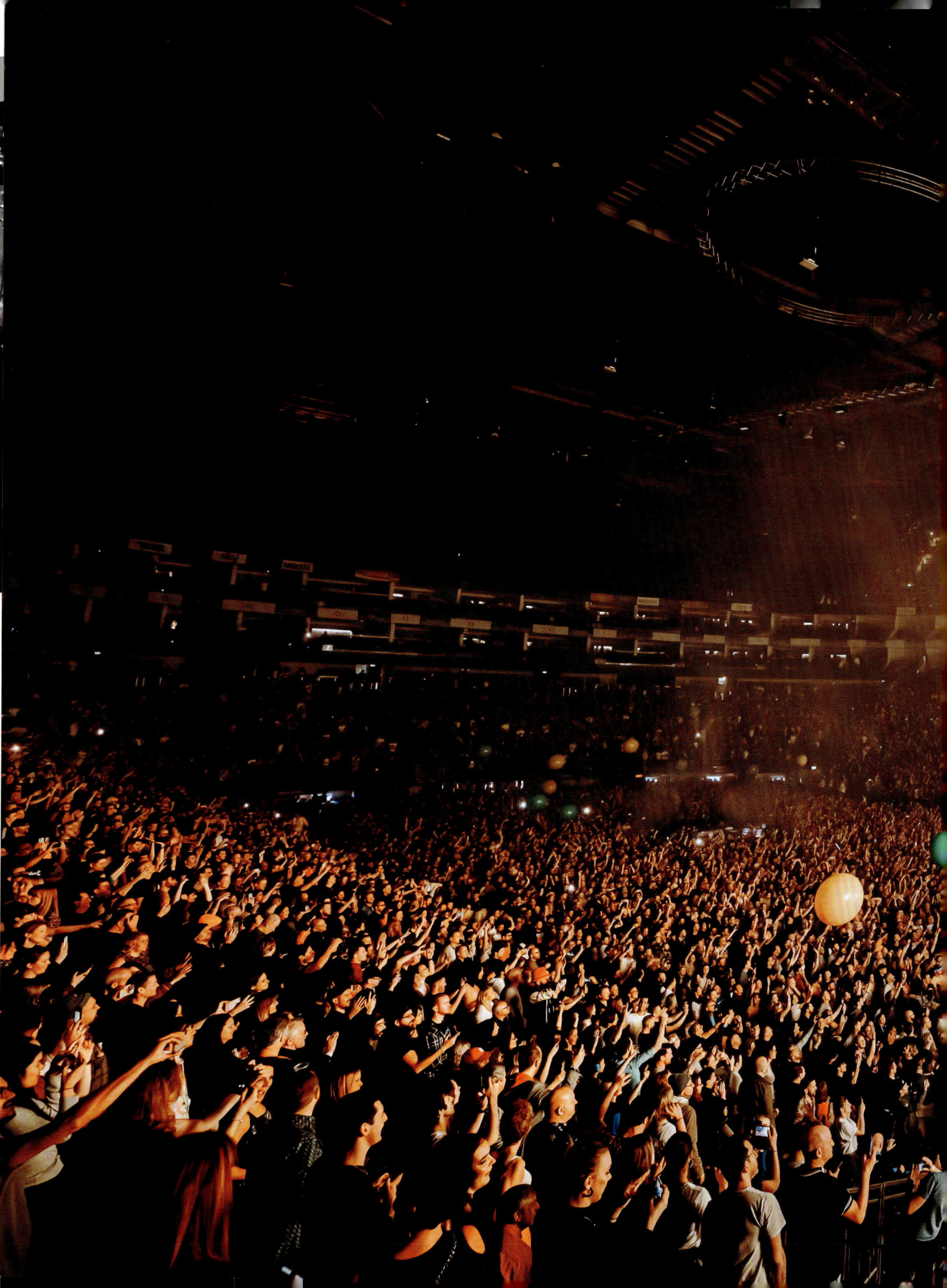

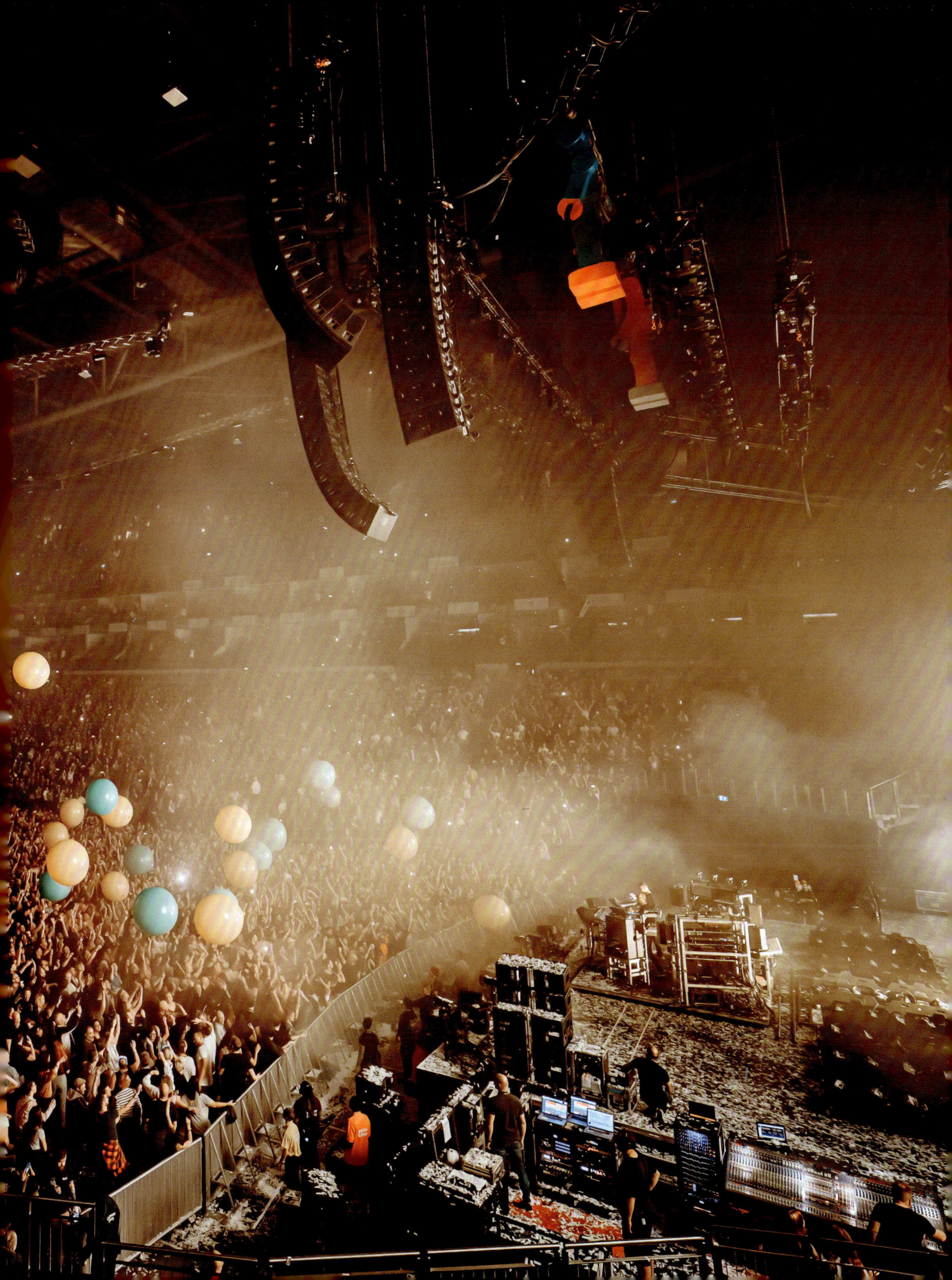

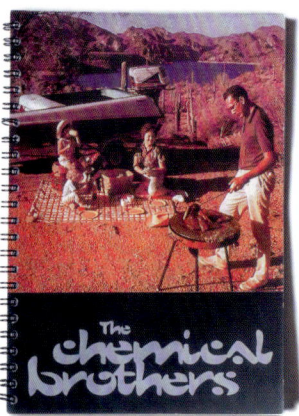

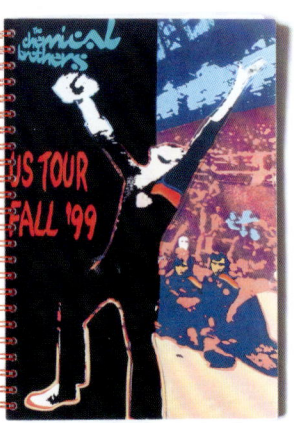

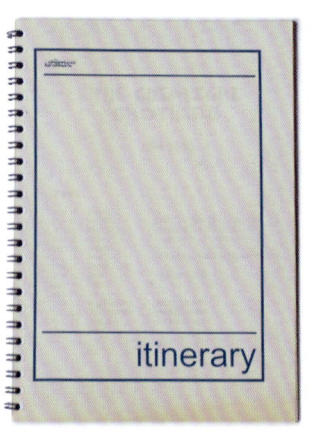

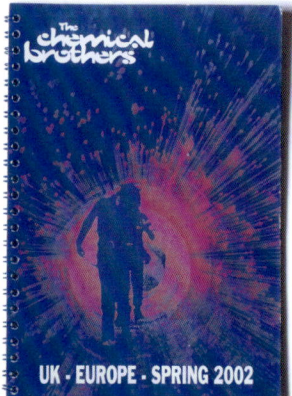

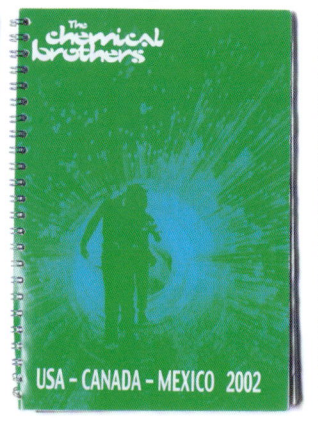

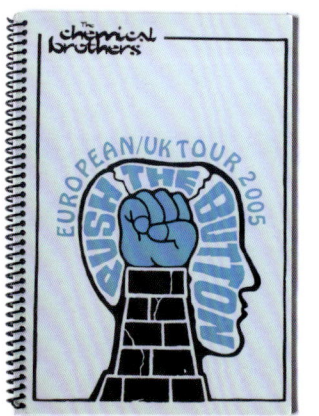

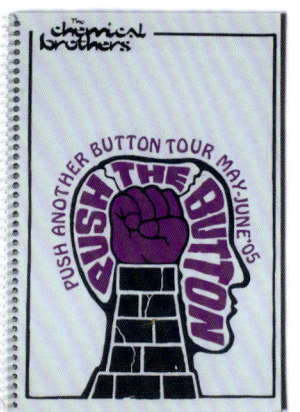

88 The Chemical Brothers

THE CHEMICAL BROTHERS
USA - SPRING '97

APRIL
WED	23	TRAVEL TO USA		
THU	24	DALLAS	BOMB FACTORY	with The ORB
FRI	25			
SAT	26	CHICAGO	ARAGON	with The ORB
SUN	27	MINNEAPOLIS	FIRST AVENUE	
MON	28			
TUE	29	DENVER	OGDEN THEATRE	
WED	30			

MAY
THU	1	SALT LAKE CITY	BRICKS	
FRI	2	LAS VEGAS	THE JOINT	with The ORB
SAT	3			
SUN	4	SAN FRANCISCO	KAISER	with The ORB
MON	5			
TUE	6			
WED	7	SEATTLE	UNION STATION	
THU	8	VANCOUVER	THE RAGE	
FRI	9			
SAT	10	LOS ANGELES	SHRINE EXPO	
SUN	11			
MON	12	BOSTON	AVALON	with The ORB
TUE	13	TORONTO	THE WAREHOUSE	with The ORB
WED	14	MONTREAL	METROPOLIS	
THU	15			
FRI	16	PHILADELPHIA	ELECTRIC FACTORY	
SAT	17	NEW YORK	MANHATTAN CENTRE	
SUN	18			
MON	19			
TUE	20	ATLANTA	MASQUERADE	
WED	21	TAMPA	RITZ THEATRE	
THU	22	RETURN TO UK		
FRI	23			
SAT	24	BRIGHTON	ESSENTIAL MUSIC FESTIVAL	

THE CHEMICAL BROTHERS
USA FALL '99

SEPTEMBER
MON	13	BAND & CREW PARTIES DEPART UK	
TUE	14	BOSTON	AVALON
WED	15	NEW YORK	HAMMERSTEIN
THU	16	NEW YORK	HAMMERSTEIN
FRI	17		
SAT	18	MIAMI	COCONUT GROVE
SUN	19	STONE MOUNTAIN	ATRIUM
MON	20		
TUE	21	NEW ORLEANS	STATE PALACE THEATER
WED	22	AUSTIN	MUSIC HALL
THU	23	DALLAS	BRONCO BOWL
FRI	24		
SAT	25	WASHINGTON	RFK STADIUM
SUN	26	PHILADELPHIA	ELECTRIC FACTORY
MON	27	WASHINGTON	9.30 CLUB
TUE	28		
WED	29		
THU	30	ST LOUIS	AMERICAN

OCTOBER
FRI	01	KANSAS CITY	UPTOWN KC
SAT	02	ST PAUL	ROY WILKENS RIVER
SUN	03		
MON	04	CALGARY	MAX BELL ARENA
TUE	05		
WED	06	VANCOUVER	PNE FORUM
THU	07		
FRI	08	SAN FRANCISCO	BILL GRAHAM CIVIC
SAT	09	INDIO	COACHELLA @ EMPIRE POLO
SUN	10	CREW PARTY DEPARTS USA	
MON	11	BAND PARTY DEPARTS USA / CREW PARTY ARRIVES IN UK
TUE	12	BAND PARTY ARRIVES IN UK	

THE BAND

TOM ROWLANDS
ED SIMONS

THE CREW

TOUR MANAGER - STUART JAMES
LIGHTING DESIGNER - CHRIS CRAIG
LIGHTING TECH - TBC
BACKLINE/MIDI TECH 1 - AARON CRIPPS
BACKLINE/MIDI TECH 2 - MATT COX
SOUND ENGINEER - JOHN JACKSON
SWAGMAN - BRADTON FOGERTY
TRUCK DRIVER - MICK KIRKCALDY
BUS DRIVER - TBC
VEGETABLE VISION - ADAM SMITH
VEGETABLE VISION - NOAH CLARK

THE BAND

TOM ROWLANDS ✓ Ness.
ED SIMONS ✓ x2

THE CREW

TOUR MANAGER - STUART JAMES ✓
PRODUCTION/STAGE MANAGER - MARK GOSLING ✓
LIGHTING DESIGNER - ANDY LIDDLE ✓
VEG VISION #1 - MATT ELLAR
VEG VISION #2 - RICARDO LORENZINI
FOH SOUND - SARNE THOROGOOD
STAGE SOUND - IAN BARTON ✓
BACKLINE - AARON CRIPPS ✓
BACKLINE - MATT COX ✓
LIGHTING TECH - BARRY MARA ✓
VIDEO TECH - CHARLES HARRIS
BAND BUS DRIVER - ROGER STONE
CREW BUS DRIVER - JARED INGRAM

USA CREW

MR PA #1 - MICHAEL SMEATON
MR PA #2 - JOHN SCHEFFEL
MR LIGHTS #1 - DAVID HEARD
MR LIGHTS #2 - DARRYL MAGURA

TOUR DJ

JAMES 'BOGGY' HOLROYD ✓

Days like this are sweet . . .

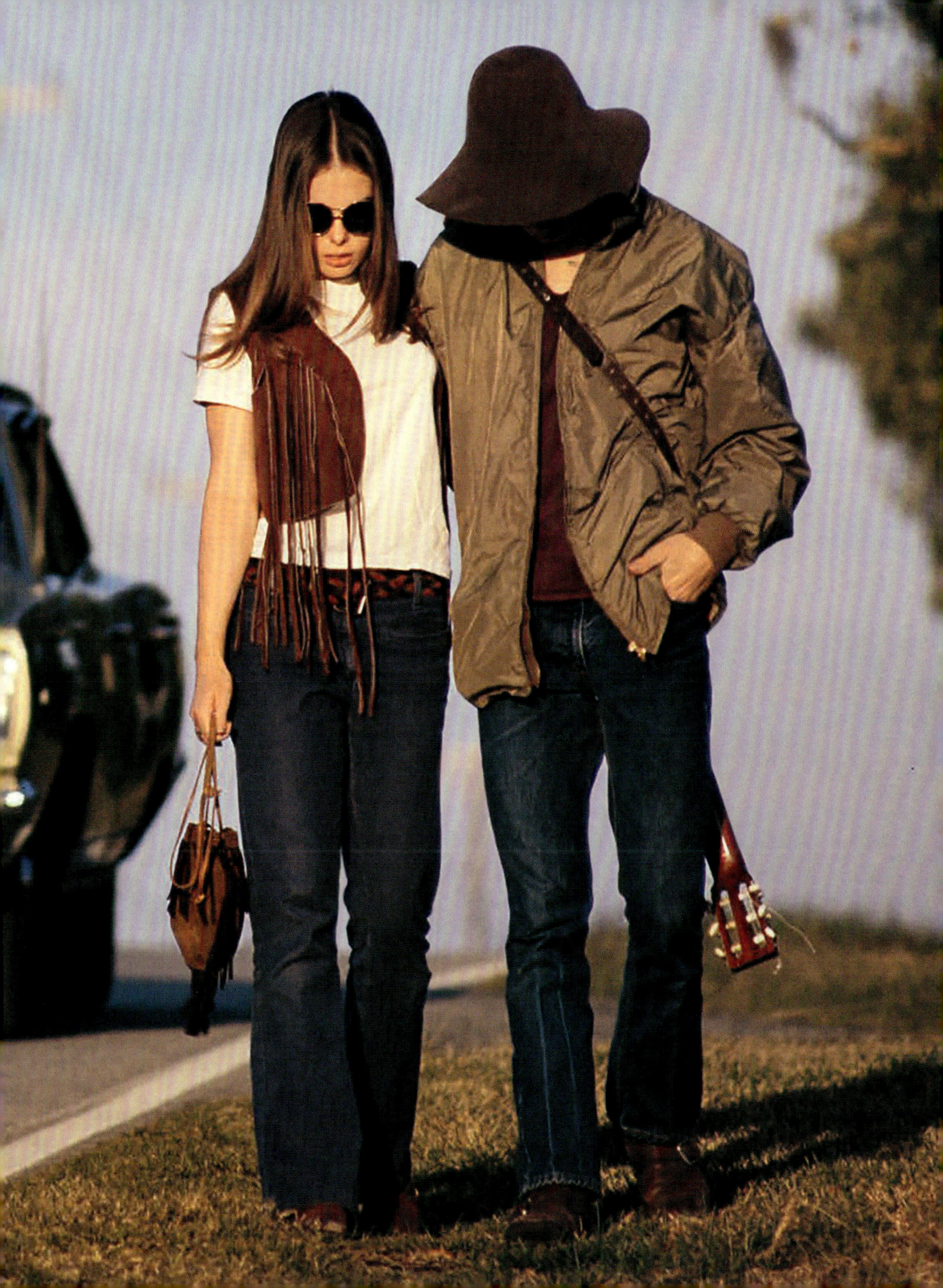

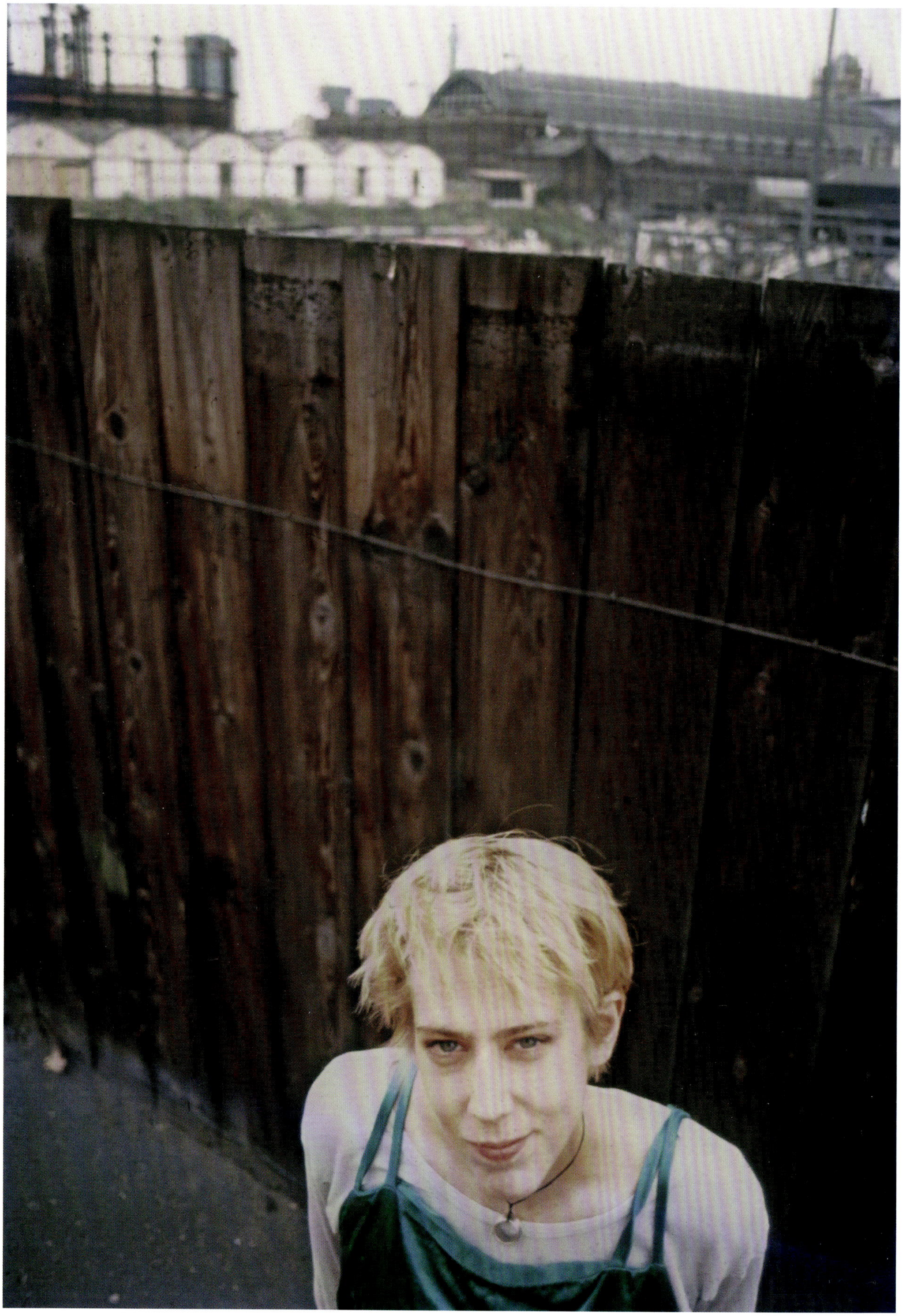

Alive Alone

'Leave Home' – *Exit Planet Dust*'s super-bass-heavy calling card – confidently predicts *the brothers gonna work it out*. Forty-five minutes later, that album's denouement, 'Alive Alone', doesn't seem quite so sure of that outcome.

So much of *Exit Planet Dust* is wired with a kind of joyride energy. 'Alive Alone' is different. Fragile in both sound and mood, it's a brace position at the end of a car chase. In some ways the song questions all that's come before it. Arriving on the heels of a track like 'Life Is Sweet', the words of 'Alive Alone' feel bleak, as if scratched out of the desperation of heartbreak or failure. *And I'm alive, and I'm alone, and I never wanted to be either of those.*

Yet the effect of the song on the listener was anything but desperate. To home listeners, 'Alive Alone' was a moment of redemption, a crack of bright white light through the curtains as the weekend ends and reality drifts back in. This was music for after the club, the soundtrack to all those new friendships that formed on the dance floor then went back home – to anyone's home – to watch the sun come up together. Over time, it would help earn the track's singer – Beth Orton – the sobriquet of 'the comedown queen'. Few singers have so perfectly captured such a specific point in time and in listeners' lives.

Musically, Beth was part of the same generation as Tom and Ed. She had been part of the Heavenly Sunday Social community, and could regularly be found dancing on the bar top as the lights went up, alongside many of the club's most 'active supporters'. She had previously made records with William Orbit and had recorded vocals for London jazz trio Red Snapper's woozy, nocturnal 1994 track 'In Deep'.

Beth would go on to sing on two further Chemical Brothers songs: *Dig Your Own Hole*'s 'Where Do I Begin' and 'The State We're In' from *Come with Us*. Both tracks occupy that hazy point where the days blur from one to another and you find yourself wondering whose bed you're in. Coming around has never sounded so attractive.

Beth Orton

I always felt like Tom wrote the words for me.

I suppose like any good song, the listener feels like it's written for them. But in this instance, I had the sense that Tom was asking me to sing the words because he knew the chaos of my life back then, how acutely those words spoke to my experience. I wasn't sure if we were friends exactly – I always felt shy around him cos he's so intelligent and I felt like trash at the time – but I felt that in these songs he was reaching out to me to speak for him as much as for myself.

I remember sitting on the floor of the shower room in Orinoco Studio with Tom whispering the words to me. I was trying to get the melody as close to what he was singing but there's some interpretation in what was recorded. The moment was so tender. It's funny because we didn't really speak a whole lot about what the song meant, there was just this real tender bridging of experiences through the song itself, this beautiful feeling of passing a secret understanding between us, as if I could say for him what neither of us had the ability to say any other way. Again, where all the best art comes from.

Tom trusting me that way felt tender. I felt seen by Tom and I was touched by this show of friendship that I could not read otherwise. I was good at being mental and we were both 'having it' but I was in pieces and he showed me a kindness I really needed through inviting me to sing his songs.

Tom Rowlands

Making music with Beth is a real treasure. Each song she sang for us was a song I'd written. And at the point of writing, I didn't feel confident enough as a singer to sing them. I was still really self-conscious about words, and I really couldn't have imagined singing them on one of our records. I'd sing things to myself in the studio; I'd never have imagined singing them in front of Ed or Dubby [Steve Dub, The Chemical Brothers' studio partner].

Beth was someone I trusted to embody those words. She was close enough to Ed and myself at that time that I felt I could privately sing those songs how I wanted them to sound before she would take them and make them her own. I always felt that she understood what I was singing to her, even if I hadn't explained what I'd meant when I'd written them. I'd never have imagined them sounding as beautiful and believable as they did. She took them and did something truly great with them, something completely natural that was how I'd imagined it would sound. It felt special hearing Beth sing my words. She amplified the emotion and really brought the song to life.

She was the first person to come into the studio that I felt that I could do that with. We'd recorded with Tim Burgess around the same time but that was a very different experience, as he'd arrived with a set of words to work with. Over time, I gained more confidence about using my own voice, partly through having more time to experiment in the studio on my own and partly through working with a lot of amazing singers like Beth who each arrived with their own methods when they recorded.

Ed Simons

I remember thinking Beth was so cool. I helped her move into this flat on Ladbroke Grove as having a car back then was quite rare. I had this shitty little beige Ford Fiesta that I'd been given by my mum when she'd decided to get something decent to drive around in. Helping Beth was a trade-off as I got to move into her old room in Vauxhall. We ended up becoming friends after that. Beth was a big part of the Social. She was starting off on a Heavenly journey at that time. She'd recorded demos for her first album and I really loved them, especially the track 'Somebody's Daughter' which has an incredible honesty and beauty.

Asking Beth to sing on 'Alive Alone' was a very spur-of-the-moment thing. It just came together on a Friday afternoon. We just called her up and asked if she was interested in singing on one of our tracks, then drove round and picked her up, brought her back and recorded. We were so young then – twenty-two, twenty-three. Things didn't need or get lots of planning. Tom had written these words, we wanted a singer, Beth was a singer who we really liked, let's give her a call and ask her. So, we set up a vocal booth in a bathroom at Orinoco and she sang 'Alive Alone', beautifully.

Beth was disarmingly honest about her emotional experiences, her feelings. In the nineties that was very unusual. And Tom needed Beth to voice that vulnerable side of himself. And it's strange and brilliant that it even happened. You wouldn't expect those songs to be beside 'Chemical Beats' or 'Elektrobank'. Beth's openness gave Tom permission to have those words on the record. That mid-nineties period was very hedonistic but there was a lot of fragility around our friends. The tracks Beth recorded with us echo those feelings in a lot of ways.

Previous page: Photo of Beth Orton, taken by director Joe Wright in King's Cross.

Next page: Stills from the 'Life Is Sweet' music video featuring Tim Burgess, directed by Walter Stern.

Paused in Cosmic Reflection

96   **The Chemical Brothers**

Paused in Cosmic Reflection 97

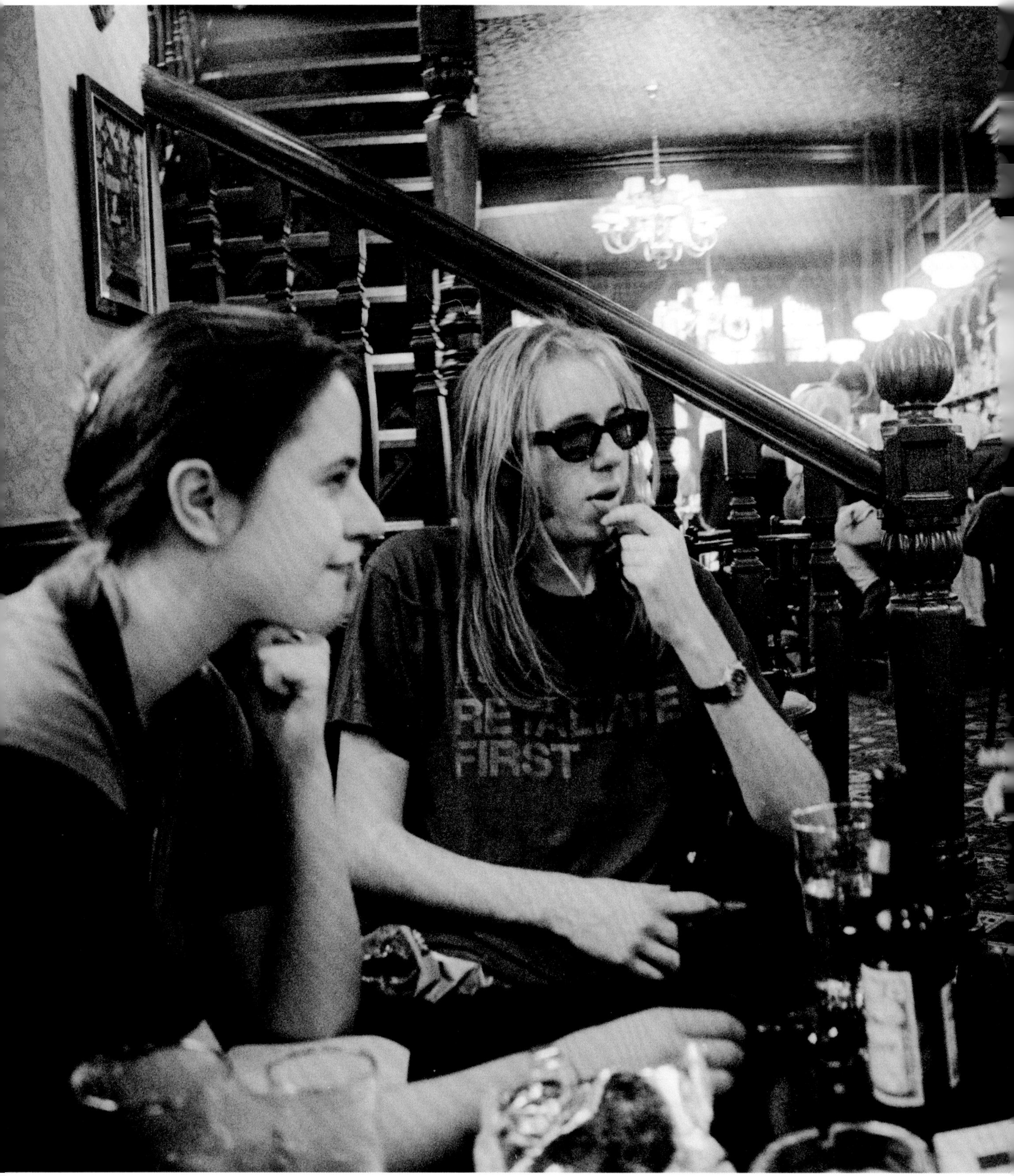
RETALIATE
FIRST

Paused in Cosmic Reflection 99

Previous page: In The Ship on Wardour Street with Stefania Malmsten (left) from Pop magazine and Sarah Cracknell (centre) from Saint Etienne during a cover shoot.

Left: The cover of the launch issue of Muzik magazine, 1995.

Centre: In Notting Hill.

Next page: Studio wallchart with notes on tracks for Exit Planet Dust.

Paused in Cosmic Reflection 101

date	working title	drums	bass
~~MAK~~	JABBA ✓ 122bpm Tom's dream edit	TASTY KIK ✓ BIT POLITE ON THE HATS	no bass required ~~YES~~ NO ✓
~~MAK~~ ~~ATARI~~	In Dust we TRUST	fucking blinding	fucking blinding
~~MAK~~ ~~VOCAL~~	SPEED ~~FUNK~~ poptastic 110bpm	oh yes very good especially the 808 beat.	big fat & Riffarama style fuzz bass.
~~MAK~~	~~SPEED FUNK~~ DELIK. 123bpm ✓	wicked BLUR loop Kwest	YUP! AMPEG Attack
ATARI vocal?	COCONUT ~~toffee~~	→	SEGGS. Gets PARTY + MINT
ATARI	Song to the SIREN mix 111 bpm		
MAK	~~Real Tom~~ 98	Yes very good	✓
MAK vocal	WAKE UP before CoCo 120bpm		
MAK	~~Chico groove~~ take vocal bit out of C-R-Rhodes back ?...	lo-slung	lo slung
~~X~~	BRRif (102) track	DOPENESS ON A PILL	PILL FRIENDLY.
	WARM	PEACE	

anything else?	vocals	comments.
ubby's kidney a bit dodgy not yet 8.8.94 5.20pm tasted zero lift Surfile sugar	Ed's guide Vox lacks the necessary PUNCH.	tasty bit of ax just mi bit pony? Ed this tr bit polite Tim
ing fuzz bass thing fucking blinding.	TIM?	dubby dubby make it dubby funky
sort out vocals ite speaks in tongues!	Maybe → vocals sorted out by Dubby — absolutely superb — backward phased/paused lovely stuff it only thin etc...	it's a winner — T.M.
+ psychodelik section! OOP, BLUR, SPIRITUALIZED together		hip hop never kno
		DUSTY'S SPRING FIELD MIX.
Breif case cable producing noise etc.	live underground Rock on! come on you freaks	PASTY + MINTY
working album title leave Home just say YO n dust we trust JUST DUST we strings me Tod made	get vaporspace or salt tank to close vocal mix Mrs WOODS.	phone manager spare re-Number possible mix? Dubby's Trance Di 8/4 - Kidney's down

Setting Sun

It's easy to forget how big a deal 'Setting Sun' was back in the autumn of 1996. The Chemical Brothers had released a handful of singles and a debut album that charted just inside the Top 10. Massively respected as part of a burgeoning electronic music scene, they would rarely trouble the pages of tabloid newspapers, which suited them and the papers just fine. A chance meeting with Noel Gallagher in the summer of 1995 changed all that.

Just over a year later, Oasis was the biggest band in Britain and heading that way in the rest of the world. Yet 'internal differences' had led to Noel walking out of a US tour, with an impending collaboration he'd recorded with Tom and Ed leading to red-top headlines: 'Noel to leave Oasis to be third Chemical Brother'.

'Setting Sun' was on the horizon and it rapidly became part of the Oasis narrative. In the weeks leading up to its release, anticipation built and built. As Sam Taylor wrote in the *Observer* (27 October 1996), 'Anything that gives Chris Evans a nasty shock has to be regarded as a good thing. Hail, then, the Chemical Brothers whose latest single "Setting Sun", featuring Noel Gallagher on vocals, was hyped by Evans throughout his radio show a few weeks ago. He hadn't actually heard it, but figured that anything featuring the great Oasis songwriter was bound to be wonderful. Then he played it, and what sounded like a fire alarm on a crashing 747 erupted from the nation's transistors. Evans took the record off, and shakily announced: "I don't think that was a very suitable record for this time of the morning."'

As Tom put it in an *NME* cover story at the time: 'It takes a lot of hard work to get a record featuring Noel Gallagher pulled from daytime Radio 1.'

Whatever the prior expectations were, 'Setting Sun' is categorically, recognisably a Chemical Brothers record featuring the voice and lyrics of Noel Gallagher. It was – and remains – utterly uncompromised, a cyclone of a track that sat as a beacon of strangeness at the top of the UK Singles Chart between a jaunty one-hit wonder (Deep Blue Something's 'Breakfast at Tiffany's') and a mawkish cover version (Boyzone's take on Bee Gees' 'Words').

Tom Rowlands

We'd been playing 'Tomorrow Never Knows' in our DJ sets for a while. It was a big record at the Sunday Social and the effect it had in an acid house environment was staggering. Every time, the crowd's reaction was crazy. It became inspirational, in that we wanted to make something that would have a similar effect on the listener – a track that took some of the strangeness and intensity of The Beatles' song. It always struck me how intense it was hearing 'Tomorrow Never Knows' in a nightclub coming out of a record like 'Lobotomie' by Emmanuel Top, which is an eleven-minute acid techno record. 'Setting Sun' was us going into the studio wanting to recreate that feeling in our world.

We wrote the track in our studio in the Strongroom. John Coxon (from Spring Heel Jack) was working out of there as well. I remember doing the early programming and writing for 'Setting Sun' in our room and John loaned me his Gibson Firebird – a beautiful, amazing guitar. That guitar was where all the noises on that track came from. The original version was called 'Mark 1', which we'd read was the working title for 'Tomorrow Never Knows'.

When we got to a certain point, we thought, 'Imagine if you had Noel singing on this now.' We'd met him in the field between the main

Paused in Cosmic Reflection 105

stages at Glastonbury a little while before and Noel was adamant that as Tim Burgess was on one of our records, he should be too. It felt like a weird confluence of inspirations coming round, like an infinite loop of ideas that all seemed to meet and meld together.

At that point, Noel had sung on a few Oasis records, and none of them sounded like 'Setting Sun'. It did feel startlingly mad when you heard it on the radio. The day the single charted, we all went round to my brother's flat to listen to the rundown on the radio at 6 p.m. on a Sunday evening. It really was an utterly surreal feeling.

Ed Simons

Glastonbury 1995 took place a week or so before *Exit Planet Dust* came out. Tom and I had gone down as punters. Even though by that time the festival itself was massive, it wasn't delineated in the way it is today with people off in all sorts of different places. Tom came back from a late-night wander saying he'd bumped into Noel Gallagher, who'd said, 'You've got Tim Burgess on your record, give us a go, I can do that.' I think we put it aside as a great, possibly mad idea. Oasis was massive at that point and already headlining the main stage.

Paused in Cosmic Reflection 107

> DEAR CHEMZ THIS IS THE MELODY IDEA FOR THE TUNE IGNORE MOST OF THE LYRICS AS THERE NOT FINISHED. THERES PROBABLY TOO MUCH VOCALS ON IT BUT MAYBE WE COULD DO SOMETHING WITH THE ARRANGEMENT TO GIVE IT MORE SPACE ALSO YOU MAY NOTICE THE SINGINGS OUT OF TUNE (HA!) AND FOR SOME REASON IT RECORDED REALLY FAST OFF ME COMPUTER SO IT SOUNDS QUITE ODD. ANYWAY GIVE US A CALL TELL US WHAT YOU THINK

Handwritten note sent with original vocal demo from Noel Gallagher.

In lots of ways, Oasis feel woven into our story. They emerged at the same time as us. I remember being at Glastonbury in '94 and being told, 'You've got to go and see this band Oasis.' This was a couple of months before *Definitely Maybe* came out, and they played the Other Stage on the Sunday afternoon. Hearing 'Live Forever' for the first time in that field was something else. When they became famous, Tom and I both had a revelatory moment: 'Oh, it's that guy!' Noel was a face at clubs we used to go to, not someone we knew but who was always out at places like Most Excellent. There was a sort of familiarity in the experiences we'd shared.

Oasis injected a lot of excitement and energy into situations in their early years. They came down to the Sunday Social one week with Mani from The Stone Roses, just before *Second Coming* was released. It set the whole place buzzing. Oasis mixed 'What's the Story (Morning Glory)' in the same studio that we had a programming room in (Orinoco). Liam used to come and take the piss out of us for hours on end, saying 'Come on, Bunsens, come and play pool with us.' It almost felt like destiny that we'd collaborate one day.

We got Noel's phone number through someone who knew Meg Mathews. Tom rung him and said we've got a track that could work. The breaks and the sound effects had existed for a while. We weren't trying to make 'Tomorrow Never Knows', but with a rolling break, distorted heavy drums, loads of sound effects coming in and out and a single heavy drone… you could say it was modelled on it a little. Plus, there was a jokey working title of 'Tomorrow Never Noels'.

Things came together really quickly. After we got him the demo, Noel came down to the studio. We didn't really know if he'd sketched anything out with regards to what he would do on the track. I discovered a few years later that there was a very early Oasis track from when they were rehearsing at The Boardwalk in Manchester that had similar lyrics and vocal tune. This was Noel reaching back into a pretty fruitful memory bank. He had a car waiting outside and he recorded the vocal quite quickly. As he did it, he kept pointing out, 'There's no tune here.'

After he left, we stayed up all night finishing the session, then both of us had a couple of hours of sleep before driving round to Noel's house in Camden to hand over a tape of where we'd got to. He was living in a rental property just off Camden High Street. Nothing particularly grand. There were no signs of life inside and we wondered whether we should drop the tape through the letterbox. It was too early to knock on the door of an in-their-prime rock star and we couldn't see any movement, but it felt like there were people in there. We ended up sitting in the car waiting to see if anyone came out. I suppose we just wanted to go round to Noel Gallagher's house, that felt like quite a big thing.

After a while sitting there, we saw signs of life and rang the doorbell. He answered, let us in and made us a cup of tea. Playing the cassette, he said 'It's good that.' That was kind of it in terms of our relationship, it didn't open a hidden door and allow us access to the heady world of members clubs and celebrity parties.

When we were mixing, I remember saying it might be good if it was hooked into more of a club sound, a softer club beat maybe. We had Noel Gallagher on there, a lot of people were going to want to play it. But it's very antagonistic, raw and noisy. It's still quite a challenging listen. I think Noel's vocal, the

NEW PRODIGY SINGLE – PAGE 3   5 October 1996   90p $(US)3.95

NME
NEW MUSICAL EXPRESS

Pipette sounds

Explosive 80 page issue!

THE LONGPIGS: The sty's the limit!

TIGER: It's getting better, man-eater

SHERYL CROW: It's only rook'n'roll!

SKUNK ANANSIE: The pong remains the same!

SUPER FURRY ANIMALS: Enough animals already!

JUST SAY TECHNOEL!
THE CHEMICAL BROTHERS
give that Gallagher bloke a good beating

THE JON SPENCER BLUES EXPLOSION ★ GENEVA
THE BLUETONES ★ SOUNDGARDEN ★ GALLON DRUNK

The Chemical Brothers photographed by Steve Double

little melody that there is, just pulls you right in. The whole thing felt really natural to us.

Interviews outside the UK would all say that we had very consciously married dance and indie music. We didn't think we'd done that at all. Everything was unconsciously done, with huge intent. The very origin of it, of Tom bumping into Noel in a corner of a field at Glastonbury late at night . . . it's nice. It's very different from how things work now.

We were really excited about 'Setting Sun'. It felt like lots of elements that had influenced us had come together to create this incredible whole. The lyrics are great, reminiscent of the way that the words on lots of old psychedelic records work. The track changed where we were positioned as a band. It was our first Number 1 single in the UK and none of the edges were softened at all. That's quite something isn't it?

Noel Gallagher

Up until the point when acid house arrived properly in 1987, everyone in Manchester was into guitar music. The nearest thing to electronic music that people listened to was New Order. Indie music was all very introspective and very angsty; the influence of The Smiths was everywhere. I can't say the rest of Oasis were versed in dance culture. The singer was not into dance music at all. Bonehead, you've only got to look at him. The other two – if they ever went out, they wouldn't have been going to nightclubs.

It was different for me. Acid house was a massive cultural revolution, particularly in Manchester because it was so easy to get to clubs, of which there were lots. And I was into it from the minute I fucking heard it. I put my guitar down from 1987 to 1990, and I don't think I picked it up during that whole period. The only songwriting I was doing – if I was doing any – was on a keyboard. I loved the groove of the music and the hope in the lyrics. Records like 'Promised Land' and 'It's All Right'. I tried to get that same spirit across in my music.

Manchester at the time was such a great place to be. What more can anyone say about The Haçienda that hasn't already been said? There were all those other great clubs that grew out of nothing to join it, amazing places like Konspiracy and the Thunderdome. Nights in those places could be utterly life-changing, and they were right on your doorstep. I used to go to a lot of the clubs that Justin Robertson ran in Manchester, the same clubs that Tom and Ed went to, nights like Spice that were absolutely amazing. It really was a great time to be young, to be in your twenties.

Early on, Oasis was accepted as part of that culture. *Mixmag* gave *Definitely Maybe* full marks and an incredible review when it came out. When I picked up the guitar and started to write again, the inclusiveness of the lyrics in house music showed up in my songs and became a big part of it. A song like 'Live Forever' would never have existed and wouldn't have been called that before acid house. It would have been melancholy. The euphoria of acid house was so engrained in me, I was so into it and what I loved about it was the inclusivity. Songs were about us, they weren't personal, they were about the collective. I adopted that and put it into my music. It's still there today. All my big songs, whether in the nineties or now, they're all about the collective. It's not about me, it's not about you, it's about us. That was really important. Around the time *Definitely Maybe* came out, I went to hear Tom and Ed DJing at the Heavenly Sunday Social at The Albany. They played 'Live

Forever', which fitted right into what they were doing there.

The next year, I recall ending up in a field somewhere. The Chemical Brothers had just released a track with Tim Burgess ('Life Is Sweet'). I remember seeing them there and saying, 'Why are you getting him to sing on your tracks, why aren't you asking me?' The germ of the idea was me telling them that I was available.

Sometime after, they sent me a rough version of what became 'Setting Sun'. It arrived on a cassette and I'd been up all night with a bunch of people at mine. It came through the letterbox, and I stuck it on to hear all these mad noises whooshing all over the place for six minutes. All the girls I was with at the time were shouting, 'Fucking hell turn it off!' I just kept putting it on again, thinking, 'Fucking hell this is amazing.' I don't tend to analyse music too deeply – I like it because of this, or because it reminds me of that. It just instantly struck me that it was going to be great. It inspired me to come up with the words, which half existed in another form as an Oasis song.

The day I recorded the vocal, Manchester City were playing. They were in the Third Division at the time, and I was going to see them play at Wycombe. I pulled up in the car and said to the driver, 'Hang on, I don't think this'll take very long.' At that point, I didn't really consider myself a singer; this was the first time I'd ever sung on someone else's song. I didn't really know how it was going to go.

Recording took no time. They had the loop going round and round and I had three sections of vocal. I sung it a few times and then said, 'Sorry, I've got to go, the football's starting soon.' They thought it sounded great and that was it, off I went and I didn't think anything more of it until I heard the rough mix. Apart from a weird effect on one bit of the vocal that I asked to change, it was as you hear it on the record. It was so painless. But this was the nineties. Nobody gave a fuck. If we'd been doing it now it would be filmed, streamed live on the internet, loads of marketing tie-ins, all sorts of shit. In the nineties, you'd meet someone backstage, say, 'I should be singing on your next single.' They'd send it to you and you'd do it. And the next thing it's fucking Number 1. Them's the days.

Hearing that first version on cassette, I would never in a million years have thought it would get to Number 1. Fucking no chance. But the fact that it knocked off that piece of shit 'Breakfast at Tiffany's', which seemed to have been at Number 1 for eleven years, made it all the more sweet. And the fact that Radio 1 DJ Chris Evans refused to play it was hilarious. I remember him being sniffy about it and thinking, 'We are on to something here.'

All the people in their field – electronic music, dance music, whatever you call it – all the greats have one amazing thing in common. And it's not skills, it's taste. Every great DJ has got great taste, and The Chemical Brothers have got great taste. It's that simple. Whether it's the sounds they use, or the arrangements, or the people they've worked with over the years, it's just cool as fuck and it's remained that way. And I put it down to great taste in music, which comes from astonishing record collections. It's not about how clever you are, or how up to the minute or how technically savvy you are. It's about great taste and they have that. Simple as that.

Stills from the 'Setting Sun' music video, the first of many collaborations with video directors Dom & Nic.

112   The Chemical Brothers

Paused in Cosmic Reflection 113

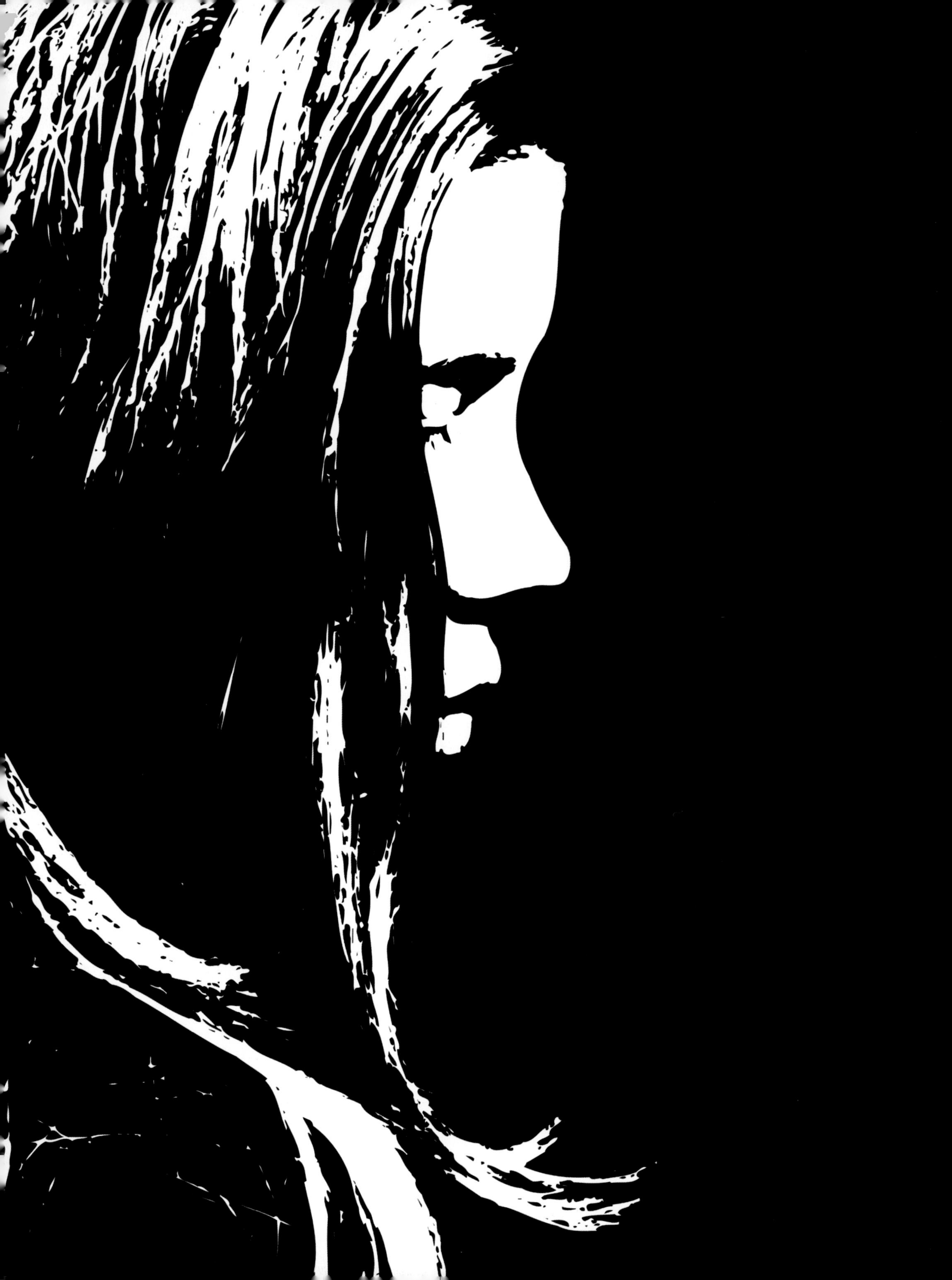

**Sunday morning I'm waking up
Can't even focus on a coffee cup
Don't even know whose bed I'm in**

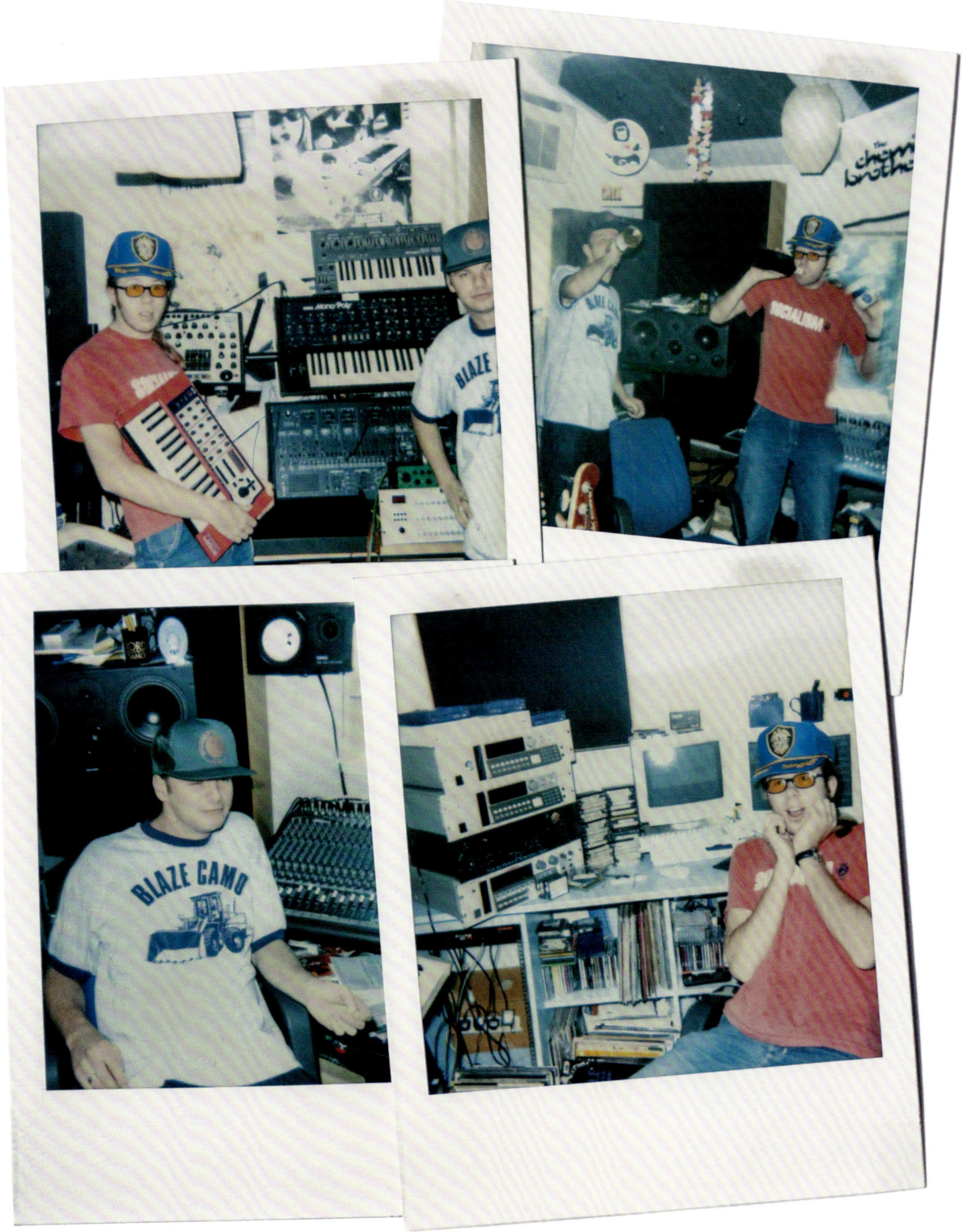
BLAZE CAMO
SOCIALISM

It Doesn't Matter

Opposite: Orinoco Studios.

Everything here is pushed to its limit, everything is in overdrive. This is music as hypnosis, set to a bass drum that lands with metronomic precision and the power of a wrecking ball. The song's central tenet, its one line of dialogue – *It doesn't matter* – is a mantra of release, a message to carry you through. *It doesn't matter*. Everything north, south, east or west of the dance floor is an irrelevance. You are here now. The rest of it? *It doesn't matter.*

The roots of 'It Doesn't Matter' lie in the kind of mind expansion one gets when discovering records, genres even, that have previously been unheard. They lie in the thrill of putting a needle to a groove to hear alien music crackling from the speakers, and they lie in falling in love with these new worlds of sound. The fair thing to do with these discoveries, that mind expansion, is to translate them back into your own music and pass on that same feeling.

Tom Rowlands

By the time we were recording *Dig Your Own Hole*, I was buying so much music from the Record and Tape Exchange in Notting Hill. They had separate shops for different genres. The classical branch had an incredible avant-garde section. It was the first time I'd ever heard people like Morton Subotnick, Pierre Henry, François Bayle or Stockhausen.

I didn't know anything about that music in 1996, it was as if they were from a different world. They weren't getting written about in magazines. Those records were often put out by universities and would come with amazing sleeve notes, all these really interesting stories from colleges that had electronic music departments back at a time when people believed that's where the future of music was headed. I got so obsessed with buying those records, most of which sounded crazy. They were a massive influence on the sound of the album. And back then, they were cheap as well.

A track like 'It Doesn't Matter' was as influenced by those records as much as it was by the stacks of psychedelic records we were buying at that time. And by experimenting with our equipment to push it as far as we could make it go.

I worked out a technique where you could move the start of the sample by the velocity with which you hit the key. And then I worked out if you did that with a micro note division – say 1,000 notes in a bar – and if you changed the velocity and had such a density in the note, you could step backwards and forwards through the sound. There's a process called granular synthesis that had first been developed in the sixties. It's quite common in recording now, but back then I had no idea what that was when I was using my own rudimentary way of granulising sound.

'It Doesn't Matter' is an approximation of granular synthesis. People would use that technique to get variations on classical string sounds to make them sound more human. I was using it in as extreme a way as possible. And the track is full of that sound. I was obsessed with that sound at the time. The bit in 'It Doesn't Matter' that sounds like time stretching, that's actually this process of changing the sample start by the velocity with which you're hitting the sound. That technique made anything fit rhythmically with anything else.

That track is one of the best showcases of Dubby's skills as an incredible performance mixer. That dynamic is one of the biggest things he brought to the way we make records in the three decades we've worked with him. Our live setup is put together in a way that's very influenced by how he set up a dynamic mix. With Dubby, it's never a case of 'that's the mix, let's record it'. He works with the desk all the time, his hands are in motion for every second of the process. It's a perfect example of that hackneyed old phrase: 'playing the studio like an instrument'.

We'd often go into a mix with loads of DAT recordings of jam versions of a track we'd been working on. I would have spent ages trying to get a really concise arrangement of a song together and we would record that. And then we'd have playtime. We'd get all the effects up in the studio and get everything spread out on the mixing desk. Then we'd spend hours and hours deconstructing the track. Sometimes Dubby would focus in on a part of the track that you'd never really paid much mind to, saying, 'I can take this thing here – that thing you've tucked away at the back of the song – and I can make this the main bit of the track.' Then you'd take a sample of what he'd done and take it away and you'd make another version of the song with a shifted focus.

'It Doesn't Matter' is the perfect example of that process. I'd sampled the Lothar and the Hand People vocal line and I had most of the elements together. I had a bassline, which had the same sound, and I had that kind of disco feel to the rhythm track. I was listening to it in my little writing studio upstairs from the main room in Orinoco thinking, 'This sounds amazing.' Playing it downstairs, it sounded a bit flat. The genius of Dubby is that he'll spend hours and hours trying to get the most ridiculous thing out of tiny elements of the track. There was a point where we thought, 'Maybe it should go really heavy for this section...' and then you'd hear where he'd taken the sound during all that time spent pushing and pushing it – and suddenly the whole thing has been reframed. That element that you'd tucked away is now the most exciting thing you've ever heard, this massive wall of bass or a kick drum that sounds ridiculously huge.

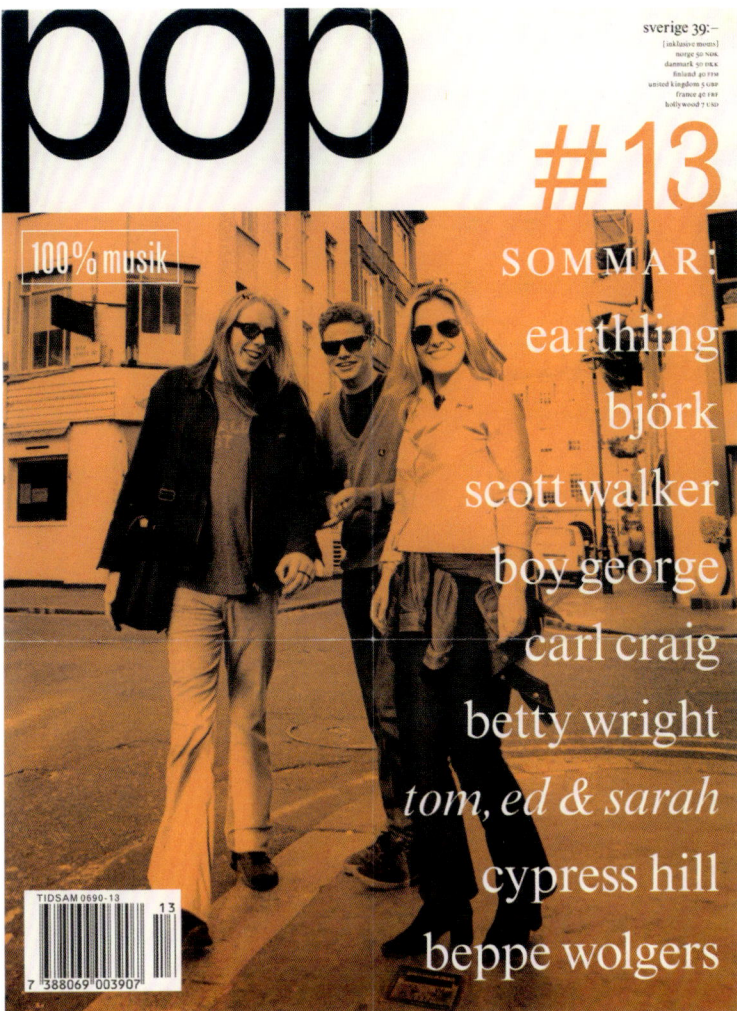

The process doesn't always work. I've got DATs full of total rubbish. But a lot of the time, certainly with 'It Doesn't Matter', the sound we end up with is way beyond anything I could ever have imagined. Dubby helped take it to a different level. We've tried to get that same psychedelic level of bass, even going as far as to use the same synth patch, but the finished version somehow achieved a weird frequency that we've never captured in

Opposite top: Tom and Ed with Steve Dub, Orinoco Studios.

Opposite bottom: Steve Dub at Rowlands Audio Research.

the exact same way since. 'It Doesn't Matter' is reduced down to its component parts. It's a triumph of its one idea and remains so pure in what it's trying to do.

Ed Simons

Tom and I both bought second-hand copies of the Lothar and the Hand People album when we were touring America in 1995. [The sample on 'It Doesn't Matter' came from the track 'It Comes on Anyhow'. A Lenny Kaye review of the band's debut album in *Rolling Stone* described it as 'electronic country, a kind of good-time music played by mad dwarfs'.]

There's a great meaning in that simple line. Lothar and the Hand People were a sonically adventurous psychedelic rock band in the late sixties who were playing with their own musical ideas. They were the first band to use any Moog instrument live. To take that mantra and put it on a very incessant, heavy disco-y techno record while keeping a sense of continuation, it's like the baton of sonic adventurism has been handed down across the generations. John Emelin and Paul Conly from the band came to a gig of ours in Denver and said, 'That was exactly what we were trying to do.' It felt like there was a really nice circularity to that, us being a continuation of something they'd been trying to express thirty years earlier.

Steve Dub

I wasn't doing particularly well at school, so I went through the Yellow Pages and rang loads of studios to see if anyone had any work going. I ended up as a runner at Radio Luxembourg, where I found myself editing records for radio, doing things like chopping out the swear words from hip hop records. After getting sacked from there, I got a job at Konk Studios in Crouch End as an assistant.

That was pretty nuts. There's Flood in one room and John Leckie in the other, and I'd end up assisting on things like Renegade Soundwave and The Stone Roses' first album. At the time I was completely oblivious to what a privilege that was, as anyone in their teens probably would be.

In 1990, I made a record with my mate George that Pete Tong signed to FFRR. With the advance for that, we bought a sampler and set up a little studio in his garage, which became Dada Studios. I started making records with lots of DJs and people like Leftfield, who used to book it a lot for their label Hard Hands. In 1993, they asked The Dust Brothers to remix their single with John Lydon ('Open Up') and they booked the studio and me.

That's where I first met Tom and Ed. We got on pretty well during the mix and they asked, 'What are you doing next week?' That led to us working together on the *Fourteenth Century Sky* EP and then a lot of remixes over the following year.

By the time they started working on their album, we moved to The Toyshop, a brilliant little studio under the stairs in Orinoco. There were two studios there – The Toyshop and a bigger studio with a Neve desk and massive speakers that we'd use if ever we had a bigger budget to work with.

Working in the studio, I've always liked to fuck about. It helps to keep the track feeling alive. Each mix you do will be slightly different because of the different ways you've pushed it. The way I approach mixing is inspired by the way dub reggae producers work. A lot of live dubbing on the desk is inspired by boredom and curiosity. *What'll happen if I put a live delay on that vocal? That sounds good, do that again.* It becomes a little performance, an hour or two at the end of the day where you see how far you can take things. Maybe it's absolute chaos and not useable. Other times, you end up making something that sounds really cool.

One of the things that Orinoco's Neve desk brought to the music was movement. Tom was always trying to bring live instrumentation into the mix, so you'd always have this mix of electronics with other things that you'd put through machines, then move around or modulate, either by hand or by an LFO or by an auxiliary send on the desk. On 'It Doesn't Matter', you'd hear a sound like a snare or a clap, which would kind of scatter around, going up and down in the frequencies. There's a lot of that in the track.

When we work together, we're always trying to make things sound more unhinged. It's almost like disrespecting the track, or at least the conventional version of what the track could be. We'd do the safe mix, where we'd sit back and not touch anything and Tom would do a brilliant arrangement based around that basic sound. Once we'd committed that, we'd plug in every effect in the studio and see what would happen. On *Exit Planet Dust* and *Dig Your Own Hole*, a lot of the weird sounds were from us messing around. Whether it was synths or effects that were moving around, that unhinged stuff might end up laid on top of or edited into some of the more static versions we'd already committed to.

One of the things that makes tracks work is not being afraid to mess with stuff. On 'It Doesn't Matter', it's got that mad kick drum on it. It ended up going up five or six channels on the desk so we could get it to sound as big and mad as possible. We were trying to get as much low end out of it while

Paused in Cosmic Reflection   121

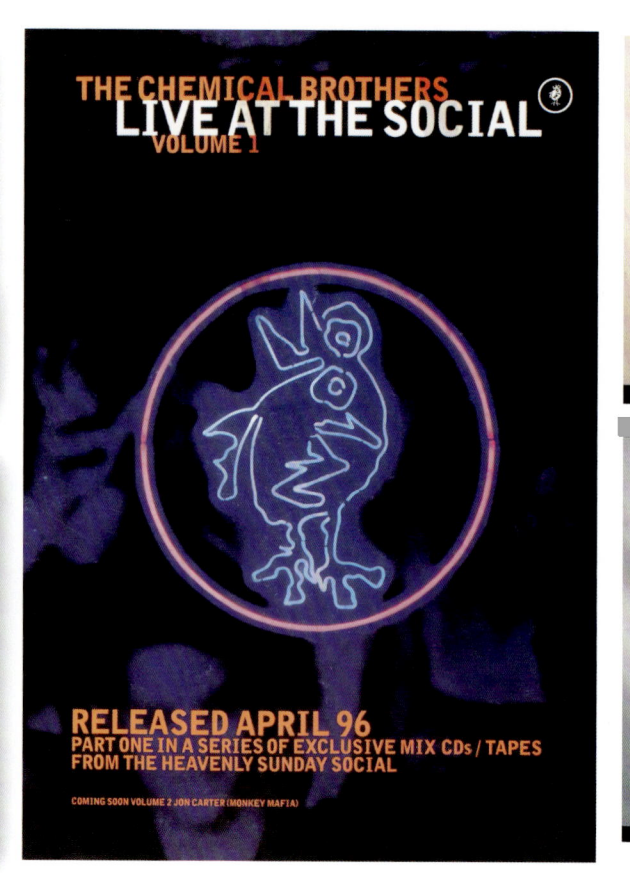

keeping clarity. Normally you'd put the bass drum up and make it sound nice while trying to balance it to make it sound good on the radio. I was a bit more mental than that. I loved the wild aspect, the interplay between the three of us in the mix. You'd go into it having locked a good version, and then you'd just see where you could take it. When we first started working together, I'd only been doing it for a few years. As we learnt together our confidence grew and the sound palette expanded, and the possibilities of what we could do expanded.

I remember coming away from the studio when we'd recorded 'It Doesn't Matter' thinking, 'Wow, we've done something amazing here.' Something that's far more than the sum of its parts. When it's at its best, you don't know how it got there but you just listen and think, 'That's really cool.' To do that in the studio, checking whether it works on the little speakers and the big speakers, and then seeing it translated into the live show, played out in a field full of people feeling the same energy that you felt when you made it, the bit where you look over at each other and go, 'This is pretty fucking good.' That really is quite an overwhelming feeling.

In our early days working together, there wasn't the technology to capture audio really well on a computer, so we either recorded on tape or, if we had a sampler big enough, we'd sample massive pieces of audio and then trigger it. It was a lot more cumbersome. After *Surrender*, audio in computers got a lot more powerful. Before that, you'd have a computer running sequencers with a tape machine and samplers linked up, machines all working with each other.

Working like that, things did have the capacity to go wrong. When we were mixing 'Got Glint?' [*Surrender*], the room we were in was getting hotter and hotter, and quite often the air conditioning would break down and the synth would end up going really out of tune. When we were printing mixes, Tom went off somewhere and there were certain bits of the track where the Moog [synthesiser] was completely out of tune, drifting by a whole tone as the room was getting hotter still. It ended up sounding brilliant – a happy accident – but it was a long way from how it was meant to sound.

Now we work in Tom's studio, which has a big SSL desk and an amazing collection of vintage equipment. Over the years, all of the

Left: Promo cassette for The Chemical Brothers' first mix album, Live at the Social Volume One, released on Heavenly Recordings.

Next page: The EMS Hi-Fli used on many early Chemical Brothers records.

Page 126–7: Stills from the 'Block Rockin' Beats' music video featuring Billy from EastEnders, directed by Dom & Nic.

stuff we've liked in studios has ended up in Tom's place. Even though the writing process comes more from the computer, it's still very machine-driven in terms of the instruments that are in the room. I think the analogue aspect is really important to The Chemical Brothers' sound.

When we mix now, we'll get a track up and it might already be sounding great. But we'll still do passes where we'll put stuff through various effects and Tom and I will perform things live, adding effects to certain parts of the track, especially in the transitions between sections. Maybe you're working on a build and then you add in some sort of filtery, delay, reverb stuff underneath, and you're doing it by hand. As you do, you're literally feeling it, you're pushing it with the music. That performance aspect is the same as somebody playing a guitar. Analogue studios allow you to play with the sound like it's an instrument. The tactile aspect of the desk and the process definitely gives you a buzz. Sometimes you'll listen back and you don't even remember how a sound has been made because it happened in the moment and you've moved on to the next bit.

Over the years, communication between the three of us of has been so important. Our working process is quite transparent. No one is afraid to say whether they like something or not. Ed's approach is very cerebral, he knows in his mind what works and he's very good at saying that aspects of a track might have been better in the morning rather than after the ten hours spent fucking around with it. Quite often as an engineer you'd be thinking something must have improved because of all the hours you've spent sweating over it.

There will be other times when I'll start doing something that I think works and Tom might immediately stop me because it's not what he's after. And that's fine too. That sort of triangulation between us means things get done, rather than us ending up in an eternal debate about whether something was better before or not. There's a confidence in what they do that serves them well. And we all still get a buzz from doing it. If you're entertaining yourself while making music, that's everything. I'm really proud of what we do together.

INPUT SIGNAL TRIGGER SENSITIVITY
Solo
Strum
OCTAVE SHIFT
Buzz
Time
Fast
SUSTAIN FUZZ
Time
Fast
SYNTHI
HI FLI
PHASE FILTER
Top Boost
Ring Modulation
Fuzz Level
Bypass Mix
Modulation Speed
Modulation Ramp Time
Modulation Depth
Frequency Shift
Vibrato
Phasing 1
Phasing 2
Waw
Waw
Meow
LEFT PEDAL
RIGHT PEDAL
Manufactured in England By Electronic Music Studios For MUSONIC INC USA

LUSCIOUS JACKSON • RAILROAD JERK • DR. OCTAGON
option
MUSIC CULTU
chemical brothers kick out the jams
NO. 72 JAN-FEB 1997
EXCLUSIVE! NOEL: THE LOST INTERVIEW PLACEBO THE ORB AT HOME SUEDE PAVEMENT 12-PAGE IMAGES FEAST
£2.30
APRIL 1997
SELECT
LIFE IS SWEET
ASH DO THE STAR WARS ALL-NIGHTER!
FREE!
8 ENORMOUS FLY POSTERS
blur
suede
The People vs. Larry Flynt
SUPER FURRY ANIMALS
Beth Orton Trailer Park
THE CHEMICAL BROTHERS
Smile!
You're massive!

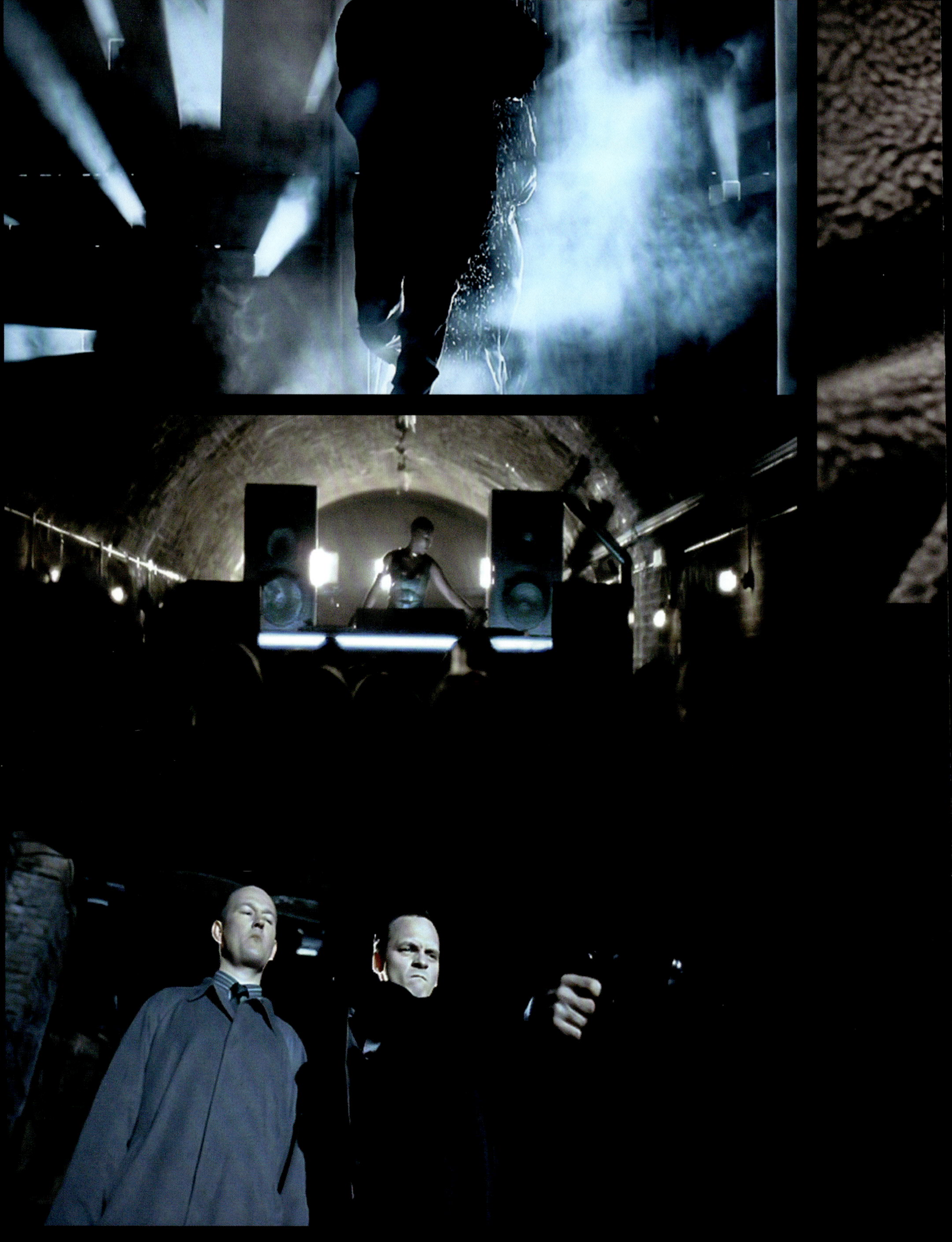

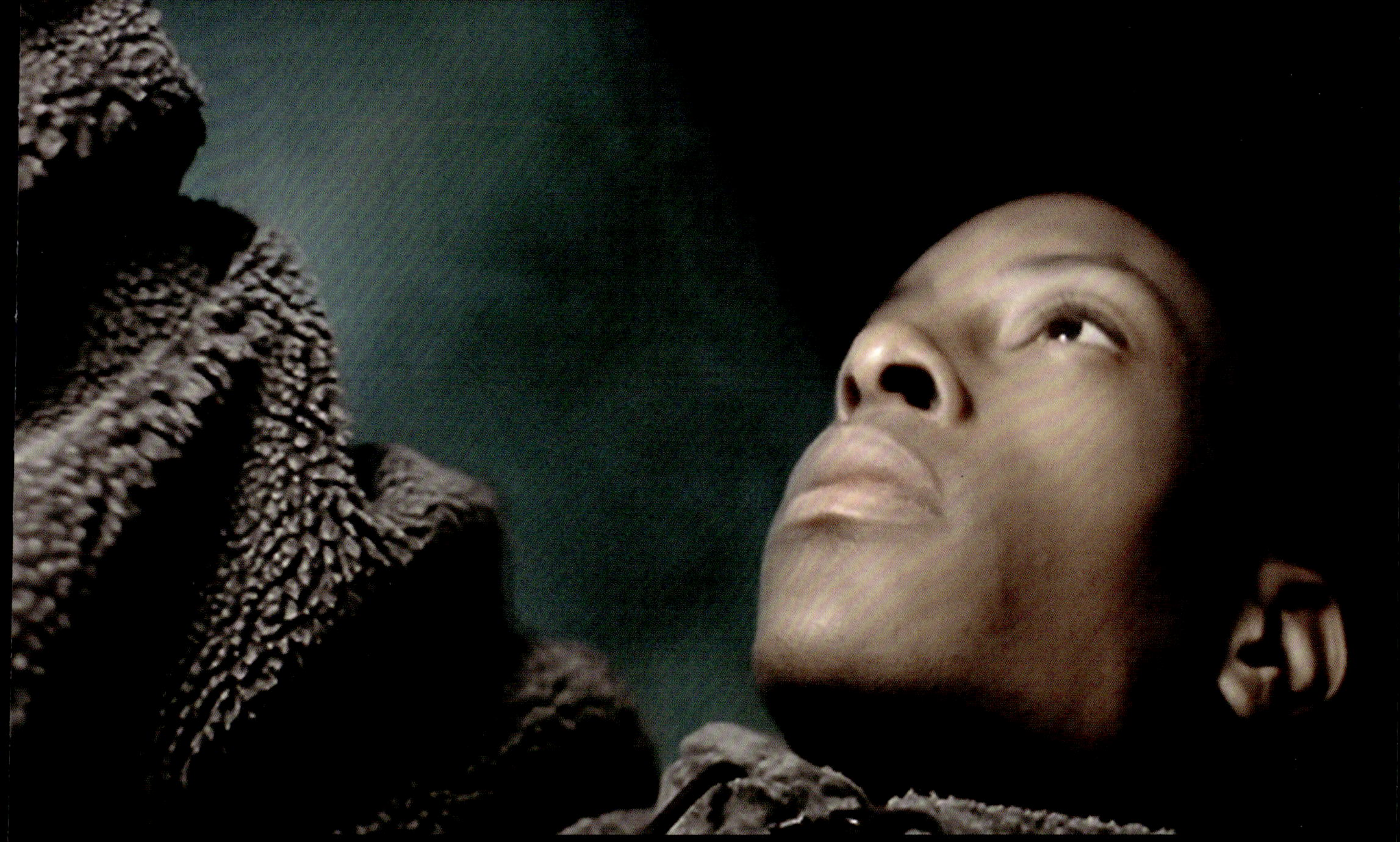
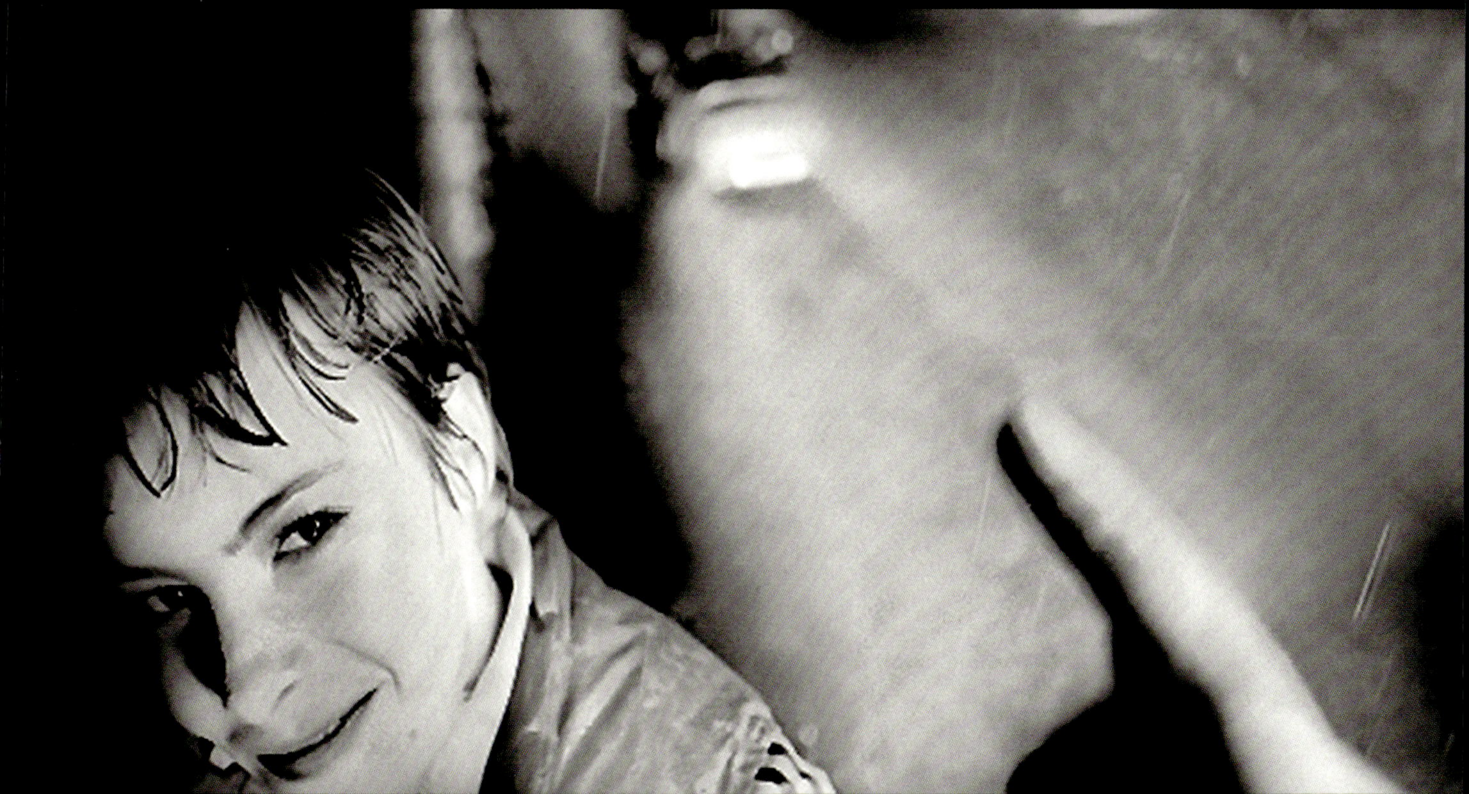

JOCKEY SLUT

IS GLASGOW THE NEW PARIS? DUB - EXPLAINED! GREEN VELVET - LIVE!

GO BALLISTIC!
with brothers ashley, dave, rocky & diesel

Schoolly D
"my trainers smell bad after one hour"

20 BIG NIGHTS OUT!

Chemical Brothers
TOM AND ED DO AMERICA!

JIMI-MANIA!
THE TENOR MAN ROCKS GERMANY

FREE!

harthouse UK present good records

freddy fresh • hardfloor
alter ego vs david holmes
hacienda • yokota • bill & ben

this cassette contains BASF tape

Vol. 2 No 9 Jun/Jul 97 £2.20

Dig Your Own Hole

In early 1994, The Dust Brothers were booked to play live in Florida. At that point their live show hadn't been seen outside of central London. Following that trip, Tom and Ed went back and forth to the States on a regular basis, building up a dedicated fanbase in the country's burgeoning rave scene. After a period of their records only being available in the US as imports, they began releasing through nascent electronic label Astralwerks.

Dig Your Own Hole came out in April 1997 and charted at Number 14 on the Billboard 200 album chart. A month and a half later The Prodigy's *The Fat of the Land* entered the US charts at Number 1.

Ed Simons

We loved going to the States. Our first trip was the first time I'd been to America, not long after we'd played our very first gigs in London in the spring of 1994. We were staying in a Holiday Inn in Orlando and we did two gigs. There was a lot of fried food, trips to Disneyworld and just hanging out. We didn't have any money but we had amazing hosts who looked after us. The first show we did was a massive club with a huge outdoor area called The Firehouse. It was one of the most insane scenes: a big shed, lots of ambulances, quite a druggy audience.

Although it was early on in our career, there was a lot of music coming out of Miami that had a similar feel. Breaks, acid, that Florida bass sound. 'Chemical Beats' had become a massive track out there. We went on a whim. We had two keyboards wrapped in a blanket, which we took on the plane as hand luggage. The two of us were so naive. We got picked up by DJ Icey, who had sorted the gigs. We went back later in the year with Justin Robertson and it was a bit more organised.

We did a small tour that took in a rave called Elevations and a gig in San Francisco. There was a lot of psychedelic energy at the gigs, they felt wild.

By 1995, there was a lot less of that in clubs in Britain. There were lots of super clubs; the mainstream had become straighter. Over in the States there was such an intensity, and people were really into the music. Different areas had different scenes. We played a few gigs in San Francisco with the Hardkiss crew and they had a whole different vibe to the Florida people. They kept the peace and love elements that had originally been a part of acid house. When we played at Irving Plaza in New York in 1995, the promoter booked two hip hop legends – Grand Wizzard Theodore and DJ Kool Herc – to warm up for us. There were lots of people from New York dance culture there, all sorts of faces. It felt like we'd made a real connection.

America was always an incredible amount of fun. Those early gigs were only about twenty-five minutes of music, and it was going down so well. You'd drive to outdoor gigs and hear *Exit Planet Dust* playing out of people's tents. Tours would see amazing contrasts: one day you'd play some beautiful old theatre in a city and the next you'd be playing a rave out in the desert. It was still a mixture. After shows, there would always be lots of people back in the dressing room and there would be lots of partying. Adam and Noah would be out there with us; there would always be some drama between them and the promoter about where they could set up their projectors. But it was such a laugh.

When *Dig Your Own Hole* came out, we arrived for a press tour and suddenly the overarching story seemed to be that this music was the future. Everything was going to sound like this from now on. Quite rightly, the press seemed a bit sceptical when they met these two dweeby guys from Britain. It felt like someone had over-promised. We'd end up doing big profile pieces for major titles, where a journalist would come and hang around for a week trying to capture a rounded picture of our lifestyle: 'What are you up to today?' 'I was really hoping to just doss about if I'm honest. Imagine the football might be on later, might go to the pub. Fancy it?' They were nothing like how the big UK music magazines did things.

In lots of interviews, people would proclaim that 'the genius of you guys is that you've married rock music and dance music'. The sense of the music connecting different musical tribes seemed very fresh in the States. There was a sense of guilt in us, as there were a lot of Black artists in Chicago and Detroit who weren't being recognised as pioneers of part of what we were doing. Our music isn't techno or house in the strictest sense, it's magpie-like.

We were on tour in the UK when *Dig Your Own Hole* charted in the States. Our manager called to say the album had charted at Number 14. When the news came through, I genuinely had no conception that charting in the States was even something that was on the cards, that one of our records could have that level of commercial success. Especially a record as uncompromising as *Dig Your Own Hole*.

Errol Kolosine

In America, The Chemical Brothers started off like a bit of a conspiratorial mission. I'd not long been hired to do a radio promotion at Caroline [Virgin's independent distribution network and label in the States]. Within that setup, there was this little upstart label over in the corner called Astralwerks. Some of the people running Caroline just didn't appreciate that kind of music; they were signing acts in the hopes of replicating debut successes they'd had with the likes of Hole and The Smashing Pumpkins. They – certainly initially – saw Astralwerks as a place for 'weird shit'. Meanwhile, I'd been promoting 'Life Is Sweet', and in many ways I was making more leeway with that as opposed to any of rock/alternative frontline bands we had. In order to push 'Life Is Sweet' further, Brian Long helped me secretly squirrel away $500 to make a CD promo of the track to send to radio stations. We actually got some legit radio ads and that really helped set the table for what was to come next with MTV's *Amp* show and *Dig Your Own Hole*.

MTV started being very good to us, beyond just the dance music specialty realm. The Chemical Brothers' videos were a big part of why that happened. 'Setting Sun' offered this unique look into a different world and lifestyle. And 'Setting Sun' was the real breakthrough, even though it's one of the maddest pieces of music to have ever been on the American charts. If I had a dollar for every person who told us, 'It's great for the specialist shows but you know it'll never get added to the playlist, right . . .?' It sounds like a bunch of airhorns going off, and it batters you with drums. But it struck a nerve.

Oasis were also pretty hot at that point and music in the US was in the midst of a shift. Indie rock had become boring for me as well: the straightness, the whiteness had gotten very stale. What The Chemical Brothers were doing – smashing together psychedelics and dance music – was incredibly valid. It was a bullseye in terms of what people were ready for. Their videos reflected a more interesting world, a more culturally exciting world. They showed the inside of clubs, and the way people were dressing in those clubs.

And when Tom and Ed came over to play live shows, they were just an amazing headfuck

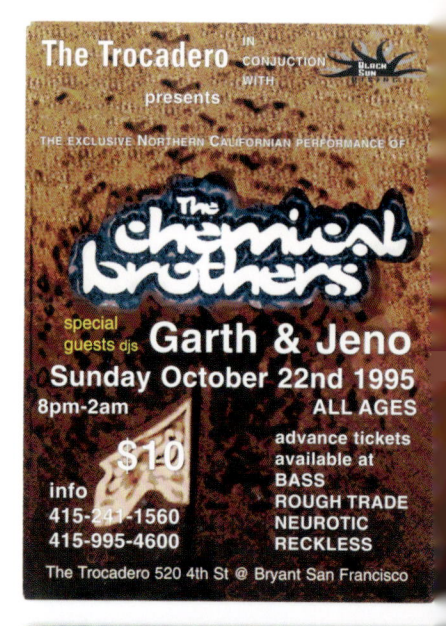

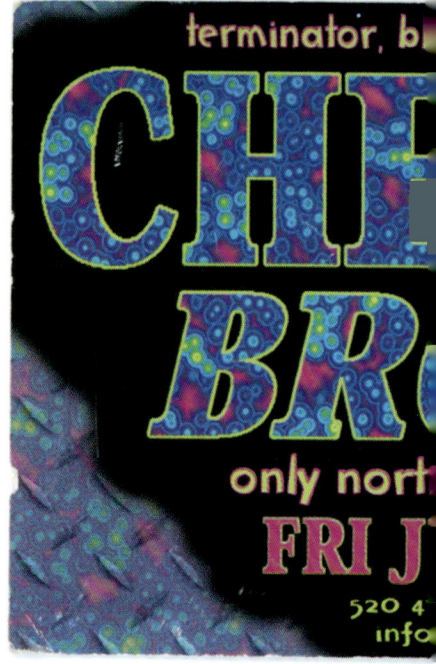

Paused in Cosmic Reflection 131

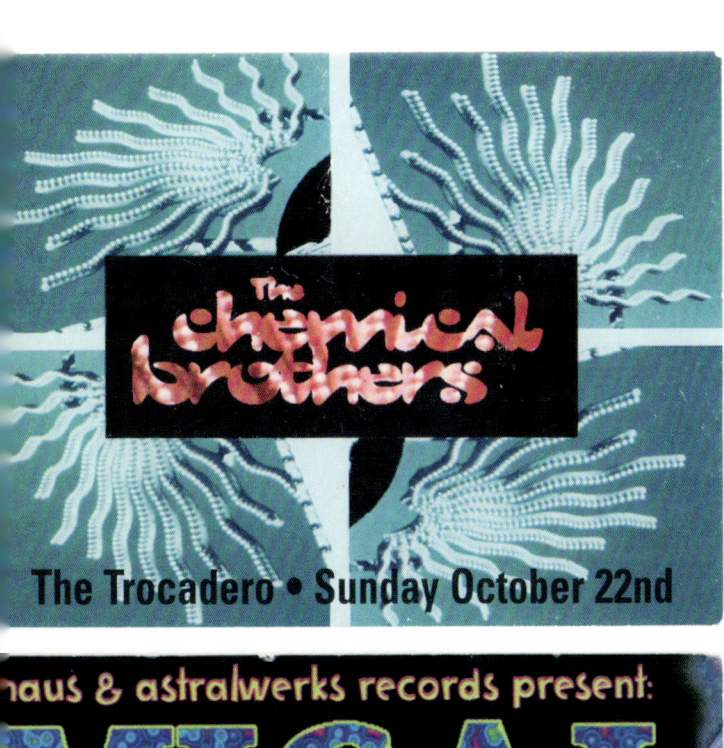

for people. The collision of styles meant it worked for dance people, it worked for rock people, it worked for hip-hop people and it worked for all people in between – because it paid respectful homage to all of those scenes while being uniquely itself. The live show had the energy to bring all of those cultures together in a way that wasn't normative. The band's music really resonated in the same way that early punk or hip hop or Jamaican music resonated. It felt like somebody was pressing a reset button.

At The Chemical Brothers' gigs, I'd insist on taking radio programmers down to the front. Because if they stood at the back, they would never understand that these people were their audience. These were kids in KROQ shirts. There was a cultural shift taking place and the band had a fair share to do with it. 'Setting Sun' was the 'holy shit' moment that created a notion that something different was possible.

Vegetable Vision's contribution in those early days was massively helpful. The hypnotic quality of the visuals from Adam and Noah veered closer to the edges of psychotherapy rather than the more common tropes of rave culture that we'd got used to. There was something about the rawness of those early shows, the 'assembled by necessity' quality, that felt like a trip without the use of chemicals. The Chemical Brothers' gigs were experiential things. They weren't places you went to have a lager, nod your head and then go home. You'd be in the thick of it and you'd talk about it afterwards. In fact, if you'd seen it, chances were you wouldn't shut up about it.

One of the real pivotal moments was Organic festival, which took place in a ski resort in southern California on 22 June 1996. It shifted the culture along both in terms of the music scene and also in how America viewed music festivals. A few promoters came up with this idea to put on a festival of all of these like-minded, mainly British bands. Underworld, Orbital, The Orb, The Chemical Brothers. For me, it was the point of full conversion. Everything made sense after that. The ripple effects of that festival can still be felt, as there would never have been Coachella without Organic. The Chemical Brothers and Underworld both played main stages at the first Coachella three years later.

There was an incredible group of people at Astralwerks around 1996/97. It wasn't a massive team, but it was very hard-working. One of the things that really helped was Virgin in the UK including us in the conversation around *Dig Your Own Hole*. If you're the American label for a British group, it can be a thankless experience. America was a highly coveted market for UK acts, but success would rarely feel like it did at home. But if you ever did get a head of steam, it got people's attention. Virgin gave us time and support, which was great because we were a very small label with very little money. Before too long, this small little upstart label in the corner ended up consuming the whole label. This is why Astralwerks was oft times referred to as 'the label The Chemical Brothers built'.

When an artist does something clever and successful, you have several years of people mimicking it until it becomes unlistenable. People get burnt out, then the next thing turns up. Bands like The Chemical Brothers – along with The Prodigy, Underworld and Fatboy Slim – didn't sound like anything anyone else had to offer. That wave of British and international electronic acts arrived at the exact point where something else had just burnt out, where rock music looked to have run out of ideas. When you walk into a radio station with something singularly

Paused in Cosmic Reflection 133

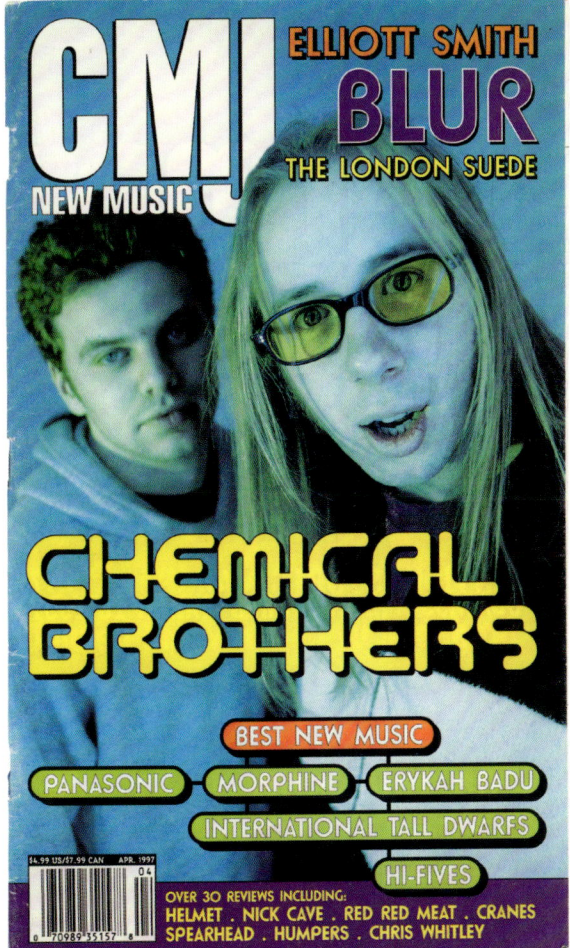

Brothers Gonna Work It Out

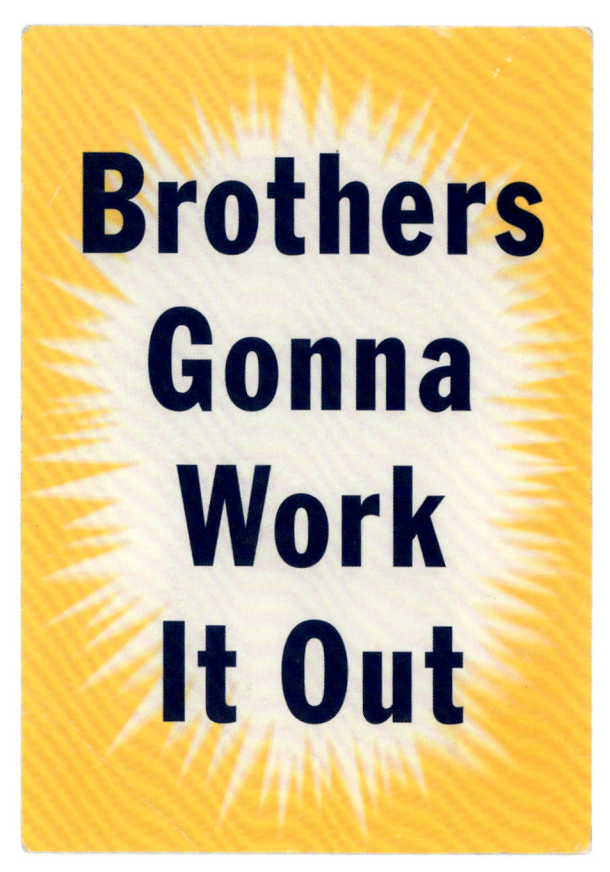

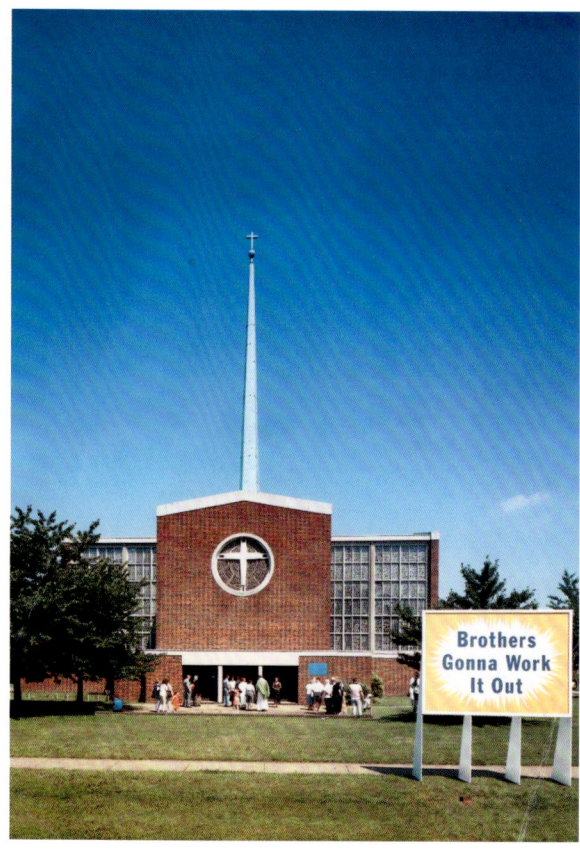

TOM AND ED INVITE YOU TO A PARTY AT THE COBDEN CLUB, 170–172 KENSAL ROAD, LONDON W2. FRIDAY 21ST AUGUST. 10.00PM TO 2.30AM BY INVITE ONLY. ADMIT ONE.

Take This Brother May It Serve You Well

"A DJ MIX ALBUM BY THE CHEMICAL BROTHERS"

ARTIST: CHEMICAL BROTHERS
TITLE: BROTHERS GONNA WORK IT OUT
RELEASE DATE: 21ST SEPTEMBER 1998
CAT NOS.: CD: XDUSTCD101 MC: XDUSTMC101 LTD EDITION CD: XDUSTCDX101
BARCODES: CD: 7243 8 46599 29 MC: 7243 8 46599 43 LTD EDITION CD: 7243 8 4660024
DEALER PRICE: CD/LIMITED EDITION CD: £8.99 CASSETTE: £6.70

LIMITED EDITION CD 10,000 SPECIAL PACKAGING

TRACKLISTING:
01 WILLIE HUTCH "BROTHERS GONNA WORK IT OUT" 02 CHEMICAL BROTHERS (WITH JUSTIN WARFIELD) "NOT ANOTHER DRUGSTORE (PLANET NINE MIX)" 03 CHEMICAL BROTHERS "BLOCK ROCKIN BEATS (THE MICRONAUTS MIX)" 04 ON THE HOUSE "THIS AIN'T CHICAGO" 05 JIMMY CASTOR BUNCH "IT'S JUST BEGUN" 06 KENNY DOPE PRESENTS THE POWERHOUSE THREE "MAKIN' A LIVING" 07 BADDER THAN EVIL "HOT WHEELS (THE CHASE)" 08 UNIQUE 3 "THE THEME (UNIQUE MIX)" 09 LOVE CORPORATION "GIVE ME SOME LOVE" 10 THE MICRONAUTS "THE JAZZ" 11 THE SEROTONIN PROJECT "SIDWINDER (313 VS 216 STOMP MIX)" 12 CAROLS BERRIOS "DOIN' IT AFTER DARK" 13 FREESTYLE "DON'T STOP THE ROCK" 14 METRO "TO A NATION ROCKIN'" 15 CHEMICAL BROTHERS "MORNING LEMON" 16 MEAT BEAT MANIFESTO "MARS NEEDS WOMEN" 17 RENEGADE SOUNDWAVE "THUNDER" 18 DBX "LOSING CONTROL" 19 DUBTRIBE "MOTHER EARTH" 20 BARRY DE VORZON AND PERRY BOTKIN JNR "THE RIOT" 21 THE ULTRAVIOLET CATASTROPHE "TRIP HARDER" 22 MANIC STREET PREACHERS "EVERYTHING MUST GO (CHEMICAL BROTHERS REMIX)" 23 SPRITUALIZED "THINK I'M IN LOVE (CHEMICAL BROTHERS REMIX)"

THE CHEMICAL BROTHERS, AFFECTIONATELY KNOWN BY ONE AND ALL AS TOM & ED, HAVE SPENT THE PAST TWO YEARS HAPPILY CONQUERING THE GLOBE, SCORING A STRING OF NUMBER ONE HITS IN THE UK (SINGLES "SETTING SUN" AND "BLOCK ROCKIN' BEATS" AND "DIG YOUR OWN HOLE" ALBUM) AND A WORLD-WIDE MILLION-PLUS SELLING ALBUM. THEY'VE PICKED UP A FISTFUL OF BRIT AND MERCURY PRIZE NOMINATIONS AND RECENTLY WON A GRAMMY IN AMERICA ("BLOCK ROCKIN' BEATS" SCOOPED THE 1997 "BEST ROCK INSTRUMENTAL" TITLE).

TAKING THEIR INFLUENCES FROM HIP HOP, TECHNO, ROCK N ROLL AND BALEARIC ACID HOUSE, THEY'RE THE PERFECT PARTY DJS. FOR THE MOMENT THEY HAVE PUT LIVE WORK ON HOLD AND DJ APPEARANCES ARE RARE BUT TRIUMPHANT. REMIX WORK IS SPORADIC AND UNEQUIVOCALLY BRILLIANT (LAST UP WAS THEIR MIND-BENDING REWORKING OF SPIRITUALIZED'S "THINK I'M IN LOVE" INCLUDED ON THIS ALBUM). WITH THE RELEASE OF "BROTHERS GONNA WORK IT OUT" TOM AND ED LAUNCH THEIR VERY OWN FREESTYLE DUST RECORD LABEL, AN IDEA THEY'VE BEEN WITH SINCE 1995.

PRESS:
CONCENTRATING ON LEAD REVIEWS FOR THIS RELEASE
FEATURE AUGUST ISSUE MIX MAG.

MARKETING:
MAILOUT TO DATABASE APPROX 70,000
OUTDOOR TEASER AND REVEAL SITES
PRESS ADVERTISING INCLUDING JOCKEY SLUT, MIXMAG AND MUZIK
INSTORE POINT OF SALE.

Paused in Cosmic Reflection   137

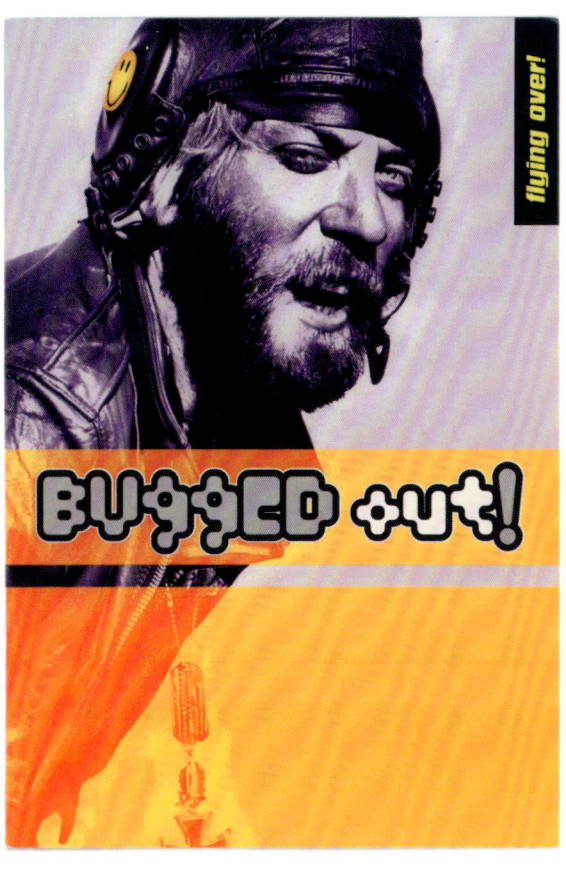

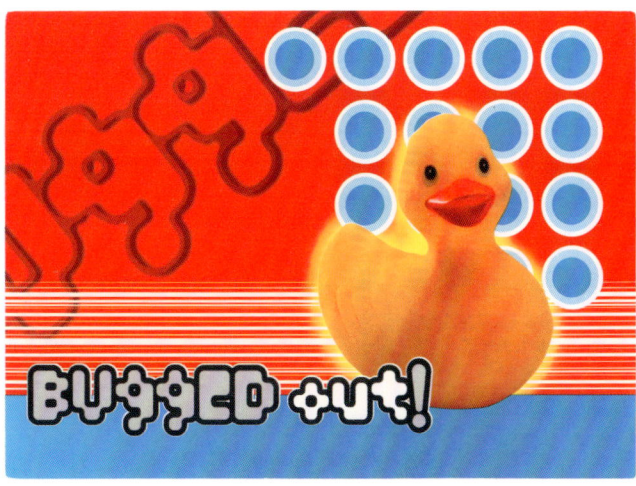

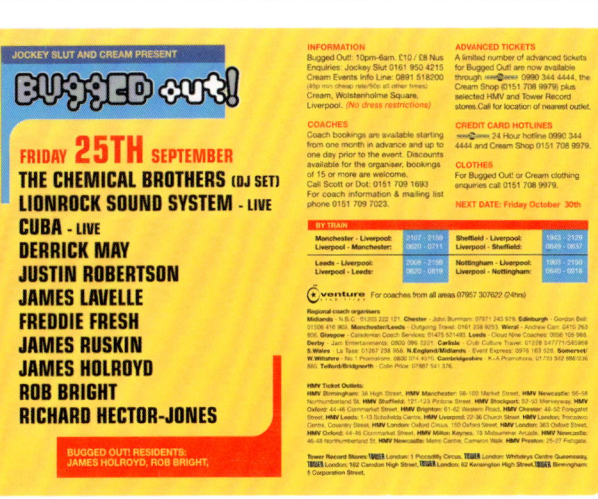

Stills from the 'Elektrobank' music video featuring Sofia Coppola, directed by Spike Jonze.

Paused in Cosmic Reflection 139

The Private Psychedelic Reel

'The Private Psychedelic Reel' is a wave. It is sound in a constant oceanic motion; a fluctuation, a wonder, a command and a goodbye. It is a deep expansion of the consciousness suited to both the crowded dance floor and the solo voyage into bliss.

Rising from a warm modulation and a golden sequence, 'The Private Psychedelic Reel' quickly encloses the listener inside a lattice of sound. Within there, the music curls around in transverse and longitudinal movement, returning again and again and again and gaining power with each new cycle.

As the 'Reel' unfolds, an orchestra of undefined instruments of the imagination swirl like phantoms through the heart of the track, phasing celestial sounds in and out of the mix. At points it is overwhelming, like trying to keep your head above a furious squall at sea, boat capsized, no land in sight. But respite – rescue – is always there, scooping you up, placing you back inside that lattice, that ever growing spiral of sound.

To be in a crowd at a Chemical Brothers show when 'The Private Psychedelic Reel' uncoils is to witness an ecstatic communion, all hands turned towards the duo who play from behind a mechanical pulpit on a stage lit by stained glass. It is the final point of a collective journey undertaken, the end of a tunnel that opens up into blazing light, a final loss of control of the horizontal and the vertical.

There's nothing else. Love is all.

Ed Simons

Between *Exit Planet Dust* and *Dig Your Own Hole*, it must have looked like we had a real professional drive. Lots of remixes, the *Loops of Fury* EP, live shows and DJ gigs pretty much every weekend at home and in the States. Really, though, that period was about us being given the keys. It was about having an audience to play to and having the money to buy equipment and pay for time in the recording studio. All of that together was hugely motivating.

During that time, Tom and I moved into a flat together in an old Victorian mansion block in Maida Vale. The flat had previously belonged to Bros in the late eighties. We both had a bit of money from the Virgin deal and from DJing out at weekends. It seems a weird idea now, us living together after the band started, and I think Tom moved in with his girlfriend quite soon after. The day I moved my worldly possessions in, Tom already had everything unpacked and set up. There was a small computer and a sampler in his bedroom, and he was ready to get down to work, writing and recording. I just wanted a day or two to sort all my stuff out.

There were lots of rich cultural inputs around that time, including the two psychedelic record shops in Notting Hill (Intoxica, Stand Out/Minus Zero) that were a short stroll from the flat. Every weekend, one of us would be in there buying these weird old records. Tom got friendly with one of the guys in the shop who started schooling him on real psychedelia. A far cry from Eastern Bloc on a Saturday afternoon but equally as much of an education.

By 1996, everything suddenly got very big and very intense. That was the year of Knebworth, the scale of which is mind-blowing even today. We were DJing at Turnmills pretty much every Saturday night, road testing a lot of tracks that we were working on. I remember about six weeks in, thinking, 'This is great, but it's also quite bananas.' It was so intense. People were very high at that club; it didn't get called Gurnmills for nothing. You'd walk in there and there would be no room, no physical space

Paused in Cosmic Reflection 141

to move, even in the DJ booth. There would be about ten mates in there, all trying to get some room away from the packed dance floor, all of them dancing inside the booth, which only added to the madness.

Dig Your Own Hole was us giving free rein to all of the different influences that were feeding into us from all around the world. It was the most extreme expression of that, one where you could have a track like 'It Doesn't Matter' sitting alongside 'The Private Psychedelic Reel'. They're completely different forms of music but they each evolved from everything that was channelled in, that fed into the making of *Dig Your Own Hole*. For us, our sound was entirely natural. It wasn't something we sat down and pondered, tried to perfect. We had no intention of making a pure electronic dance record; we always wanted all of those external forces to be reflected.

'The Private Psychedelic Reel' has a certain portent to it. I love the fact that it comes steeped in religious imagery at the live shows, and I love the way the very long drawn-out intro isn't afraid to be quite serious and maybe a little pretentious. It's all about wild release and escape. When we play it live, it leaves a real magic in the air, a kinetic energy. It's such a cool combination of things – relentless drum fills, release and escape. In the live set, it feels like permission to really surrender yourself to the music. At a good Chemical Brothers gig, the audience is pretty wild, unfettered and untamed. 'The Private Psychedelic Reel' serves those people by building such a peak of intensity, and it comes with the added knowledge that it's the last chance to dance.

I remember the riff coming together in the Strongroom quite late on a Friday night, back in the days when I definitely wouldn't have wanted to be in a recording studio in a pre-gentrified Old Street on a Friday night. I was twenty-five and eager to be out and about, but the track was developing with this sort of sitar riff coming together. That was the first thing that arrived, on top of some simple building blocks for the drums. There was already something mesmerising enough about it for us to get lost in it that evening, even in its most simple version, before we started adding layers to it.

And there are so many layers, even before Jonathan Donahue and Mercury Rev added their parts, so many small fragments of sound, so much careful sampling. Over the years, all these big memories have built around the track where it's the final point of an incredible show, a rapture almost, but there's also this moment of intimacy where Tom and I were cut off from the rest of the world, building this piece of music in the Strongroom.

In the early days of the band, we'd always talk about how much of an influence 'Tomorrow Never Knows' was. People seemed to think that we'd sampled it but we never did. We just loved the sound of the record, particularly the drums and all those fragments of sound that spin around inside it. We played it at the Heavenly Sunday Social and it made a big impact in that little basement.

Wanting to know and hear more about 'Tomorrow Never Knows', we read somewhere that there was a fabled, unreleased hour-long version of the track called 'The Void'. When we were touring Japan, we'd head to the most obscure bootleg shops. There were lots of vinyl collectors' shops over there, places that specialised in Beatles bootlegs. And we would trawl them, all in the hope of one day finding 'The Void'.

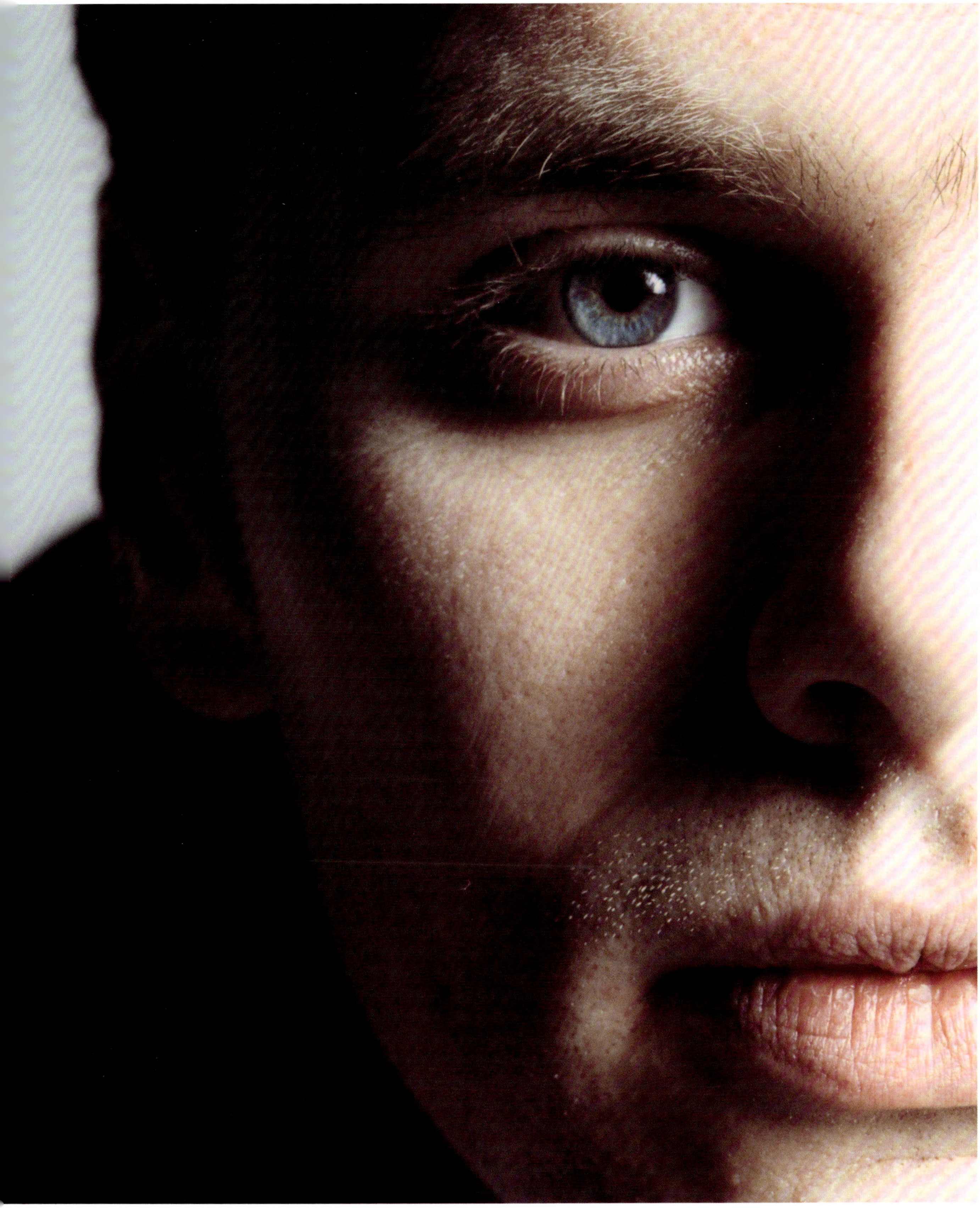

In a way, 'The Private Psychedelic Reel' was our version of 'The Void'. It's what we imagined or hoped 'The Void' would have sounded like if ever we'd found it. Since then, a lot of Beatles bootlegs have come out through the *Anthology* series and the album reissues. It's never emerged, so it probably never existed. But we have our version. 'The Private Psychedelic Reel' is actually a title of a Beatles bootleg that I bought in Japan back then. It was a great title. Although I loved the idea of something that just exists for the people in the band, their own world, this was our own way of making that 'Private Psychedelic Reel' public.

Tom Rowlands

It might sound blasé but it was exciting just to be able to make another record. Just to be in the world of making records, having people listening to them, that really was the main thing. We were playing live a lot and DJing a lot and making lots of music. And we were still working out of a programming room in the Strongroom on Curtain Road that was a hangover from Ariel days.

Every day we'd head from west London to the studio to work. I loved being there because it had a real sense of community about it. There were always people there who were happy to help out. The Beatmasters were in a room upstairs and famously Orbital were based out of there. Our programming room was tiny so we'd often go down and see Phil and Paul [Hartnoll] in their bigger room. They had an engineer called Mickey Mann who worked with them. Mickey was very generous and would always help us out; he would always share floppy discs with loads of amazing bass drum samples on them.

The first inspiration for 'The Private Psychedelic Reel' was seeing Mercury Rev supporting Spiritualized at the Astoria [2 November 1993]. I loved the chaos and the wonder of those early Mercury Rev records like *Yerself Is Steam*, there was something so beautiful in the heart of the chaos that they captured on record and at live shows. At that gig, they ended the set with the whole band stood in a line on the front of the stage. They had a flute player and a brass player and the lot of them were just making this absolutely amazing cacophony, building up this towering wall of noise. I came away from the gig wondering how could I get the feeling that they just gave me into the music that I wanted to make. That thought stuck with me for a while.

There was one other major inspiration. After *Exit Planet Dust*, I had it in my head that I wanted to create something that channelled the kind of feelings that a track like 'I Am the Resurrection' invoked. There's an incredible, infectious energy created by all those fills and the utterly relentless nature of it. I love The Stone Roses' first album; I love all the detail, how all the tiny little bits became so engrained in our generation. 'The Private Psychedelic Reel' wasn't so much a direct stylistic influence from 'I Am the Resurrection', but it did take the idea of ending the album with a towering, epic final song. The kind of track that nothing could possibly come after.

One of Ed and my spiritual influences when we made the record was what we called the Blackburn Rave moment. Whenever we'd make music, it had to have some connection to the spirit of the original Blackburn Raves. Those raves felt like they were the epicentre of a certain kind of manic euphoria, which was obviously something we were after. Even a track like 'Where Do I Begin' or a song recorded with someone like Hope Sandoval

Paused in Cosmic Reflection 145

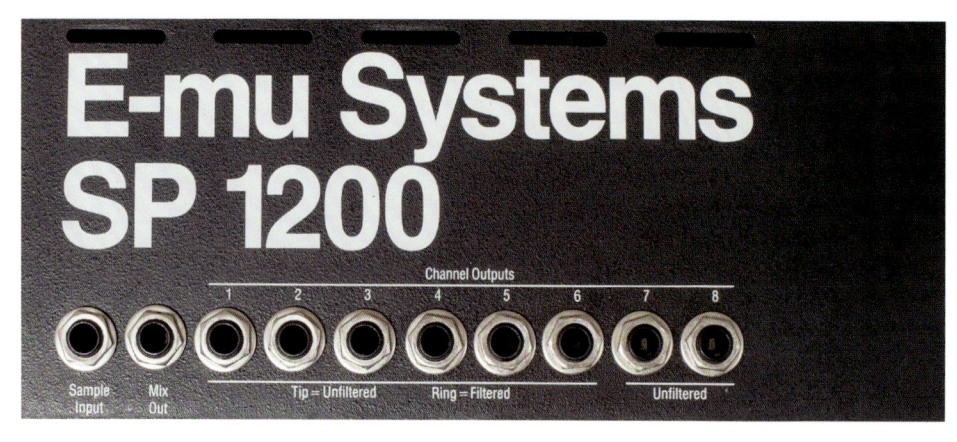

had to recreate that feeling of spontaneity and madness, a moment that feels entirely natural even though it's been programmed in a room just off Old Street. That feeling is in 'The Private Psychedelic Reel' in the moment where there's a little suspension in mid-air, a second that lifts the listener before the music fills out around them. That didn't really happen in a lot of the electronic music that was being made back then.

One of the key moments in the song coming together was programming the fill. Working out that pause, the moment that it all hangs in the air. The drums and the organ came together early on. The sound at the start of the track is a guitar played with an E-Bow that I sampled through my E-mu sampler. That machine is very much the bedrock of our early records. There's an edit page in that sampler where much like with a modular synth you can assign a modulation source to any destination. In this case I was modulating the sound's filter with one LFO, then a much slower delayed LFO comes into bend the pitch of the notes towards their end. Delaying the pitch change and the sound at that right moment so it swooped down into the note was a really important part of the track. After I had that, the organ and the drums, the sitar part came easily.

As much as I love it in other people's records, I've never really liked that strong, linear way of arranging when it comes to our music. I'm obsessed with arrangement. I love the alchemy of arrangement. I love how it can feel like a puzzle where you combine all these disparate ideas and sounds to make something that feels complete and whole. Even when you're using samples, it's part of the magic that makes it feel like everything naturally works together. I've always looked for that kind of *disjointer* record. Something that's going to disrupt the DJ set, rather than act as a smooth transition with eight bars of this or sixteen bars of that or thirty-two bars of drums at the start to get things in time when you're cueing it up. I want our music to twist away and have some kind of difference to it.

Often when we collaborate with people, it's because the track we're working on reminds us of what they do, how they sound. A drum part or a sequence that sounds like someone's band might be enough to send us down that path. It's not always the greatest imaginative leap; sometimes it's a blindingly obvious choice. With 'The Private Psychedelic Reel', I was definitely still drawn towards the power of that Mercury Rev live show. I wanted it to reflect the sort of freedom that created, the looseness.

We approached Jonathan Donahue in the days before email, before file sharing. There was no work in progress from them, no prior knowledge before an ADAT [Alesis Digital Audio Tape] came back from him. Sticking it on in the studio, I was floored by what they'd done. He'd got the clarinet player Mark Marinoff to play on it and they'd created all these mind-blowing sounds, which they'd labelled with strange, evocative names like the 'Dub Tetix Wave'. Even just reading the names of the parts, all I could think of was putting these sounds through our processes; it all felt so cool even though they were probably just far-out names for guitar parts. He clearly understood exactly what the spirit was that we were going for and delivered accordingly.

I think the track feels alive. It careers around in total freedom. Making it, it felt equally as important that it was beautiful as well as chaotic. It needed to invite you in. I've always felt there's a sort of magic to it, something that's pure and different. I don't know what that is; I can't put my finger on what that magic is, something just happened when we made it.

An E-mu SP-1200 sampler was 'very much the bedrock of [The Chemical Brothers'] early records'. (Tom)

Next page: Original flyers from the Heavenly Social at Turnmills and a one-off Heavenly Stockholm party.

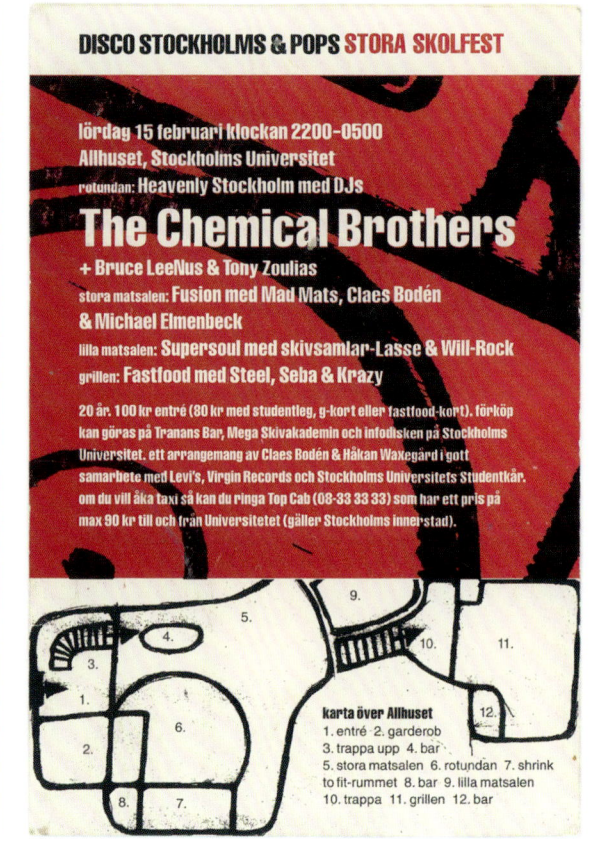

And I don't know why it's there so prominently in that piece of music, but I'm very glad it is.

'The Private Psychedelic Reel' has been the encore at our live shows for a long time, and, like 'I Am the Resurrection' in a Stone Roses set, it is a clear signifier that there's nothing coming after, that nothing *can* come after it. *This is it*. It has a finality to it. When it's playing against the projections of stained-glass windows, there is a real resonant feeling. It all just connects in an emotive way . . . you know, hang on . . . hang in there. We're going there together. I never tire of playing it, all the stops and the releases and the moments of stillness. I'd play it every day if I could.

Jonathan Donahue

In 1995, Mercury Rev had released an album called *See You on the Other Side*. Myself, Grasshopper and producer Dave Fridmann really thought it was a gem of a record, the best thing we'd ever done. It had choirs and flutes and oboes and brass sections. I really felt it was the one. And it fell on deaf ears. It came out almost the instant that Britpop hit and it sank like a stone.

For a year, we toured the album across America and Europe. Those shows were very poorly attended, and we were going broke. Everything was shattering. Foundations that I thought could not be rocked were crumbling. Self-doubt kicked in and really it broke me. Spiritually, creatively, financially, emotionally.

By the spring of 1996, touring had wound down and myself and Grasshopper had each sunk into a low point. I sank into alcohol and I was finishing up a heroin addiction. I was at – what I felt was – the bottom. I never thought we'd get the opportunity to do another album. I didn't think anyone was waiting for another Mercury Rev record. And out of that darkness, something unforeseen happened, like the one ring in *The Lord of the Ring*s being found again.

The phone rang and it was The Chemical Brothers. While it may have been one of a hundred phone calls they made that day to other singers and other artists, that particular call was to us. They asked if we'd like to contribute to an upcoming record they were making. It changed everything. It was not just clouds parting, it was something inside of me opening up saying, 'Hey, someone out there is listening.' It brought life into what was – if I'm honest with myself – a dead man walking. Musically, emotionally, enthusiastically . . . it was a shot of courage.

To be honest, I only barely knew in my brain that they were a 'dance band'. In whatever consciousness I had, I knew they were a UK dance band and I knew that they were weird. I remember them saying, 'Make it like you guys . . . psychedelic and far out.' To be honest, even if it wasn't a call from what would become a legendary band, even if it was just two unknown musicians out of the hills in Wales, it meant the world to me.

And it changed everything that would come after this point. Not just because I did some work with The Chemical Brothers, but because it gave me a renewed enthusiasm to make what would later become [Mercury Rev's 1998 album] *Deserter's Songs*. That year a DJ saved my life. That statement could not be more true. I'm well aware that we might have been one of many people they reached out to, but they reached me at a time when I felt I was unreachable.

The cacophony we made at shows in the early days was very central to what we did, but it was only later that we'd feel the ripples that that noise made, whether it was heard in other artists' records or at their live shows. It was something that was so specific to us that I'm not certain whether it held us back or propelled us forward. Maybe it was both. Maybe the best things in music are these moments, where artists like ourselves go both ways, creating a polarising moment. In a way, it defines you, but only in hindsight.

When the phone call came in, I didn't have a lot to work with. We'd sold all our instruments for pawn just to survive. I only had the barest bones left to create music we added to 'The Private Psychedelic Reel'. We had created a lot of electronics at that time. We'd have a friend rewire broken pedals, which did something unique with all the bits we had lying around. These bits were the only things we hadn't pawned to pay the rent, or, in my case, buy heroin.

I took it to heart when they said, 'Be you.' Whatever that meant in Tom and Ed's frame of reference, I knew what it meant to me. It meant adding the crazy Balkan clarinet pieces, some electronics. The final version features a lot of that clarinet. At the time I can remember piecing together the few things that we still had left of us. Not just the music stuff, it really was the sound of the fumes that were left in us. They called right before I took my last breath. Thankfully, that breath was still there.

Grasshopper and I weren't really speaking much at that point; we were like two astronauts staying in touch through short bursts of crackly communication on the moon. This invitation brought us together for a moment, a moment that would later lead to us creating *Deserter's Songs*.

Between *Dig Your Own Hole* and *Surrender*, I believe the Brothers themselves changed. On 'The Private Psychedelic Reel', you begin to hear the beginnings of *Surrender*. That album had real definitive 'song' moments. Not track moments or piece moments, not beat moments. It had song moments. It opened me up, as I'm sure it did the fans and maybe the Brothers themselves. The idea that there were songs there, not just riffs and heavy beats. I thought, 'Who's done this? Who's made dance music rock before this?' *Surrender* had these songs that I would have wanted to write. Regardless of the rhythms and the bass. The songs themselves. It was a ripple effect back from the Brothers, certainly to me.

The Brothers' music brought a deep emotional context to a genre that – I'll be honest – I'm not an expert in. And that emotional content immediately struck me as it was very consistent with a lot of the groups I grew up loving that weren't dance-oriented. I didn't have to question, or search the tracks for it. Their music already had that aura to it; it's there on the initial demo versions. I was astonished by that quality, the song part, the emotional content.

There's that transcendent quality to 'The Private Psychedelic Reel'. I understand why it would come at the end of the live show. It's allowing the people at the concert, and the listeners at home with headphones, to open up without the thinking part that goes with any show or album. There's some part of it – whether that's the Indian instrumentation or the clarinets or the *surrender to the void* moments – there's a transcendent quality that most of us artists look for at least once in an album.

If we're fortunate there's a few times in a career where a song we have has this indescribable, unpurchasable, unmixable, unproduceable quality to it. You can't buy someone or pay some studio to do this; it can only reveal itself out of itself. And if you're fortunate, you catch that on tape. For me, 'The Private Psychedelic Reel' may have been one of those songs. For them, it was already there. All they had to do was capture it on tape as accurately as they could.

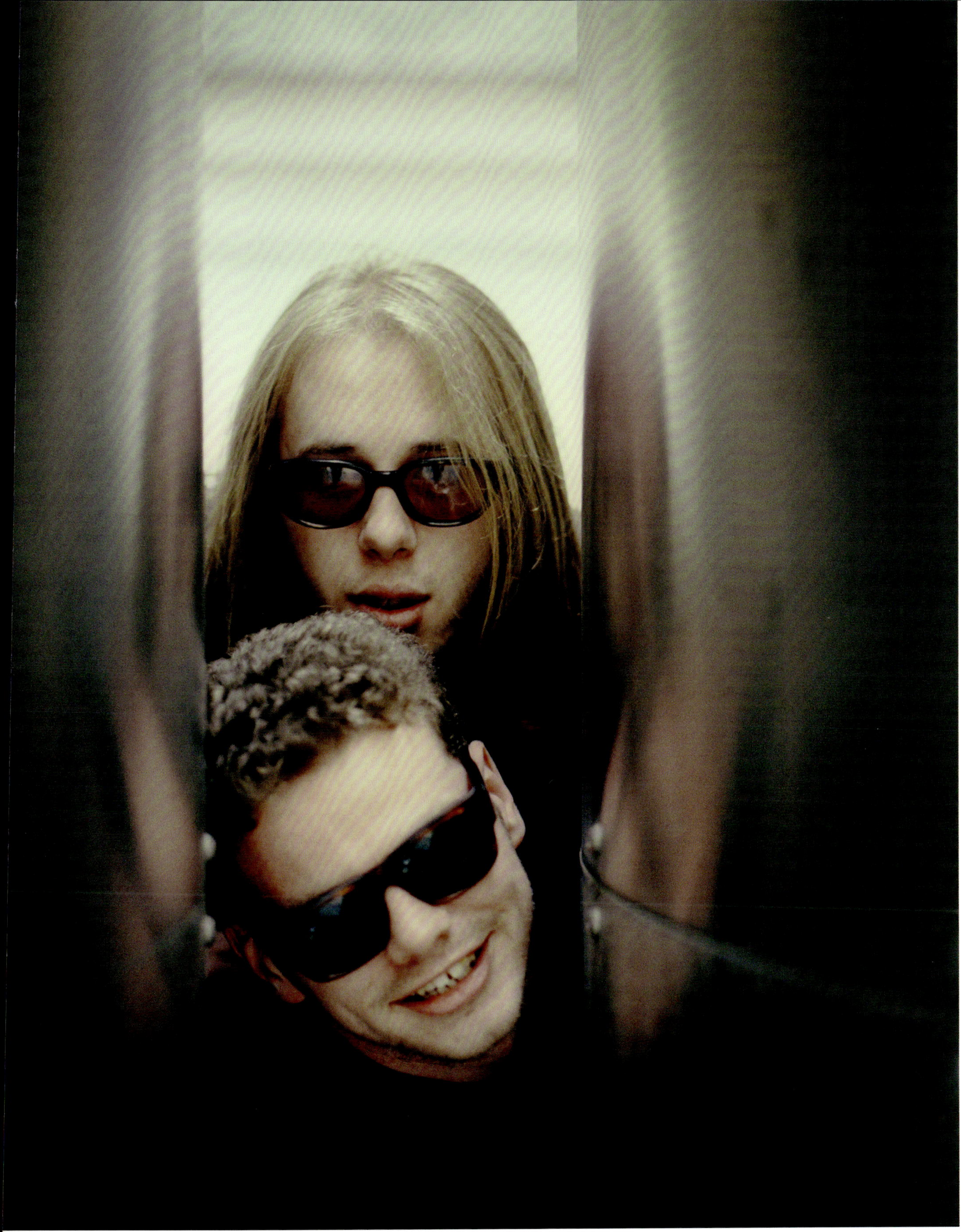

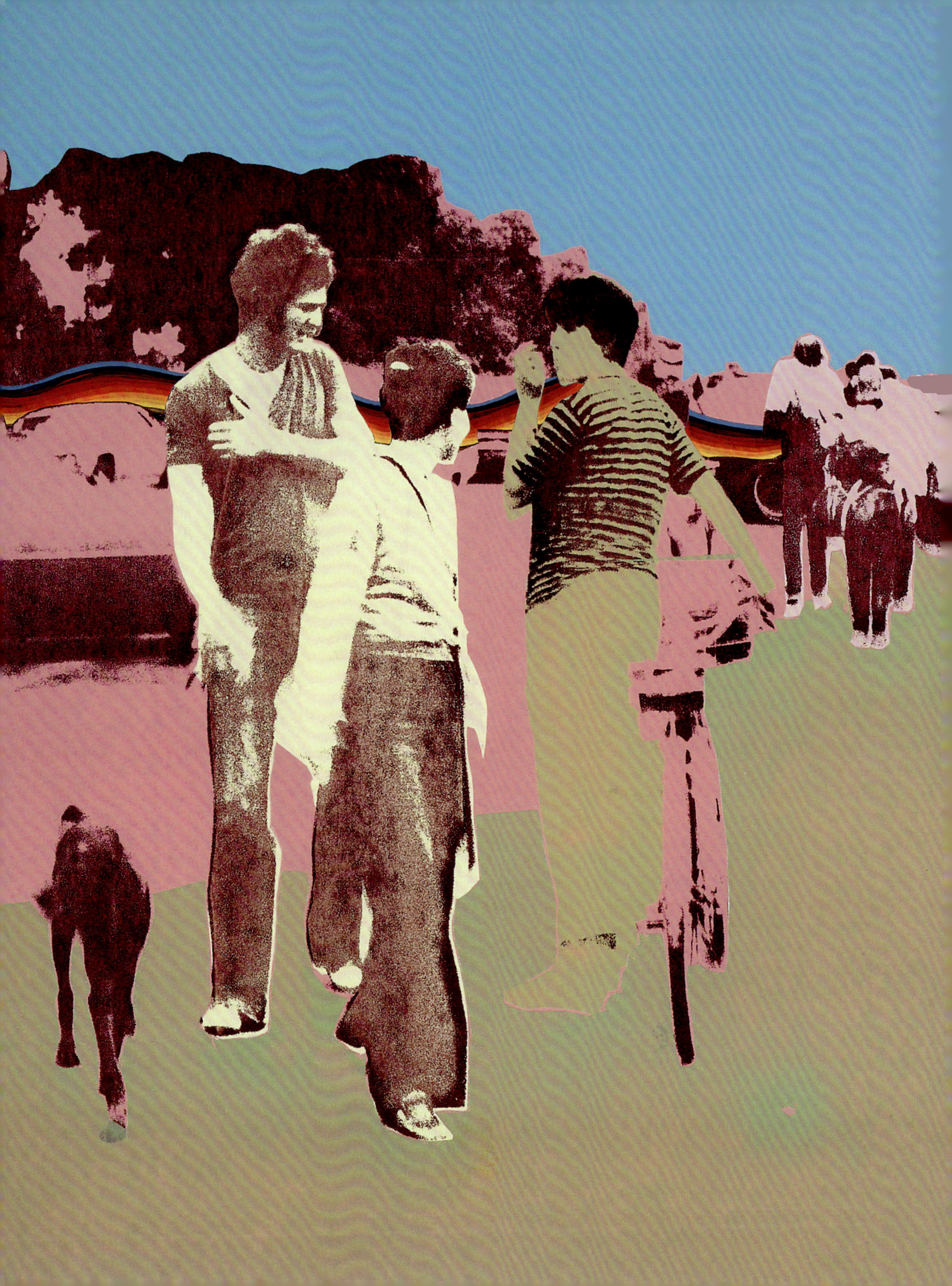

Hey Boy Hey Girl

If *Dig Your Own Hole* had been the sound of underground clubs and dimly lit dance floors, 'Hey Boy Hey Girl' flipped the switch and turned everything technicolour. The outlier for *Surrender*, it was bold, bright and relentless. Its whirling riff, steady propulsive pulse and lone vocal line (sampled from Rock Master Scott & the Dynamic Three's 1984 hip hop track 'The Roof Is on Fire') were instantly addictive, the audio equivalent of catnip.

Over two decades after its release, 'Hey Boy Hey Girl' still exerts an almost primal, hedonistic power over the listener. It's the very definition of dance music, in that it's made for dancing and demands to be played loud.

Ed Simons

Dig Your Own Hole was such a big record and we toured it a lot. When we came back, we used to spend days and days together in Orinoco. We had a fully functioning room with lots of new keyboard and vintage synths. I think we were both ready to make something more colourful.

In 1998 we DJed occasionally and released the mix album [*Brothers Gonna Work It Out*], but other than that we were in the studio solidly. I think I used to say in interviews that 1998 was the best year of my life. It was the first time since we were students that we had time to stop and enjoy ourselves. Tom is always happy to be in the studio but that was the first time we'd had a bit of money and weren't out on the road every weekend. I think that does come out in the album. It's not glossy and pleased with itself, but there is a kind of contentedness in the psychedelia.

If you look at the press at the time, there was a lot of talk of how we'd gone to Gatecrasher and had some kind of epiphany. We were in Sheffield to DJ at a cool, Mo' Wax-y club. Our set was made up of the same sort of records that we'd been playing up to that point. It all felt a bit flat. A friend of ours in the city was working for Gatecrasher, so we thought we'd check it out as it was infamous at the time. Walking inside, the first thing you noticed after all the mad dressed-up kids was this incredible sound system, one that seemed to hit you with both volume and depth. Back then, I would never take my coat off in clubs. I was wearing a parka. It was like a blast furnace. Paul Van Dyk was DJing this really mesmerising music. Tom and I were both thinking, 'This is wild.'

We'd had a version of 'Hey Boy Hey Girl' for a while that was quite breaky. And we thought, 'Let's not make it difficult, let's make a big superclub dance record.' There was something about it – and maybe us – that was hiding away in a metaphysical backroom. A spiritual backroom. People often talk about the big colourful cover of *Surrender* being a move away from darkness; I feel like we made a record that reflected where the energy was being generated in clubland at that point. It didn't need us to come back with Day-Glo earrings and Darth Maul make-up, it just needed us to turbocharge what we were doing.

There was something about the energy being generated in that room at Gatecrasher that felt infinitely more exciting than the club we'd been playing in down the road. It was glamorous and fun, and we felt like joining in. It's not like all of *Surrender* is like that, but the big statement that preceded it – 'Hey Boy Hey Girl' – was informed hugely by what was going on in that room and rooms all around Britain just like it.

Weirdly, the Americans really didn't like 'Hey Boy Hey Girl'. They didn't get it and didn't want to release it as a single there. To us, it didn't really feel that different from the music we'd made before.

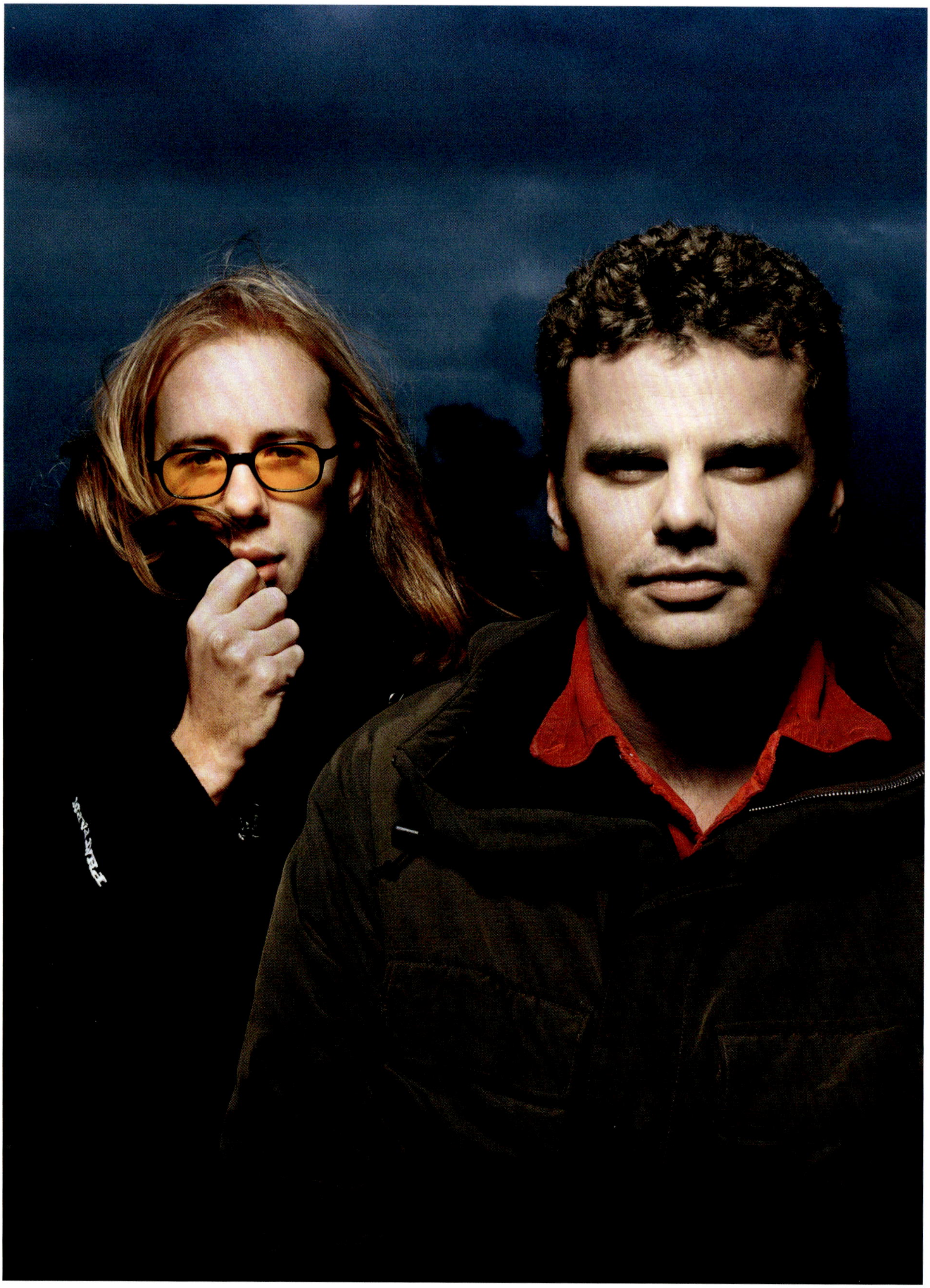

ARP SEQUENCER
ARP INSTRUMENTS, INC., LEXINGTON, MASS.

SUPERSTAR DJ'S...HERE WE GO!

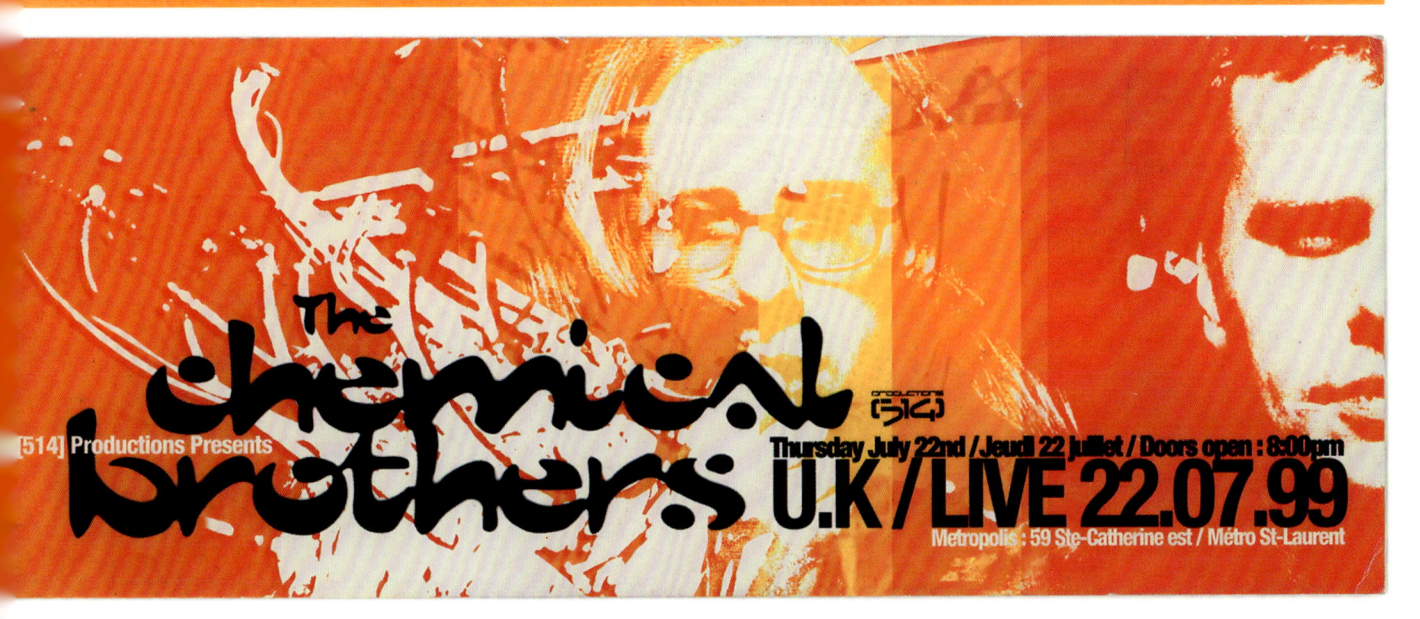

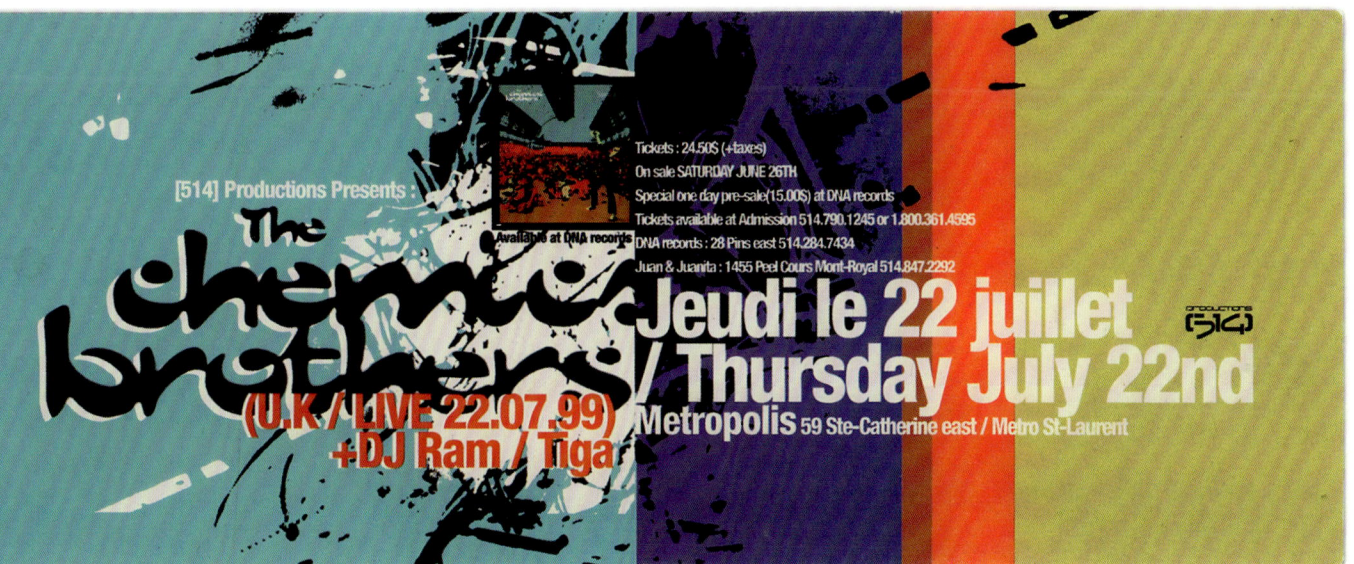

www.astralwerks.com

[514] Productions Presents

the chemical brothers
U.K / LIVE 22.07.99

Thursday July 22nd / Jeudi 22 juillet / Doors open : 8:00pm
Metropolis : 59 Ste-Catherine est / Métro St-Laurent

[514] Productions Presents

the chemical brothers
(U.K / LIVE 22.07.99)
+DJ Ram / Tiga

Tickets : 24.50$ (+taxes)
On sale SATURDAY JUNE 26TH
Special one day pre-sale(15.00$) at DNA records
Tickets available at Admission 514.790.1245 or 1.800.361.4595
DNA records : 28 Pins east 514.284.7434
Juan & Juanita : 1455 Peel Cours Mont-Royal 514.847.2292

Jeudi le 22 juillet
Thursday July 22nd
Metropolis 59 Ste-Catherine east / Metro St-Laurent

Paused in Cosmic Reflection 155

156 The Chemical Brothers

Paused in Cosmic Reflection 157

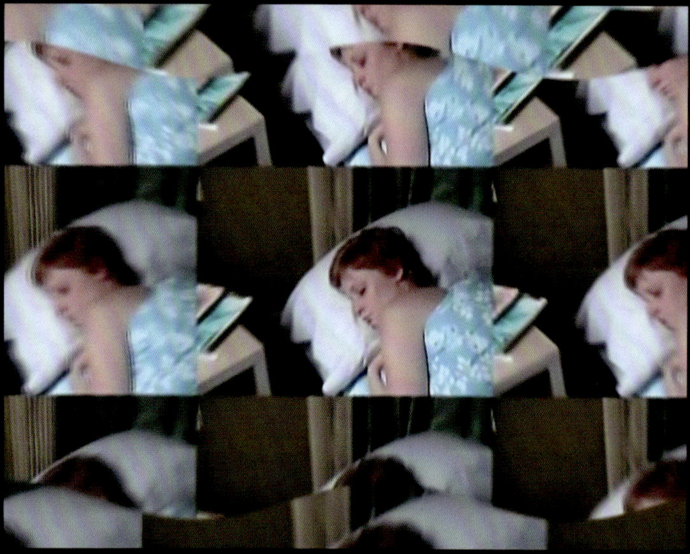
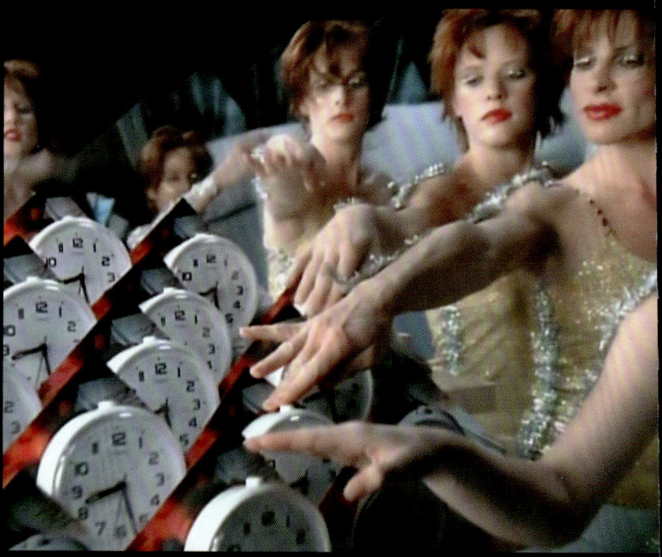
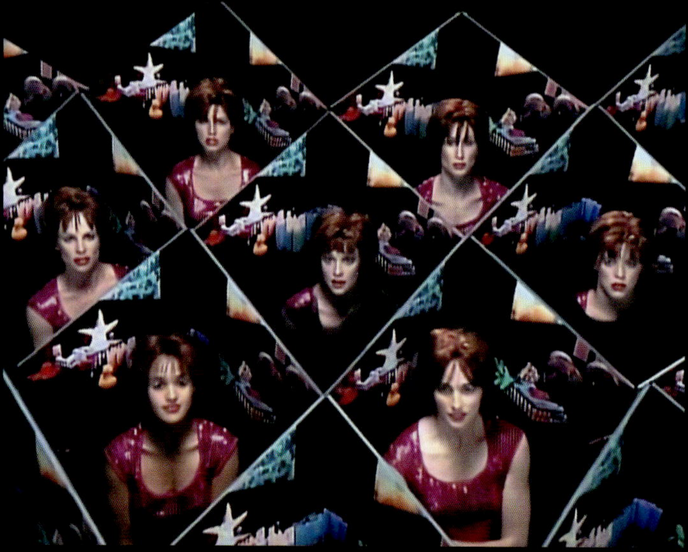
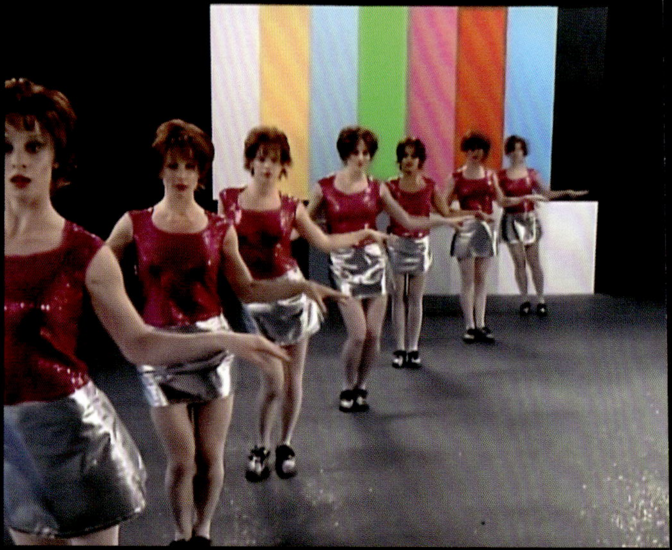
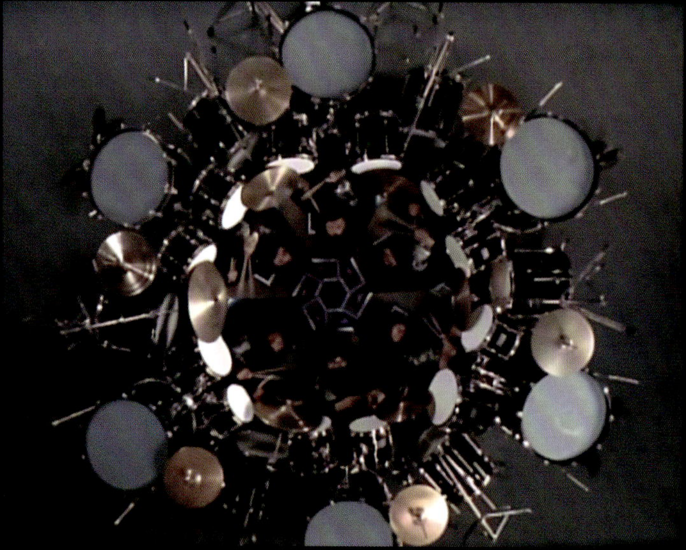
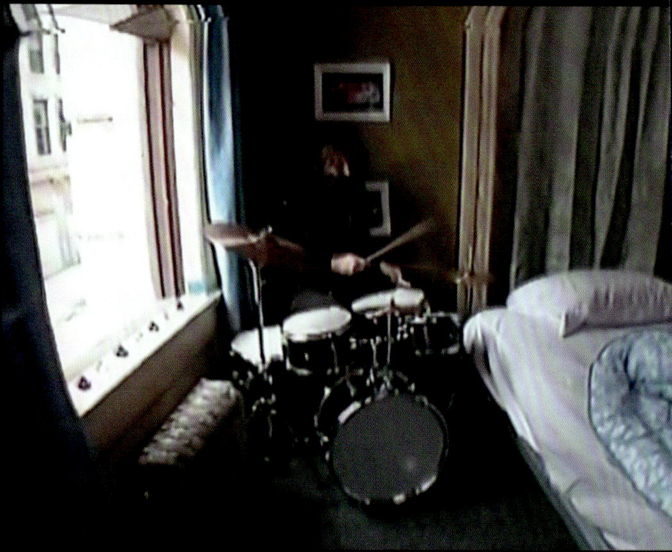

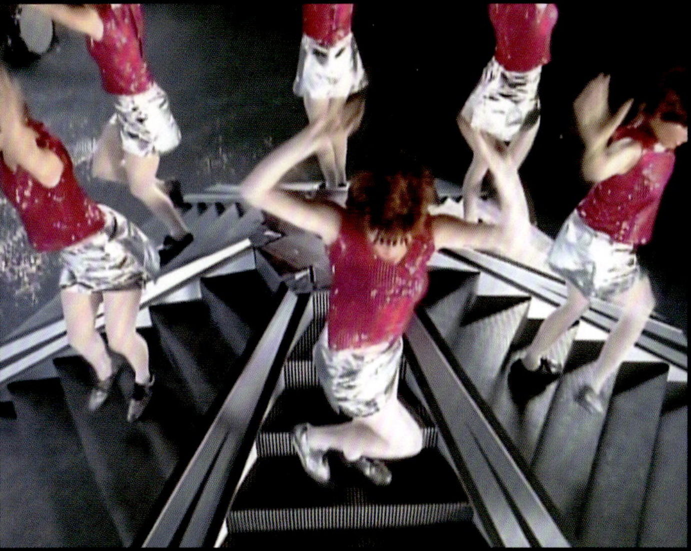
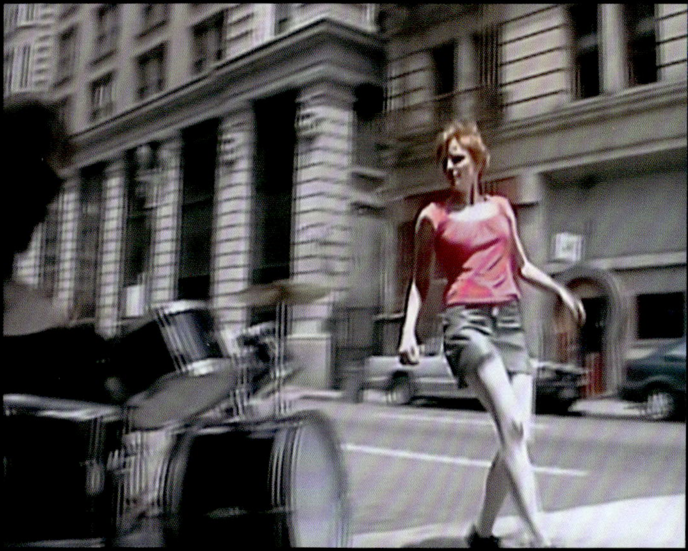
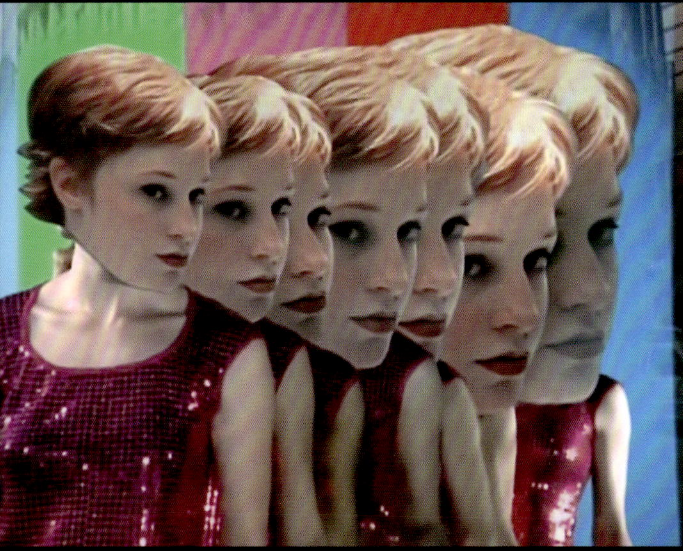
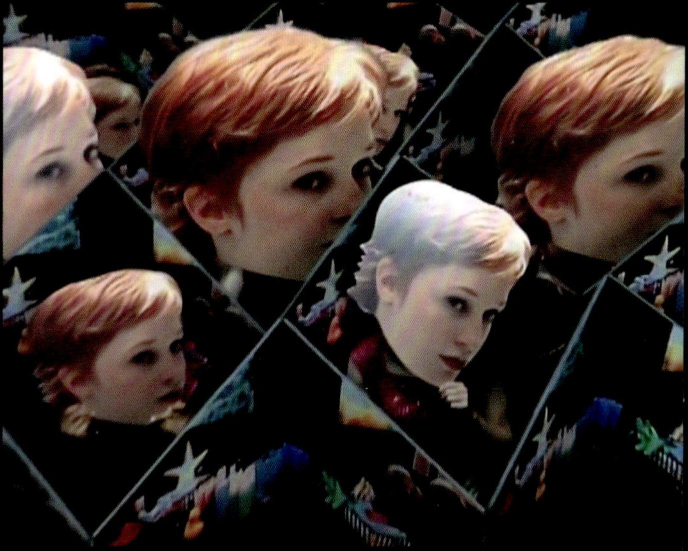
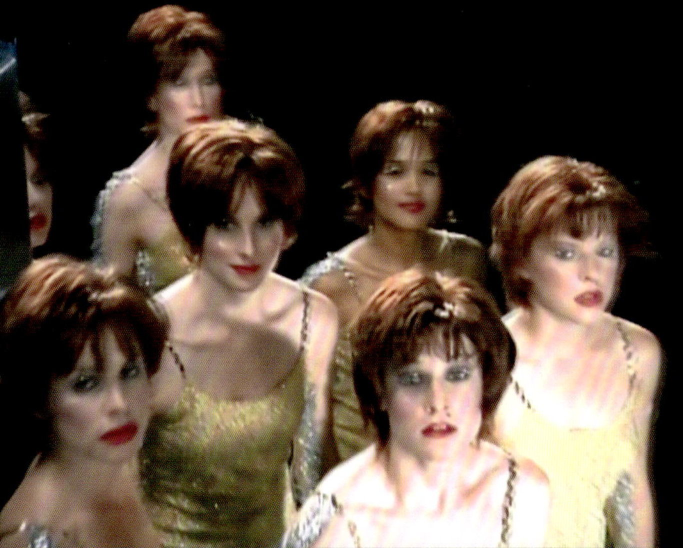
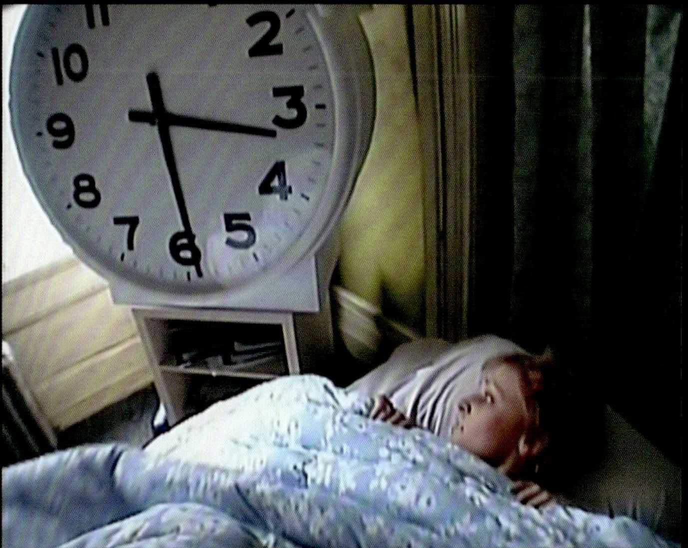

162   The Chemical Brothers

Surrender

This *Surrender* is clearly a state of mind. It's a willingness to give in and let the music take over. To allow a ripple of wild electricity to flow through you and take control of your next move, and the one after, and the one after that.

The picture on the cover of the album sums it up better than my words ever could. Olympia in West Kensington is a vast hall that dates back to the Victorian era. On the night the picture was taken, it's full of fans sprawled out on the floor. There's palpable boredom among some, the interminable wait for something to arrive on the main stage clearly dragging on. That's not the case for the main figure, the one that our eyes are drawn to: the shaman, lost in music that no one else seems to be able or willing to hear. He's like an air dancer on the forecourt of a car dealership, freed from whatever shackles everyone else in the room is clearly held down by. Everything about the scene is a world away from how the Victorians must have envisaged the hall would be used. Good. That's progress.

That shaman – Jesus Jellett – was a regular fixture at London gigs from the late sixties through to the early nineties. A man with seemingly relentless energy, he was often seen wielding percussive instruments, waving slogans on hand-drawn placards or playing bongos or a penny whistle on stage. He could often be found preaching at Speakers' Corner in London, devout in beliefs that blurred the lines between biblical reincarnation and hopeful hippy philosophy. A true child of the peace and love era, Jesus was a totem for rock acts in the period before punk (and many that flew the flag for that era in later years). His death was announced in 2021. It is not known whether he ever experienced the rapture at a Chemical Brothers gig.

Kate Gibb

I wasn't long out of college when I got asked to pitch for the artwork for a new Chemical Brothers album. I was an indie kid back then. I knew who the band were, but I didn't know masses about them. Two brothers who aren't brothers, quite noisy, late night, that sort of thing. I got sent an image that the band liked and they wanted something in the same vein. I spent the whole weekend in my studio and didn't come up with anything remotely good. Nothing worked, I binned it all. On the morning that the artwork was being presented to the band, Mark Tappin (designer at Blue Source) called to tell me that the meeting wasn't until 11 a.m. In two hours, I pulled together three tiny pictures that got me the job.

Everything started with the titles. From there, we'd try to find images that would marry with each title and reflect any feelings they might evoke. We knew there would be four singles, and for the album cover, we knew we were looking for images that captured a sublime moment of rapture. The main source of original imagery was the Hulton Archive – an immense historical photographic archive. We'd do searches for pictures that showed festivals and people uniting, big communal experiences and moments where audiences were coming together in the moment.

For each cover, we'd have a pile of black and white photographs that we would sift through to work out which were best. It was a fair, democratic process that we all got involved in – band, designer, record label and myself. Tom and Ed had lots of ideas of the kind of feeling they wanted the sleeves to capture. They'd found a piece of art they loved that had the spectrum flowing through it – a stripe of colours dancing across the artwork. From there, we put together a storyboard of

Paused in Cosmic Reflection

164 The Chemical Brothers

Paused in Cosmic Reflection 165

other artworks they liked, print styles and inspirations. The essence of this, the tone of that, the colour of something they loved.

When we came across the image of Jesus Jellett throwing his arms up in Olympia, it was such an obvious fit for the album title [Surrender]. It stood out so much, it was perfect. I felt like it was the kind of image that would lend itself beautifully to a screen-printing process. He was clearly surrendering to music.

The first image I worked on was the crowd shot against a cyan sky that ended up in the gatefold of the record. The original shot was of a group of fans at an Osmonds concert. The image you see is a silk-screen print that's been created in layers – like a collage – with a hand-painted spectrum floating through the piece. That spectrum that The Chemical Brothers loved became a theme, spilling through the various cover images. There was always a thought about what the spectrum element could represent. As an artist, colour is my thing. Most of the photographs we sourced were black and white, and we were injecting colour and vibrancy into them.

My studio was in Westbourne Park, which was round the corner from where Tom and Ed lived. Mark's office was nearby, and Virgin was within walking distance too. Everybody would come over to the studio and take part in the process. Each person brought something to me and I remixed it into the artwork. For each image, I'd work on several different colourways. The decisions got down to tiny preferences, such as someone liking a lavender tone on one version, or someone not liking the brown on another. If there was a version I really liked, I'd sometimes leave it around the studio so someone could find it and feel like it was their discovery.

The music was a total revelation for me. To first hear it, I had to go into Virgin and sit in their A&R man's office to listen to it at full volume. I was a little indie kid just out of college; I genuinely didn't know what to do with myself in front of this incredible sound. Towards the end, Mark Tappin turned to me and said, 'It's not Belle and Sebastian is it?' I couldn't really conceive of how it was even made. One time we all met up on a Friday and I asked Tom what he was up to at the weekend. He said, 'I'm writing music.' I had no concept of how music like that was *written*, I just couldn't work it out. He patiently explained to me it was a bit like how I make a collage. It was all a massive learning curve for me.

Previous page: The fold-out inside sleeve of the Surrender *album.*

Above: The test prints for the Surrender *album cover by Kate Gibb.*

Next page: A selection of Kate Gibb's sleeves.

Page 170–171: The Oberheim Xpander used on the Surrender *LP.*

The whole process was special because there was time and collaboration and space. It was a deep project, which you just don't seem to get these days. It was freedom. We had the time to pull all the elements together, which you don't seem to get now in an age where everything is digital.

When the album came out, the record company made lots of merchandise with the cover art on it. I ended up with a holographic mouse mat printed with the cover on. I was absolutely mind-blown, I thought it was amazing. Back then, I didn't have a computer, let alone a mouse. I found it in my studio the other day and it looked so shit, but I loved it so much at the time.

When I came to work with The Chemical Brothers, I'd get on with the work and go back and listen to whatever guitar bands I was into afterwards. And then I went to see them live and thought, 'Fucking hell.' They were amazing. I understood. I saw them make music how I might make a piece of art.

As a band, The Chemical Brothers are constantly evolving but their centre – their heart – remains the same. There are bands you could go and see, and you'd think, 'I still love them, but they don't sound as good anymore' or 'they're not really up to it'. The Chemical Brothers are the real deal, constantly. I think it's because of how much they care, all the thought that goes into what they do both behind the scenes and on record and on stage. The Chemical Brothers allow the people who make the creative components that surround them freedom, while also giving a shit at the same time. I think *Surrender* was so successful because of what they put into the process. They cared so much about getting it perfect.

Richard Young (photographer of *'Jesus' Amongst Fans, Olympia Music Festival, London, 1976*)

I didn't know who the hell he was. I'd never met Jesus before; he was just this figure standing in front of me. I had no idea what he was doing or why. But there he was. It was at a Rod Stewart concert at Olympia back in my early days of being a photographer. I went out into the crowd and that scene just seemed to happen in front of me. I hadn't asked him to do anything. But the image was immediately interesting. Everyone was sat down looking pretty miserable and then that happened, that moment of freedom. People were waiting for the show to begin. After I took the shot, I photographed some of the gig then ended up in the dressing room afterwards with Rod and Britt Ekland, which was more my kind of scene back then.

I never ran into him at a gig again. I didn't have a name for him, that came along much later when I found out he was notorious; he was this guy who was famous on the scene and was even known to turn up to gigs naked. I'm quite glad he was wearing clothes on the day that I shot him. There were always characters around, certainly back then anyway. It's not the same now as it was back then; I don't think it ever will be again. Maybe people aren't so flamboyant and as crazy as they were. It was very enjoyable to see those things when they happened in front of you.

I'd gone out into the crowd before the gig and taken the picture. I didn't think anything more of it. Years later, The Chemical Brothers put out this breakthrough album – it happened to have that photo on the cover, which they'd licensed from an agency. I'm not sure The Chemical Brothers would have even been born when that picture was taken. The album title – *Surrender* – does suit the image pretty well though.

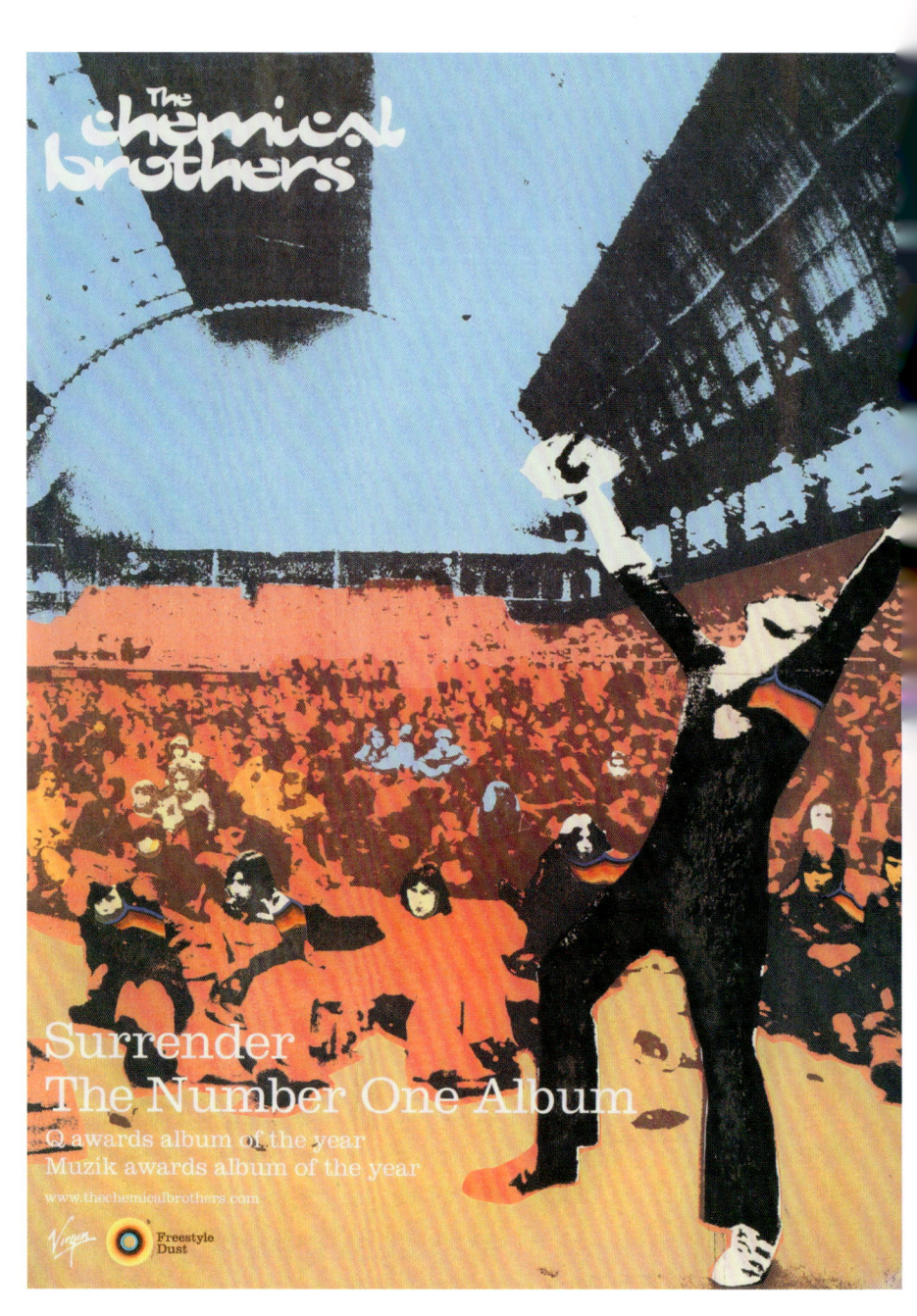

Paused in Cosmic Reflection 169

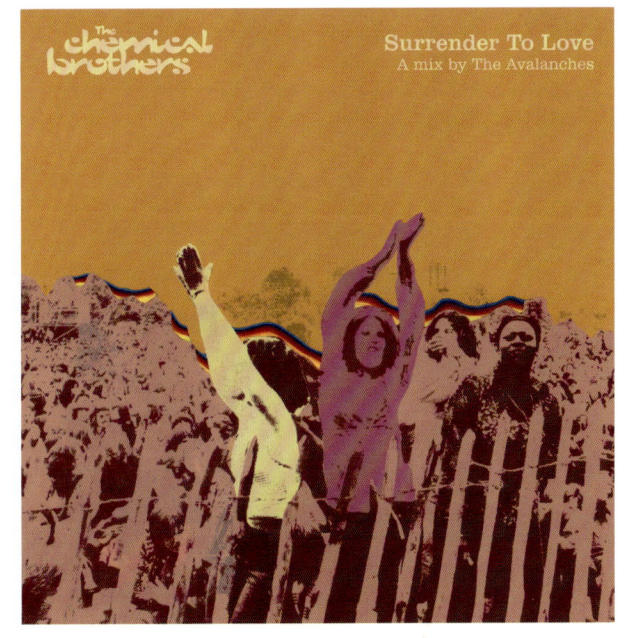

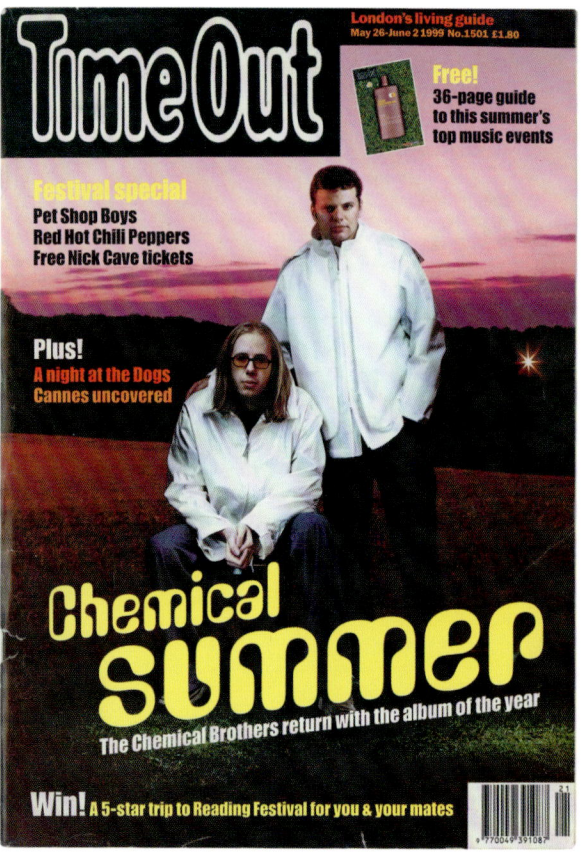

170   The Chemical Brothers

Paused in Cosmic Reflection 171

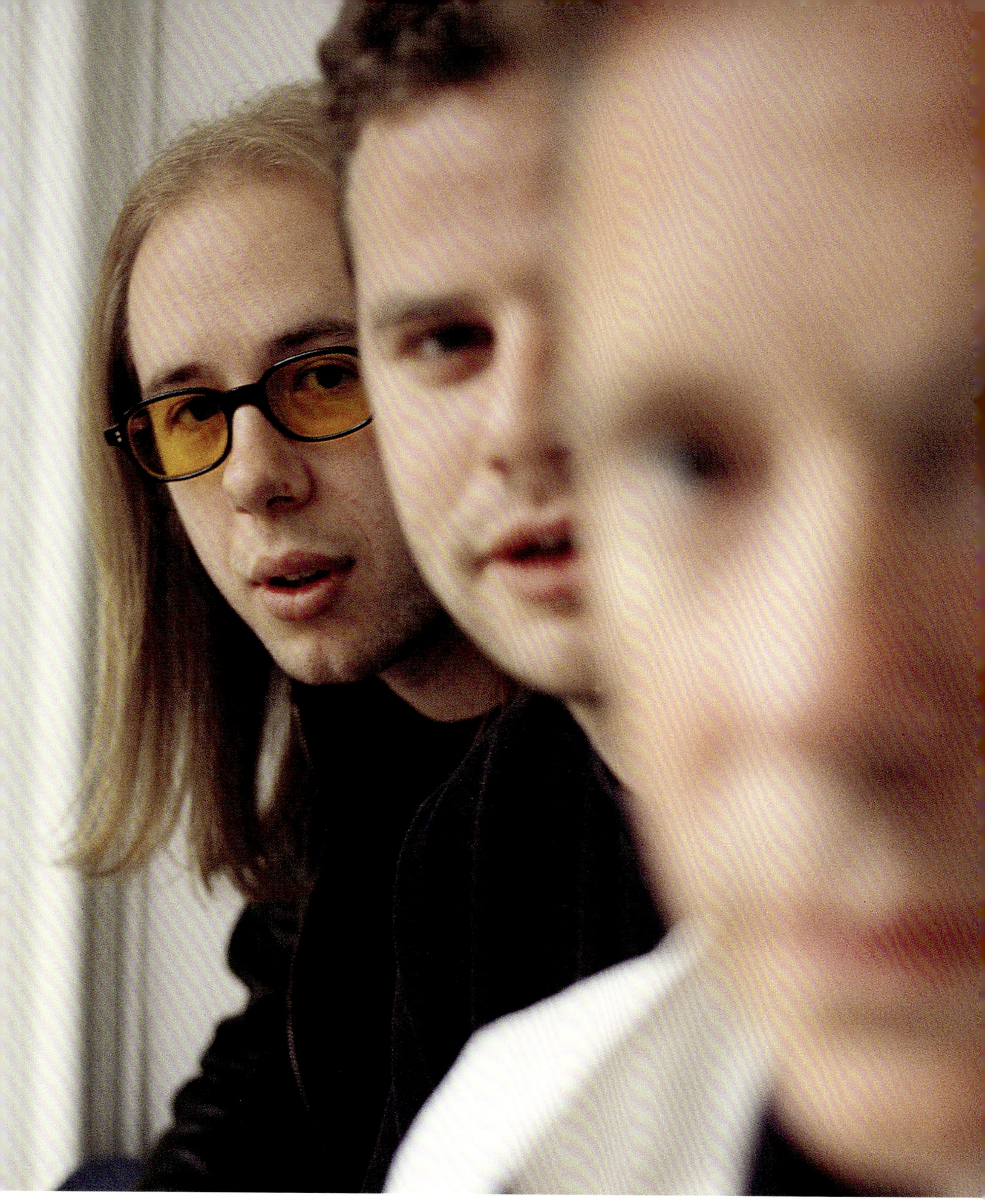

Out of Control

'Out of Control' is built on a bass line that feels like part of the UR-coding of electronic music; a variant of an insistent rhythm that's been a core piece of dance floor DNA since Giorgio Moroder first fired up a similar sequence in the mid-seventies. The percussion is splintered and frenetic, almost racing ahead of itself but never missing the beat. Twin voices crest above everything, circling each other, locked in perfect harmony. They offer complete contrast to the electrically charged chaos going on all around them. When a guitar arrives, simple and clear, it's almost as if the moment has been framed. It's a pure noise that stops you as it splits the whole track apart, pauses the whole thing and lifts it off the ground. It's a rush, a shot of adrenalin. As the beat returns, you're plunged back into that chaos, that electricity. The whole thing is irresistible. Surrender is inevitable.

The third single from *Surrender* taps a musical vein that connects different eras of Manchester music, from Joy Division to New Order to the basement of Eastern Bloc Records via too many lost nights at The Haçienda and Most Excellent, Sankeys Soap and the Warehouse Project. It's as if that bold, beautiful city has been imagined in sound.

The accompanying video – directed by WIZ – trains its eye on the consumerism and the exploitation of youth culture. Conceived over a decade before the rise and rise of social media, the video now looks acutely prophetic, to the point where it appeared to be imitated by an ill-advised and deeply controversial fizzy drink advert nearly two decades later.

Tom Rowlands

Getting to work with Bernard Sumner was a dream for us. You don't tend to analyse things at the time, there's not a point where you step aside from things in total wonder at what's happening. Getting the seal of approval that happens when someone agrees to come and work together with you, it's a massive thing.

Ed and I had a tendency to drive each other mad in the studio talking about who might work on a track. Usually, though, it's the piece of music itself that dictates who you get in touch with about collaborating. Quite often, there's something in the track that reminds you in some way of the artist you'd end up approaching. You think about the song and you imagine what it could be.

With 'Out of Control', the earliest versions had a similar feeling to lots of New Order records that we both loved. Although it didn't really sound like one, their seed was definitely there in the toughness of the Donna Summer-esque bass lines and in the way the drums were programmed.

So you listen to that early version and you get an idea and then you end up thinking, 'Do we dare? Do we dare ask, because it means so much?' And if you ask, what if that dream you had of what it might end up sounding like isn't fulfilled? In the case of 'Out of Control', the two elements came together in a way that was as strong as we'd ever hoped – stronger even. It felt completely natural and not in any way bolted on. To be able to listen back to a track and say, 'I can't think of a better way of us collectively making a piece of music together.' That's the beauty of a successful collaboration and it's a really good feeling. And that's how 'Out of Control' felt.

Being in the studio with Bernard was really instructive. He was key to the direction the song eventually took. We sent him an early version of the track (later released as 'Enjoyed'), which had a big, distorted part that sounded like a sitar on it. He ignored that sound and focused entirely on the groove and synth parts, taking the song in a more coherent direction. It was his idea to bring Bobby Gillespie into the studio, knowing that their voices would work well together, which they really did. He convinced us the track needed another singer and literally within about half an hour Bobby was in there with us. They were a good pair in the studio, really happy in each other's company.

Although Bernard worked on a lot of guitar parts that weren't used in the final track, it's his guitar that really gets its own moment in the track. He recorded parts all the way through but they didn't feel necessary. I really wanted to let it shine and have a moment where it can really stop time.

Seeing how he worked in such an obsessive way made me realise that all of those records he's been involved with over the years, those incredible records, they didn't happen by accident. They were the result of a massive amount of effort and inspiration. He was obsessive about everything, even down to which guitar leads sounded best, auditioning so many different types before finding the exact one he liked and thought would work. The whole time, he would keep doing it and doing it and doing it, striving to get everything exactly right.

Ed Simons

Surrender reflected our increasing confidence as a band. We were consistently in the big room of Orinoco, spending long periods in there writing and mixing. 'Out of Control' took a long time, and Bernard Sumner spent a long time in the studio with us. He came down and recorded several times and he took the parts away to work on them back at home.

Beth Orton and Tim Burgess were people that we knew socially prior to working together.

Noel [Gallagher] was someone who we'd met through our bands and through him being at things we were DJing at. The first time we reached beyond our social circle was Jonathan Donahue for 'The Private Psychedelic Reel'. Pre-internet, that would take someone reaching out to a potential collaborator on the phone. I do look back and think we really must have had some chutzpah, thinking 'Who do we want to sing on this track?' then approaching them. But people wanted to work with us.

Bernard has a long history of collaborating with other artists, and New Order have been open to working with different producers over the years. He knew what he was doing. When he came to the studio, he immediately made us feel really comfortable. He arrived straight after recording *TFI Friday* where New Order had been performing 'Regret'. His guitar tech came down and set up, then Bernard turned up and retuned his guitar by playing 'Love Will Tear Us Apart', which was quite a statement. He put off writing the words for a long time, as it seemed like his confident place was writing guitar around synths and bass. I used to get nervous when singers turned up to record but his manner is such that his presence is enough to put people around him at ease.

A couple of years later, we worked on a track with Bernard and Hooky [Peter Hook] for the soundtrack of *24 Hour Party People* ('Here to Stay'). They were both in the studio to oversee us mixing and arranging a new version of the track. On one of the days, they both left at teatime. We both had tickets to see *The League of Gentlemen* live at Drury Lane Theatre, so we finished early, thinking they wouldn't know, and snuck off to the theatre. Only Stephen and Gillian from New Order were at the same show, and they told on us. For the next few days, Bernard and

Paused in Cosmic Reflection 175

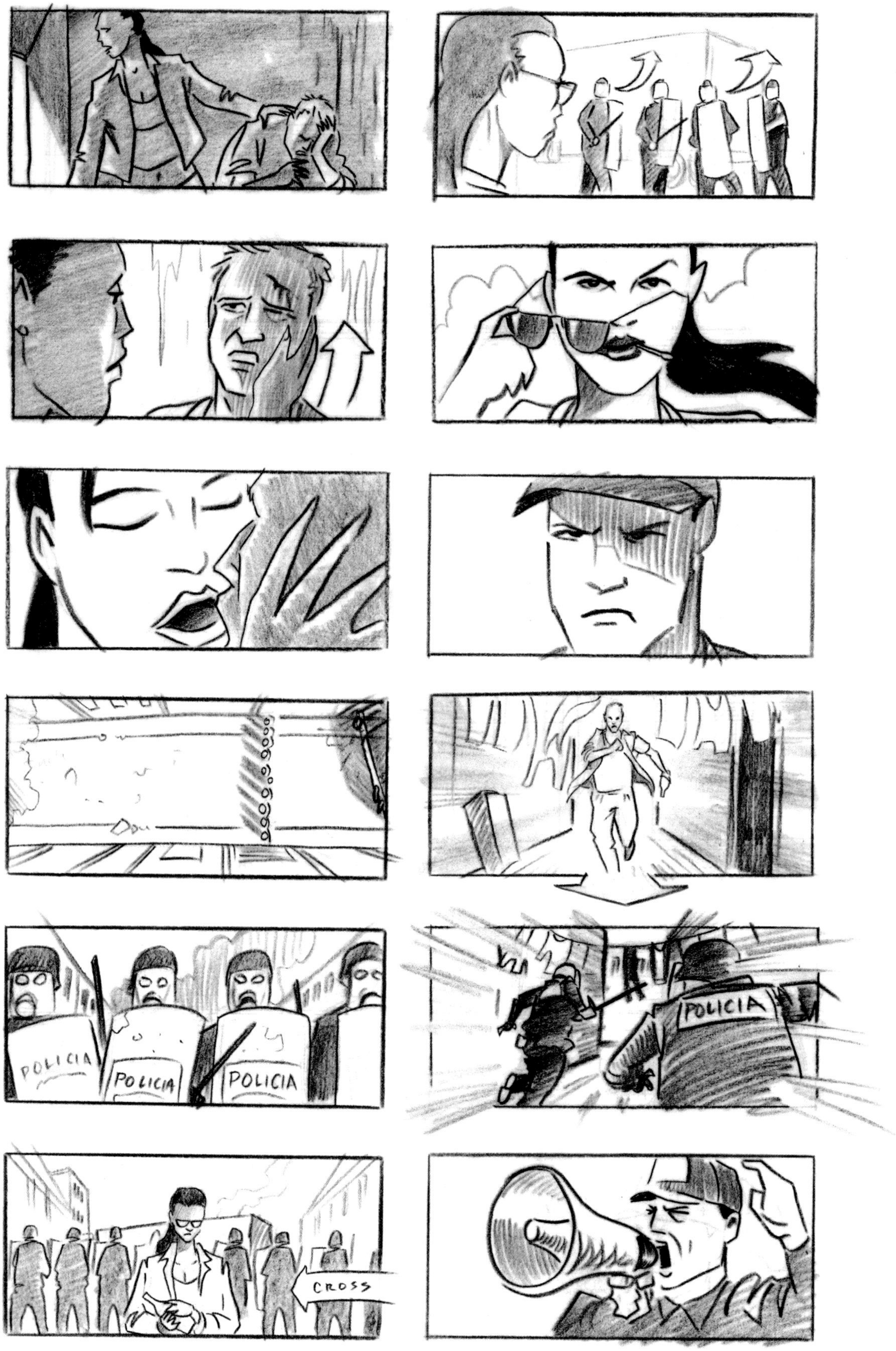
POLICIA
POLICIA
POLICIA
POLICIA
CROSS

Paused in Cosmic Reflection 177

Hooky mercilessly took the piss out of us for going out when there was studio time being paid for. Happy days.

Bernard Sumner

The first thing they sent me was pretty much a four-bar loop. It was a very good loop, with some great effects on it, but it was hard to write a vocal on something like that because there wasn't much support. It's almost like coming up with a vocal to no music at all. So I recorded quite a bit of rhythm guitar to give me some chords to play off. That made writing easier. I played a whole lot of guitar all the way through and then I wrote the vocal line and sent it to Tom and Ed. Tom got back to me with a very basic monitor mix. He asked what I thought. It sounded really great. He'd taken it somewhere I really hadn't imagined. But he got rid of all of the guitar. 'Where's the guitar you fuckin . . .?' 'Er . . . what guitar?' I really didn't mind at all. I'm not precious about stuff like that. The guitar was there to serve a purpose, which it had done.

The track they sent me had loads of fireworks on it; it really sounded alive, even though it was still just a demo. They asked if I'd come down to London to record it properly, so I went down to their studio. I had an idea to get Bobby Gillespie involved as I thought our voices would work well together on that track. Even at that stage, the track was pretty anarchistic and wild, and Bobby's a bit like that so I figured it would be a good fit. The tonality of our voices is a little bit similar – it's maybe hard to tell the two different tones apart – but Bobby's vocal style is quite fluid and relaxed, which I thought made my vocals sound a bit uptight. I felt like I was there singing with a suit on when I heard Bobby's voice.

A few years after it came out, I played it live with them at a gig at Brixton Academy (9 December 2005). I was a bit worse for wear and I missed the solo completely, or I fucked it up completely, not sure which. That night's probably best forgotten if I'm honest. I think the night of that gig I ended up staggering around my hotel corridor trying to find the toilet. I got caught short. Everyone's done it. I'm sure even King Charles has done it. I was less well behaved in those days.

Apart from me being inebriated at the gig, the guitar solo was actually quite hard to play as it uses some very unusual two-note chords. It was definitely more of a studio thing; I never expected to be asked to play it live. All their records sound screwed up, fucked up and not straight in any way, so I didn't really want to put straight guitar on it.

Tom and Ed are definitely kindred spirits. We feel relaxed around each other which is always a major bonus as you get older and you work with people. For years and years, Joy Division and New Order were very closed shops. We were self-taught musicians who stopped using producers for a while so we only had each other to bounce off, and that ball had been bouncing between us for very many years. We didn't really know what we were doing, but we just carried on and did it. So for me, it's always interesting to work with other musicians because you can learn different ways of working. Working with them, it felt like they were kindred spirits who were on the same wavelength. And that makes for a great creative environment.

WIZ (director, 'Out of Control' music video)

I've always felt that there was a real revolutionary potential in acid house. People talked about opening up minds and paradigm shifts and for a while that really seemed to happen. Young people behaving with independent thought in vast numbers. I've always been inspired by that, but I wanted to nurture that potential, in my modest film-making way. I'd first tried to communicate the

Previous page: Original storyboards for the 'Out of Control' music video drawn by Mark Bristol.

Below: WIZ on set with Rosario Dawson, filming the 'Out of Control' music video in Mexico City.

emotional arc of the acid house phenomenon with 'Weekender' [Flowered Up, 1992]. I'd tried to bring a conscious dimension to that film rather than just reflect an escapist drug experience. A real imperative to me is that there always has to be some substance to the style. 'Weekender' was one of the first critiques of that hedonism.

Seven years later, I was much more of a confident filmmaker. I heard *Surrender*, and all the incredible songs on it, and 'Out of Control' really spoke to me in a succinct and powerful way. It had all these ingredients that lifted it above so many other records. It's got that undeniable dance floor rush. But also, what really worked for me is that it has this contradictory side, this vulnerable, melancholic, wistful vocal from Bernard Sumner and Bobby Gillespie. So the track addresses the listener on two levels. That's a sweet spot for me.

I always want to stimulate the audience and elevate the expectation of what a music video can do. And the planets absolutely aligned with 'Out of Control'. I had this wonderful song that touched me emotionally and intellectually from a band that trusted me to visualise it. One of the reasons The Chemical Brothers' videos are exemplary is that as a band they have the self-confidence to find a director that they have kinship with and let them make the film. They don't impose. When you have that kind of trust, interesting work gets made.

There's a Guy Debord quote: 'Every new lie of advertising is also an avowal of the previous lie.' Sometimes the relentlessness of advertising makes you feel ineffectual, like giving up. Powerless. But you never know what's round the corner. Who would have predicted acid house? Those moments of despair I always have to remind myself that

Paused in Cosmic Reflection   179

180 The Chemical Brothers

Paused in Cosmic Reflection 181

IN THE HEAT OF THE MOMENT

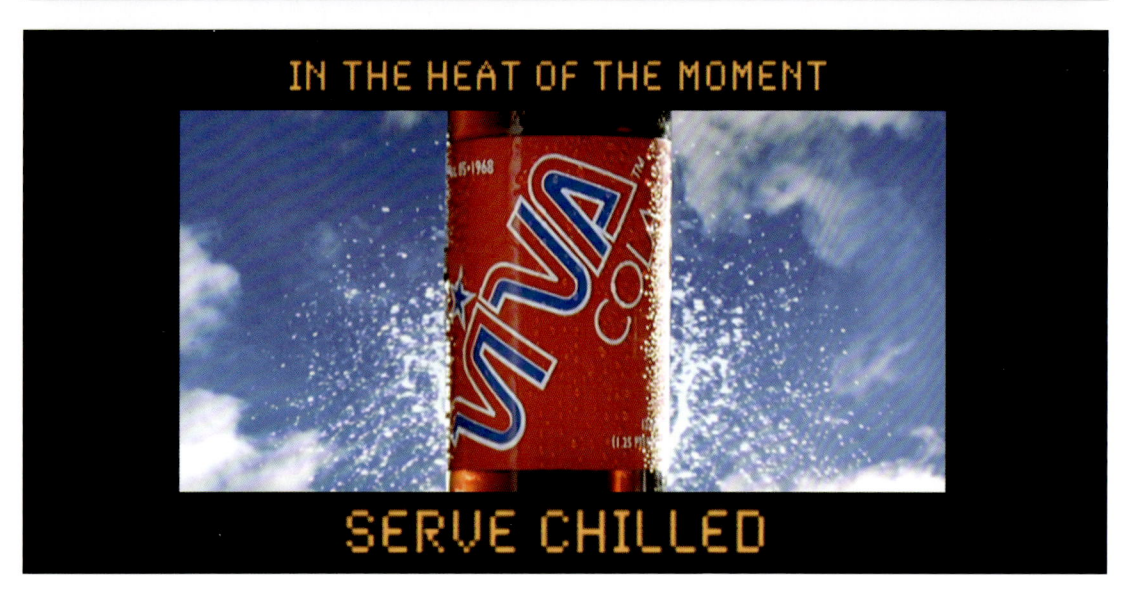

SERVE CHILLED

Paused in Cosmic Reflection   183

Previous pages: Stills from the 'Out of Control' music video, directed by WIZ.

Opposite: Prop bottle of cola used in the video.

Page 188–9: Stills from 'Out of Control (The Avalanches Surrender to Love Mix)'.

things happen when people aren't expecting them. People know that real existence comes from human exchange. From conversation, from communal experience, from dancing. It's the reason that something like acid house affected so many lives so strongly, and why you hang on to hope.

When I was planning the video, I wanted to reflect on modern methods of advertising and the fact that youth culture gets completely appropriated to sell product, to sell capitalism itself. There's no holds barred when it comes to consumerism; it would co-opt Marxism if it thought it could use it to further sell capitalism. The Clash put it best when they sung about turning rebellion into money. I thought that would be a wonderful irony to explore. And I asked myself what's the epitome of a useless product that everyone consumes, and it's cola. It's a universal product that everyone in the world knows. The Chemical Brothers got it – of course they did. They got it straight away.

Taking that idea, I wanted to embrace that visceral fantasy that we all have at some point where you want to throw a brick at the police. The David and Goliath scenario. Whether we do it is a different thing entirely. I believe in the power of the collective and in solidarity which I think is illustrated in the second half of the video.

All the casting and locations were wonderful gifts. I knew exactly what I was doing, and I had immense good fortune along the way. Originally, we wanted to shoot in Havana. We had to send the treatment and the shot-list to the culture department of the Cuban government. They came back saying they couldn't allow it to be filmed on their streets. Whether it was deemed too inflammatory, who knows.

We ended up shooting in Mexico City. The police in the video are real police we'd hired as extras. When I first arrived in Mexico, I briefed the location people that I needed something that felt real. They took me to all these lame, pedestrian tourist spots that were really uninspiring and didn't work. As we were driving across the city, we went past this district, and I pointed to a street saying, 'That's it.' Their faces went pale because if we shot there, we would have been completely exposed. It was really dangerous; almost as if we'd gone into a riot zone.

Thankfully, because we had a platoon of riot police, we could go in with relative safety and shoot on that street. I can remember at 5 a.m., this huge army-like bus pulled up looking like something out of *Full Metal Jacket*. This helmeted, jack-booted legion of policemen trooped off and did a little bit of square bashing, flexing their muscles, not letting us forget who was in charge. Soon after, a whole case of tequila was delivered. I asked what was going on; this was the start of the shoot, why were people starting drinking? The producer said, 'Just don't ask.'

The shoot was eighteen hours. A really long day. It wasn't a residential place where the riot was filmed so the police – our police – were happy for 150 kids to turn up and act up. The week we were there, there had been student riots, real student riots, in the city. It was heated, a proper life-imitating-art situation.

Casting the video was a gift from heaven. I was walking along Old Compton Street in Soho and I went into a newsagent to buy some cigarettes. I saw a magazine in the rack which had Rosario Dawson on the cover. She wasn't hugely famous at that point; she'd been in Harmony Korine's film *Kids* a few years before but not a lot else. Seeing that cover, I knew she'd be perfect. There was resistance from my production company as we hadn't budgeted for a proper actress but I wrote to her sincerely and she got the idea and was totally up it.

One of the interesting things about the 'Out of Control' video is that it's – and I hate this word – meta. It's making the experience an experience; it's trying to make you conscious of consciousness, of the omniscience of consumerism. And it parodies revolution.

When the video came out, it might have looked like an act of defiance but it didn't get people out on the streets. Some people recognised what it was trying to do, not least The Chemical Brothers themselves, but most people at the time were pretty complacent. It was the end of the nineties, which was a relatively peaceful time in the world, before the May Day riots of 2000, before 9/11, Iraq and austerity.

I think it's one of my best videos. There's a vitality to it and a timelessness to the story. It flew in the face of a lot of music videos at the time and it changed the expectation of what a Chemical Brothers video could be. Lots of their other videos play with the idea of psychedelic, out-of-body experiences. This wasn't interested in that. In a way, it addresses the whole bread and butter of music video in general, which is that they're often four-minute-long advertisements made up of beautiful, glamorous, manipulative imagery. But the saving grace from it being overly intellectual – or even pretentious – is that it is very watchable. And that it's a truly fantastic song.

Paused in Cosmic Reflection 185

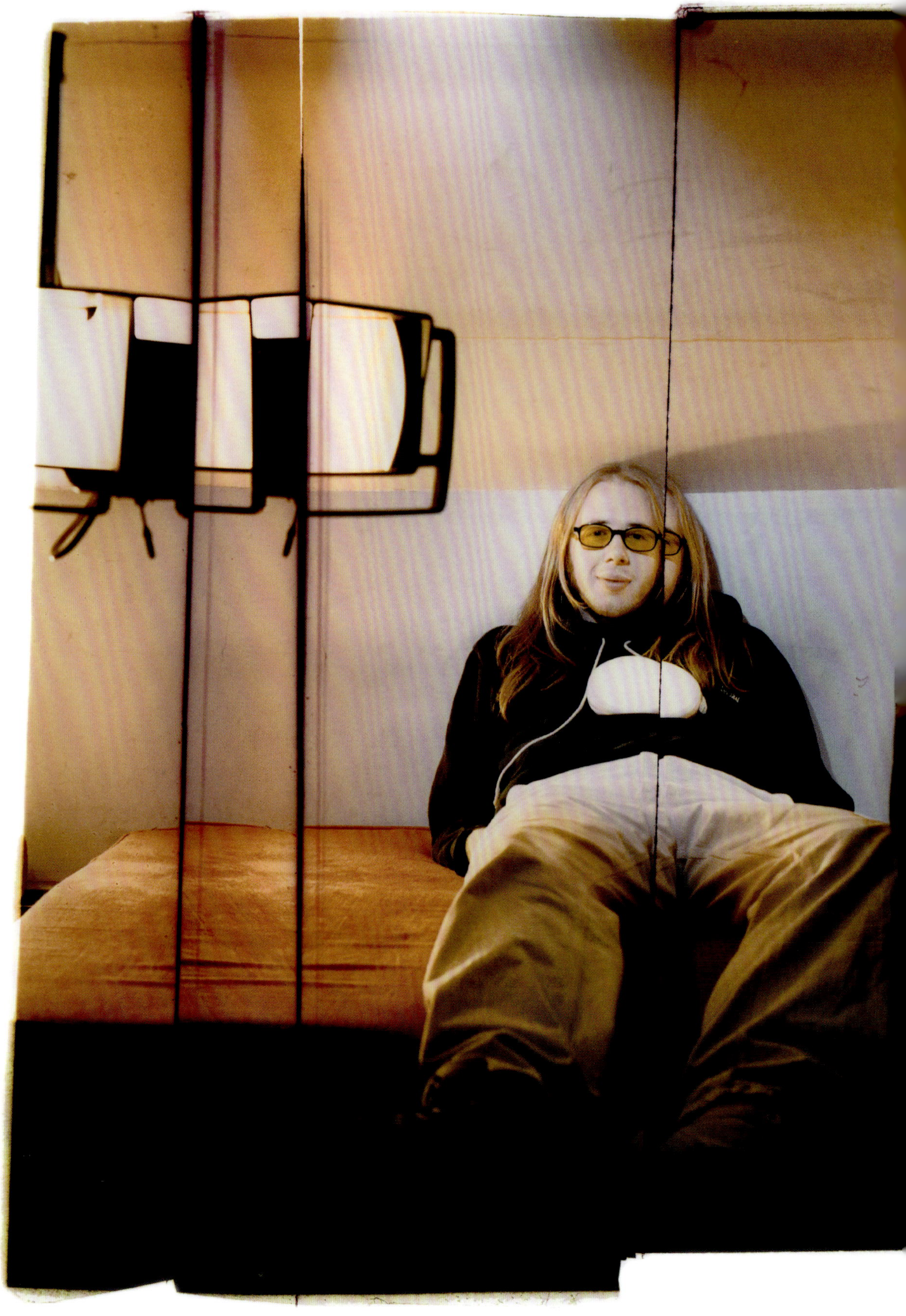

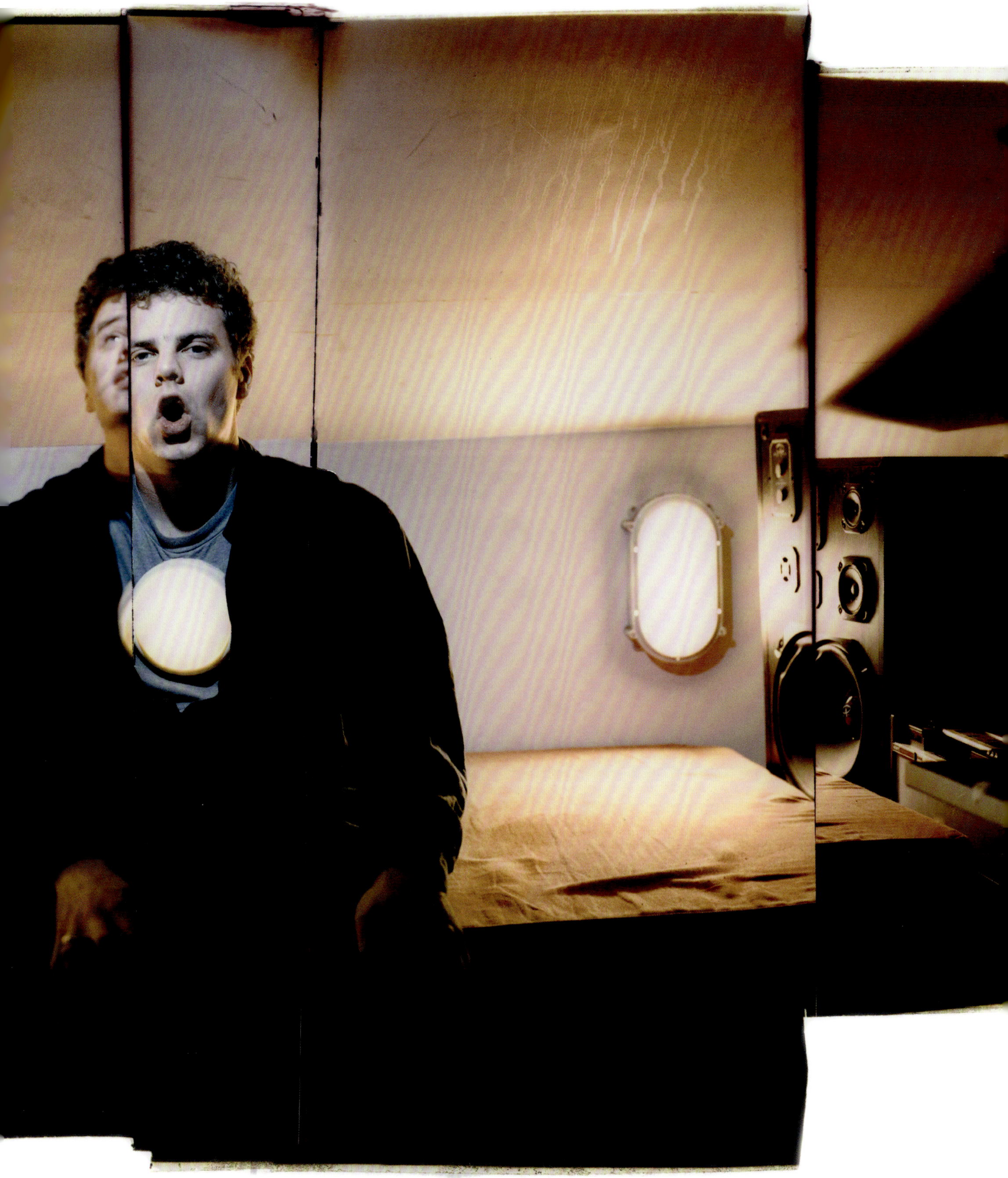

You always get up

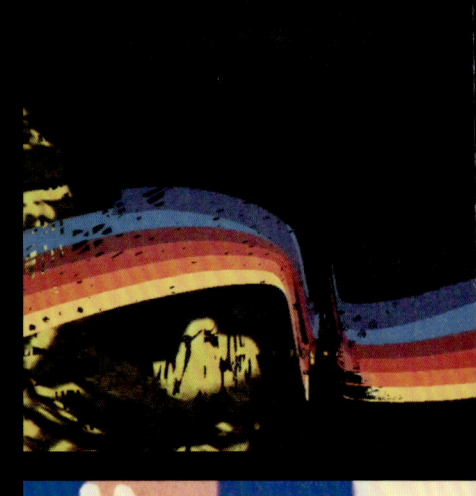

it's a sound
it's a sound
it's a soun

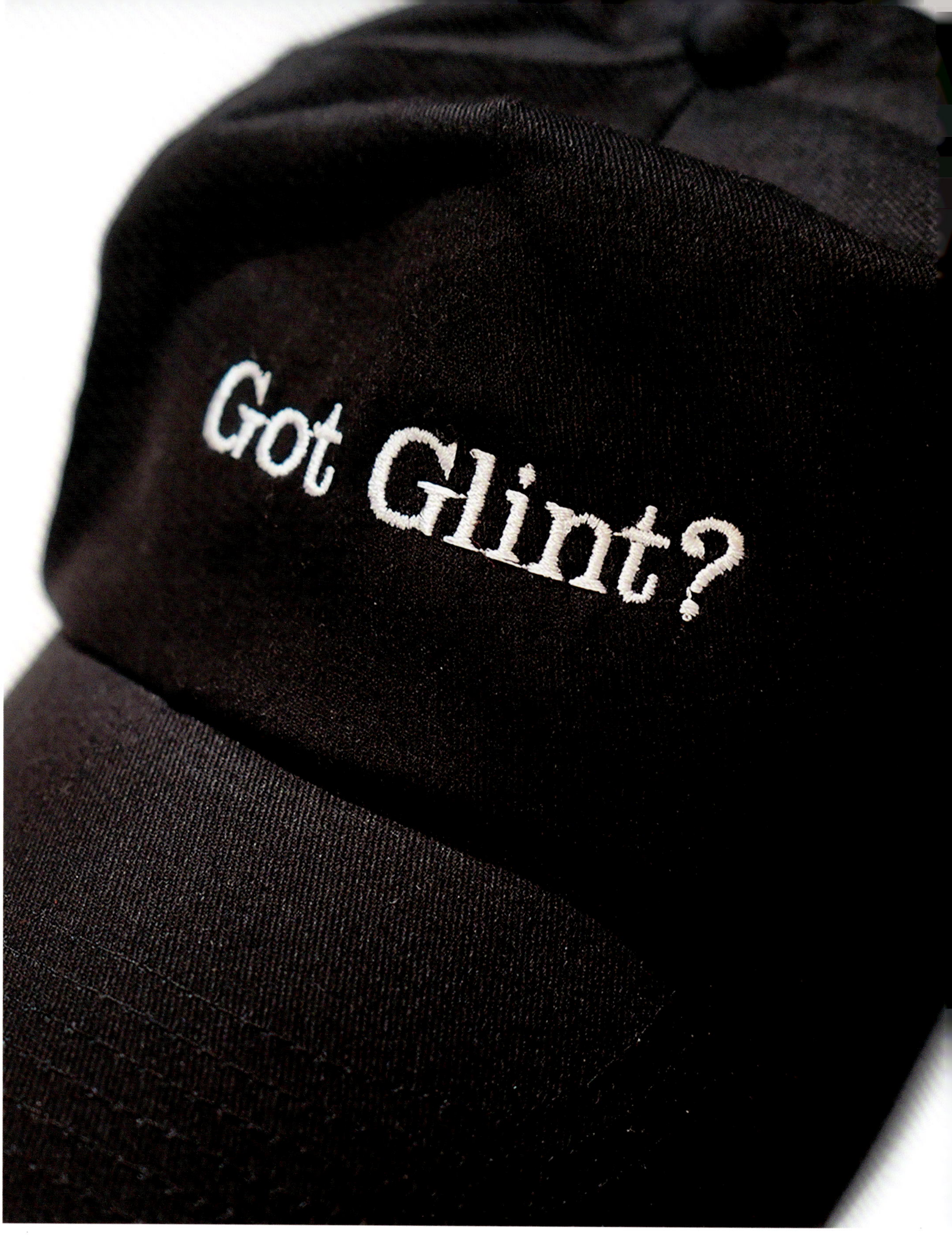
Got Glint?

Got Glint: DJing as The Chemical Brothers

The spirit of dance music – of dancing itself – can often be summed up in a well-chosen song title. 'Lost in Music', 'Let the Music Use You', 'Jack Your Body'... Each of them is a knowing wink to the effect that a great record – or a set of great records segued together by a DJ who can read a room – can have on the listener; insider knowledge passed from the original artist to the people on the dance floor. Add to that list 'Got Glint?'

Glint is a turn of phrase and a state of mind. It's the view from the heart of the room just as things begin to take off. It's the psychic connection between friends, the unspoken bond one might be lucky enough to share if the conditions are right and the music is loud. It's a link that connects generations, a sense of humour, a flow of energy.

An essential part of The Chemical Brothers' DJ set, glint is the reason to get up there and play. If you've ever heard them DJ, whether in a tiny, dank sweatbox or a huge, laser-lit hall, chances are you've experienced the very same thing.

Nathan Thursting (aka Nathan Detroit, Glint promoter, DJ and tour manager)

Everything changed on the night of the Millennium. Prior to that, Tom and Ed weren't DJing that much, certainly not like they had in the mid-nineties. They'd spent a few years busily making records and being a live band. Then they played Gatecrasher at the Don Valley Stadium in Sheffield with Paul Oakenfold, Sasha, Paul Van Dyk and a load of other massive DJs. It was a huge gig: 20,000 people or more. And it all felt weird, just not quite right, disconnected. After that, we put on our Millennium 2000 novelty glasses and drove down to London where Tom and Ed played Turnmills at 3 a.m. in the morning. Turnmills was a brilliant club that felt like a small room, even though it held nearly 1,000 people. The contrast was remarkable. And it inspired them to start their own night – Glint.

Glint was a proper *heads down, lost in music* dance floor. It was in the basement of El Dorado, a Portuguese coffee shop in Westbourne Grove that had a legal capacity of 180. We'd push that to about 300. Glint was somewhere where they could develop records. It had a suspended ceiling and the amount of sweat that got absorbed into the ceiling tiles made it look like it was perpetually on the verge of collapse. The second night, there were 1,500 people outside when we opened. By the third one it was really out of hand. There were *Big Brother* contestants trying to get in but refusing to pay.

In a way, Glint was a reaction against an idea they'd inadvertently helped invent – that of the 'superstar DJ'. Tom and Ed were never that, but 'Hey Boy Hey Girl' was so big and the phrase so widespread that you'd often see it stuck to them. They worked better in intimate environments where they could play long sets. There, they could be face to face with the dancers, really engaged in a boiling hot room where they could just let rip.

It couldn't last at El Dorado. I'd been promoting it, trying to keep a lid on things, but it was way too crazy to carry on at such a small venue. The knock-on effect was that a lot of people clocked The Chemical Brothers were back DJing and they started getting requests from all over for DJ gigs. Since then, they've done cute little runs of DJ gigs whenever they're not in a live cycle. I'll go out with them as warm-up DJ and tour manager. It's a tight travelling party, very unlike how the live show goes out.

Because they're not jobbing DJs out playing every weekend, their gigs always feel exciting. Being at every DJ show, I end up hearing three hours of truly mind-blowing music. The set is never a monotonous sequence of nondescript 4/4 records. It's a journey, and an incredibly well-choreographed one. They spend ages putting the sets together, creating mad edits and cut-ups of things especially for DJing. And during the sets, you always hear where the next album is going. With each album, the tracks evolve over the course of half a dozen or so DJ sets, sometimes starting off as raw ideas before ending up as massive numbers that go on the records.

When most DJs go to play a club, there's a presumption that either the people there are regulars at the club or they're into them as a DJ, maybe having heard a few tracks they've made. With The Chemical Brothers, there's a different audience. I'd say the majority are mad, passionate Chemical Brothers fans. And that includes people from different generations, all mixing on the dance floor. The reactions are intense. These days, Tom and I like to have a little explore before the gig, work out where the weirdos and the freaks in the crowd are, the kind of people who'll lose control and kick the party off. I might then go and dish out some beers or water to those people to make sure they're ready.

Glint remains such a key word for Tom and Ed. It's about the cheeky look in the eyes, the moment you share when magic's happening. It's where you'd look at someone and there's a little glimmer, you're both thinking: 'This is what it's all about.' Playing at clubs where people actually want what you're offering, where everyone in the space is on the same wavelength as you. All connected and losing their shit on the dance floor. That's how you get glint.

Tom Rowlands

When you play music you've made when you're DJing, it's more about how you feel yourself while you're playing it. I remember playing a really early version of 'Music: Response' in Glasgow. We were so excited to play it straight out of the studio. Within about thirty seconds of putting it on as the first track in the set, we knew something was wrong. Back to the drawing board.

DJing can be such a brilliant, immediate way of knowing whether music works, right or wrong. Something that might have sounded immense in the studio might suddenly sound completely wrong in a different environment. It might not even be that it's sonically wrong – this bit's not right, that bit sounds odd – it might be that you just don't enjoy it as a piece of music. You can change things in the studio endlessly, but playing it out in front of a room full of people after another record you've made or a track that you love by someone else can provide a really stark contrast. 'This one just doesn't make me feel good.'

John Burgess

The Chemical Brothers trusted Bugged Out! to find somewhere good for them to play in London. They'd still do Fabric occasionally, but we found a couple of gay clubs in Vauxhall – Fire and Area. They loved them because they reminded them of their roots, where the clubs were quite gritty and weren't shiny in any way. They would always want to have someone cutting-edge on the line-up, which was important to them and us too. Tom and Ed have carried that through to now, when they play places like Printworks. What's always amazing is that new up-and-coming DJs who probably weren't born when 'Song to the Siren' came out can't believe they're on the bill with these legends.

...Turnmills, London

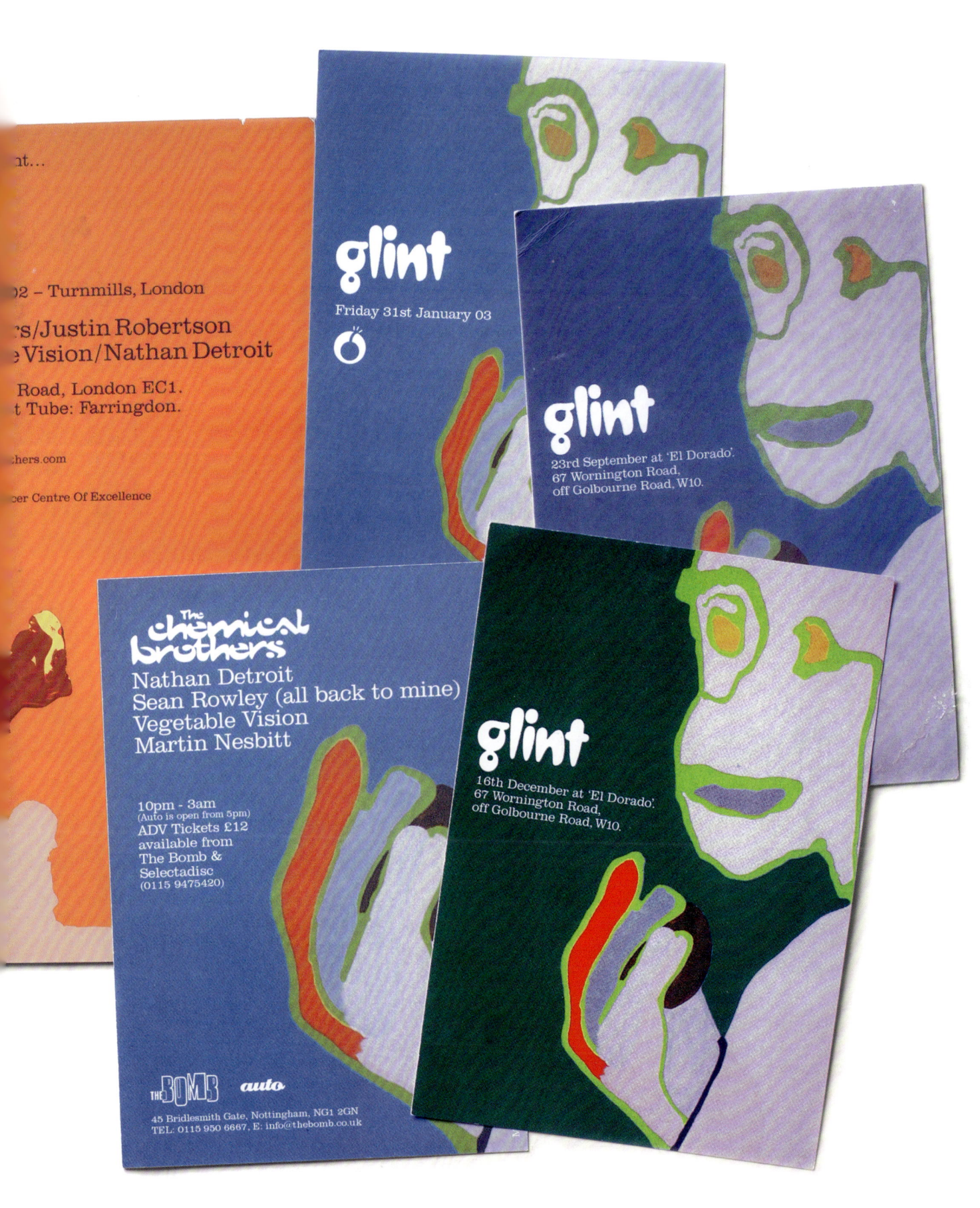

.../Justin Robertson
Vision/Nathan Detroit

Road, London EC1.
Tube: Farringdon.

...thers.com

...cer Centre Of Excellence

glint
Friday 31st January 03

glint
23rd September at 'El Dorado',
67 Wornington Road,
off Golbourne Road, W10.

The Chemical Brothers
Nathan Detroit
Sean Rowley (all back to mine)
Vegetable Vision
Martin Nesbitt

10pm – 3am
(Auto is open from 5pm)
ADV Tickets £12
available from
The Bomb &
Selectadisc
(0115 9475420)

THE BOMB   auto

45 Bridlesmith Gate, Nottingham, NG1 2GN
TEL: 0115 950 6667, E: info@thebomb.co.uk

glint
16th December at 'El Dorado',
67 Wornington Road,
off Golbourne Road, W10.

Paused in Cosmic Reflection 193

In 2017, they started showcasing *No Geography* material. Bugged Out! has always been somewhere where they felt confident to road test new tracks. They played 'Galvanize' for the first time in Sankeys Soap in Manchester and 'Go' in our night in Area. The audience at our clubs are always supportive. At one of the Printworks nights, they played a track featuring the sample from 'Weekend' by Class Action ['Eve of Destruction']. Afterwards, Tom was saying, 'That worked, we need to get that sample cleared.' When they play, it's an excuse to have fun, play with their peers and lots of new faces, and to play new tracks on a massive PA in front of 5,000 people.

When they DJ, they don't sound like anyone else. They have this slavish acid house attitude. In today's terms, they play quite slow – somewhere around 125 bpm – whereas a lot of younger DJs will consistently play around 140 bpm. They always play long sets, four or five hours if they can. It's pure acid until the end where they might play a track like 'Swoon' or 'Star Guitar'. They always play 'It Doesn't Matter', which is the epitome of their sound when they DJ. That sums up their DJ gigs. They like it really dark and so full of smoke so you can't see your hand in front of your face.

No Geography definitely connected with a younger audience, partly because The Chemical Brothers' festival gigs are so incredible and so many people get to see them live. If you're twenty-two you're going to watch that show if you have any passing interest in dance music. When we put them on, the audience seems to stay young. There's a guy who regularly comes up to me at their gigs who now arrives accompanied by his eighteen-year-old son. Both of them gurning their faces off, both of them loving The Chemical Brothers.

Erol Alkan (DJ, producer)

The Chemical Brothers have been one of my biggest influences, as far back as the *Fourteenth Century Sky* EP. As an avid *NME* and *Melody Maker* reader, I was totally immersed in the alternative music of that era. I was also obsessed with acid house and rave. When they emerged – first as The Dust Brothers – it felt like those worlds were all being brought together in perfect sync. In photos, Tom and Ed looked like outsiders, so different from other dance music producers. I was a massive Manic Street Preachers fan and there had been lots of crossover between the two groups in 1994. They remixed 'Faster' and 'La Tristesse Durera (Scream to a Sigh)' and they DJed at the Manic's The Holy Bible gigs at the Astoria. Like the Manics, they felt very relatable to me growing up.

I didn't really pay much attention to DJ mixes in the early nineties, but after reading about their sets I was intrigued as to how they'd mix The Beatles with techno and acid house records. What they did in those early days ended up being an influence on me, and on a lot of my peers. A lot of people will try to imply that they're doing something original in dance music, but it's quite likely that The Chemical Brothers have already done it pretty brilliantly years before. When I became known as someone who mixed dance music with a lot of alternative music, I always put it down to my personal taste. It's something I'd like to think I've got and I think taste is the foundation of what drives The Chemical Brothers.

Over the twenty-odd years I've been DJing in dance clubs, their music has always been in and out of my sets – whether that's records from the past or new things they've sent me. They'll often send me tracks to road test, and there's music I've played out that never ended up being released. If I play a six- or seven-hour set, dropping 'Star Guitar' in the last half hour can bring a room to its knees beautifully. It's a phenomenal, emotional club record. A lot of their music is absolutely timeless – tracks like 'Saturate', or 'It Doesn't Matter', which is one of the greatest embodiments of psychedelia ever made in dance music. There's been moments where I find myself wishing that I had another hour and fifty minutes of tracks that sound and feel just like that.

When I DJ with them, they're always inspiring to watch and to listen to. Their sets are brilliantly cohesive. They're true to what they stand for, and they have an ability to be immediate and deep at the same time, which may sound a bit odd to say but it's not an easy thing to pull off. Every time we've played together, I always listen and watch. Listening to them playing nearly twenty-five years after I first played with them, I can still hear that taste come through in their sets. It's the one element that can't be taught. I always walk away inspired.

Ed Simons

At one of the DJ gigs we did recently, I stopped for a second and found myself thinking, 'This really is incredible. There's 5,000 people here properly into it.' The atmosphere and the electricity in the room was genuinely palpable. Lots of friends and DJs like Erol were stood around with us on stage, along with Tom's son and all of his mates who had never been to a proper nightclub before. And I found myself thinking, we've been making this happen together for a long time.

Although it felt very far removed from the Old Steam Brewery in Manchester, the spirit was the same. When we first DJed together back there, Tom was in Ariel so there was already a bit of a buzz. But even at those first DJ gigs, people went crazier than you'd ever have expected. I think that's because we've always had something that's connected with people on a deep level. Our DJ gigs seem to give people permission to be together in a different way. And the fact that Tom's teenage son – who's now taller than me – was there seeing his dad do this thing that we've been doing together since well before he was born. That felt pretty mind-blowing.

The band and family on stage at Bugged Out! Printworks, December 2022.

Paused in Cosmic Reflection

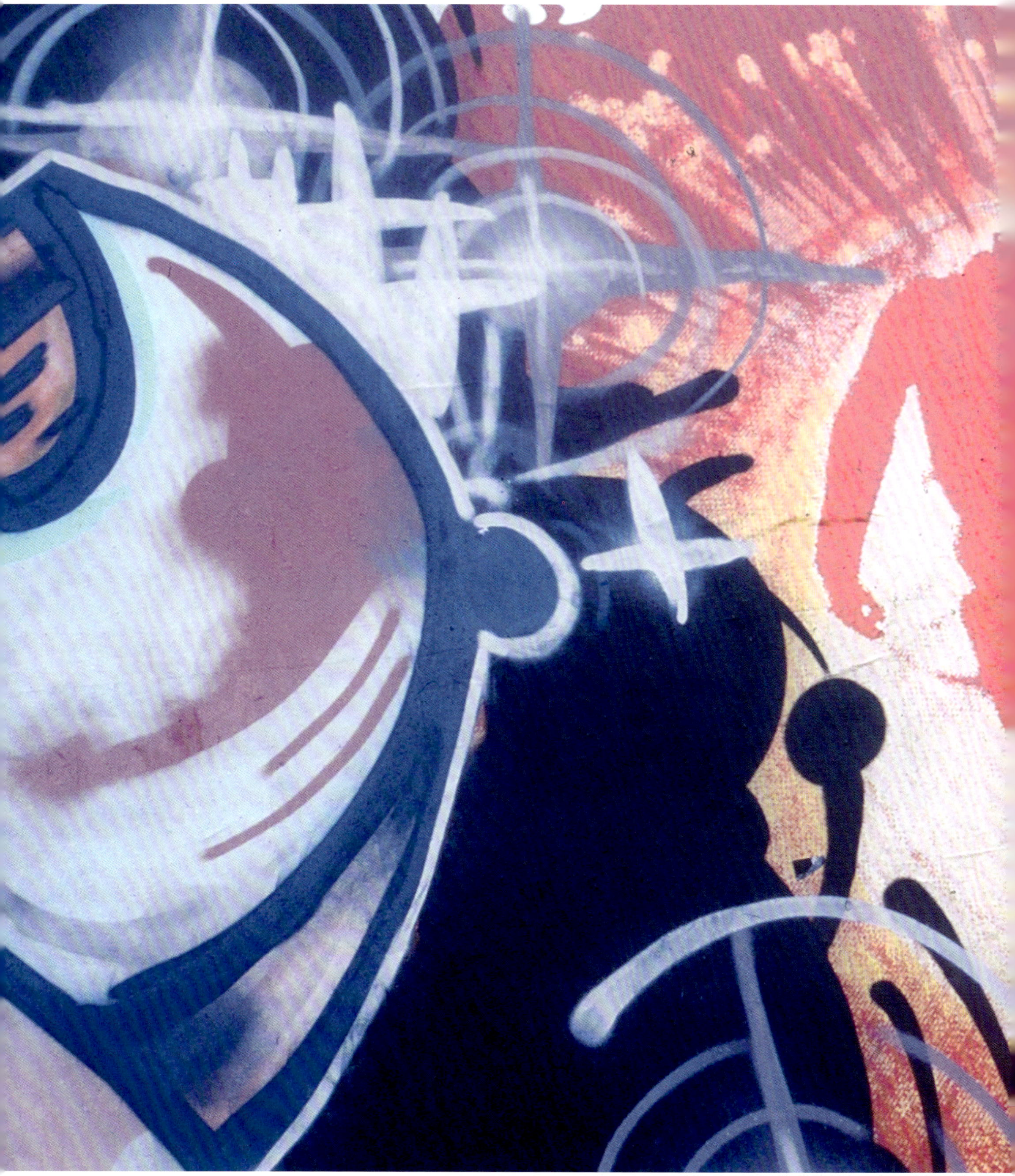

Star Guitar

Trying to describe 'Star Guitar' is like trying to pin down the finer details of a dream.

It's an evolution and an elevation, a change in the atmosphere. The track's guitar chords shift and shimmer just out of reach, like a heat haze on the horizon in the dog days of summer. Closer to the ground there's a supremely forceful rhythm track that punches the gut with every whip-crack clap and kick-drum thump.

Setting that endless swirl of melody set against such a measured, mechanical groove was inspired. As was the addition of a vocal refrain that perfectly captures the moment where you cede control to the higher powers of the dance floor, the point where you give in and let the music move you.

A shift in tone and mood from The Chemical Brothers' previous album outliers ('Leave Home', 'Block Rockin' Beats', 'Hey Boy Hey Girl'), 'Star Guitar' was released as a single a few weeks before *Come with Us* in January 2002. The video for the track was made by French director Michel Gondry, who had previously created the kaleidoscopic fantasy world for 'Let Forever Be' and would later go on direct clips for 'Go' and 'Got to Keep On'.

Tom Rowlands

'Star Guitar' started with the drums. I wanted something that had that real tough New York house sound. At first, the drums don't sit in a standard pattern, they're not four to the floor. As it built up, I wanted them to sound different, even though they're nodding to classic nineties NYC house, like something that might come out on Strictly Rhythm or something that Masters at Work might make. Those records have a kind of hypnotic power that almost forces you to dance. It was about building a drum pattern that was memorable in its own right.

When you're making music, there's not a conscious thought of, 'What's the unique thing that this track can be?' but there's something nagging away in your brain that's always asking the question. With 'Star Guitar', somewhere in my brain, I was thinking that what would fit with a really jacking house rhythm would be a phase-y, almost My Bloody Valentine type of sound. That contrast could be brilliant; that's what I wanted to explore. I wanted the drums to be as tough and as forward as those records that I love, and then to have a fluid, phased sound, a kind of modern psychedelic sound. Chasing a thing that feels totally natural to me is probably what makes the track memorable.

When the intro drums were in place, I wrote a guitar part based on what I thought the chords to 'Starman' by David Bowie were. What I ended up with had a totally different feel because of the way I played them, with one chord held for ages. We also had a new phaser – the Mu-Tron Bi-Phase – which we were really excited about. We'd used it a bit on *Surrender*, but this was its time to shine. The sound is a sample of my real guitar being re-played by my MIDI guitar. I'm a terrible guitar player and a terrible piano player. I can play chords on a guitar, but I can barely play chords on a piano. So, if I play chords on the MIDI guitar, playing a sample of my real guitar, I'll find a way to make it work.

When 'Star Guitar' came out, I think it felt very different to songs we'd released before, certainly the tracks that had led off our previous albums. I'm not sure people took to it immediately. With the video, I remember waiting ages for it to be completed. It took a long time to come together. When we finally saw it, you could see why. It was the early days of computer manipulation in video production, and they just made it look so seamless. I

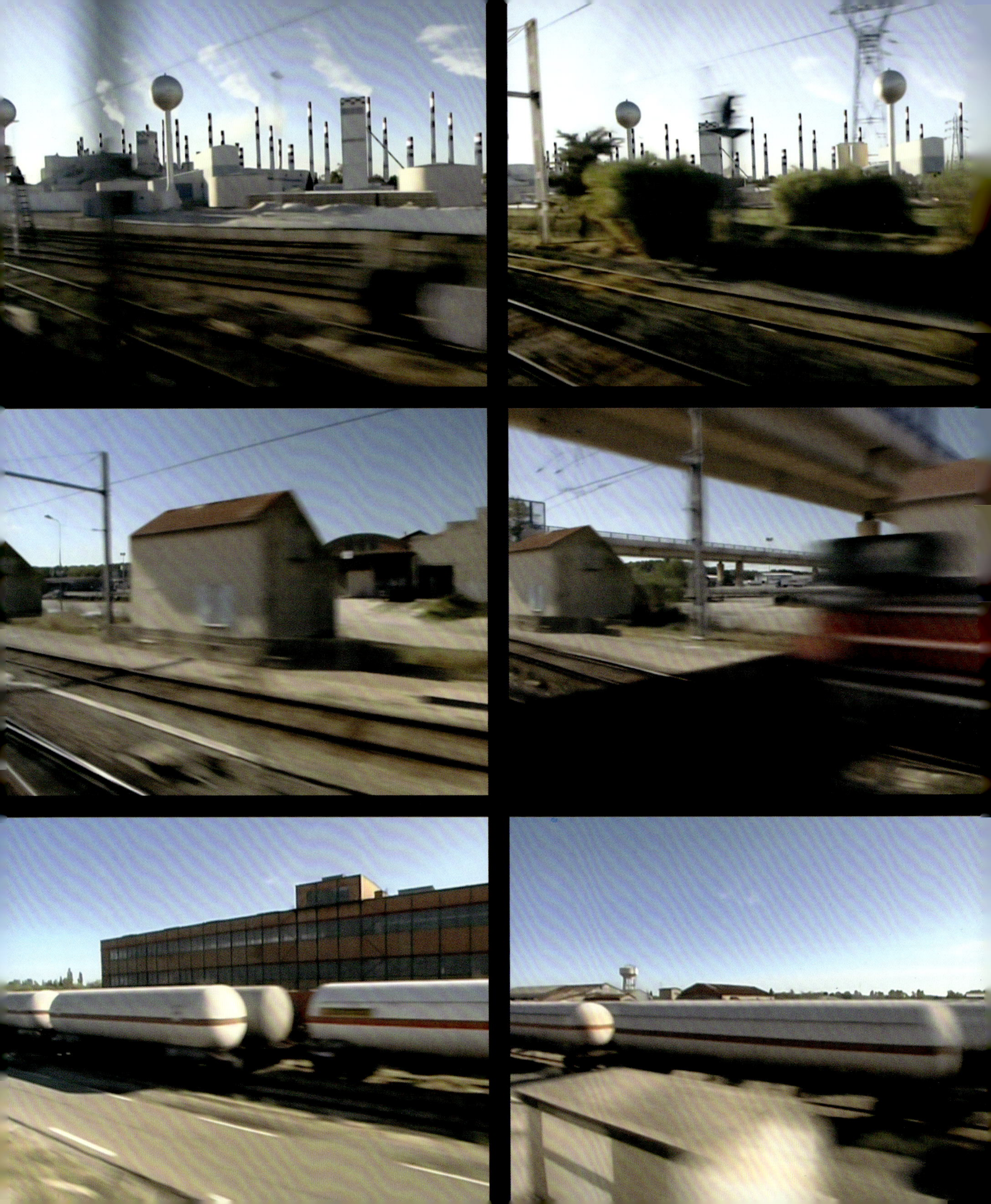

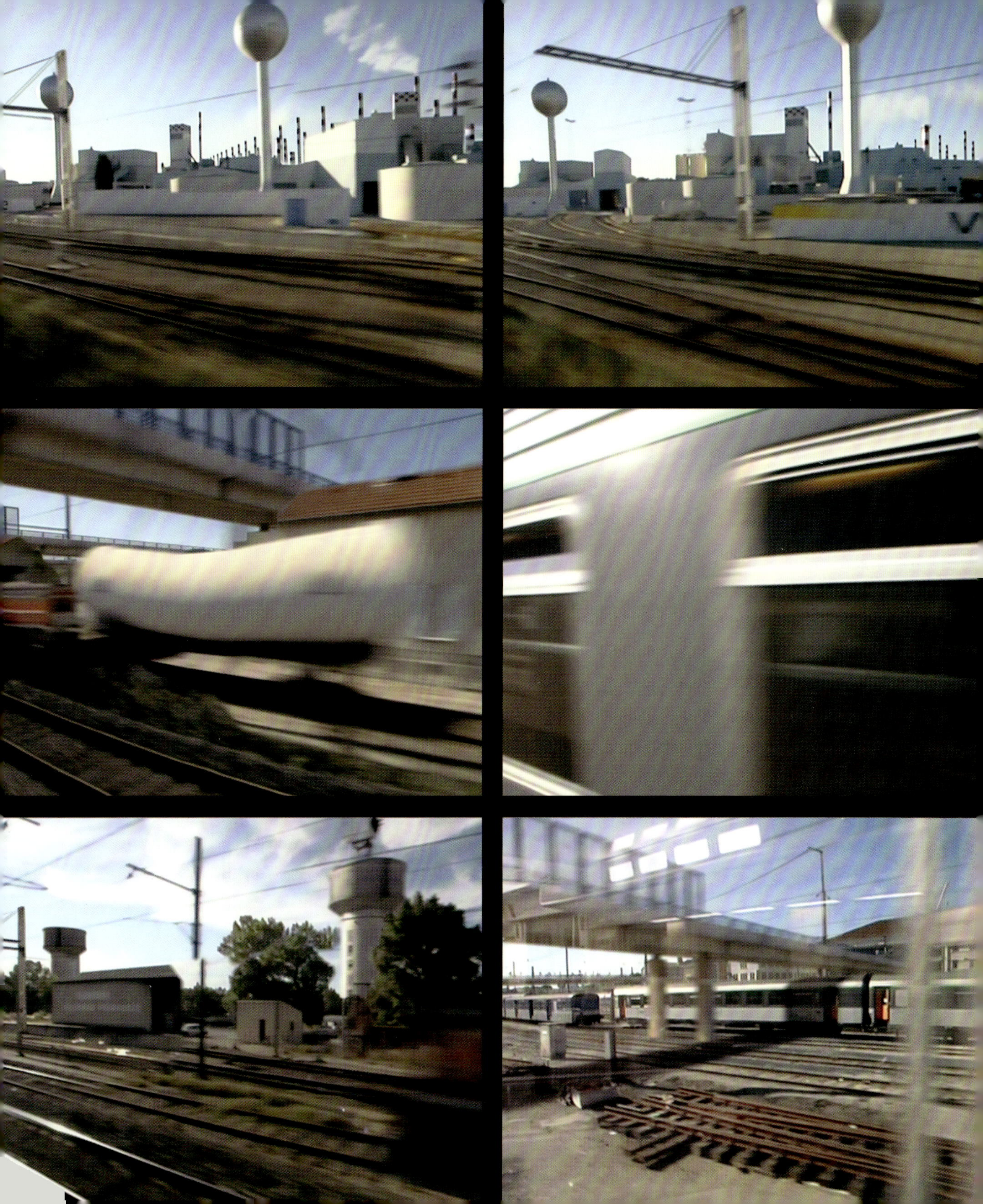

Previous page: Stills from the 'Star Guitar' music video, directed by Michel and Olivier Gondry.

Below and opposite: More sleeve artwork from Kate Gibb.

love the way it's become a meme on social media over the years. You're sat there looking out of a train window and immediately you're thinking of 'Star Guitar'.

Michel Gondry (co-director, 'Star Guitar' music video)

I think I first heard The Chemical Brothers when Spike Jonze showed me 'Elektrobank', the video he did with his future wife [Sofia Coppola] as the gymnast. As always, it was great. I thought the music was cool, and I should also direct a video for The Chemical Brothers too.

I don't like the word psychedelia to describe my work. I would rather use words such as fractals or recursion to define what I do. I think if magic is grounded into magic, it's not magic anymore. It's extension. Magic must grow out of the normal to be magical. In other words, inspiration for the video could have come about because my beautiful girlfriend had left me after a sleeper-train trip in France. In truth, the inspiration came from a phone call with one of the two Chemical Brothers. He just told me: 'Escape, trip.' That was enough.

To film the video, I sent my brother with his camera on French train tracks between Valence and Marseille. There are factories, towers and smoke there. He did the trip three times at different hours of the day.

Like many of The Chemical Brothers' tracks, 'Star Guitar' is unapologetically funky. It's music that was invented to dance to.

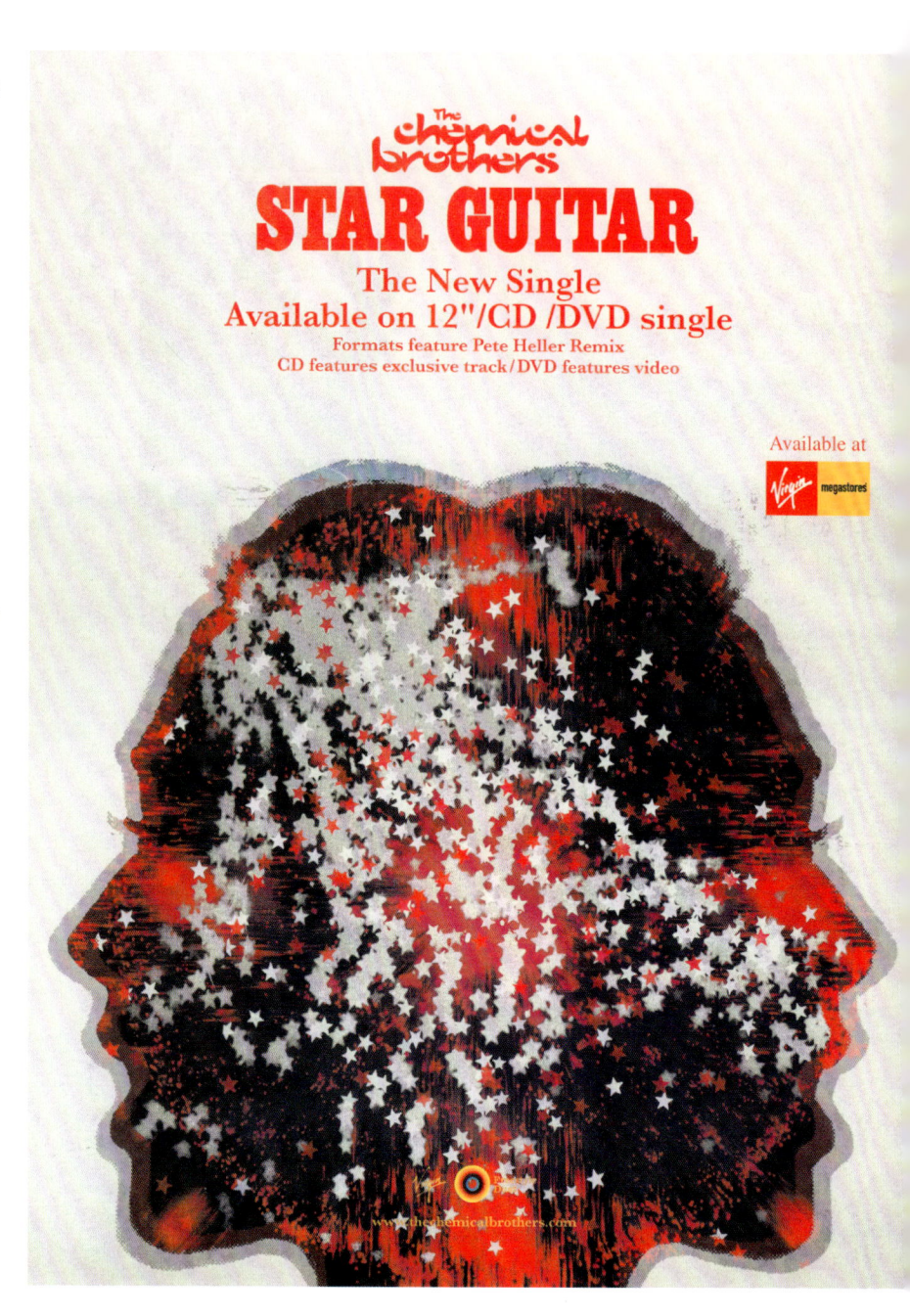

Paused in Cosmic Reflection 203

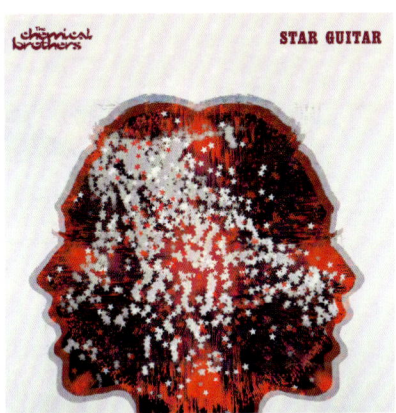

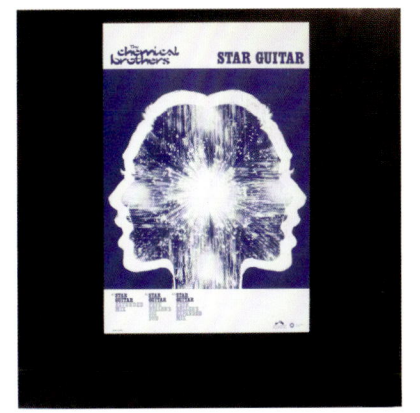

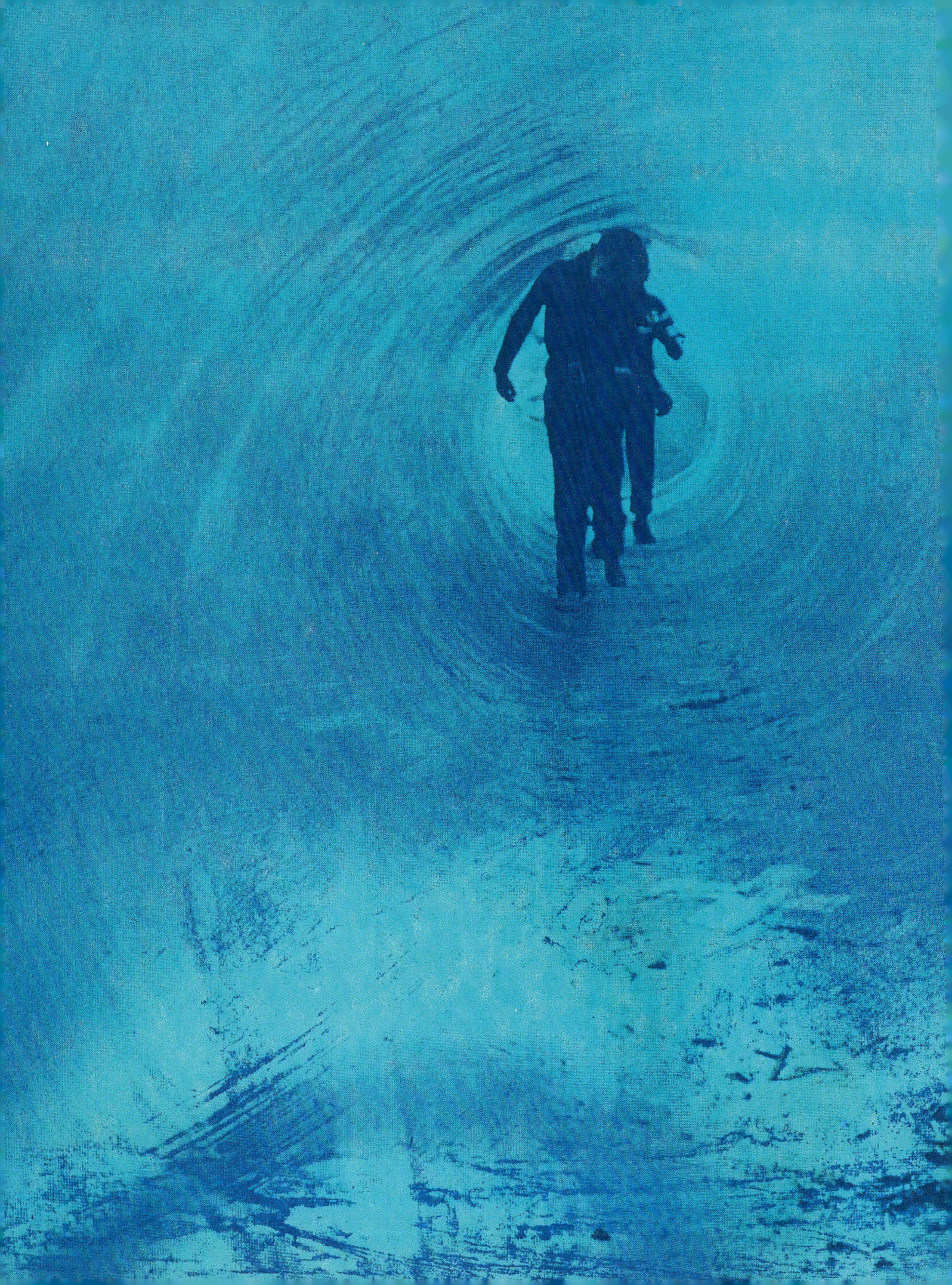

Come with us
    Leave your world behind

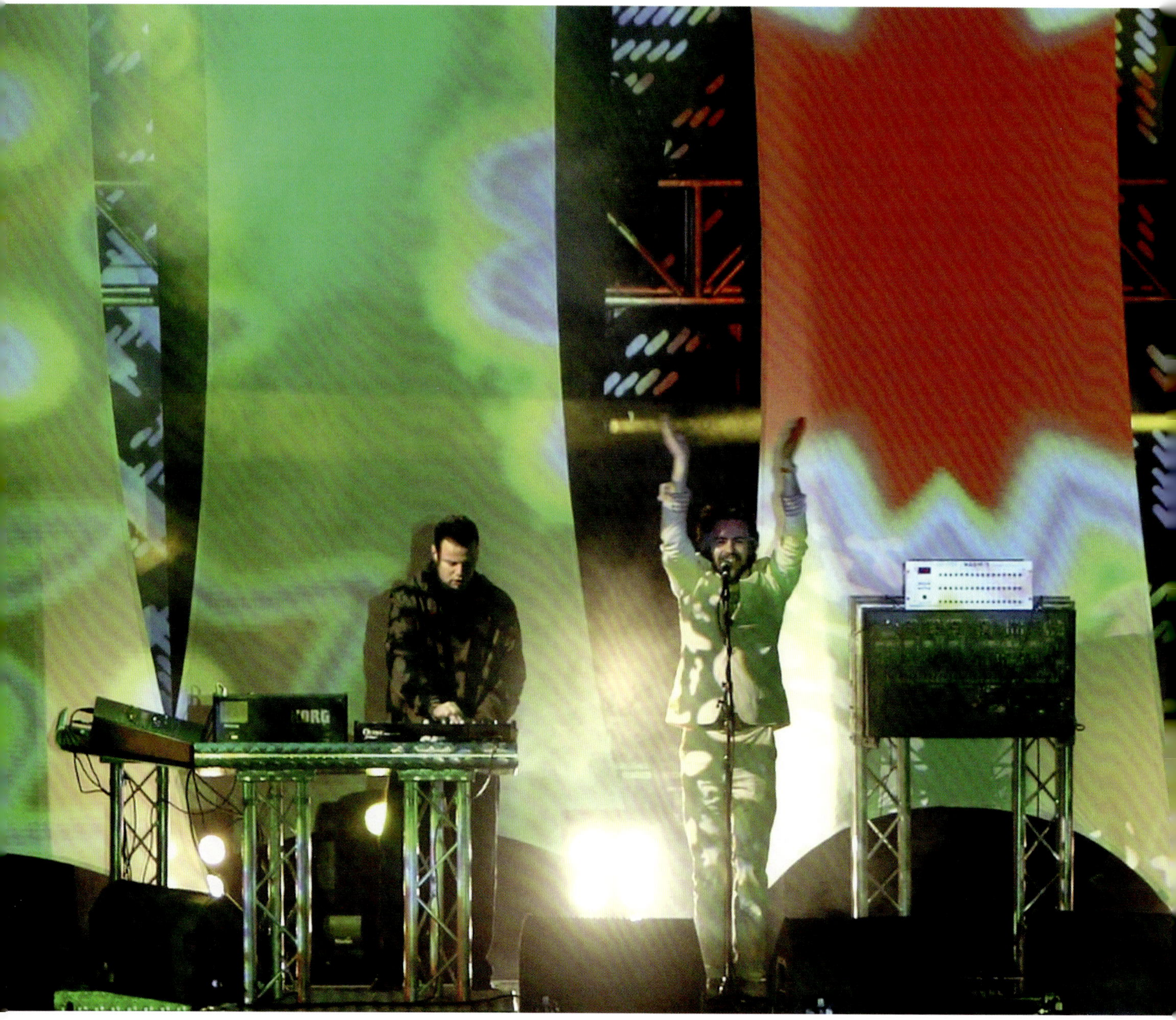
KORG

The Golden Path

'The Golden Path' is an anomaly.

A futuristic trans-dimensional pop song that poses existential questions across a relentless rhythm. A sermon from a satellite heart that's still unexpectedly beating away in the afterlife. *Paradise Lost* rewritten by Ken Kesey and soundtracked by aliens.

The song's message is broadcast from an astral plane somewhere nearer to the underworld than any celestial nirvana, a place the song's narrator doesn't understand how he got to. By the story's end, he will find himself pleading forgiveness for the eternal future of his soul. All the while, the music flows, like lava, like blood through the veins, an ecstatic counterpart to the narrator's plea for redemption.

Released as a standalone single before the compilation *Singles 93–03*, 'The Golden Path' formed a temporary union between The Chemical Brothers and The Flaming Lips – two sets of psychedelic practitioners from different sides of the Atlantic, each laser focused on rewiring the audience's brains, both on record and in concert.

'The Golden Path' was performed live once on an outdoor stage in front of Edinburgh Castle as part of the 2003 MTV Europe Music Awards. The live version used a short section of 'Hey Boy Hey Girl' as an intro.

Wayne Coyne

The Chemical Brothers never made a record that we didn't love. They've always been amazing, creative, cool guys. We loved their music but we didn't ever really think that they'd ask us to get involved. But, of course, that's one of the things they do; they get great guests to work with them. Once they ask, you immediately answer, 'Fuck yes.' We would have done anything with them, and we'd have

Previous page: The Chemical Brothers performing live with Wayne Coyne and Steve Drozd of The Flaming Lips at the MTV Europe Music Awards in Edinburgh.

Opposite: Original handwritten note from Wayne Coyne, sent with The Flaming Lips' contribution to 'The Golden Path'.

tried to make anything they sent us work. They sent us a couple of different tracks to have a think about but for us it was obvious straight away that the great, stellar one was 'The Golden Path'.

Even though we were in different countries, it felt like we were all working on tracks together. I'm always glad to make decisions but I loved even more that they were making decisions. I thought I'd just do whatever came into my mind, and Steven [Drozd, The Flaming Lips' multi-instrumentalist] could do whatever came to him, and if they didn't like it we'd give it another shot. It really takes a lot of pressure off to think, 'They do this all the time, they know what they're doing.'

One of the big inspirations for us was the song 'Spill the Wine' by Eric Burdon and War. It was a big, big hit in America in the early seventies. Eric Burdon does this kind of rap as he's telling a story. He dreams he's in a Hollywood movie and he's the star of that movie and then he gets all cosmic and journeys to the top of a mountain and he meets all these crazy women. It's him embarking on a psychedelic journey. And in 'Spill the Wine', there's even a flute, which is why Steven added the flute that follows along with me.

Added to that, I had a desire to use words that would make it sound like I'm from the South. Oklahoma is more the Midwest and I would have never used a phrase like 'over on yonder hill' in real life, but I thought if someone's listening to The Chemical Brothers and they've got these weirdos from Oklahoma on their record, why not make it stranger for them by including a kind of biblical dialogue in the song. As I was recording it, I was thinking, 'If they think this is all too cornball, I'll just change it.'

When the track arrived, it already sounded great. It had pretty much the same arrangement as the finished thing. I probably listened to it twenty times before I started to get an idea. Back then, I would take a long bike ride to think things through. I remember riding out and thinking, 'I can fit this whole story in there.' And then I had an idea to add a kind of 'Hey Jude' ending, one where you roll out this other vibe for the last couple of minutes. The end of the track feels more like a typical Chemical Brothers collaboration, a moment of rapture where you latch on to some cosmic truth, then repeat it with harmonies and whatever else is flying in from the edges.

The final version wasn't wildly different from what we'd already done. Even the effects on the vocals were pretty much as we'd recorded them. We loved it. We were just pleased to do anything with them. If they hadn't have used it, we'd have thought, 'Fuck, it was cool doing it anyway.' Everything about it was just a joy, including getting an insight into the way they record their music. Just to be a part of it was just amazing. And it's still thrilling today, knowing that we did it. Even if we hadn't recorded our parts for the song, I'd love it anyway. It's just a great rollicking, very original-sounding track.

Playing the track live in Edinburgh was utterly frightening. There's a lot of things you can do when you're recording that you can't do in a performance. Suddenly I'm on stage in front of thousands of people having to remember all those strange lines. It's not like the track has a typical melody where you can latch onto little pointers, so it was pretty scary on the night. 'Oh shit, we're doing this song in front of all of these people with the real Chemical Brothers and all their crew and all their stuff.' It was frightening. In hindsight, how great to be able to actually get together and perform. At the time, though, 'Oh shit.'

HEY TOM N' ED. - WE FUCKIN LOVE BOTH these new TRACKS...HERE'S A STEREO MIX OF OUR CONTRIBUTION - the computer files will be forth coming - we've only BEEN ABLE to WORK on the FIRST ONE SO FAR....
TALK TO YOUS GUYS SOON..
LOVE
WAYNE

君の知っている人は皆、いつか死ぬ。

FLAMING LIPS 2003

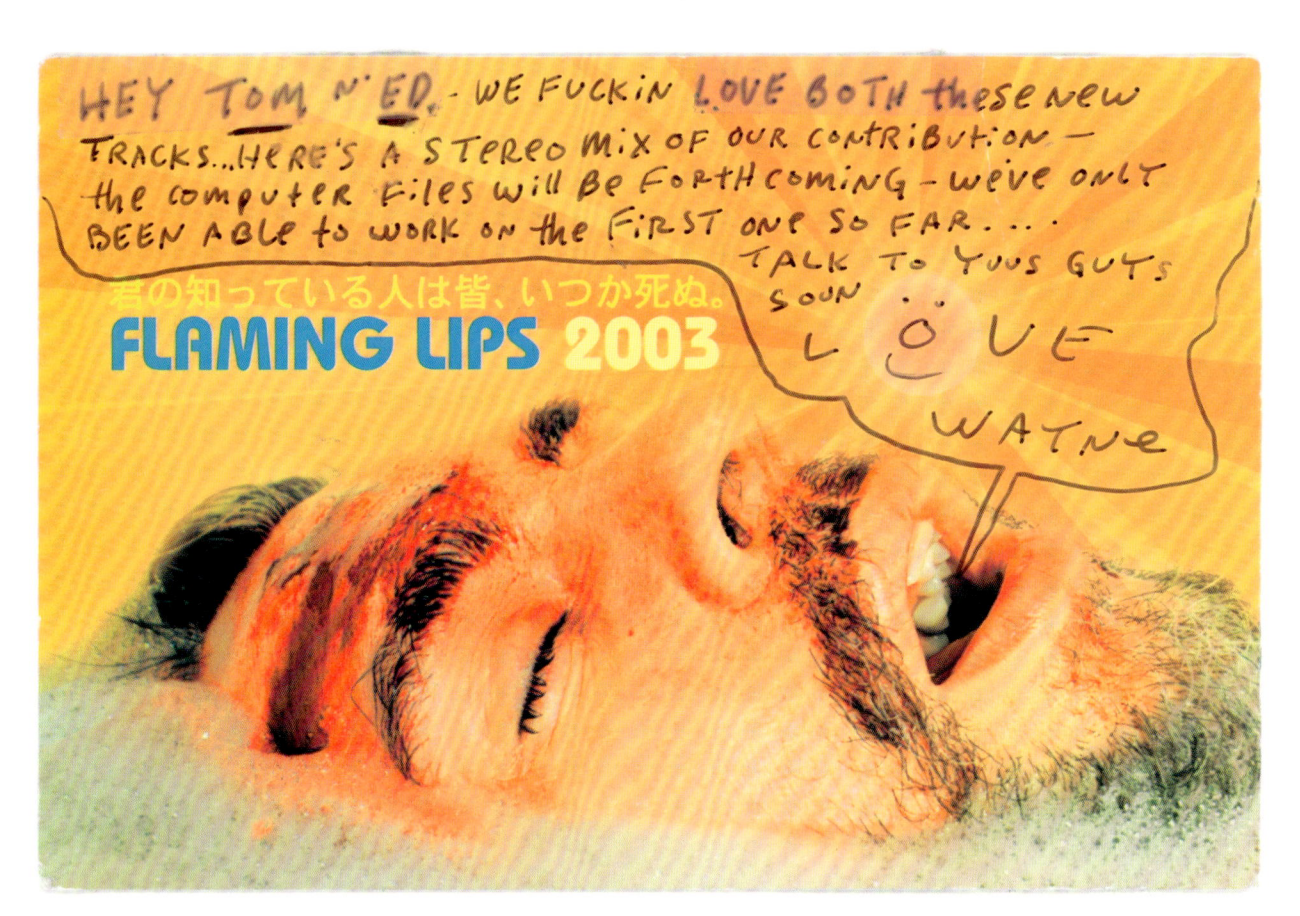

Tom Rowlands

I grew up playing the guitar, which I've always felt much more comfortable playing than the keyboard. Sometime after *Surrender*, I started experimenting with drop tunings. I used to spend a lot of time sat on the sofa watching TV with the sound off, playing and recording with a MIDI guitar. The beauty of MIDI guitars is that you can play the synthesiser with your guitar. I loved the idea of being able to control all aspects of the sound after it's recorded. The basis of the track is the MIDI guitar mixed with real guitar. 'The Golden Path' and 'Surface to Air' [from *Push the Button*] were experiments with that setup.

I loved The Flaming Lips album *Transmissions from the Satellite Heart*. I'd seen them play live and be this incredible, enveloping psychedelic freak show. When we got in touch and were talking to them about collaborating, they said how much they loved *Exit Planet Dust*. The track they loved the most was 'Playground for a Wedgeless Firm'. That was the last track I'd imagined anyone falling for, but Wayne put me right saying, 'No man, it's the sound of spiders!' This weird instrumental track, fun to make but you'd never imagine it would be the one track to freak out America's greatest living psychedelic rock 'n' roll band.

It was one of the easiest collaborations we've ever done. They sent what they thought was a rough version of the vocal and the flute part. We thought it was awesome already, we loved it. They'd thought there might be some back and forth, but it was all there in that first take. The combination of the journeyed voice and the flute... it really reminded me of 'Going up the Country' by Canned Heat, which was an early obsession of mine and Ed's in university days.

We didn't give any guidelines for what we wanted from them; we don't really do that with collaborations. Making the decision to collaborate with an artist is to trust in their work, their performance. If it came back and it needed steering or it didn't quite fit, then you try to make it work, but with The Flaming Lips what we first heard was amazing, that's what we used. It's all we ever imagined it could be. I wish they were all like that. The decision is the trust.

The fact that it came out on the *Singles 93–03* gave it licence to be this weird little thing on its own. It didn't need to fit into an album; that compilation gave it a space to be its own, standalone thing.

It did take on a different life when we did the Edinburgh show, which was pretty surreal and so unlike anything we'd normally do. The Flaming Lips were very keen, and I think that was enough to get us on board. We'd never done a playback before, so it seemed like a good chance to get the guitar out. I don't think the Lips had ever done anything to a backing track like that before either. I think a massive part of us doing it was the excitement of meeting Wayne and Steven, those amazing, inspirational people.

Recently, Wayne's vocal has ended up in the most intense point of the live set. It's one of our favourite points – a disembodied voice that comes in a breakdown section halfway through 'Escape Velocity' that we pile all these crazy effects onto before the whole thing erupts. Night after night you see it having the same kind of effect on the audience as the one we got when we first merged those two tracks in the studio. The voice is taken from the original recording they sent us. If you listen closely to the sample, you can hear him rustling the papers as he's reading back the lyrics. I always love that when we play live and you can hear something so real, the unaltered sound of the track being originally recorded.

'The Golden Path' is quite restrained, a contained piece of music. But in that live context as part of 'Escape Velocity', it really is the opposite of that.

Ed Simons

We both loved The Flaming Lips. When we first started touring the States, you'd often find yourself in a hotel room with jetlag at some mad hour. Their track 'She Don't Use Jelly' seemed to always be on MTV, no matter what time you turned the TV on. We've loved their vibe since then.

Collaborating with Wayne and Steven felt very different, in that we weren't going to meet to record. Everything up to that point had been done in person. In those days, we had a belief that if we approached someone we liked, then they'd be interested in working with us. That sense of 'If you build it, they will come'.

It's quite a natural fit, us and them. They're part of an American psychedelic culture that developed in a different direction to the one we work in, but the two things quite easily lock together.

When the fully formed song came back, the vocals just immediately jumped out, and then you really lose yourself in Steve's flute part. It's hard to imagine a more perfect Chemical Brothers vocal. The metaphysical experience and a big moment of transcendence – it was all so perfect when it arrived.

When I brought it home from the studio, a group of mates ended up back at my house and everyone was just dancing to it on an endless loop, into the night. Those are some of the most exciting memories of that track, seeing the look of disbelief on friends' faces.

There was a big DJ at the time who was dismissive of the track, saying he couldn't even understand what it was, incredulous about the rhythm track. Maybe it was quite different, and harder to pigeonhole. A driving Krautrock beat, a guitar line that's been synthesised, and this mad acid-fried lay-preacher vocal. It's quite an idiosyncratic production, a definite sidestep. I remember being at a club in Ibiza and Justin Robertson played it in the middle of a set. Just hearing it over there felt like a putsch, a crazed intervention.

We'd never been interested in doing live television before; it didn't really seem like the most effective way of getting our music across. But the MTV Awards was a huge thing, and the fact that Steven and Wayne were coming over meant the die was cast. We did a rehearsal in the afternoon which went OK, but the thing I remember most was being looked after by Wayne. He was the motivation we needed. On the night, they got Vin Diesel to introduce us, just after a warm-up DJ had played Seal's 'Kiss from a Rose' to get the crowd going.

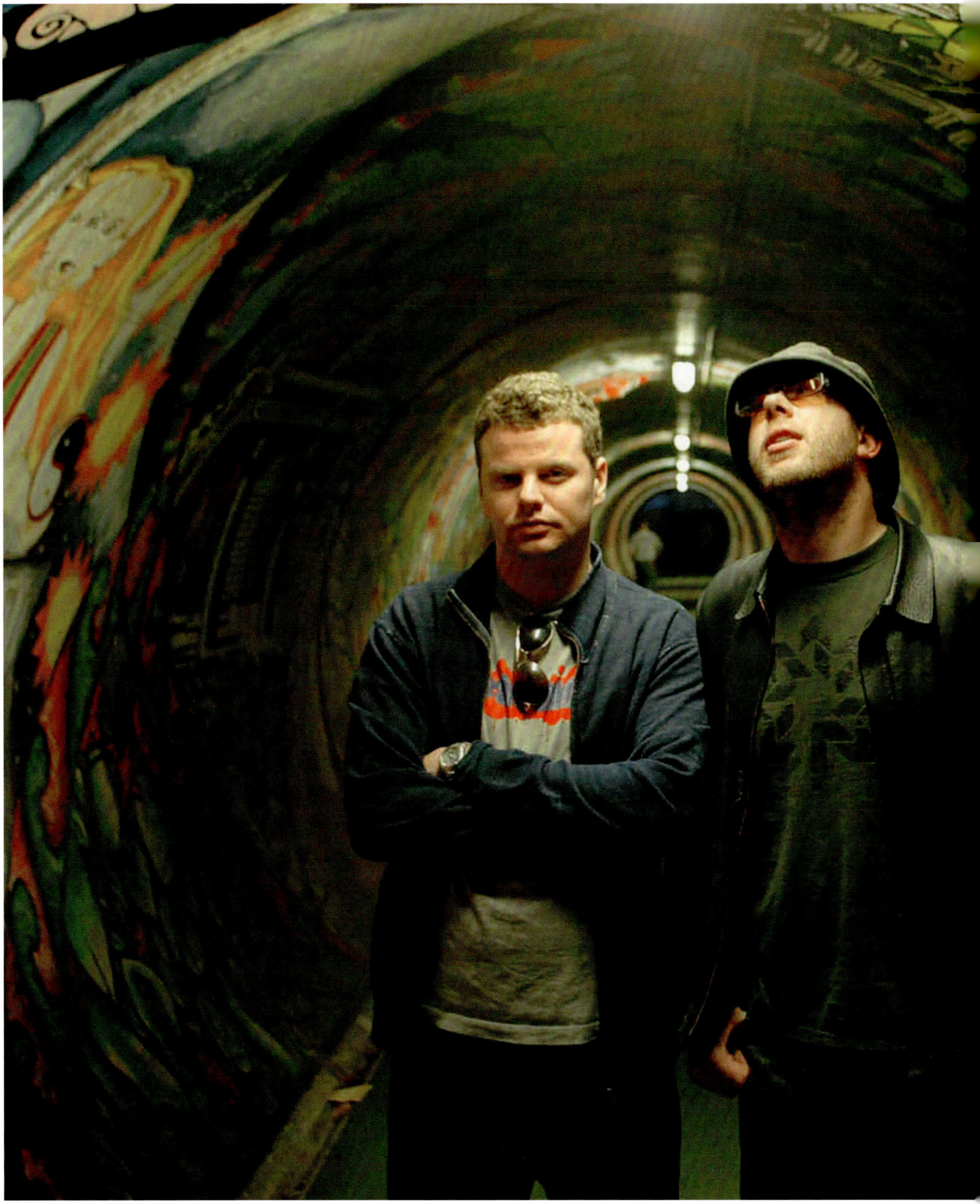

Tom and Ed in the tunnel that leads to the main stages at the Big Day Out. Auckland, New Zealand, 22 January 2005.

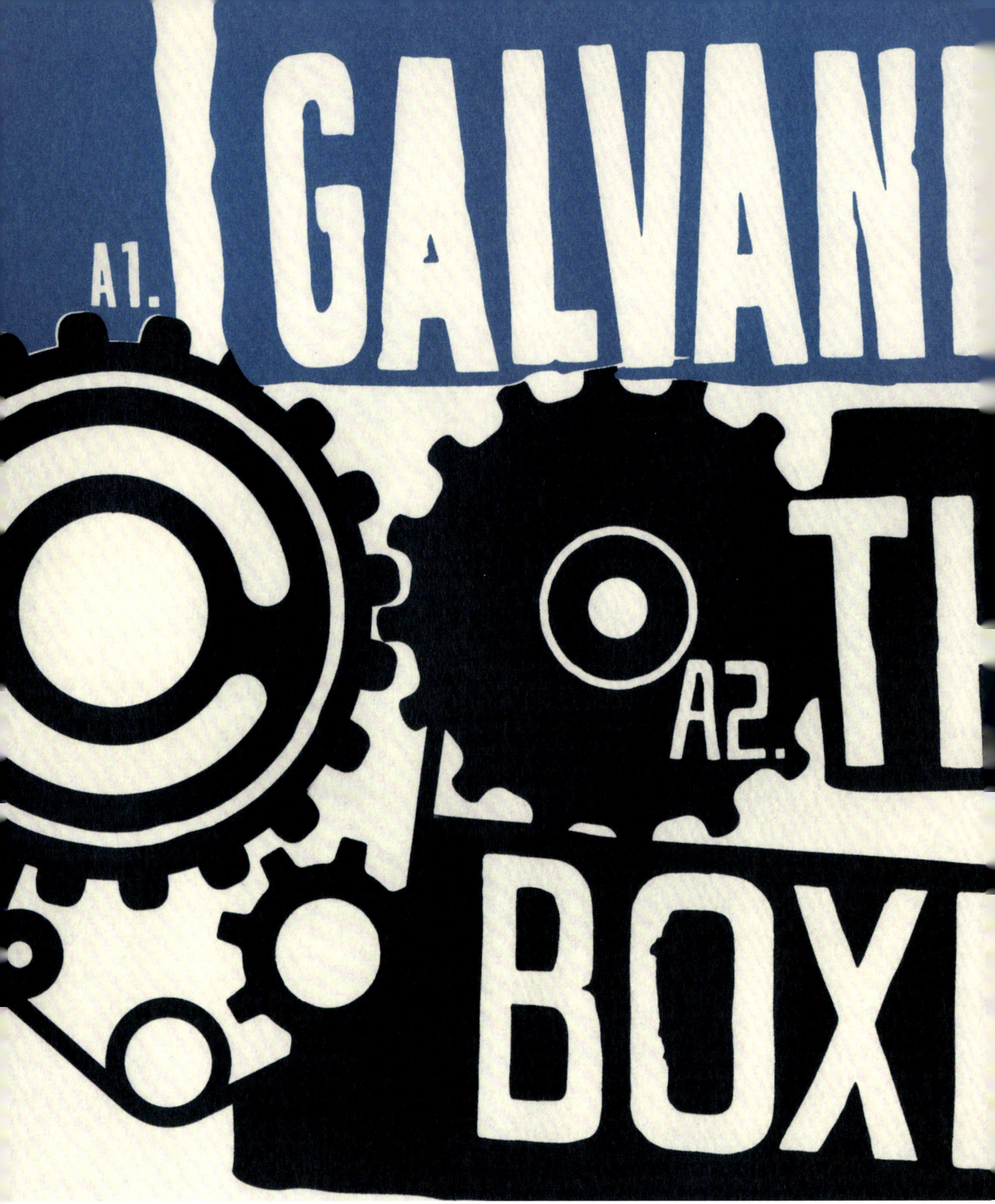
A1.
GALVAN
A2.
TH
BOX

Galvanize

Although constructed from wild and disparate elements – sampled North African strings, rhymes from New York rap royalty and a resolute groove that's equal parts hip hop block party and illegal acid house rave – 'Galvanize' makes perfect sense. It takes the irresistible feel of a classic Native Tongues record then transplants it onto a bold, bright electronic chug. In doing so, The Chemical Brothers spin a musical globe, creating a beautifully borderless sound that plays out like clashing radio stations blaring from car windows, somehow fusing together for a few glorious minutes.

During The Dust Brothers' early years, Q-Tip's inimitable voice was a cornerstone of their DJ sets thanks to Beastie Boys' peerless track 'Get It Together'. His unique unhurried flow was instantly recognisable among crazed 303 meltdowns, clattering drum loops and transcendent psychedelic rock 'n' roll. 'Galvanize' somehow channels the frenzied spirit of those sets, with the sample (from Moroccan singer Najat Aatabou's 1992 track 'Hadi Kedba Bayna') having the same kind of discombobulating effect as the whoosh of 'Tomorrow Never Knows' or the relentless wah-wah riff of 'Chemical Beats'.

The video for 'Galvanize' was directed by Adam Smith – his first for the band after a decade of working on their live visuals. It manages to capture the thrill of sneaking into a nightclub when you're too young to be in there – a rite of passage for generations of kids besotted with music and dancing from an early age.

Tom Rowlands

We'd played a gig in the States where someone had given me a bunch of CD compilations on a label called Ellipsis Arts. I'd put them in my bag because they looked pretty cool and promptly forgot about them until a long time after we'd got back home. Quite often I'll get records and then trawl through them, dropping the needle to try to find interesting sounds or voices that might be good to sample. I was in the studio absent-mindedly listening to one of the Ellipsis Arts CDs while doing something else, when 'WOAH. What is that?' What was that blast of sound? The strings just sounded so powerful, I was immediately back in the room.

It took me a long time to figure out how to make the sample work and bring it into a kind of 4/4 world. I had the sample for ages, and I'd always try to work out how we could use it. It was always the sample we had, the one that I'd intermittently try to write drums for. Finding a way to make it fit was almost like unlocking some special power. We'd keep coming back to it as an idea, always thinking that it would be amazing with a rapper.

We were so excited about the demo of the song; it was one of those rare times when you use a sample and drop it into disparate sounds and rhythms, and it all still feels connected. All those things came together and didn't feel bolted on in any way – in fact they accentuated the energy of the track.

We sent the track to Q-Tip for him to record in the States. We were so excited about what might come back. When the DAT arrived from him, it had 'Same Old Song' written on it. That didn't sound like the kind of title I'd imagined as a response to the track. We put it on and all the dreams we'd had of having someone as inspiring and brilliant as Q-Tip on a record were immediately quashed. It was depressing. I couldn't stop thinking, 'This can't be it.' It hadn't fulfilled my dreams of what Q-Tip would be like on a Chemical Brothers track, and that track in particular. The instrumental did not sound like the 'Same Old Song'.

We'd paid him some money already, which was a good thing because it forced me to

Opposite: Stills from the 'Galvanize' music video, directed by Adam Smith.

say, 'This could be better.' It felt like we had to pursue it. Q-Tip gave us another day of his time, so Ed and I went to New York to record with him at the Hit Factory in New York. The Hit Factory is legendary, one of the last real old-school studios. Everyone has recorded there over the years.

Going into the studio with Q-Tip was totally transformative. We'd gone in knowing that what we made on that day, in that studio, was really important to us. How were we going to get from this bland idea to greatness?

We came to the studio with the *Don't hold back* line, which gave him a jumping-off point. Q-Tip started freestyling and one of the words he used was 'galvanized'. I stopped him as I thought it was such a cool word, and the kind of word you'd never hear in this kind of record, ours or his. From there on, he was absolutely incredible. The whole time, we were floored, thinking, 'This is why you're so good.' It was absolutely natural.

Often you work on an extended timeframe where things can keep rolling on. There's no pressure as you can tweak this or come back to that in a few weeks. This was really not that. When you have to make something happen, and you've got six hours or so to make it happen, that's daunting. When we walked in there, we genuinely didn't know how it was going to go. You're in the studio with Q-Tip and you're there because you're in love with his records and his voice. You just want it to work and hopefully get entertained in the process. 'Hit me with it, do the thing!'

When we left, we knew we had something fantastic. We were lucky to record the session with a phenomenal engineer called Vaughan Merrick. He did a brilliant job capturing the vocal and letting the session really flow. When I brought it back home and worked out the *Push the button* call-and-response section and the drop, the whole thing just felt ridiculously exciting. 'Galvanize' went on to be the most played record on Radio 1 in the UK that year.

Adam Smith

I'd wanted to direct music videos for Tom and Ed for ages, but I was very much thought of as the visuals guy. Away from The Chemical Brothers, I'd been working with The Streets, graduating from their visuals to making a video for 'Blinded by the Lights'. People loved it and it proved to Tom and Ed and the record company that I was up to the job of making one of their videos. When they played me 'Galvanize', there was something so magical about the melody and rhythm of the sample. It's utterly hypnotic.

I started thinking about the film *La Haine*, specifically the character Saïd, and also a documentary I'd loved called *Clowns in the Hood*. It was directed by filmmaker and fashion photographer David LaChapelle, and later became a feature film called *Rize*. *Clowns in the Hood* showed a new style of dancing called krumping. Dancers would battle each other in these really physical showdowns and a lot of the dancers wore clown make-up, which had been a major part of the live backdrop for The Chemical Brothers' gigs for years already.

Those two influences meshed together in my head, and the idea and look for the video was there. It would follow three kids getting ready to sneak out to a club for a dance battle. That idea resonated with how I'd grown up going to clubs as an underage teenager, leaving the house to the sound of protesting parents. I was very lucky because London clubland was really exciting back then, both in the big West End club nights and in the empty buildings where people were putting on illegal parties playing electro, rare groove and hip hop.

Paused in Cosmic Reflection 217

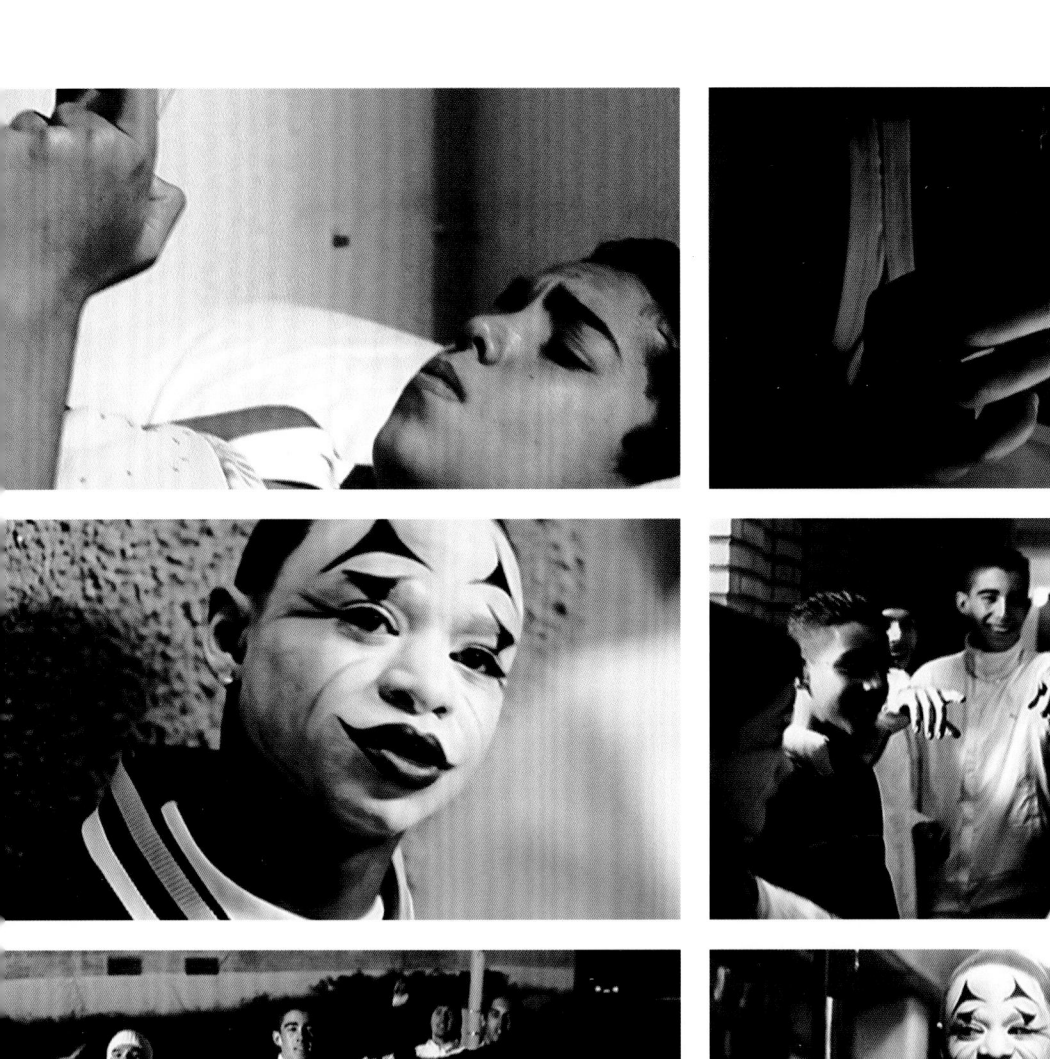

I've always loved watching dancers ever since going out to clubs – that kind of motion has been a big part of the band's live visuals since the early days. I wanted the video to reflect the euphoria of being young and being out at night, heading to places where you really shouldn't have been.

When the kids go into the club space in the music video, it flips into colour a bit like in the Wim Wenders film *Wings of Desire*. It wasn't the most subtle idea, but it chimes with seeing things through the eyes of a kid who's just walked into a club and everything suddenly gets a lot brighter. And as much as the video references lots of art house films, it also nods to John Hughes's films in the way the kids acted and got treated by other people, the way they got the piss taken out of them before they went out. Kids rebelling and daring to be different. All those ideas were thrown into the script.

I'd originally wanted to shoot in Paris but we ended up shooting in Spain. We cast kids out in Malaga, none of whom had ever done any acting before. I was determined to get the real krumpers over from LA. We ended up flying three of them over. One of them (Lil PeeWee) was quite short, so with clown make-up he could pass for one of the kids. During the shoot, Lil PeeWee pushed himself so hard when he was dancing he had to go outside to be sick. He kept saying it was normal.

The element of the video where the kids get caught wasn't based entirely on personal experience of underage clubbing, but it was based on the nagging idea that it might happen when you're underage in somewhere you shouldn't be. Are you going to get in, are you going to get thrown out? One summer, me, Joe Wright and our friend Simon were in the Café de Paris and I nicked a whole packet of plastic tickets that ended up being VIP free entry cards. We spent the whole summer selling those to people. Maybe in some way, the kids in the video got the payback that we never got.

Even though I'd worked on their visuals for years, it felt like such an honour to be making a video for Tom and Ed.

Watching The Chemical Brothers' videos back at Adam Buxton's Bug event, I was struck by just how amazing that body of work was. They're artists who understand artists. It's very different to commissioners, or financiers, or executive producers. Tom and Ed pick the right person and they trust that person. And they realise that sometimes it doesn't work. If you don't have freedom to fail, you're never going to make anything that isn't diluted and mediocre. Tom and Ed take risks. I really think they deserve a lot of credit for that, as collaborators and creative curators.

Paused in Cosmic Reflection

220   **The Chemical Brothers**

Paused in Cosmic Reflection

Stills from the 'Midnight Madness' music video, directed by Dom & Nic.

222 The Chemical Brothers

Paused in Cosmic Reflection 223

The Salmon Dance

Did you know . . . that I could go to Japan . . . and back?

You're kidding!

'The Salmon Dance' is an infotainment guide to the lives and loves of migratory fish set to a chunky, skipping hip hop rhythm track. A *Finding Nemo* for the edibles generation, the track features Fatlip – hip-hop star and one of the four original members of West Coast group The Pharcyde – who introduces his friend Sammy the Salmon, along with a brand-new, not-complicated piscine dance routine.

Dom & Nic's video for 'The Salmon Dance' picks up the baton proffered by the track to create a perfect moment of baked wonderment featuring an aquarium packed full of fantastical fish. Some of them are rapping, others beatboxing and a few more are swimming in beautiful fractal formations, all in front of a bombed teenager.

Amazing. Jeez.

Tom Rowlands

The working title was 'Cartoon'. The song always had a weird, childlike quality. The groove is funny and odd, but it was addictive and I kept coming back to listen to it. Fatlip tapped into that side of it and brought the cartoon idea to life with his talking salmon. Definitely one of our more divisive songs but we love it, and we love the joy it brings.

Fatlip

So, let's talk salmon.

I was very excited to collaborate with The Chemical Brothers and when I heard the track, I started writing and brainstorming ideas about a concept. I always start with a theme or hook when I write, and there was already sort of a vocal hook on the track. The now famous line *I'm floating upstream again* was my main focus.

Cut to four weeks later and I still hadn't come up with anything good. I tried many, many angles but nothing seemed to work with that line. I even thought the song could be about reincarnation . . . get it? *I'm floating stream again . . .*

Cut to seven weeks and ten studio sessions later – the record company told me I had one more session to finish before the deadline . . . I still had nothing.

Literally in the final hour of that last session, I thought about a fish and in five minutes I had the entire song written. I thought to myself, The Chemical Brothers are either gonna love me or hate me for this. The engineer (Cort Pfister) looked up some salmon facts on the internet and recorded them at the end of the song. His voice was exactly like how I would think a talking salmon would sound. That song became one of YouTube's first viral videos with so many people getting into doing the dance.

And that is how the legend of Sammy the Salmon was born.

Ed Simons

After it came out, we met the track's engineer, Cort, at a gig we played in an incredible venue in Brooklyn (McCarren Park Pool). It was like something out of *The Warriors*. He was a total dude, and he seemed to have got all the way back to the dressing room through every stage of security by telling people he was Sammy the Salmon.

Paused in Cosmic Reflection   225

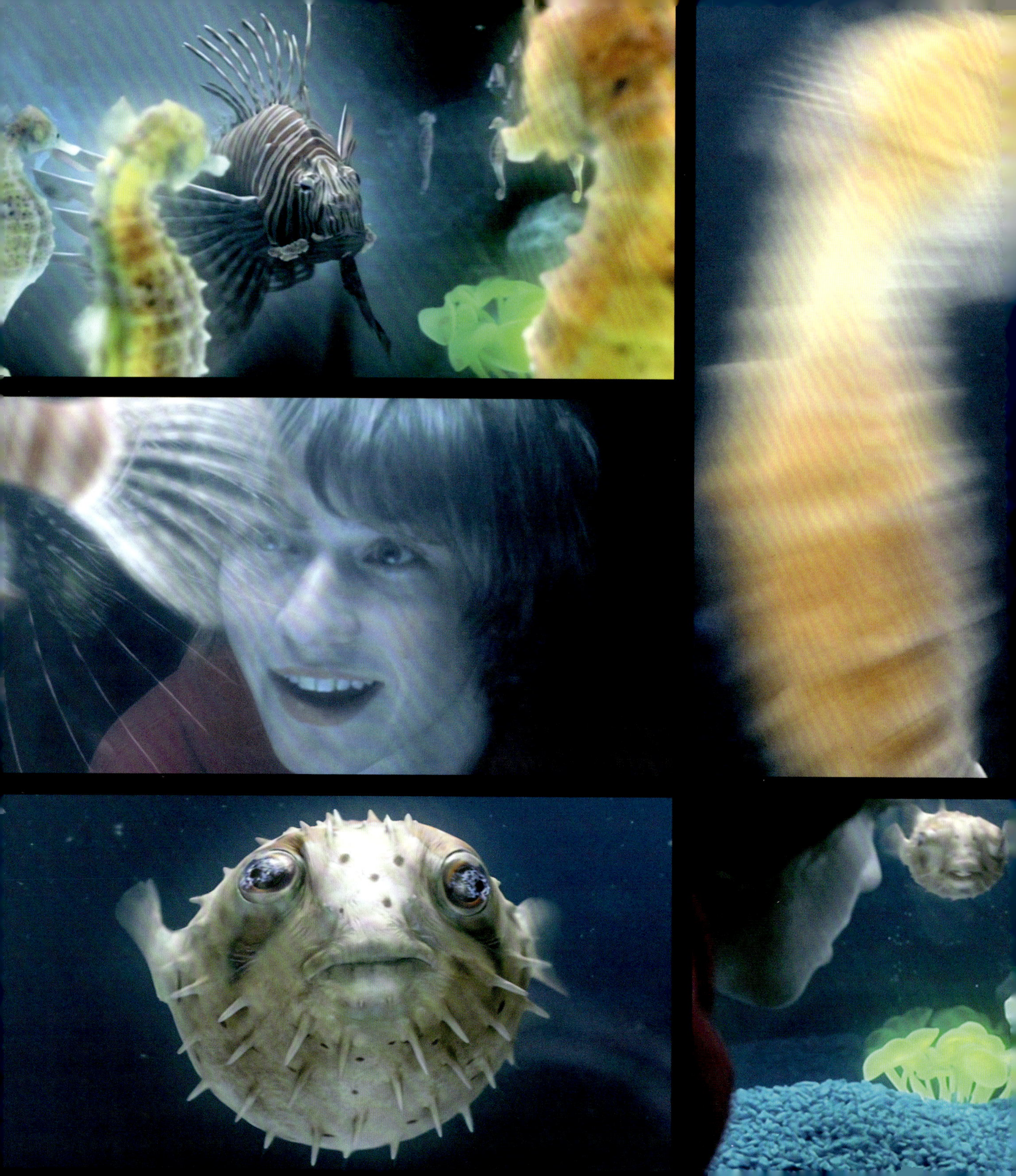

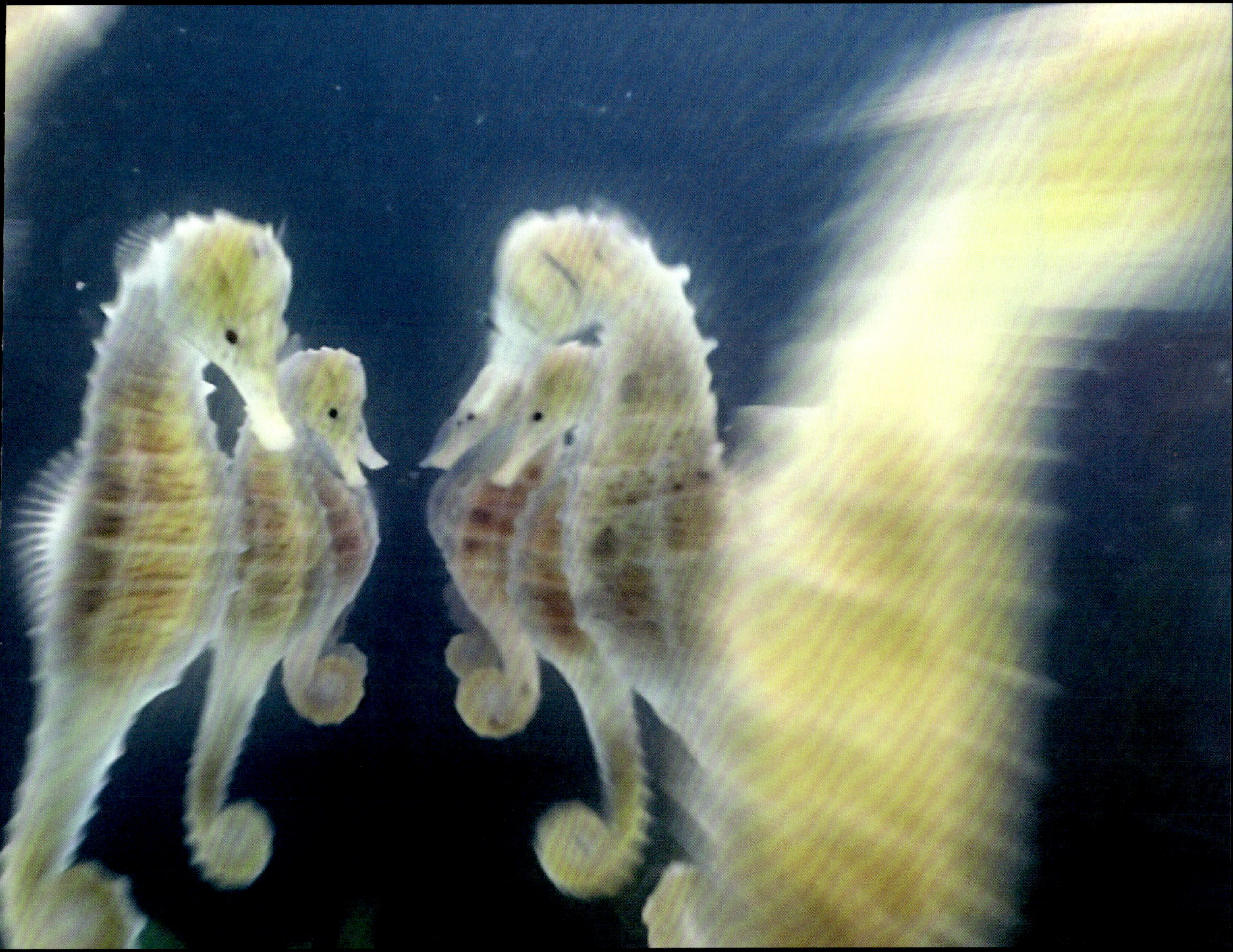

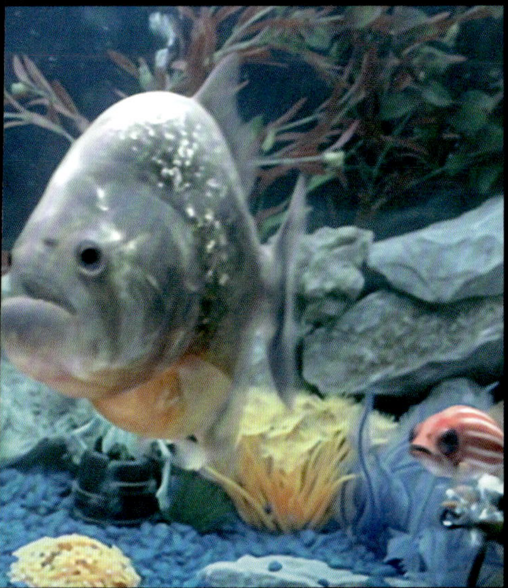

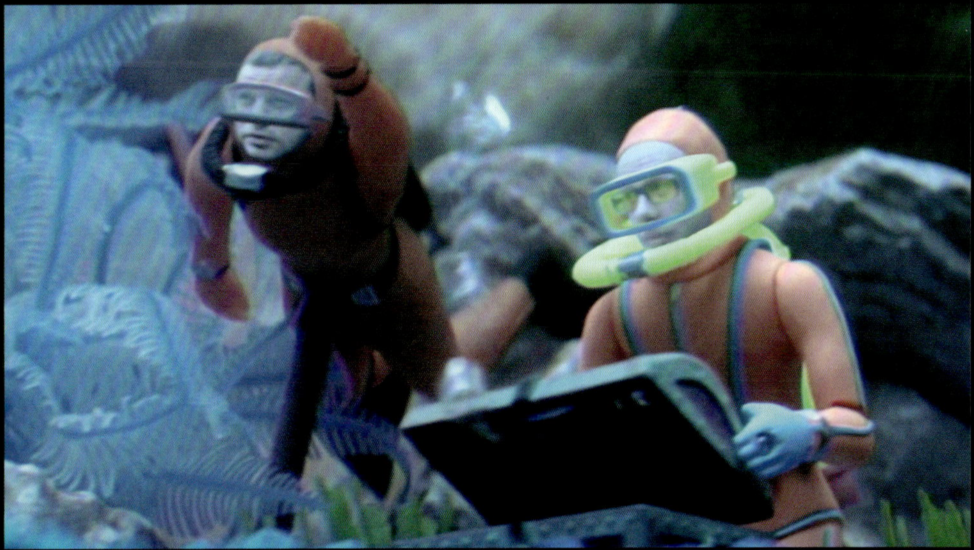

Previous page: Stills from the 'The Salmon Dance' music video, directed by Dom & Nic.

228 **The Chemical Brothers**

Paused in Cosmic Reflection 229

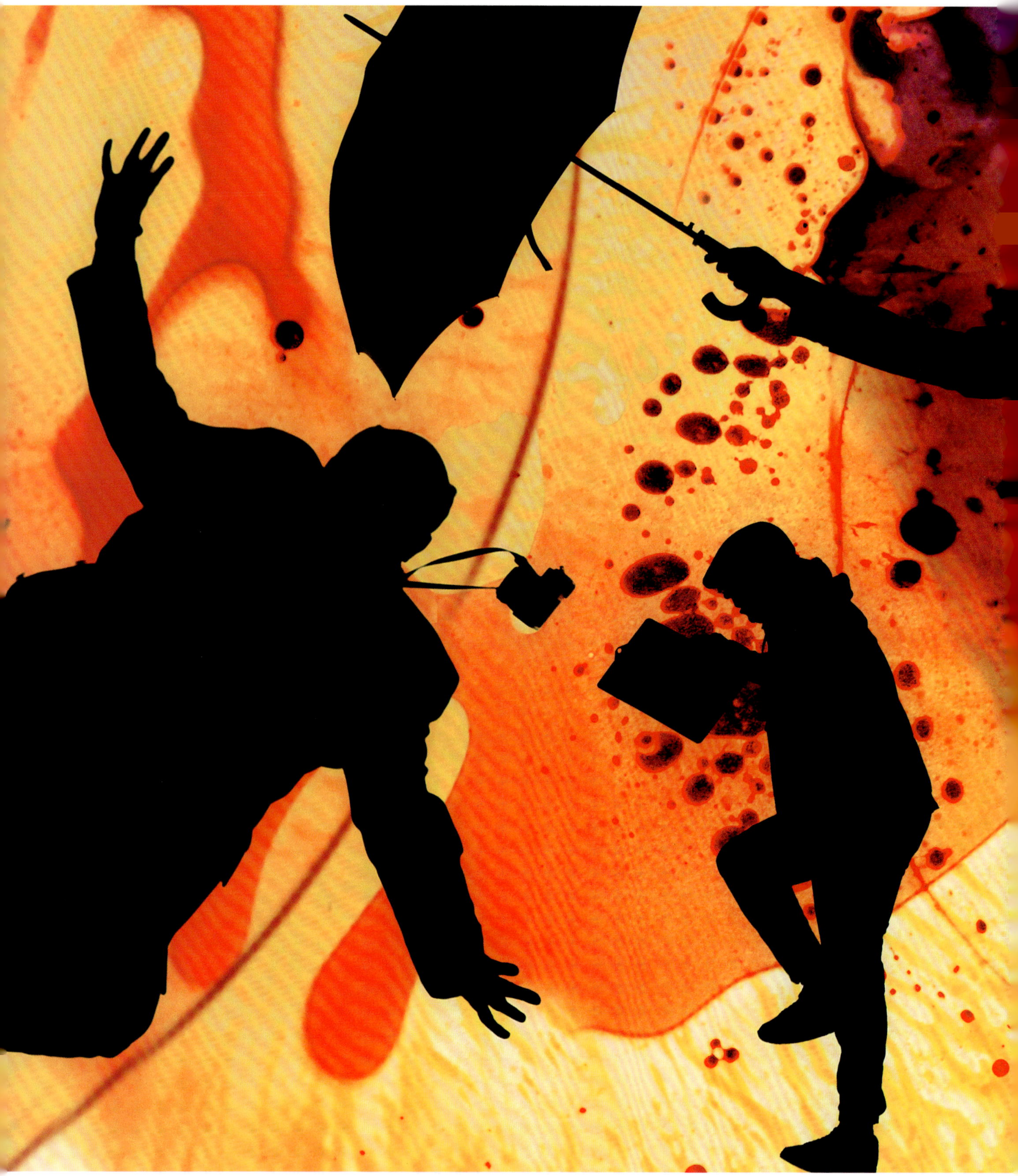

Further

It starts with a signal, like Marconi's morse code transmitted through a feedback loop that bounces across the airwaves. A female voice joins, looping around and around, higher and higher, a siren's enchantment that could crash you against the speakers. This is an entry point into a world mapped out in analogue sound, a world full of dusty old machines that have been pushed beyond their limits and rattle, overheating to the verge of meltdown. *This might be the one to finish them off, might as well push them harder, take them further.*

The Chemical Brothers' seventh album was a departure in that it eschewed guest voices and internalised the band's work process. It is the sound of freedom. It fuses hard, exploratory electronic music to moments of unalloyed beauty, melodies torn and shaped out of distortion until almost celestial.

Although 'Escape Velocity' was released as a 12-inch, *Further* was always meant to be listened to – or watched – as a whole piece. The accompanying visuals by Adam Smith (and Marcus Lyall) were shown as an integral part of the band's gigs at The Roundhouse in London, where the album was presented in full for the first time over four nights prior to its release (20–23 May 2010).

Tom Rowlands

Each record you make is in some way a reaction to the one you made before. And *Further* was definitely a reaction to *We Are the Night*. The earlier record had a lot of brilliant, disparate voices on it. The reaction was to do the opposite, to follow one idea and one feel for the whole record. It was definitely a record that wasn't made with an eye on the outside world. *We Are the Night* had been very open, open to voices and ideas and welcoming things into our world. This was definitely a retreat into sound, with a real freedom to mess around.

When we started recording *Further*, the studio at my house was at a point where I could record and mix properly. I'd used it for writing before but by then it was the equivalent of any studio we used to work in in London. Everything was up and running. Having the studio at home reminded me of how I used to work at my parents' house. I'd often work on something, and then I'd leave a loop going round and go and do something else like make lunch or listen to the radio. I'd still be able to half hear it going round from upstairs; I'd still have one ear on what was going on. It's a really good way of telling you what needs to happen with the track. *Further* was the first time I could work on music at home and really marvel at the power coming out of the speakers, never more so than on 'Escape Velocity'.

The working title for that track was 'EMS Monster', because it's mainly played on an EMS Synthi AKS. On top of the EMS, it features pretty much every synthesiser I owned up to that point too. There's a freedom in the album and especially on 'Escape Velocity'. Sometimes when you're working on a track, there's often an internal nag that says that it has to be a certain thing or has to make sense in a certain way to fit in. It has to be precisely structured and edited down. Part of me loves whittling something down to its core, creating the tightest possible arrangement. Some tracks benefit massively from that. After *We Are the Night*, I wasn't worried about those kinds of constraints. There was no compulsion for a track like 'Escape Velocity' to be anything. It could – and should – develop in its own time and go where it needs to go.

I can remember being stood at the back of the room while playing the track at full volume through the massive sound system. The whole room was vibrating and rattling with layer upon layer of synthesiser. It was ridiculously exciting to listen to; I felt like I was levitating. Often when you're making records, you have an idealised vision of what effect a record might have on the listener. The power it had listening to it then, at two o'clock on a Tuesday afternoon... what the hell would it be like at Fabric or Glastonbury?

A few months later, I was out driving when Zane Lowe played 'Escape Velocity' on the radio for the first time. It sounded incredible. And then he played it again. It's nearly twelve minutes long. It was such a great feeling, and it reinforced the idea that you didn't always need a track to fit into any particular box. The form is important to what it means as a piece of music. Part of the excitement is the length, the idea that you're going on a trip. It's going to last as long as it needs to last. It remains an awesome point in the live set – it feels like a reset, a point to strap in.

We were lucky to have Stephanie Dosen as the voice of the record. Stephanie is always such a nice presence in the studio. I love her voice and how open she is in how we work together. And there's a lot of me singing on the record, which was something I'd never really pushed before. My voice had only been used as a texture on our records before that point, meshed into the mix. When Boys Noize did a remix of 'Swoon', they had a section of my vocal on its own. Hearing that was quite a shock, but when it's not you mixing it yourself there's less of a barrier to being able to hear it.

When we were making *Further*, we wanted to play the album in its entirety to an audience. It would be the first time we'd ever presented a record like that: showing the way that it all worked together as a whole. It was envisaged as a homogenous thing and lent itself to being played start to finish. Then came the idea of visualising every song for the performance, bringing all of those ideas to the screen. Looking back, maybe playing a new album in its entirety to a room full of people who had never heard it before was a bit of a crazy idea.

Ed Simons

One of my most powerful memories around the making of *Further* was the impact 'Swoon' had on me. During the period we wrote and recorded *Further*, I suffered quite a serious bout of depression. I guess, like many, as midlife came into view I became quite lost. The depression manifested as an experience of invasive, negative, panicky thoughts going round and round. I remember at this time driving down to the studio and working on mixes and arrangements of 'Swoon', and I became completely absorbed in that beautiful redemptive swirl, the powerful lyric of hope. 'Swoon' became a balm for the soul. It was an instant tonic; I'd take the latest mix home and just have it as a source of comfort. Even now when we play it, I can become overwhelmed by the connection I feel to it and how that music helped me find a way back to serenity.

Stephanie Dosen

In 2002, I was just starting out as a singer-songwriter. I was living in Wisconsin and somehow I managed to get one of my songs on the CD that came with CMJ's *New Music Monthly* magazine. It was just me singing with my little guitar. It was a really big deal back then; we always used to have that magazine sitting around the house. And The Chemical Brothers were on the cover of that issue and 'Star Guitar' was on that same CD. I was a fan of theirs already, and it felt pretty cool to me.

A few years later, Simon Raymonde found my songs on MySpace. He got in touch asking if I needed a producer. I almost died because I was the biggest Cocteau Twins fan. Just totally obsessed. I was thirty at the time and was thinking of giving up music as it wasn't working – then my main inspiration from my favourite band reached out. There was no coolness to me, I was just putting my music up on MySpace, but, for the first time ever, it was possible for someone overseas to hear music and connect. Obviously that message completely changed my life. I sold everything I had and moved to London to make music.

I'd love to say there was something magical about how I met The Chemical Brothers, but I think they heard a record of mine and got in touch with Simon in 2009. I was working with Massive Attack at the time, and I remember being really shocked and really excited about the fact they'd got in touch. Another example of someone reaching out when you least expect it.

I went to the band's studio and Tom had all these things for me to sing. He kept saying he wanted me to fill in wherever he couldn't. I said, 'What are you talking about? Your singing is great. You don't need me, you have this.' Listening back to the album, I love the way our voices work together. Maybe me being there helped him to channel something in himself. Sometimes having another person there can give you the confidence to try things out.

There was a real synergy in the room when we worked, everything was very open and open-ended. Tom never said, 'You're going to be on the record.' I left the studio without really knowing how my voice would be used and that was fine. Maybe he'd use what we did, maybe he wouldn't; it had been nice to do it all the same.

A while later, they invited me to one of their shows at The Roundhouse. I went with Simon, still not knowing what had come of the recordings we'd done. The Chemical Brothers had invited me backstage, so I went to the green room before the gig and had a drink and Twix bar or something. They were going on, so we said good luck and went to our seats to watch the show.

The first thing I heard was my voice blasting out from the stage. They were playing 'Snow', which I still hadn't heard. I figured at that point I'd made the cut. I looked at Simon, who asked, 'Is this you?' And then I turned to the woman sat on my other side and shouted, 'This is me!' She must have thought, 'Who is this crazy, crazy American I'm stuck next to?' It was such a strange trip, from Wisconsin with an acoustic guitar to meeting heroes and working with incredible people, and then eventually hearing my voice coming back at me real loud with all the lights and the visuals. It was such a fun way to find out that I was on a Chemical Brothers record.

Adam Smith

I got the music for *Further* when I was filming the first *Doctor Who* episode with Matt Smith in Cardiff in 2009. There's a lovely trail along the River Taff that takes you from the castle right up the river. I used to use it as an escape route; it was the perfect place to go and clear my head from all of pressure around filming.

So, I went for a really long walk with the music and immersed myself. My first thought was that we had to work out a way to bring it all together as a film. When I came to the fourth song – 'Dissolve' – I was hit by the lyric that goes: *Caroline, Caroline/Did your heart just fuse with mine?* I thought, it's all about her, isn't it? It's Caroline's journey. That idea seemed in line with lots of the band's videos

The Chemical Brothers

Further

Paused in Cosmic Reflection 235

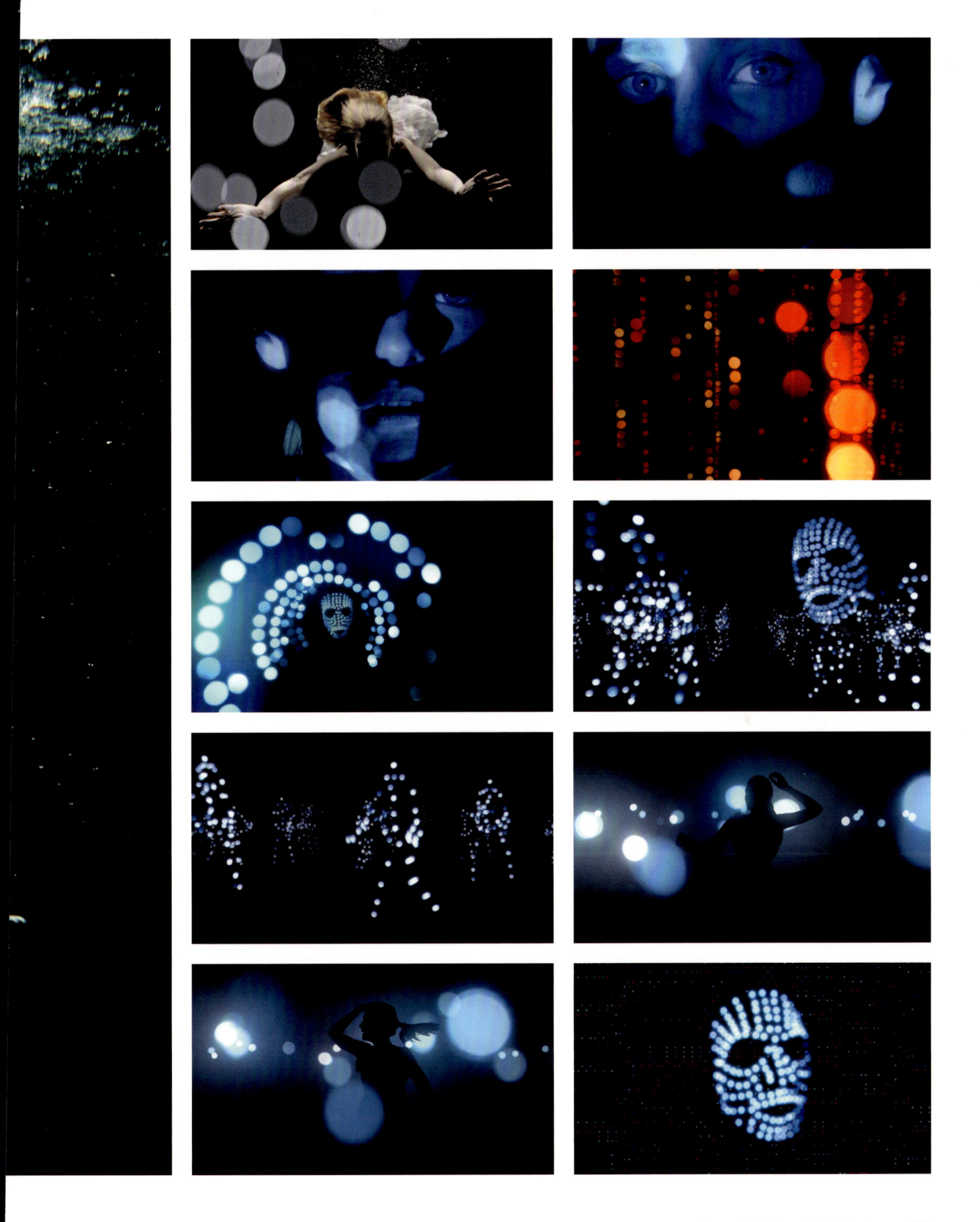

236　**The Chemical Brothers**

Previous page: Stills from the *'Escape Velocity'* music video, directed by Adam Smith.

Opposite: Actress Romola Garai on set for *Further* visuals.

Paused in Cosmic Reflection 237

– ones by Dom & Nic, Spike Jonze and Michel Gondry – which had female protagonists at the heart of the stories. So, the film for *Further* would follow Caroline's journey down the rabbit hole.

From there, Marcus and I went through each track and tried to connect them in a loose way. We cast the actress Romola Garai as the main character. She was brilliant, so patient all the way through the process. Marcus had this idea for the first track that was inspired by the work of American video artist Bill Viola. In it, the camera would track Romola moving underwater in slow motion. We filmed it in the underwater tank at Pinewood Studios. Romola – and a swimming double – had quite a hard job trying to hit the mark underwater. They were both incredibly patient with us.

Motion was incredibly important as it needed to work as a piece of film and also as a visual for The Chemical Brothers' live show. With that in mind, we commissioned two friends (Steve and Sarah) to film a starling murmuration over the derelict West Pier in Brighton. I was obsessed with that movement; there's no reason why they do it, they're just having a good time. There's a freedom and a togetherness to the way they dance. That got used in the film for 'K+D+B' in the *Further* shows, and now sits in the live set when the band play 'Wide Open'.

On another song we decided to submerge all these household objects underwater. It felt nice to have all these everyday mundane objects doing things you don't expect in the middle of a live show. We dropped them through the water: things like a teapot, a high heel, knives and forks, a shopping trolley. We ended up making a game of it, where the people dropping in the objects at the top of the tank didn't give the people filming at the bottom any warning of what was coming down next. After half an hour of guessing, Marcus snuck up there and jumped in himself. Sadly, that only made it into the director's cut.

With 'Escape Velocity', we decided to take Caroline – or the viewer – into dot world. In there, you've got an army of dot men, a lord of the dots and a dot tunnel. There was definitely an inner logic that made a lot of sense to us at that point, even if it sounds odd now. We used bokeh light, which is very out of focus, and we wanted to use motion capture but we couldn't afford to do it. The solution was to make a kind of tight nylon gimp suit with LED lights on it in the spaces where the main parts of the body are. We put the camera out of focus and it looked absolutely wicked. And no one needed to know it was a man in a gimp suit.

The actor Mark Monero played both Dot Man and Lord of the Dots brilliantly. For the latter, we painted his face completely black and put these little white balls all over. We then put the aperture down on the camera so all you can see are the white balls. He put in an incredible performance, and then went home like that and went to his local pub for a pint in the full Lord of the Dots get-up.

Paused in Cosmic Reflection 239

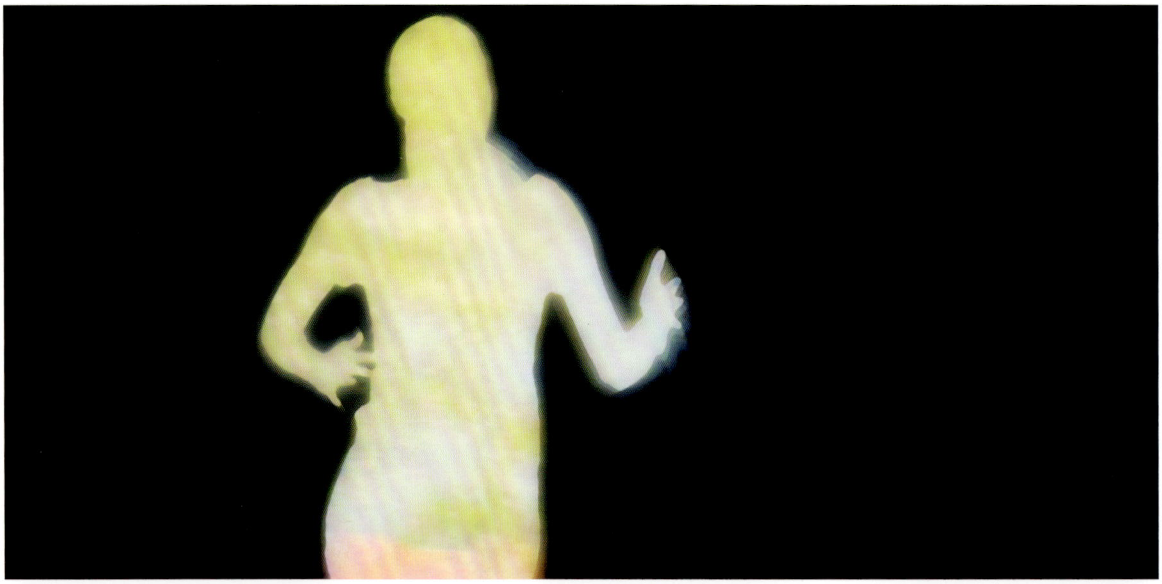

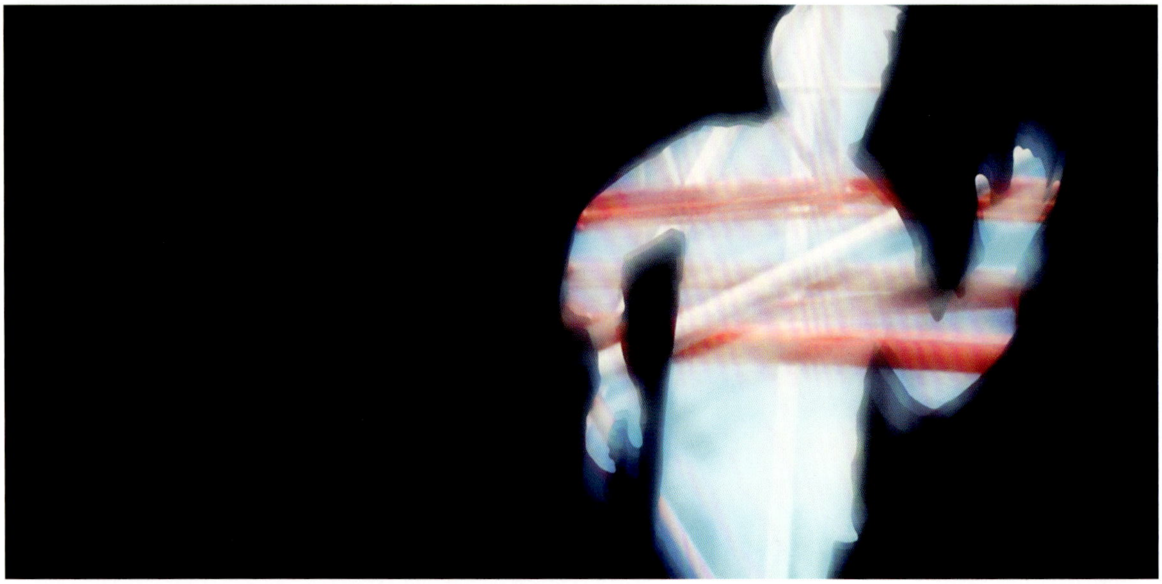

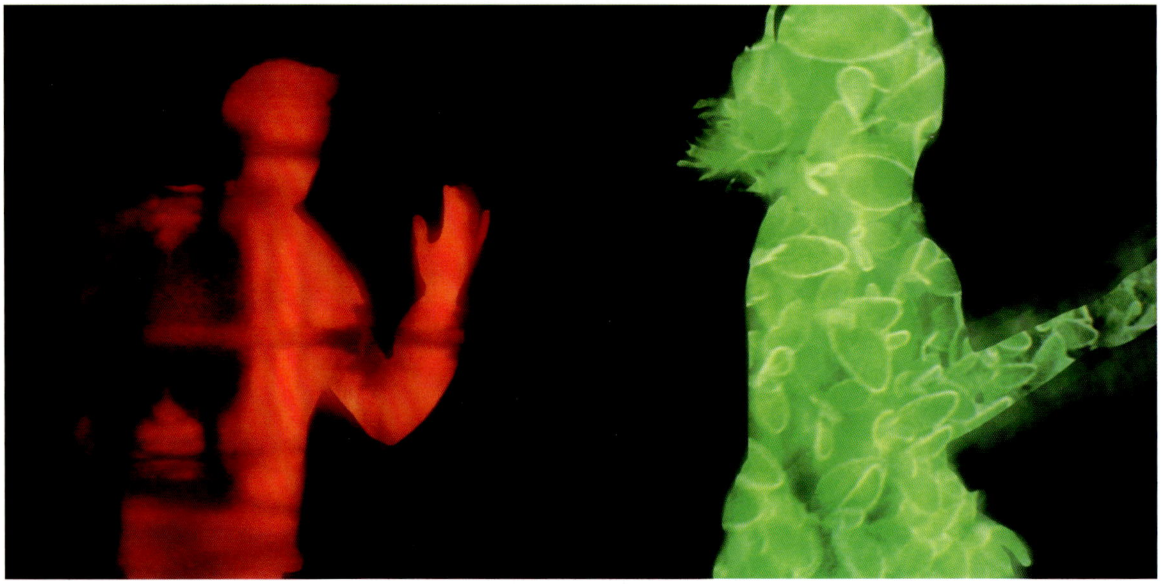

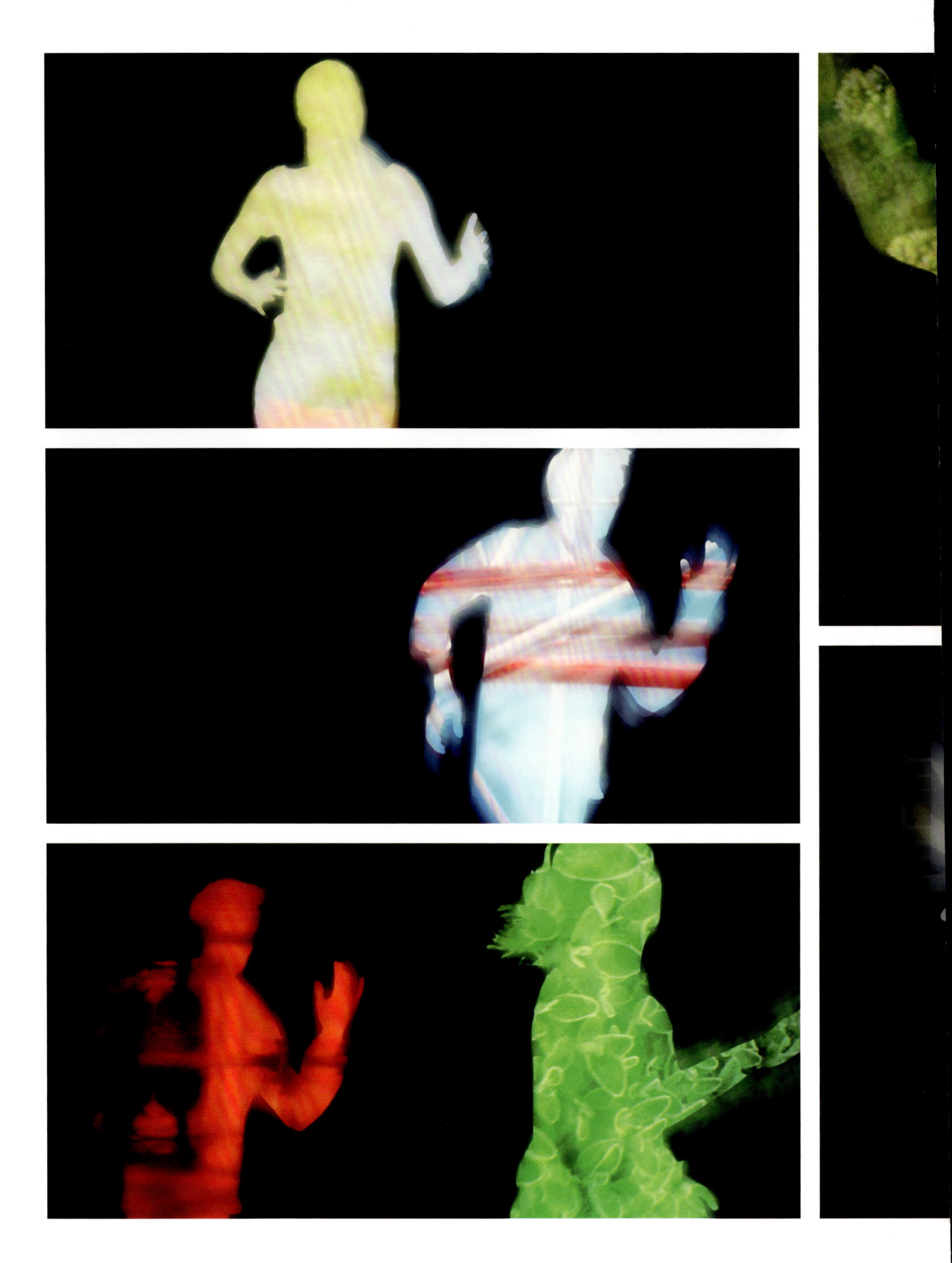

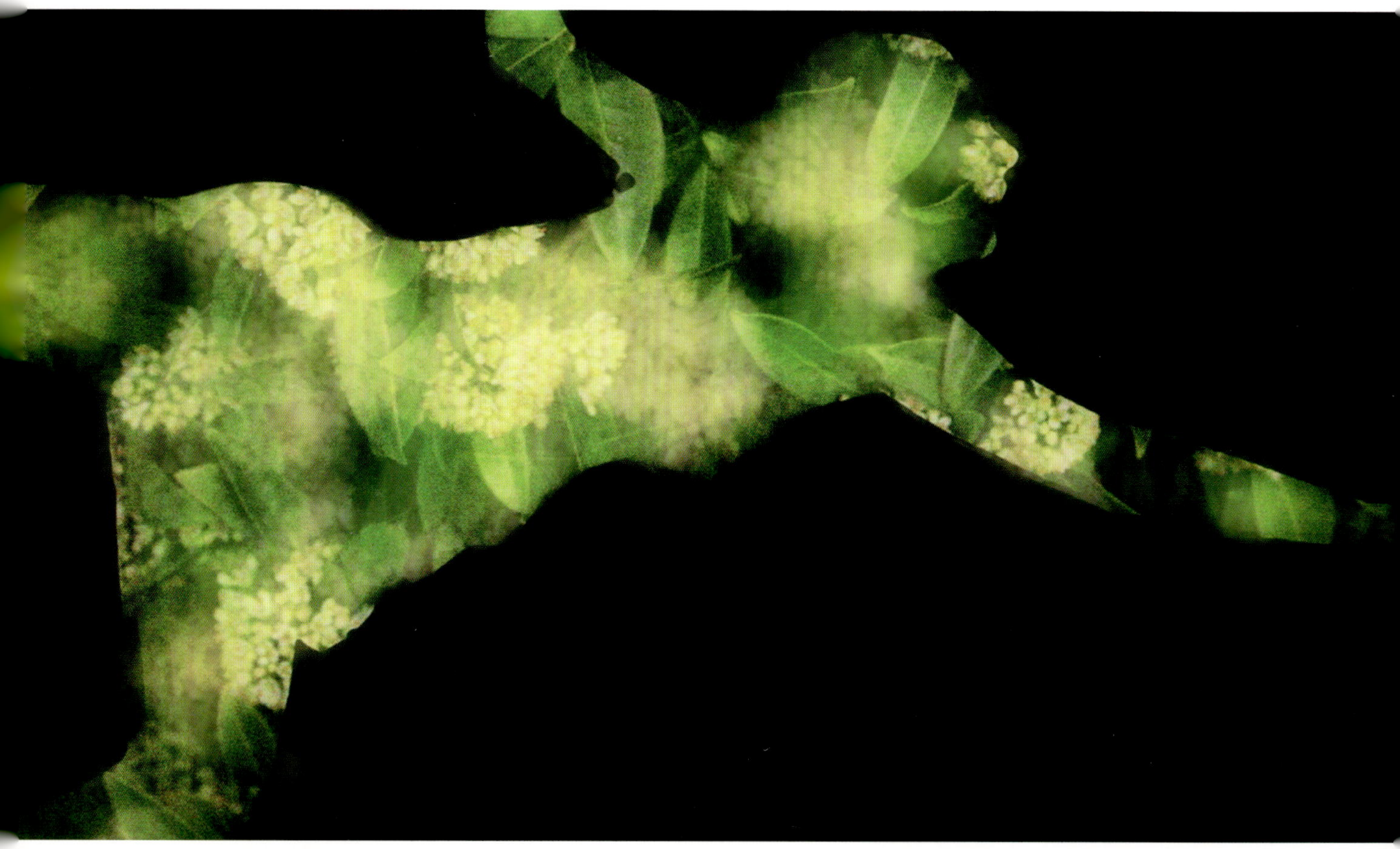

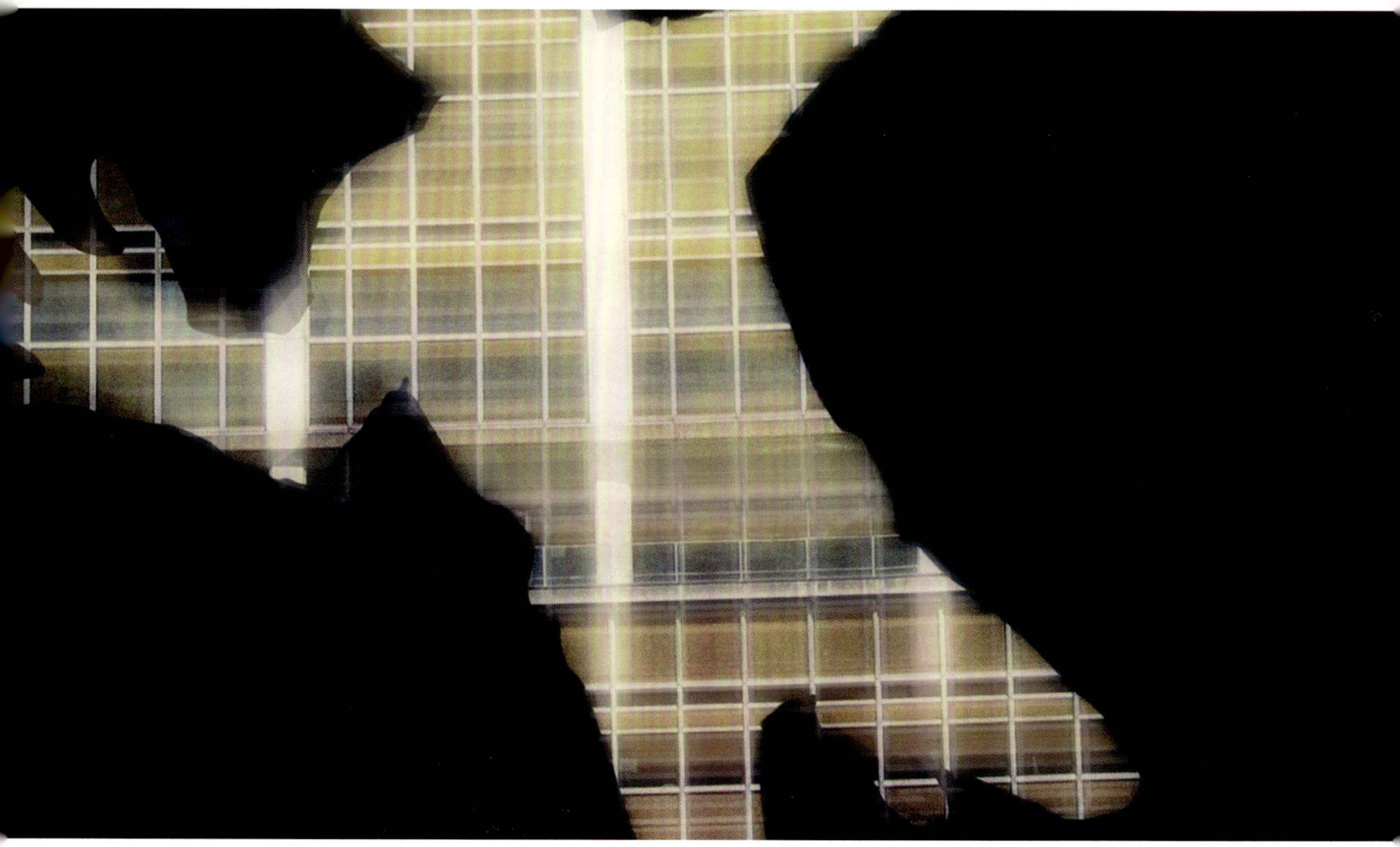

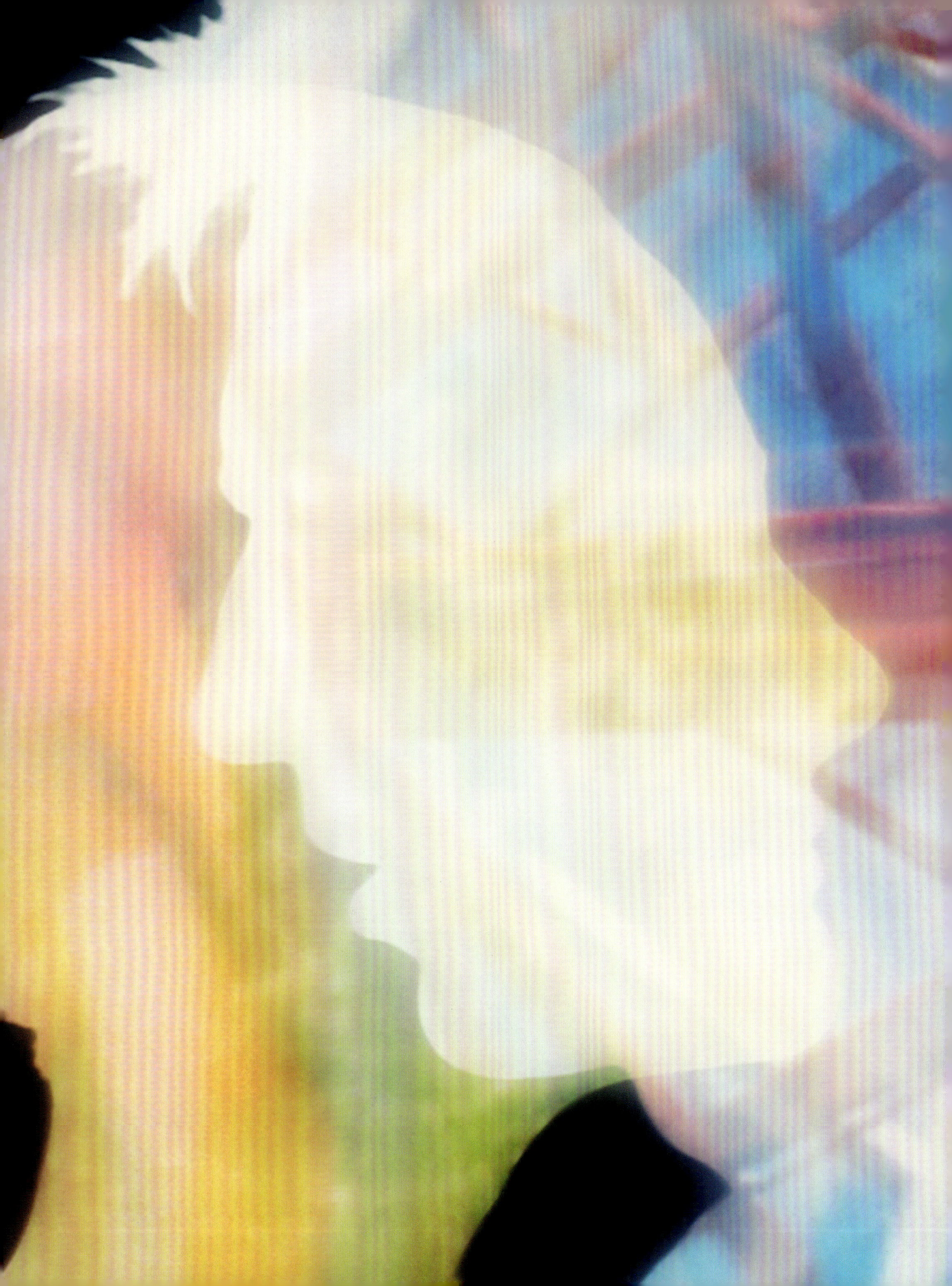

Just remember to fall in love
There's nothing else
There's nothing else

Below: The EMS VCS 3, used on everything from early remixes and 'Leave Home' up until today.

Opposite: The Buchla 219, used on *Further*, *Born in the Echoes* and *No Geography*.

244   **The Chemical Brothers**

Paused in Cosmic Reflection 245

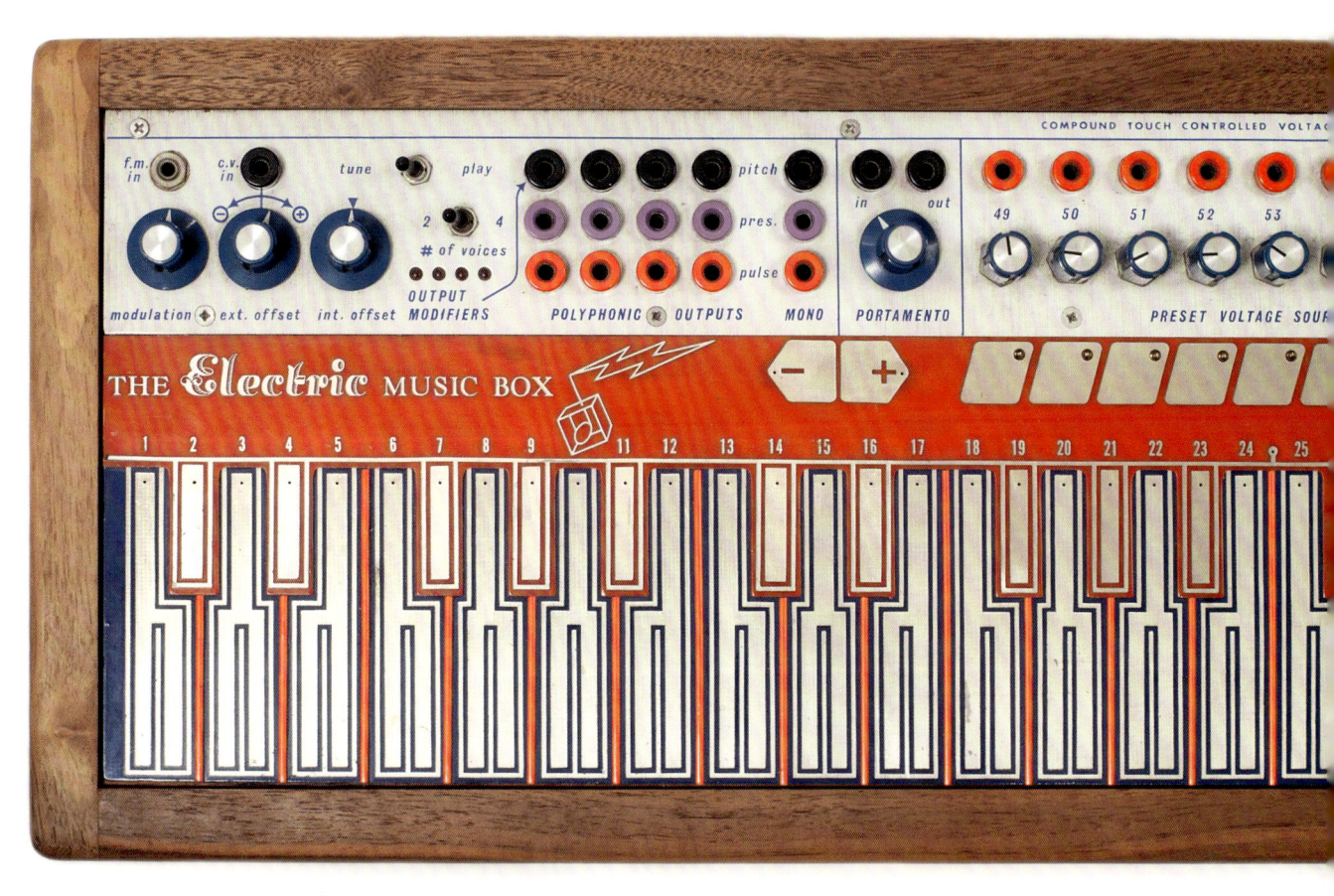

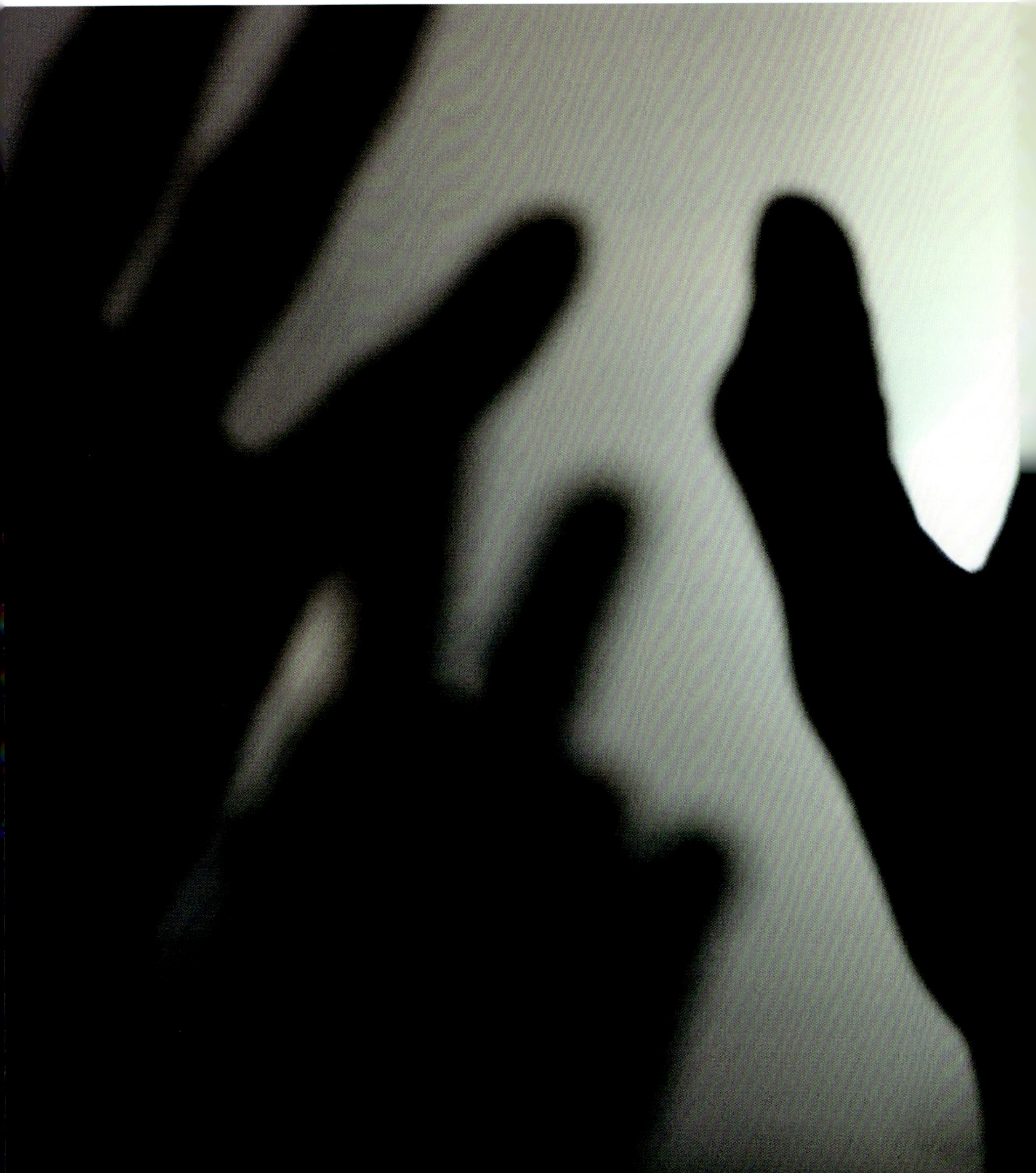

Don't Think

On Sunday, 31 July 2011, a twenty-person camera crew gathered on a rain-swept mountain to shoot the final headline act at Japan's Fuji Rock Festival. Over the course of the evening, the team secured a series of vantage points. Some were on stage with the band; others sat right at the heart of the 50,000-strong crowd. A few more were set up outside the arena, deep in the heavily wooded festival site. Battling the elements later that night, they helped to create *Don't Think* – the definitive visual document of one of the twenty-first century's most phenomenally psychedelic live shows.

The Chemical Brothers had played Fuji Rock several times (1999, 2000, 2002, 2004 and 2007) and the love between the band, their crew and the festival was mutual. In 2011, they were booked to headline on a bill that included Yellow Magic Orchestra and Mogwai. Back home, a plan was hatched to capture the band's performance on film, something that had only happened before on rare occasions. While the plan was perfectly simple, the practicalities of filming the show at a festival were fraught with issues.

When *Don't Think* was released in cinemas, screenings blurred the lines between a visit to the local Odeon and a night out at Fabric. It was transgressive cinema made for dancing to. That's a genre as old as rock 'n' roll itself – one that harks right back to when the Teddy boys tore up the Trocadero – and it's one that's explored all too rarely.

Adam Smith

The Chemical Brothers' live show had never really been filmed apart from the times that they'd headlined Glastonbury. There, the festival and the BBC would let us have some control over how the performance was shot and edited for broadcast. At most other festivals, the band aren't filmed or broadcast. Part of that was always down to a belief that the show is a magic moment for people who are there, and filming it dilutes a magic that should be reserved for the people who are at those shows.

Although I'd always agreed with that previously, I became convinced that the show had grown to a point that it needed to be documented and we really needed to capture it. It took a lot of persuading but eventually, when we did, we began to plan how we'd get it on film.

Originally we were going to film a gig at the Arena of Nîmes, an incredible Roman amphitheatre in the south of France. That fell through and the idea moved to Fuji Rock in Japan, where the band were headlining a three-day festival on the last night. They'd played there several times before; it has both an incredible site and audience. Apart from Glastonbury, there's no other festival that feels like Fuji Rock. There's something magical about the site and how people act when they're there. You enter another world and there's so much creativity poured into it.

The cost nearly stopped it happening; we didn't have a lot of money. Nick Dewey from the band's management said, 'Look, if we don't do it now, we might never do it.' That was the final motivation to actually make it work.

In the planning stages, Marcus and I worked out a different look for each track. We wanted to really take the viewer there – to the gig itself. We didn't want it to feel like it was footage filmed for TV coverage of a festival, because that's what we'd collectively avoided for the past fifteen years. And it had to feel like the festival, which is in an out-of-season ski resort three hours' drive from Tokyo. I don't have any issues with the way festivals are usually shot, but it's not how I experience a gig. I don't fly over the crowd on a crane; I don't have multiple vantage points on the stage. I'm looking past people's heads to try to see the band. The film had to reflect that experience. It had to take people there, to that place, on the ground level.

Over the years I'd been filming quite a lot of TV drama, which led me to thinking, 'How do we emotionally connect the viewer with the show?' We decided to heavily feature characters from the audience, with the idea that you see the whole thing through their eyes. It meant you could treat it like drama and cut from gig to character and back, allowing you to build a connection and become a part of the experience.

The one person we cast was Mario, an amazing character and a massive Chemical Brothers fan. She's married to Jonny, an editor we worked with for years. She's a very gregarious, charismatic woman. Although she'd never done any acting before, I knew she was clearly a natural performer from nights out that we'd had.

We set her up in the audience of the show and I wanted to film her in the festival itself too. One sequence in the film goes inside her head. I quite often find myself closing my eyes at a gig and letting my mind go off places as the music envelops me. The idea was to film Mario and, as she closed her eyes, it would cut to her at the festival as a flashback or a flight of fancy, and we'd explore Fuji Rock through her eyes. We got her into a camera mount – like the type used so effectively in *Mean Streets* – and she totally froze up. She was really nervous and very self-conscious. Suddenly it looked like the whole thing wouldn't work. Thinking quickly, I took her to the bar and got her three or four shots. After that, she was great. I'm not advocating the intoxication of performing artists, but from there she came into her own, loving having the mount on her and all of the attention it brought.

We used all the cameras from our crew and all the cameras the festival was filming with. Despite bad weather, the best footage we shot was from the vantage point of the audience in a style that was inspired by YouTube clips that people have filmed on their phones. As well as that, we wanted to find ways to get the cameras to move through the festival without it seeming gratuitous. We made a mount that would

Stills from the *The Chemical Brothers: Don't Think* film, directed by Adam Smith.

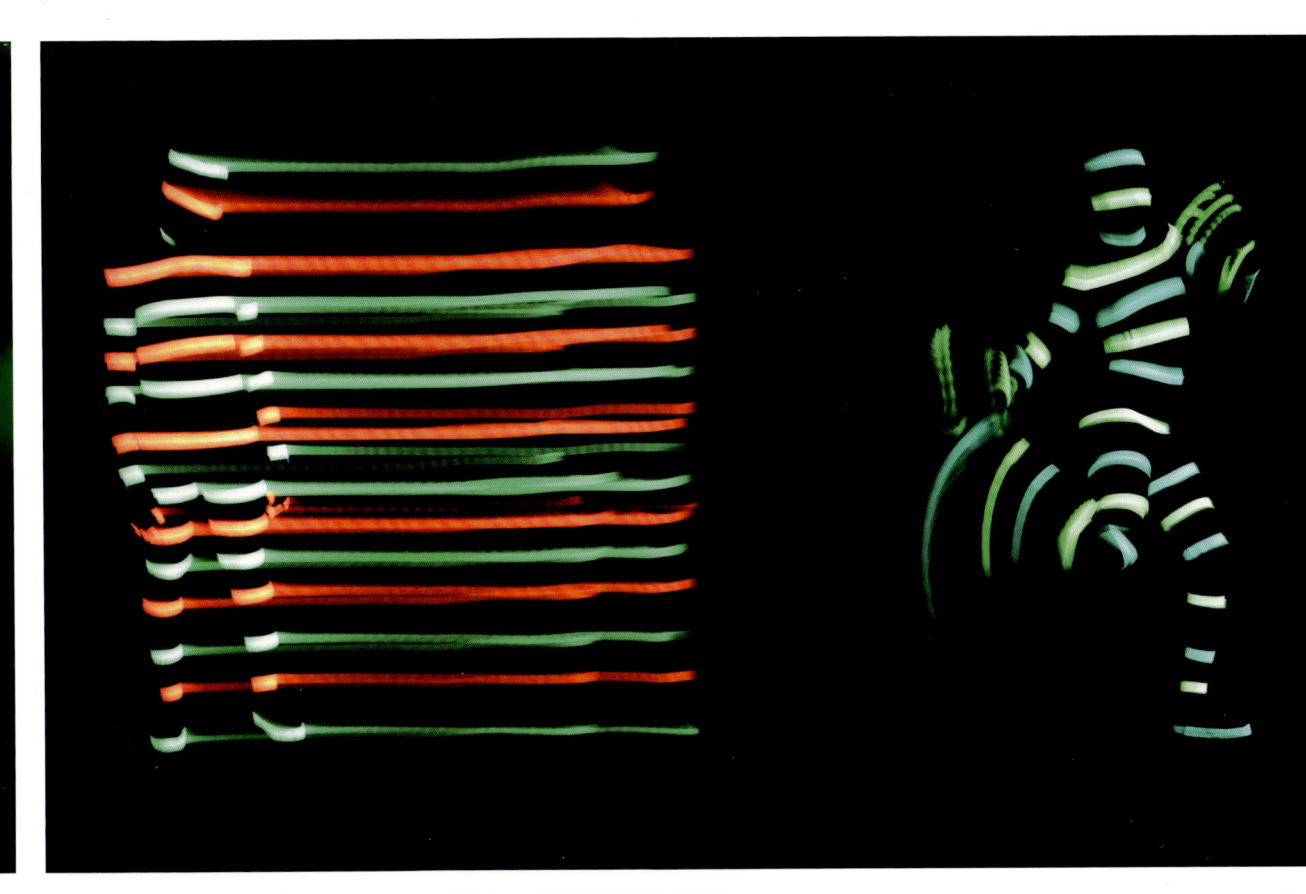

carry a small projector, and then we walked around the site and projected images from the visuals wherever we wanted: on the ground, people's T-shirts, food stalls, anywhere. Because Fuji Rock is such a magical place, filled with beautiful people all with a real sense of playfulness, everyone loved interacting with the projections and got really involved.

Tin toy robots have been an obsession of mine as my mum had a collection when I was growing up. They've always featured in the live shows, even before we had four-metre-high ones on each side of the stage. We bought a bunch of the same robots and filmed them in various places at the festival. There were three-inch robots everywhere – wandering about on the bars, on the floor or walking across bridges.

After the band played, Marcus went off with one crew and I went off with another and we shot as much as we could until dawn. We only had that night as it was the end of the festival. We had to get everything we needed despite the weather conditions, so we just kept going. And it was amazing, so exciting to stay up until

Paused in Cosmic Reflection   249

dawn, filming anything that caught your eye at a festival you adore.

At the end of the night, the sun came up and we had to stop filming. The whole film was set at night so we couldn't break that up with day shots. As it got light, I noticed all these people going to the river to wash their wellies. It's one of the things that makes Fuji Rock so different to any other festival I've been to; it's incredibly clean and tidy, in the same way Tokyo is clean and tidy and London isn't. I'd been up all night, sober as a judge, but high from the excitement of shooting at the festival. In my head, there was something sacred about the ritual of washing wellies in this river. I went over and put my own wellies in the water and was immediately transported back to childhood, to that point where you first wear wellies and jump in puddles or in the sea. It was so intoxicating.

When we got back, the editing process was incredibly slow. The record company kept trying to get us to say it was finished but I wasn't happy with what we had on the screen. We had to keep pushing it and pushing it. I wanted it to feel like an entirely different concert film. The Chemical Brothers' show is different to most live shows, and I thought it was essential that we reflect that in what we made. The process needed to take a long time, and on something like this, you need the time that you need. And you need the right people in that process, which was lucky because everyone working on it was so into it. The film editors were working every hour – to the extent that one time I found them in the middle of the night putting Berocca tablets into straight vodka to make some kind of cocktail.

A lot of times when the film was shown in cinemas, you'd find people getting out of their seats and dancing. The first time it happened was at the premiere at the Hackney Picturehouse. Seeing people getting up, I was thinking, 'What's everyone doing, sit down and watch the film!' It very quickly dawned on me that this was people having a brilliant night out, in a cinema, and we'd pulled it off. We'd got people in the mood to the point where they wanted to unshackle themselves and party. It may well have been Tom's wife, Vanessa, who started the dancing at the premiere, but the same thing happened at the BFI and at the ArcLight in LA, where they stopped the film and threatened to call the police if people didn't sit down. When it inevitably started up again, some guy tried to clamber over the seats to get to the front to dance and dislocated his hip in the process. It was absolutely crazy, unlike any traditional cinema experience.

Tom Rowlands

Ed and I both agreed very early on that being on live TV in an antiseptic studio really wouldn't serve us well. What that meant was that over the years there's no footage of the band playing apart from on camera phones. We'd played a lot of festivals where we haven't allowed them to film; it's a policy that's served us well over the years. People couldn't believe how resistant we were. But I began to take stock and started thinking that this thing we're doing was worth documenting, especially as we were doing the show the way we wanted to do it, as uncompromised as we could possibly make it.

When the idea to film the entire show came up, Ed was very resistant. There was a lot of argument of whether to do it. I loved the idea. We were putting on such an amazingly visual show, it seemed nuts that we weren't going to capture it. I understood Ed's belief that it should be for the moment and for the people there, but I also wanted to have a record of what we were doing because at some point we won't be doing it anymore. And the idea that we would shoot it at Fuji Rock – this amazing place that we loved playing so much – was irresistible.

It was quite a mad idea to do it there. Usually when you film a gig, you shoot your own concert and maybe film in the same venue across multiple nights so you can fill in the bits you've missed in case something goes wrong. Because there's enough things that can go wrong at your own gig, let alone at a festival halfway up a mountain in the rain. But I loved the idea of having one night and one chance to do it. It was a brave decision. Adam was so excited. He wanted to represent the thing he'd been working on for so long in the best possible way.

Our connection to Fuji, all the amazing experiences we'd had playing there . . . we knew it would work. I love how the camera goes off into the night – it really captures the randomness of festivals, how incredible things happen away from the stages at night-time.

Adam captured the feeling that you'd want from a gig. He's someone who's so entwined with the live show, and he has the skill to get across the feeling that you'd want. Casting the characters, filming the crowd... those are the things I enjoyed the most about the film. I'm really happy we did it.

Ed Simons

I was very resistant to doing *Don't Think*. I don't like a big fuss. I've never loved the gigs being filmed. I think every time we play it should be about the people there and the atmosphere generated. Putting a camera in front of us or the screen for just a moment can potentially take something ineffable away from the experience. Up until this film, only the BBC with their on-the-fly recording of our Glastonbury shows had ever vaguely captured the vibrancy of what we were attempting to present.

Such an important part of gigs – especially our gigs – is the crowd response and that magical transcendent crackle in the air. I really didn't think it was possible to capture that. I think Adam considered this and managed it by taking the cameras into the crowd and creating a narrative around Mario. I love that there are periods where the camera isn't even fixed on the stage. With the best will in the world, even at the most mind-blowing gigs there are periods when the mind wanders. Suddenly you're more concerned about whether that rucksack on the guy in front is going to bosh you during the next big track. One of my favourite things about Adam's direction of the film is the recognition that the gig is just one of the things happening on that night.

Fuji Rock was the most perfect setting for it. It was a rainy one and the mist had settled serenely on the hills when we came on. That crowd are always just so into it. Love it.

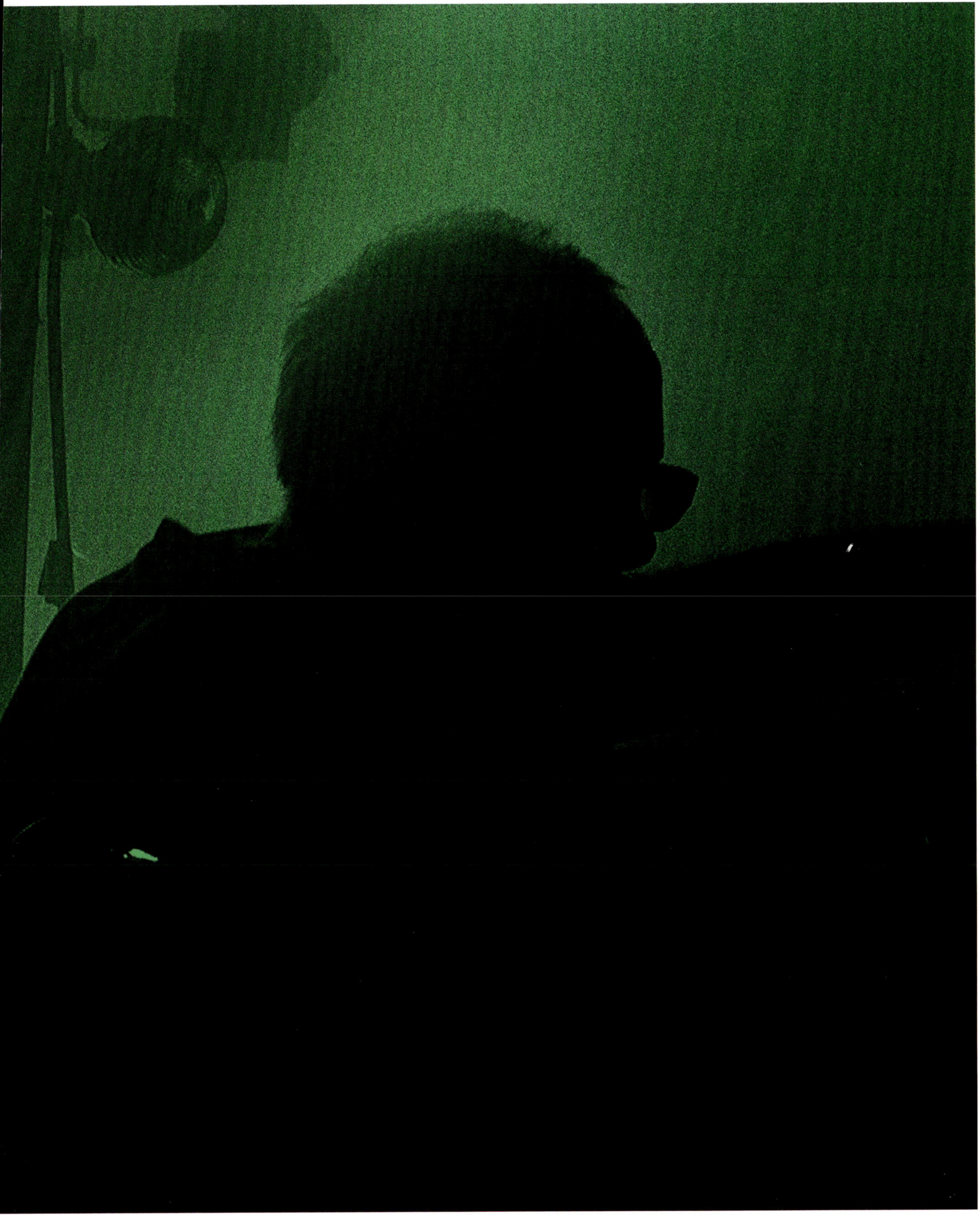

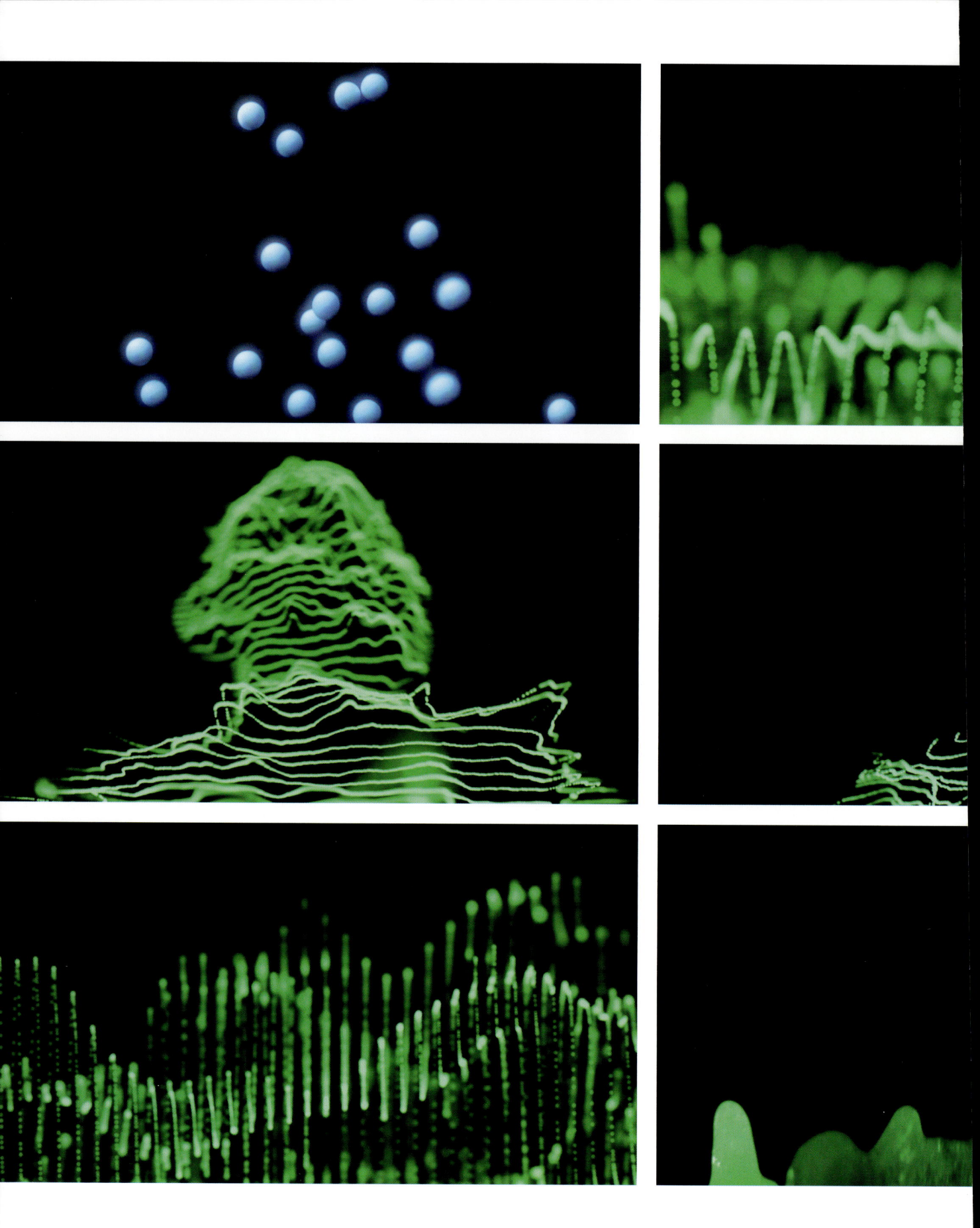

254   The Chemical Brothers

Paused in Cosmic Reflection 255

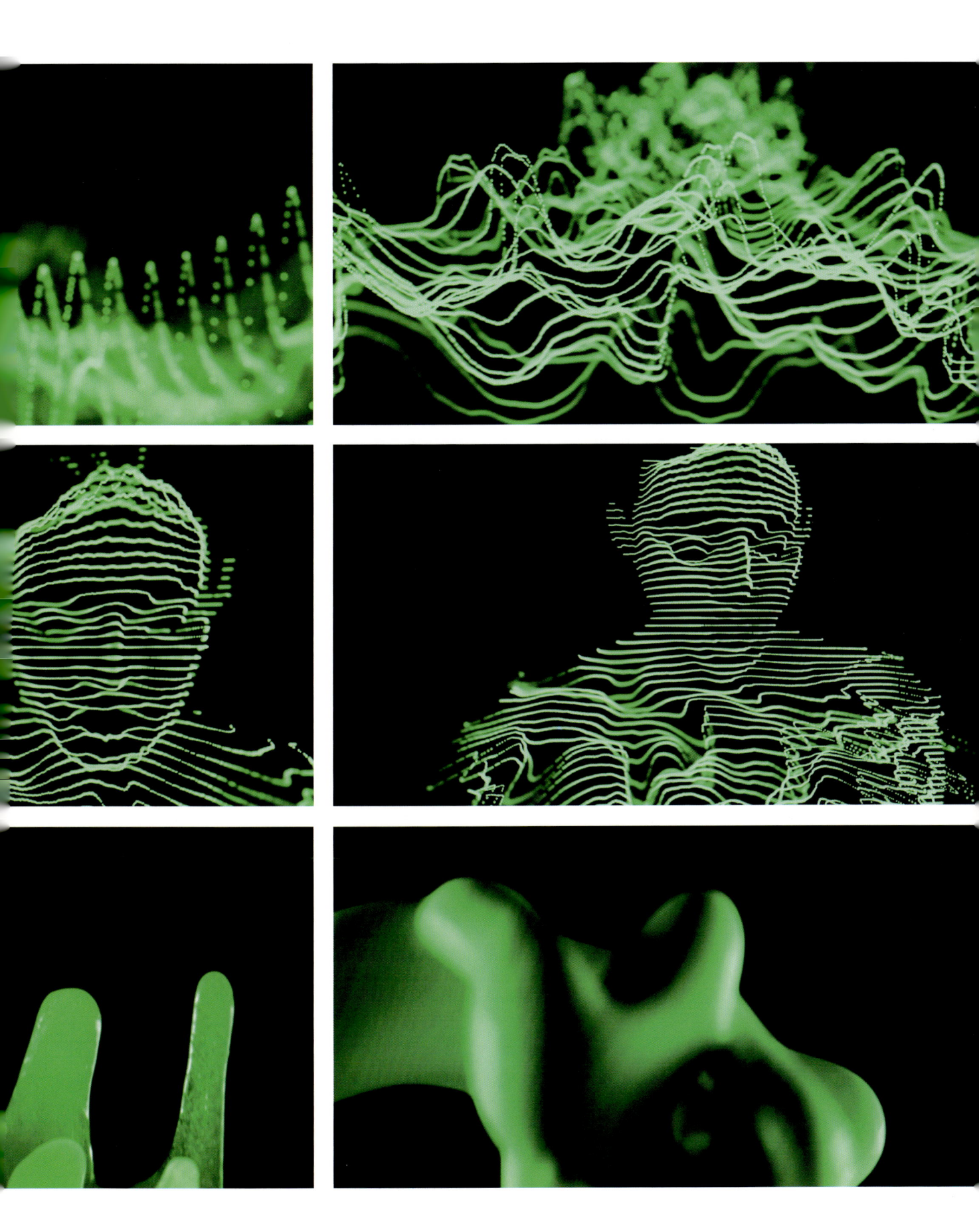

SAOIRSE RONAN ERIC BANA AND CATE BLANCHETT
HANNA
ADAPT OR DIE
DIRECTED BY JOE WRIGHT | ORIGINAL SCORE BY THE CHEMICAL BROTHERS
FOCUS FEATURES PRESENTS A HOLLERAN COMPANY A JOE WRIGHT FILM "HANNA" SAOIRSE RONAN ERIC BANA TOM HOLLANDER OLIVIA WILLIAMS
JASON FLEMYNG AND CATE BLANCHETT MUSIC BY THE CHEMICAL BROTHERS SARAH GREENWOOD
DIRECTOR OF PHOTOGRAPHY ALWIN KÜCHLER, BSC EXECUTIVE PRODUCER BARBARA A. HALL PRODUCED BY LESLIE HOLLERAN MARTY ADELSTEIN STORY BY SETH LOCHHEAD
PG-13 PARENTS STRONGLY CAUTIONED
Some Material May Be Inappropriate for Children Under 13
FOR INTENSE SEQUENCES OF VIOLENCE AND ACTION, SOME SEXUAL MATERIAL AND LANGUAGE
SCREENPLAY BY SETH LOCHHEAD AND DAVID FARR
COMING SOON
www.HannaTheMovie.com
DIRECTED BY JOE WRIGHT
FOCUS FEATURES
A Division of NBC Universal

Hanna

Previous page: Stills from the 'Another World' music video, directed by Smith and Lyall.

Opposite: Promotional poster from the cinema release of Hanna.

Next page: Stills from the 'Go' music video, directed by Michel Gondry.

It starts with a gorgeous nursery rhyme melody played on a xylophone and echoed in a human voice. It's a tune that's infectious enough to stop time as it unfolds all celestial and sun-kissed. Each repetition brings a musical undercurrent, a new backdrop that changes the context of the original refrain. The final cycle adds a distortion that unsettles everything. It adds a moment of uncertainty, and the track becomes a portent.

Hanna was the fourth feature film directed by Joe Wright, starring Saoirse Ronan as a fifteen-year-old trained by her father to be a killer. Wright had known The Chemical Brothers since the mid-nineties when he worked with Adam Smith and Noah Clark as an occasional part of their Vegetable Vision setup.

Tom Rowlands

We've had a few film scores almost happen over the years. Early on, when we had our studio in Orinoco, there was always this massive script that we'd been sent with a view to writing a score for it. It sat by the door for ages and got used as a doorstop. All we knew was that it was about boxing, which didn't sound like the kind of thing Ed or I would have any interest in reading or watching, let alone working on for ages. It was called *Fight Club*, and we didn't engage with it at all. It eventually got taken to the original Dust Brothers who did the music for the film to massive acclaim. It was only years later when the film was released that we realised what that doorstop had been.

Hanna was the first score we did and it's one of the things we've done that I love the most. We've known Joe Wright since we first started working with Vegetable Vision on our gigs in 1994. He was part of their crew and came to a few shows to help out with visuals, but he had his own thing going on, which ended up with him becoming a very respected film director.

Working on *Hanna* became a totally different experience of making music. One of the things that's hardest about making music is finding an internal reason for the music to exist in the first place. *Why does this track do this? What point is it trying to make?* With a score, the reason is right in front of you on the screen. You have a structure and a tangible emotion you're trying to hit. Working that way was so freeing, having an immediate reason to express something. In film, there's a point to everything and everything has a meaning. Those strictures, those reduced parameters, they were the most liberating thing ever.

I worked on the score at home. I had a screen set up next to my computer, which meant I could watch the film as I wrote. A lot of the synth stuff was done live to the film, jamming along to the scene before turning it into something more nuanced. We worked with a sound editor called Mike Higham, whose enthusiasm for the project – married to his technical excellence – allowed me the freedom to get on with writing and exploring.

I only realised later how free Joe had let me be with the music, and how lucky I was there. Quite often that world is incredibly proscriptive. With *Hanna*, it felt like Joe was encouraging me to take little things further and explore different ideas more. I really respected how he managed to make me feel so liberated, which in turn got the best out of me.

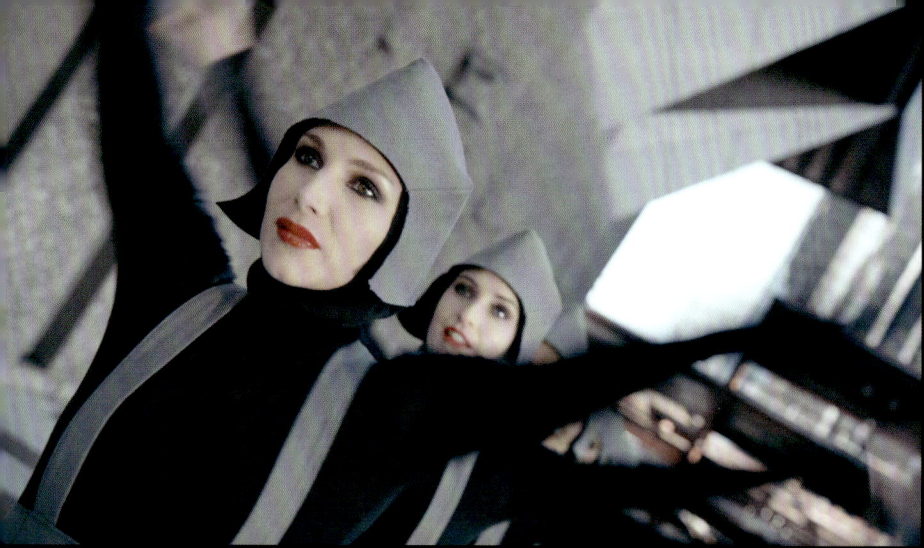
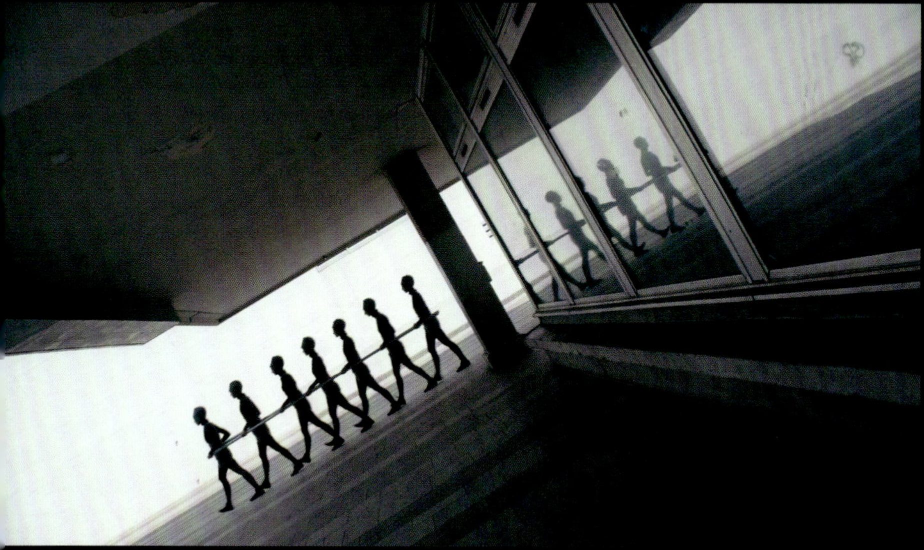
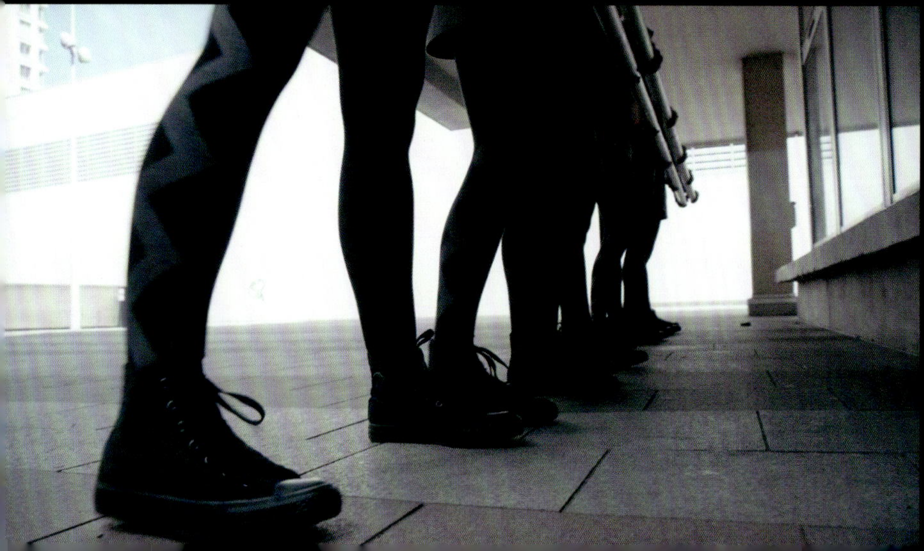
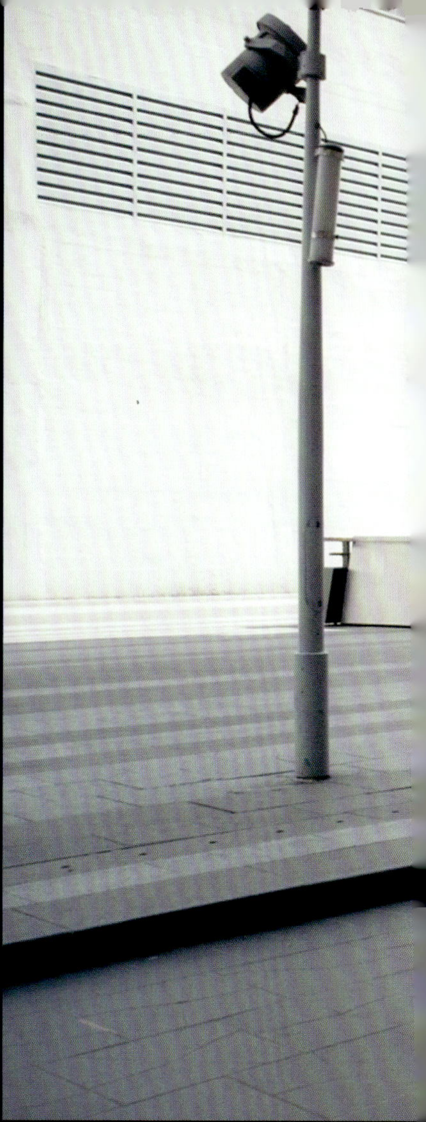
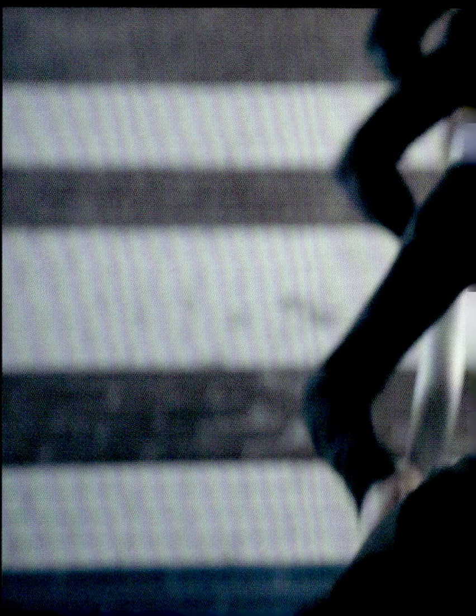

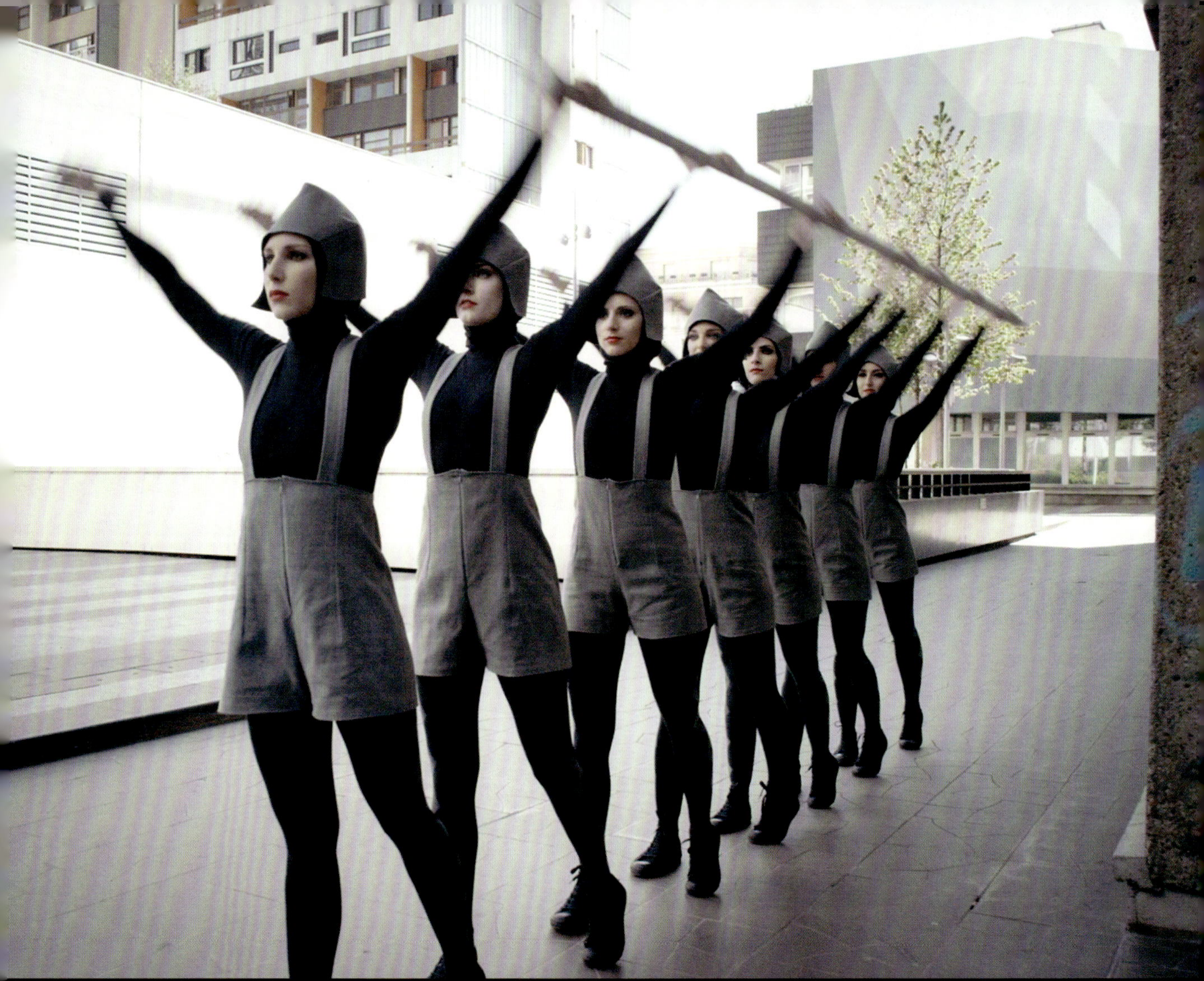

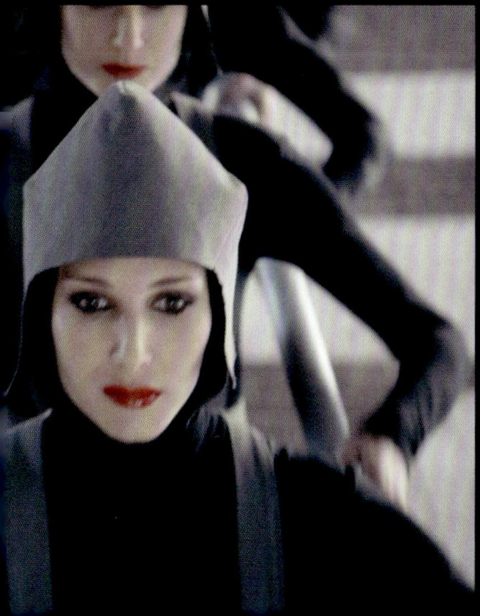

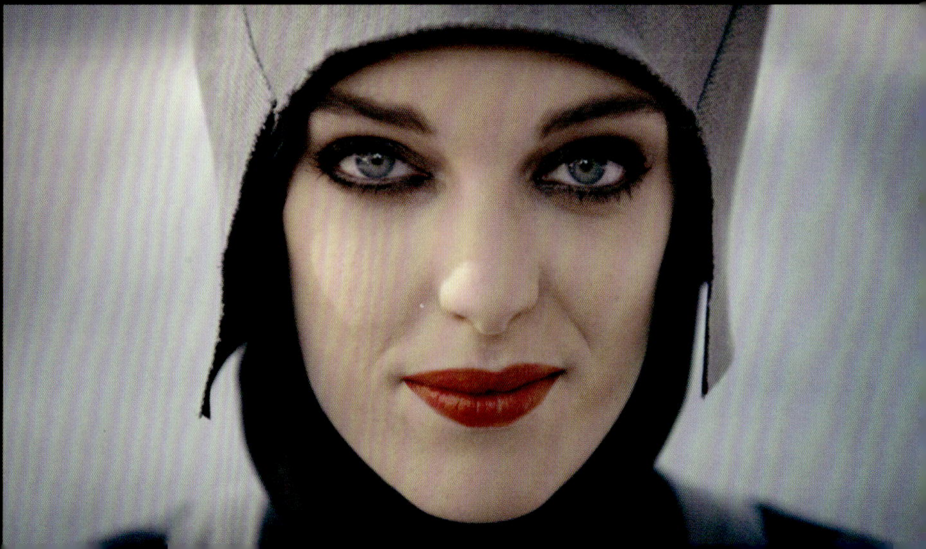

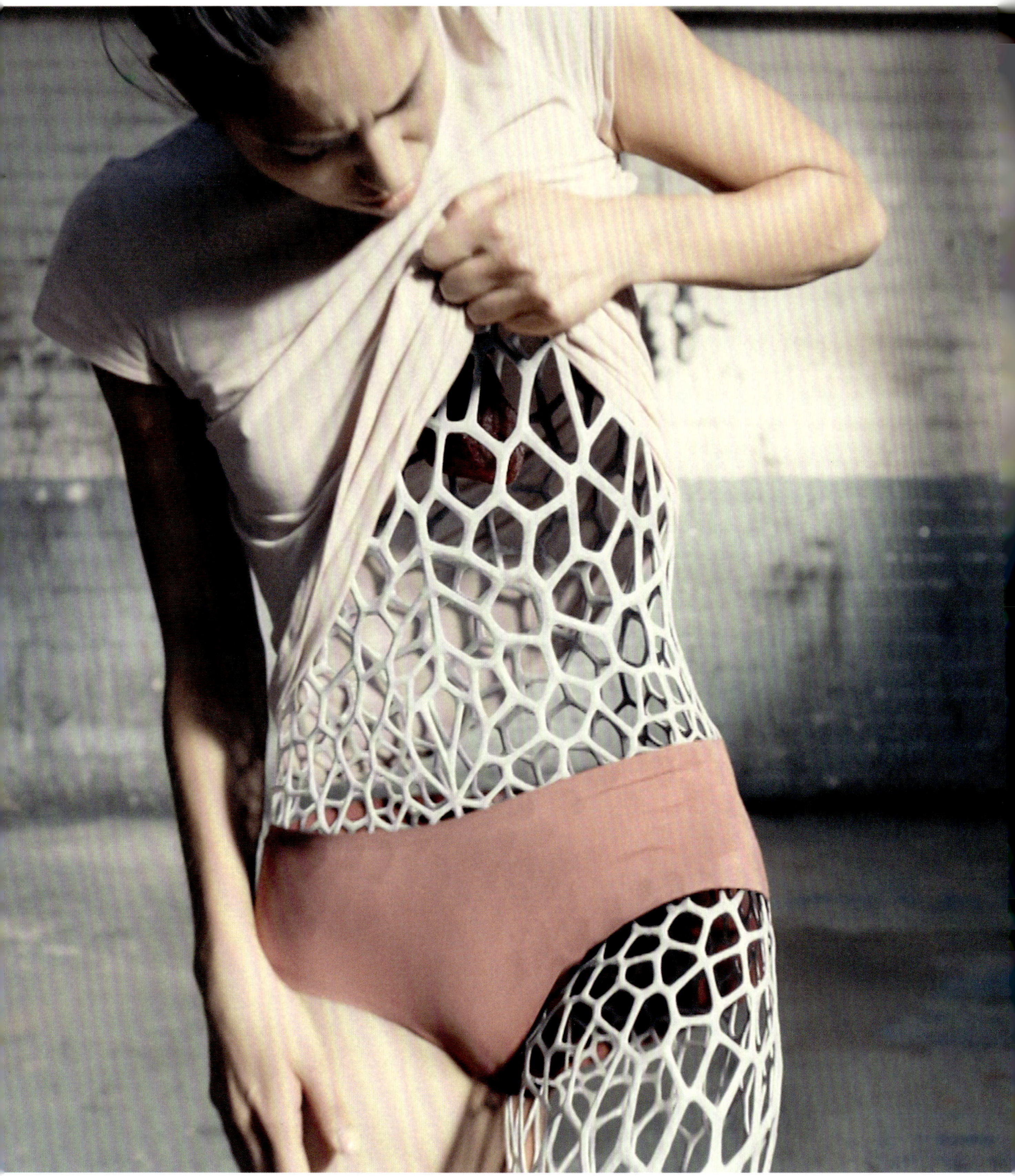

Wide Open

'Wide Open' is a country song. The closing track on *Born in the Echoes*, it is pure synthesised soul music, a sweet song of heartbreak sung to a 4/4 kick drum, a low-end-bass pulse and an orchestra of analogue machines.

'Wide Open' features a vocal by Beck Hansen, who lends a tenderness reminiscent of his own classic albums *Sea Change* and *Morning Phase* – two records that effortlessly manage to place the listener right at the heart of a troubled relationship at the point it untangles.

While the track might echo the emotional palette of those records, its real precedents are the songs Beth Orton recorded with The Chemical Brothers on their first two albums. Like 'Alive Alone' and 'Where Do I Begin', 'Wide Open' is a moment of uneasy reflection, an uncertain blink into sunlight as a new day dawns.

The award-winning video for 'Wide Open' was directed by Dom & Nic.

Tom Rowlands

'Wide Open' was originally a song I'd written called 'Emotional Rescue'. It was me wanting to say something more direct and outwardly emotional. It took me back to 'Alive Alone', which also has a vulnerability to it. I think there must be a strand of that which runs quite strong in me. The music was an exercise in restraint, while still landing with a lot of impact. We were aiming for warmth and simplicity.

The demo I sent Beck had me singing the main part. He sang it back brilliantly and added and ad-libbed new sections of the track. There was a lot of back and forth with where to pitch the rhythm. One thing I knew I wanted was a muted feel to the drums so they could then bloom towards the end of the song.

Ed and I have both been big fans of Beck since his early records. His voice is such an iconic thing, the way he can move so effortlessly between feelings yet remain so identifiable and unique. One of the reasons we were inspired to collaborate on this was down to our deep connection with his *Sea Change* album. It's a truly beautiful record I always find myself coming back to. It was so exciting to hear his voice and words with our music. He communicated the exact feeling we needed.

Dom & Nic's video is such a bold and pure expression. Everyone involved really went deep, from Sonoya Mizuno's central performance and Wayne McGregor's choreography to all the team at The Mill. They created something truly special. It's impossible not to be moved by it.

Ed Simons

When we play 'Wide Open' live, you can feel from the stage how much it connects to people. If you look into the audience, you see closed eyes as people get lost in the track, couples kissing, camera phones going up in unison like a wave of light. We love those moments of beauty that allow people time to drift away. It's as far from a pulverising, noisy moment as you can get.

Beck's vocal and the synths combine into something transcendent. I don't think someone would necessarily need to be a Chemical Brothers fan to fall for it; it has a universality and a fragility. I think Dom & Nic's video has given it a massive reach beyond what it originally was.

Beck Hansen

The Chemical Brothers came up at the same time as me. I first heard of them when I was working on *Odelay* with the Dust Brothers, who were producing. It was early 1995 and they had a 12-inch of this record by another group from England calling themselves The Dust Brothers. Apparently the original Dust Brothers were sending some sort of cease-and-desist notice so these other Dust Brothers would have to change their name. I remember the English ones sending a note saying that they were big fans. They said they'd only named themselves as a form of tribute and hoped there were no hard feelings. I don't know if anybody was sure if they would hear from them again, but of course they renamed themselves The Chemical Brothers and put out *Exit Planet Dust*, which I've always assumed was a sly reference to the Dust Brothers moniker. I became a fan as soon as I started hearing their songs on the radio. 'Block Rockin' Beats' was huge around the time of *Odelay* and I think it shared a similar ethos.

When they first sent me 'Wide Open', I thought it was so incredibly economical and brilliant in its simplicity. I think when I got the music, there were only four tracks on it. I was working on an album that had so many parts and tracks; there were some songs with over a hundred tracks. This was a complete antidote. It was refreshing to work on. I remember greatly admiring the discipline of how spare yet effective it was, like 'this is all you need to make a good song, nothing more'.

I wrote lyrics and melodies, and worked on it for a while until I felt like I had something to send them. We ultimately just kept the *Slow me down* section of what I originally sent, but they got inspired and came up with a new idea for the main 'Wide Open' vocal melody. I stacked it with lots of harmonies, but they preferred just one single vocal. Very bare and direct.

The track felt very warm and vulnerable, not like any typical electronic or dance-based track. To me, it had a distinct yearning and emotional quality. I was relieved that we were ultimately able to capture that. It's a quality that my favourite electronic artists have, all the way back to Kraftwerk and Depeche Mode – bands who were able to catch that intimacy and openness using electronic and digital instruments. The video very much mirrors the simplicity of the track. It's difficult to pull off a long clip essentially filming one thing in one location. They pulled it off brilliantly.

After 'Wide Open' came out, we were both playing at a festival in France. Watching them, the breadth of the tracks in their set went from complete electronic bangers to psychedelic trance and rave meltdowns and everything in between. In that context, 'Wide Open' felt even more unusual and impressive. I'm really happy we got to make something together and for it to be the kind of song that adds another dimension to their live show.

Ultimately, I think The Chemical Brothers have a great predilection for exploration. Their records always seem to take you to different places. They kind of sit in an unusual place between different eras of electronic music and DJ culture. It's like they have one foot in multiple decades at the same time in a way that is utterly unique among their peers. They are rare in that they are always making stuff year in year out and amassing such a rich and impressive body of work.

Dom & Nic

Nic: I'd been to the Royal Opera House to see a performance of *Chroma*, which was a ballet set to the music of The White Stripes. The show was choreographed by Wayne McGregor, who was resident choreographer of the Royal Ballet. Wayne had worked with Radiohead and Atoms for Peace previously and I loved *Chroma*, so I left with the idea that Dom and I should try to work with him one day.

Opposite: In pre-production on the 'Wide Open' music video.

Opposite bottom: (L–R) Nic Goffey, Dom Hawley, Wayne McGregor and Sonoya Mizuno.

Paused in Cosmic Reflection 263

Stills from the 'Wide Open' video, directed by Dom & Nic.

Dom: We'd pitched on 'Go' from *Born in the Echoes*, but there was a very tight turnaround time and we couldn't make the video. When we first heard the whole album, we both absolutely loved 'Wide Open'. When we talked about the track, the lyrics quickly gave us that repeated idea of someone slipping away. We wanted to portray someone physically slipping away in front of your eyes, which are represented by the camera's view. So, we got in touch with Tom and Ed saying, 'If you ever want to make a video for "Wide Open", we'd love to pitch.' At that point 'Wide Open' was planned to be the third single off the album. Pitching an idea that early meant we had more time than we usually would to make the video, which we needed all of. And a lot more besides.

Nic: We came up with the idea of a one-take film of a dancer transitioning into a 3D mesh model of herself throughout her performance. We were looking into the 3D printing of prosthetic limbs, 3D-printed body parts. That was very much the idea with the mesh.

Dom: One of the 3D artists at The Mill introduced us to the idea of a Voronoi diagram, which is an irregular mesh that still keeps the structural integrity of a shape. It has a strangely organic feel to it, as well as being quite tech-y.

Nic: When we talked to Wayne, he suggested a couple of dancers who were brilliant but they looked too much like ballet dancers. They had these almost bird-like physiques. We were worried about going back to ask if he could try to find someone a bit more . . . real. Thankfully, he knew exactly what we were talking about and came back with Sonoya Mizuno.

Dom: Sonoya is an actress and a dancer. She'd just been in *Ex Machina*, the Alex Garland film. She fit perfectly. She came over

Paused in Cosmic Reflection 265

from LA for a weekend. She and Wayne had a day together to rehearse at the Royal Ballet, then we had one day on location where we could develop the choreography with the camera in the room. We also worked out where the performance would begin and end.

Nic: Wayne was a really big Chemical Brothers fan and he loved the track. He had a lot of connection with their music and had a real passion to make it all work. He was determined to make the movements in the dance connect with their music and had worked out these building blocks of movement. It was a case of working out where they fitted into the whole performance, which was almost like an edit before we'd started filming.

Dom: The original treatment was a one-take performance at sunset or sunrise on a really open beach, like Holkham in Norfolk. Pure sand, beautiful sun.

Nic: We talked about doing it in a forest as well.

Dom: There were so many technical reasons that meant we ended up shooting indoors. A room meant the background could be consistent; there were no moving waves or variables like tree branches. That would have added another element of craziness for post-production to deal with. We ended up using an old black-cab workshop in the East End that was being looked after by a group of property guardians using it as a studio space.

Nic: On the day of the shoot, there was a guy who set up multiple GoPro cameras around the room to capture the movement from different angles. He was a bit of a character and before every take, he'd shout, 'Wait for me!' and he'd run around with a remote control firing off the cameras. This happened every time we did a take. Some were OK, some were really close. When we got to take thirteen, everyone was holding their breath as the camera moved out, then went mad at the point we cut. We knew we were running out of time at the location – it was the end of the day – but the thirteenth take – unlucky for some, lucky for us – was perfect. We'd packed up and gone home knowing we had an amazing performance. Then the GoPro guy came back saying, 'Did you really like take thirteen?' *No, it* is *take thirteen, that's the one.* '. . . Because only three of the cameras went off on that take,; the others didn't fire. It will be mind-bendingly difficult to track the movements without the others.' We didn't really know what to say; that was the take. Sonoya had flown back to LA, Wayne had gone on to his next project, there was no way we were going to get people back in the room to reshoot. An impossibly complicated job had just become far more impossibly complicated.

Dom: The video looks so simple that people often can't understand why it took so long to make. The reason was that we wanted it to be one take and we wanted it to be live with moving cameras, not motion control. In order to see through Sonoya, you needed a clean background. Normally you'd shoot motion control, and you'd do the shot once, take Sonoya out and shoot it again – but we didn't do that. So the team at the post-production house The Mill started writing software and doing mind-bending stuff to make it work. But that wasn't the difficult bit. Sonoya had to be scanned and we had to make a CG version of her, then a CG version of the 3D-printed version of herself. Every single movement of the wrist, arm, leg, finger . . . everything had to be matched throughout the whole film. It's still the longest 3D-tracked shot ever.

Nic: Although there's so much digital technology in there, the core of the video is a one-off human performance. It's pure. We were under a lot of pressure to use a few different takes spliced together because technology had failed us. But we resisted. People were tearing their hair out, but we knew it had to be that one perfect take.

Dom: 'Wide Open' is first and foremost a music video, but we wanted it to be an authentic dance film too. It's a dance between Sonoya and the camera. Add to that the transition into the 3D-printed version of Sonoya and you had something that could only exist as that film; it couldn't be performed live to an audience. That's why it was vital that it was one take, even though that may have added two months' worth of post-production work. And so many people gave their time for nothing. The runners got paid and everyone else waived any fee. It would be impossible to make a video like that now, and it would have been impossible then but for the team at The Mill and their creative director Neil Davies. He was one of five collaborators on the video, along with us, Wayne and Sonoya. He had the clout to take it on. The Mill worked on it for five or six months, which at book rate would have been an insane amount of money.

Nic: They were making stuff, developing technology in order to finish the job. Neil had to have a shareholder meeting every week and he'd have to justify this ongoing Chemical Brothers production, which was taking months and months.

Dom: It was a perfect storm. A brilliant track, the fact that we heard it and contacted them early on, finding Wayne and Sonoya, Neil getting so into it. As much as Tom and Ed and the label were desperate to get hold of the video, they were patient and didn't try to hurry what was a very slow process. They'd check in and we'd tell them it was taking longer, and they'd come back in a month to check in again. It couldn't be finished any quicker.

Nic: Once it was in post-production, it was like a huge juggernaut that couldn't be sped up and couldn't be stopped. It was one of the toughest things to stand firm. There was a lot of pressure on us to cave in but that would have destroyed the idea of an authentic one-take dance. It's not a combination of different shots from different takes, it's a real in-the-moment, once-in-a-lifetime performance. If we'd cut two takes together, we'd have debased what we set out to do. You can definitely get into a mindset of 'they'll never know', but to us this felt different: it was important. It was a one-off moment with the help of huge technology to get the desired look. To have shot it all, got the perfect take and then had that snatched away would have been a bit too much. We had to really stick firm – it did cause a lot of problems but it was worth it.

Dom: When you work on something that's absolutely reliant on the effects process, you don't get to create the illusion until it's almost entirely finished. And because it was all one shot, that was even more the case. It wasn't like you could say these six shots are finished, this is what it'll look like. So no one experienced it properly until it was entirely done. Watching it during the process broke the magic of it. It became scary towards the end because it wasn't finished, and everyone had committed all this time and work. You're watching the edit thinking, 'That looks a bit stupid', or 'That's a bit crap.' You find yourself longing for the original dance, which was authentic and complete. There was a last push, and Neil – who'd stopped working in hands-on production years before – and his colleague Fergal got involved in comping things together. They did two all-nighters and suddenly it was finished. You could actually watch it and go on the emotional and visual journey without seeing rough edges. Up to that point, there was a genuine fear that we'd wasted everyone's time. When we stuck the titles on the end, it wasn't an indulgence. It was more than just our film and we needed to thank everyone. So many people had worked on it for so little payment.

Nic: One of the last things we did was add the sound of sirens recorded on a New York street, which gave the impression that it might have been shot in America. We didn't want it to feel like it was shot in any one specific place, so we used that bit of sound design to wrong-foot the viewer. Years later, I saw some YouTube comments where people were saying, 'This is in Denver, I used to work in that building!' I love that people can write their own stories and create their own illusions around it as they watch.

Next page: Stills from the 'Free Yourself' music video, directed by Dom & Nic.

SJM Concerts by arrangement with EC1 presents

The Chemical Brothers

ALEXANDRA PALACE

FRI 5TH & SAT 6TH OCTOBER 2018

Show Direction: Adam Smith & Marcus Lyall

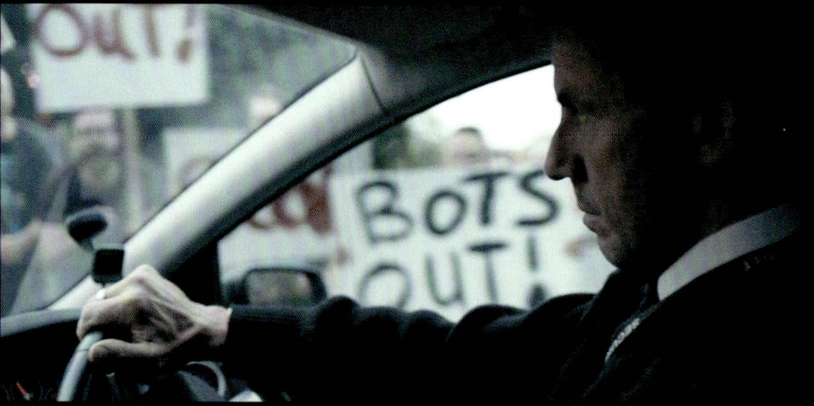
OUT!
BOTS OUT!
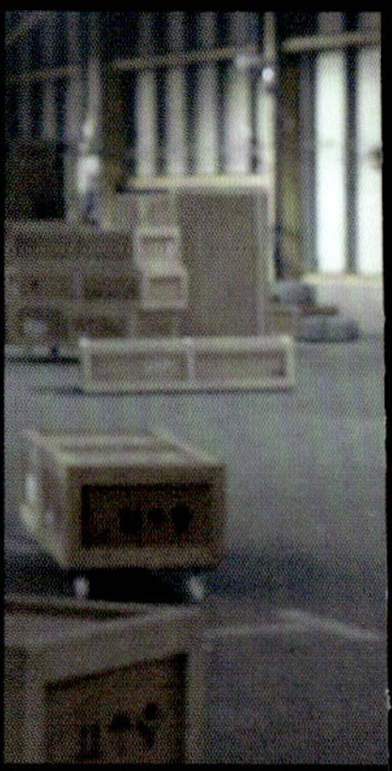
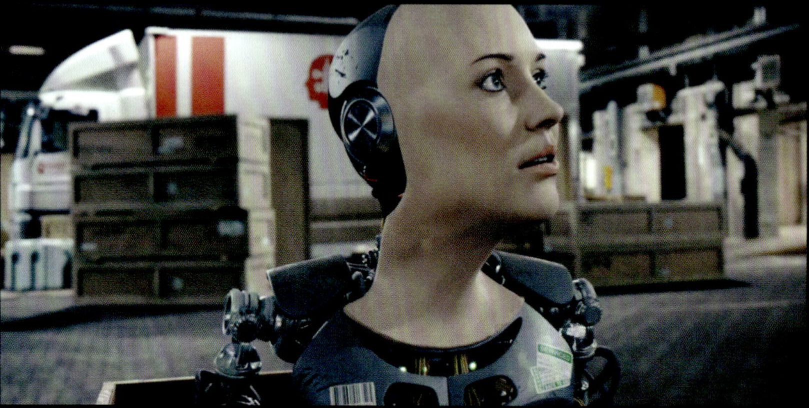
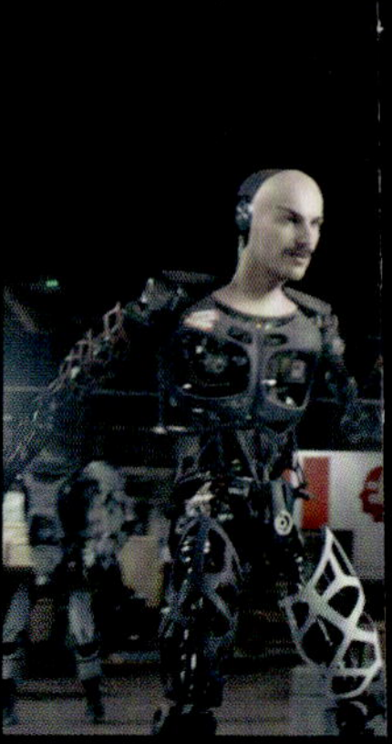
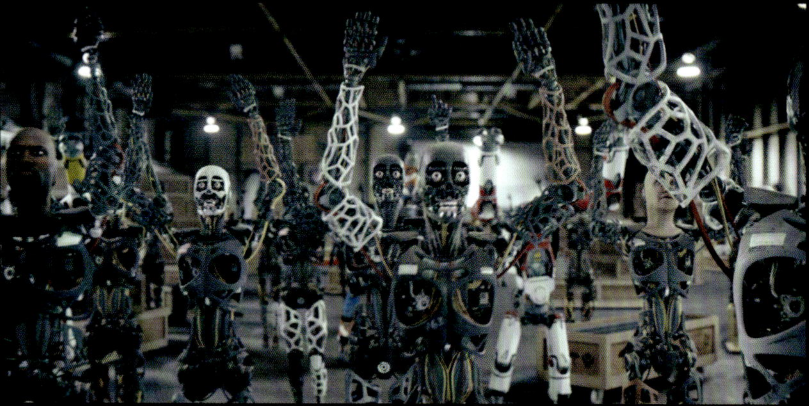
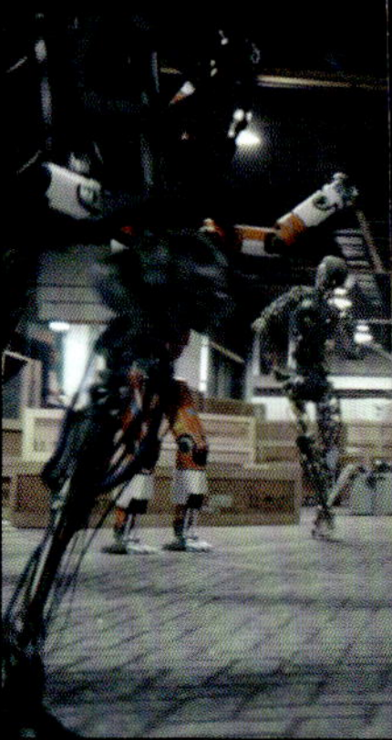
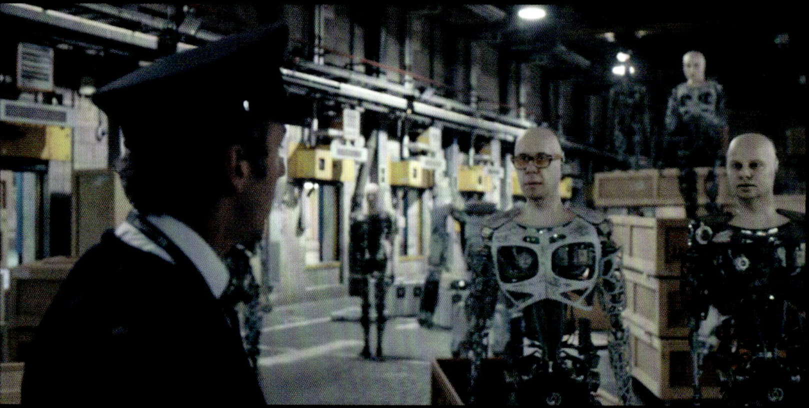
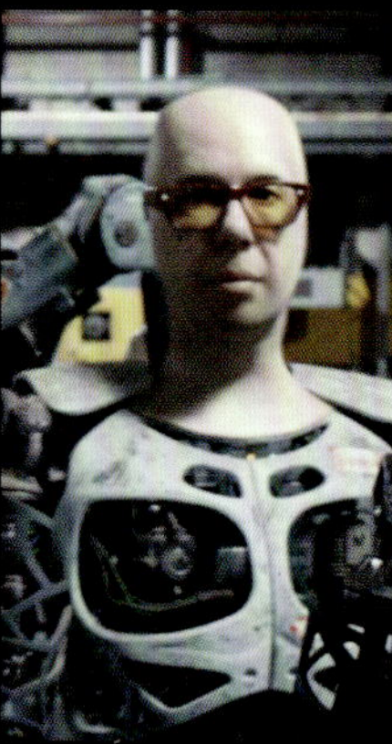

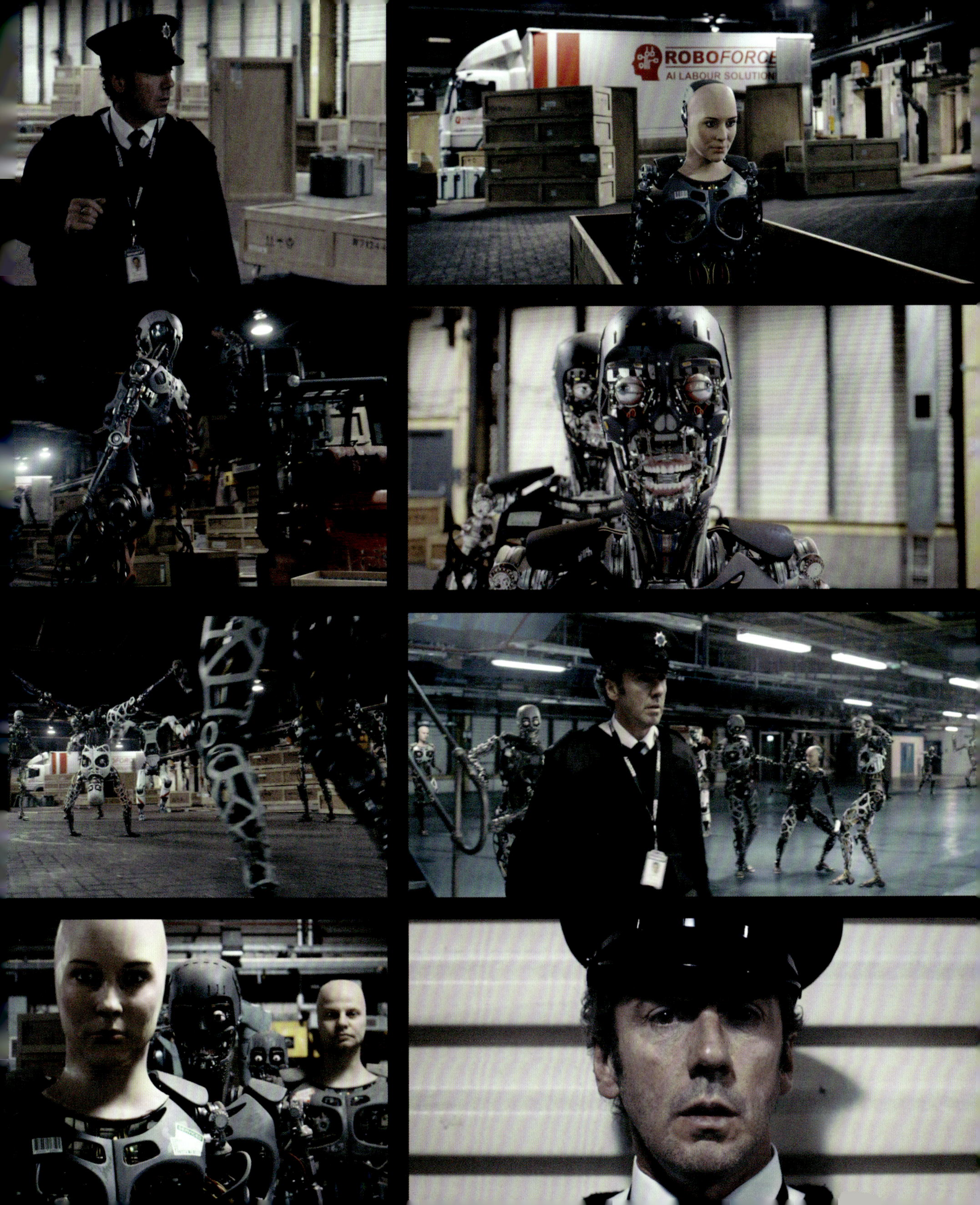
ROBOFORCE
AI LABOUR SOLUTION

272 The Chemical Brothers

Got to Keep On

In late July 2020, London's Design Museum finally launched an exhibition delayed by the advent of Covid-19 earlier in the year. 'Electronic: From Kraftwerk to The Chemical Brothers' was a multi-room tour through the history of electronic music, heading from Düsseldorf to Detroit and Chicago, then on to London via Paris and Berlin. It brilliantly reflected changing trends and evolutions in the associated culture while threading a consistent line through the seventies to the second decade of the twenty-first century. And it did it all at a time when clubs were shut and gigs were being postponed for the second or third time.

A stroll through the exhibition was a poignant reminder of what was lost at that point in time. It wasn't just the odd cancelled club night but an entire culture reliant on human contact that had shut down. No one knew if or when it might be switched on again. We were collectively both paused and reflective, but not in a cosmic way.

As you reached the end of the exhibition, you left the main space and its walls of fliers, sleeve art and rave memorabilia to enter a final inner sanctum. This room presented an immersive extract of The Chemical Brothers' live show, specifically the film Smith and Lyall had made to accompany 'Got to Keep On' for the *No Geography* tour.

A *Guardian* reviewer wrote: 'The exhibition culminates in an installation by Adam Smith and Marcus Lyall which reconfigures their stage visuals for The Chemical Brothers' "Got to Keep On" in a small room full of noise, smoke and lights. It feels like electronic music's proof of concept, pulling together music, film, fashion and modern dance into one dizzying sensory experience.'

The effect was almost overwhelming. Each small group of socially distanced, mask-wearing museum goers was offered a five-minute glimpse behind the curtain into a forbidden world, one where the volume was cranked to ear-splitting levels and the strobes were set to stun. The visuals showed a hypnotic, surrealist dance routine complete with costumes that seemed to doff a cap to both Leigh Bowery and some of Doctor Who's stranger nemeses.

And the soundtrack to the piece was perfection. 'Got to Keep On' is a piece of pure musical escapism that seems to pay homage to so much of dance music's glorious, globe-trotting history, not least the New York discos of the 1970s and the Detroit techno clubs and M25 Orbital raves of the eighties. For a few months, that room was as close to dance floor heaven as it was possible to get, anywhere in the entire world.

Tom Rowlands

'Got to Keep On' followed a really long, twisting path to get to where it ended up. It had so many iterations, some much more song-y than the final track. The first recordings date back to 2011. At one point it was called 'Fantasy' and it had a real techno feel, much more like a track we released on the Japanese version of *No Geography* ('Fantai'). That had the techno stabs that are still in the finished track, and it had Stephanie Dosen singing lyrics along with the wordless melody part that we ended up keeping.

The main vocal line was taken from a big old disco track (Peter Brown's 'Dance with Me'), but it's not sampled. I heard a seventies album of people doing choir versions of disco records and it really intrigued me. So we got a choir of people to re-sing the words. I liked the idea of those brilliant, sweaty old disco records reimagined completely differently just by changing the style of the voices. Taking the spirit of the original sample line, then putting it into this different context. I'm not sure what the impulse to do it was, but we just got carried along by the idea and the final song started to form from there.

When I got to play with the track in the studio with Dubby, the whole freak-out section in the middle (*And the rain . . .*) really came to life. It had always been there but not with anything like the same degree of intensity as it ended up having. Often in the studio, you're looking for a wildness where you push things as far as you can, almost to the point where it's too much. If you can bring that wildness into your structured version, that's where a track really takes flight.

There's a weird mix of stuff in there. When we were making it, I kept thinking, 'This all works', and then when it was finished I was struck by how odd the elements are when stuck together. It connects a lot of dance music that we love as a band and, thankfully, it all glued together. I often find with making music that you can be working on a track that isn't quite making sense, then, after spending ages toying with it, you change one tiny aspect of it and it all works perfectly.

But exploring so many avenues can be hugely frustrating. When you start out, you can only really do one thing, so recording is a simpler process. The more you work, the more skilled you become at the technical side – the craft side – and the more maddening it becomes. You start thinking you can do this to a track, and do that, and they're all long processes to explore. Music ends up being more complicated now than it ever has been; there are so many paths once you know where the paths are and how to access them.

Making tracks, I often visualise the kind of space I imagine it being played in, what the crowd would be like, how they'd react. The first time we ever played 'Got to Keep On' out anywhere was at a party we were DJing at in a friend's flat near Old Street roundabout. It was an amazing loft apartment that looked like it could have been straight out of New York. I played the track to a crowd of up-for-it people and it immediately felt like how you'd imagine proper 1970s loft parties would have been. Cool-looking people having the time of their lives. And the music seemed perfect for that feeling, like a realisation of a daydream. It has a heaviness to it but it's also light and trippy and fun. All those different things that had stuck to it on its path to becoming a finished record all helped make it what it was.

Since we've played it live, Adam and Marcus's visuals have become so synonymous with the song that it's hard to hear it without seeing that imagery. The track is fun and groovy, and Adam and Marcus brought that exact same feel. When their visuals were shown at the Design Museum, I took the kids along to see it. Stood in that room, I couldn't believe the amount of strobing going on while it was playing. I kept saying, 'Fuck, is this what our gigs actually look like?'

Right: Promotional poster for the 'Electronic' exhibition at the London Design Museum.

Next page: Costumes for 'Got to Keep On' visuals.

Next page centre right: Adam Smith with Mike Shepherd (in mask) on the 'Mad as Hell' visuals shoot.

Page 278–9: Stills from the 'Got to Keep On' music video, directed by Michel and Olivier Gondry.

ELECTRONIC

THE EXHIBITION

FROM KRAFTWERK TO THE CHEMICAL BROTHERS

276   **The Chemical Brothers**

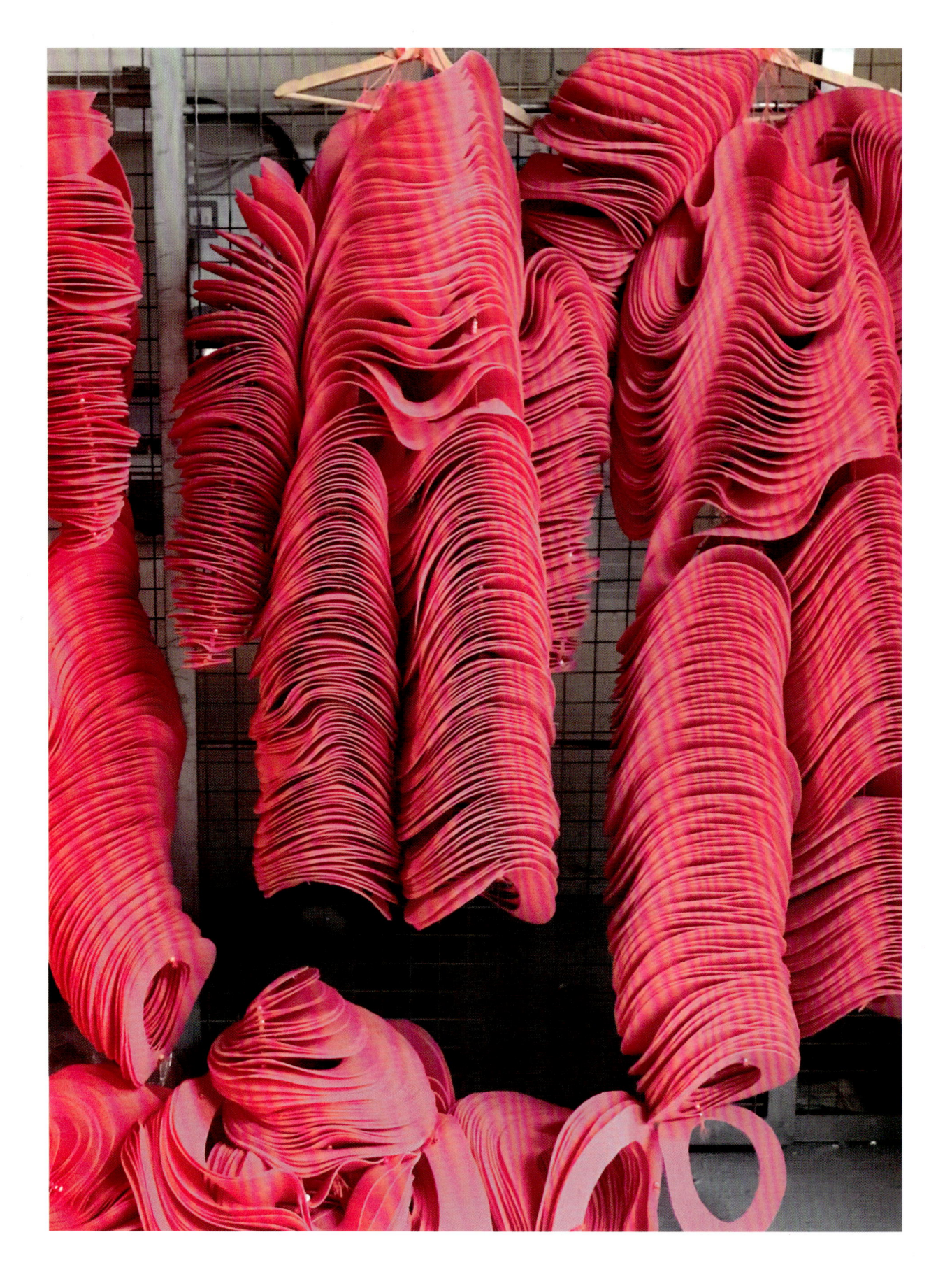

Paused in Cosmic Reflection 277

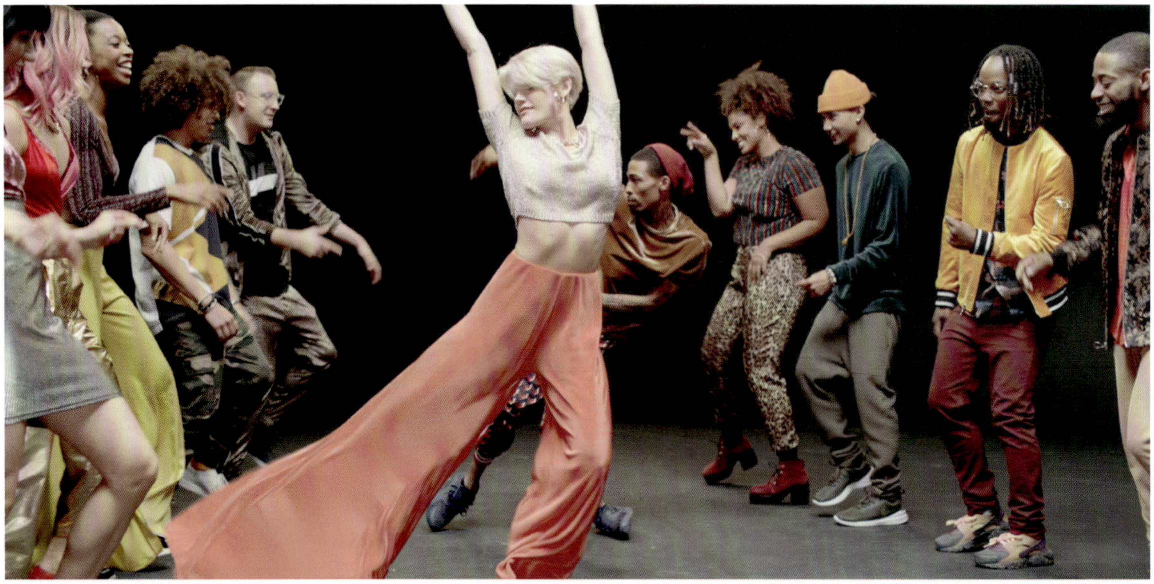
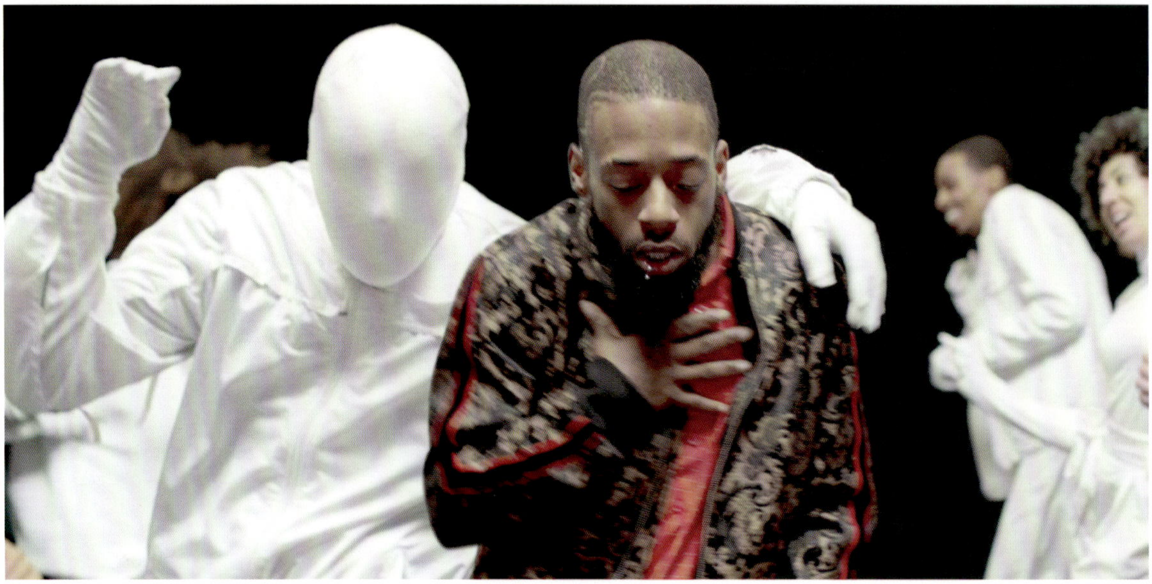
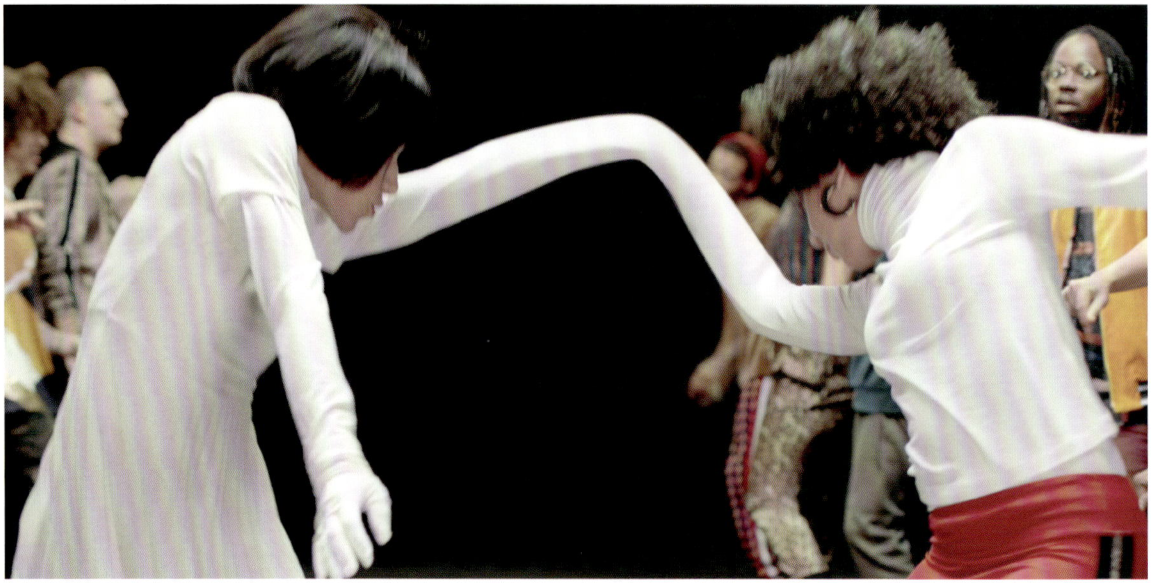

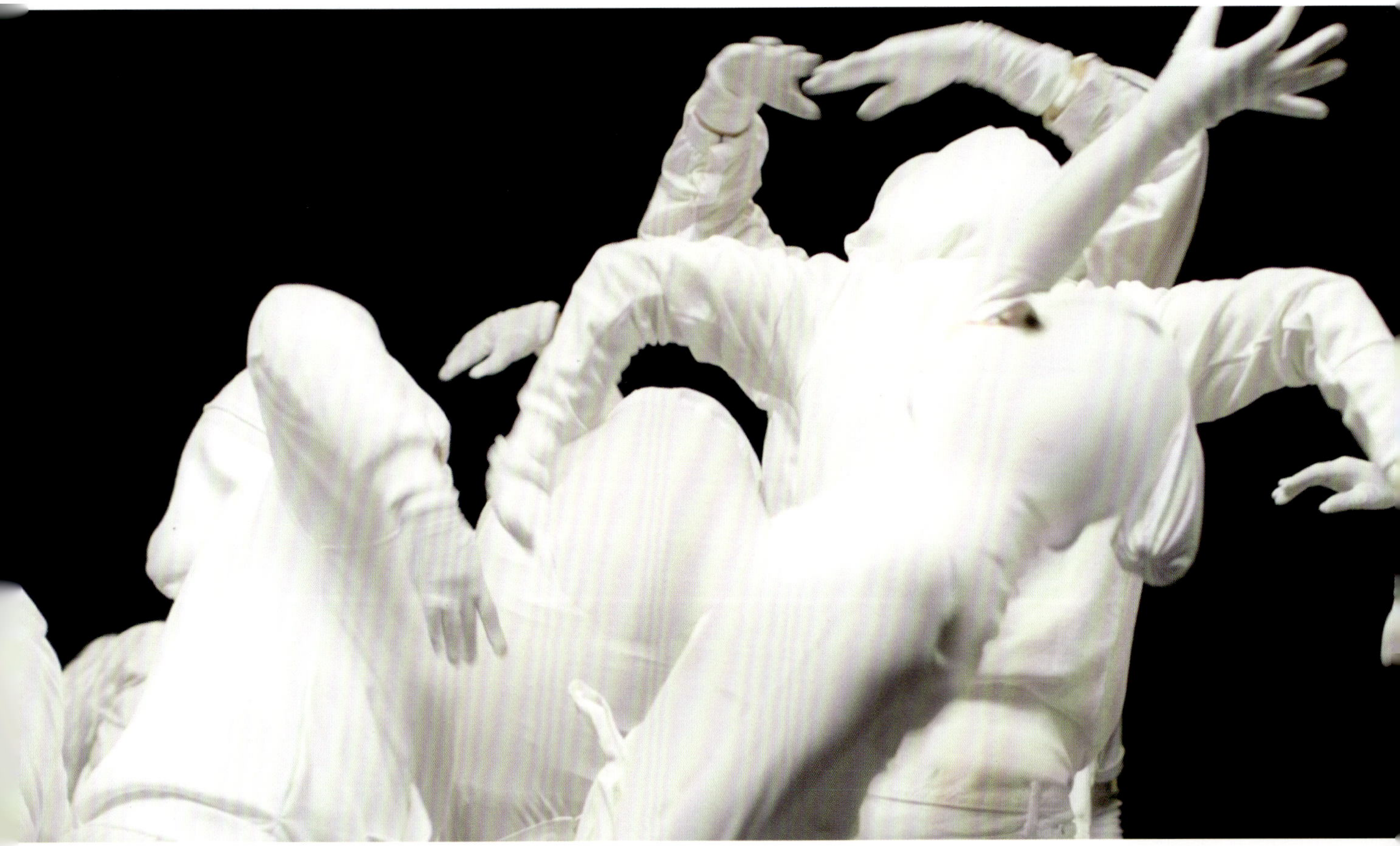

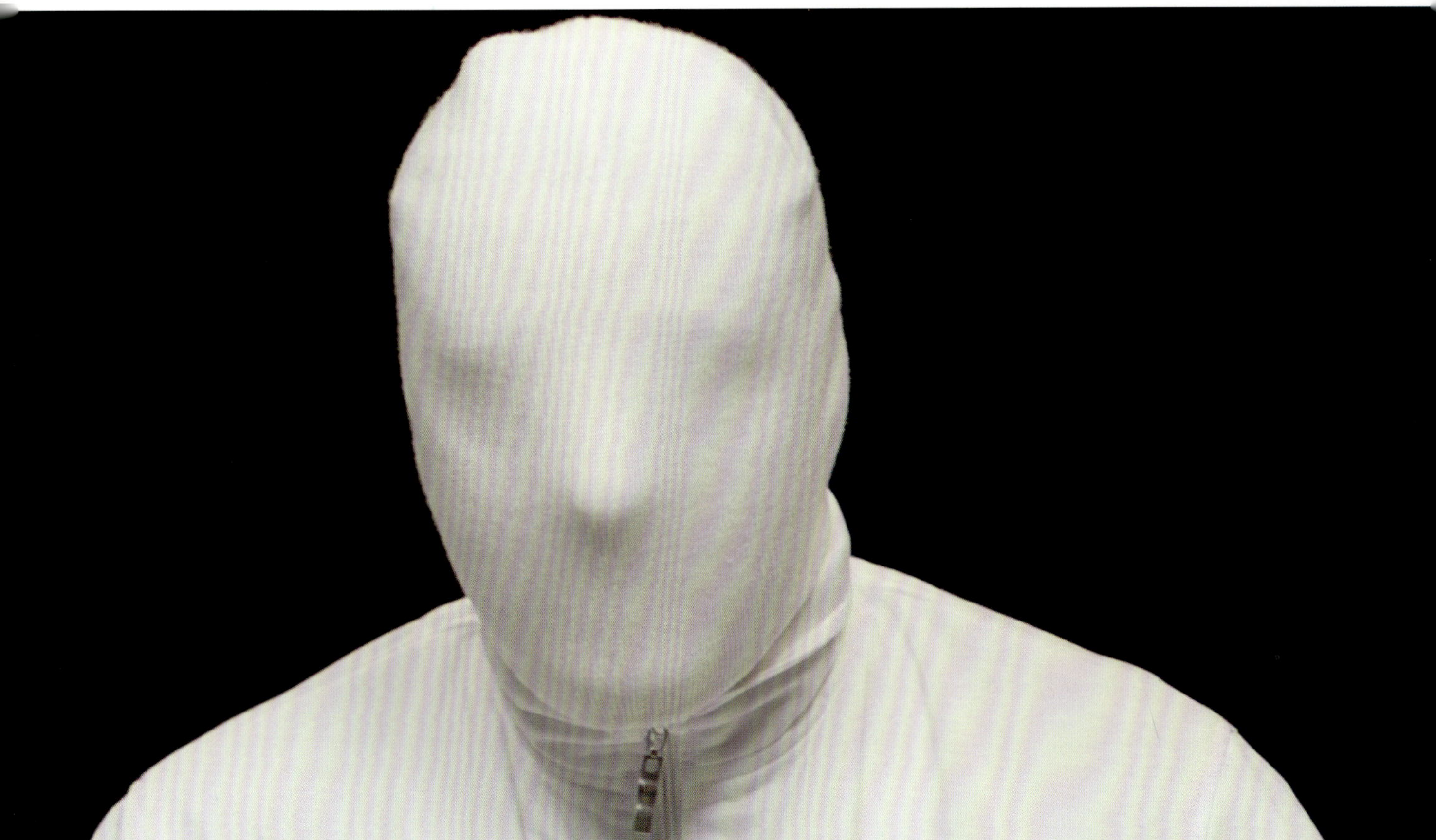

280 The Chemical Brothers

Eve of Destruction

A fully choreographed, ultra-futurist kaiju movie where humans fight impossible beasts from the deep. An office worker by day is a ninja superhero by night, battling a phalanx of electrically charged manga monsters, all under the watchful eye of a blonde Norwegian girl dressed up and ready for a night out in the thirty-first century.

Both the track 'Eve of Destruction' and its accompanying video spin the globe and stop at various points to harness more power. It splashes down in the Pacific just off Japan, crosses an expanse of Eurasia to stop off in Bergen before powering back to the south coast of England and that studio, hidden away from the rest of the world.

Like the rest of *No Geography*, 'Eve of Destruction' was recorded in Rowlands Audio Research during a period reconfiguring The Chemical Brothers' sound. For a while the recording of the album was frustrating: myriad ideas banged up against each other without quite connecting. Old equipment used for recording the first couple of albums was dusted off for the first time this century, and old methods of sampling and song construction were explored. Then, a Scandinavian singer in her early twenties arrived in the studio with a headful of ideas and enough imagination to inspire a complete rewiring of the entire process.

Tom Rowlands

Sometimes when you're recording, you have to go around the houses, almost to the point where you drive yourself mad trying to find the right path. With *No Geography*, it took a while to get the right feel, where it was almost a bit naive and sounding a bit wrong. Lots of electronic music is made to sound really tight and sharp and bright. I was determined to make something that sounded a bit wrong but that worked in the environment you're hearing it in, whether that's live or in a club or on headphones. I didn't want to make something that sounded 'awesome' or precise; I wanted to make something that sounded human, something with the ability to wrong-foot you. A lot of music is made from sounds that are pre-maximised and inflated. I want our music to be more idiosyncratic and I wanted the samples to become like collaborators, like on our early records.

One of the things that helped focus the record was working with Aurora. Her contribution to the album was so important. I'd seen her live on the John Peel Stage at Glastonbury in 2016. I didn't know her music at all but seeing her, I thought she had an amazing voice and this incredible presence. And she brought that presence with her to the studio.

Aurora arrived in the studio at a point where I was questioning how all the ideas I had were going to fit together. She was the human glue that made it all fit, so energised about music, pulling lots of loose ends together. She came to my house to work and she had a brilliantly wide-eyed approach to making music, a natural response to ideas. We'd be looking at two ideas that were meant to sit in the same song, that weren't written at the same time and she'd say, 'Yeah, of course we can put that with that.' The freedom in her approach while being exacting – and confident in what she did – became really exciting and infectious and informed so much of the record. A complete inspiration.

Aurora

I grew up quite isolated in a very small town in Norway and we didn't really have a lot of access to music. I grew up listening to people like Leonard Cohen and Bob Dylan. The Chemical Brothers was the first thing

Previous page: 'Eve of Destruction' live visuals.

Opposite: Aurora on set for 'Eve of Destruction' visuals shoot.

I discovered for myself. It was something I found in the world that sounded like nothing I'd ever heard before. It wasn't in my life just because it was there, it was something new that became very much all mine. So I've loved them for most of my life. When I first heard the *Hanna* soundtrack, my mind began to understand something about music that I'd never known had existed before. I didn't know a lot about music growing up; I still don't. But their music did something really special to me.

Tom sent me an email asking if I wanted to work with them. It was a few days before I answered. I needed to still my hands and calm my pulse. I felt flabbergasted that he'd got in touch. It was fascinating getting that email saying they'd love to work together, so I answered, 'Yes, I'd love that.' He invited me over to England, to his studio. I stayed in this beautiful, small inn with these beautiful people. It was such a special experience.

I'd been touring all throughout 2016, so much so that I'd lost a lot of the things that made me *me*. I think it's very usual for artists to overwork themselves. Being invited by The Chemical Brothers over to this beautiful calm place where there was no phone connection, no 3G signal, was exactly what I needed to reset. Staying in this small house with a family and walking along the small road from the inn to Tom's house. Just doing whatever we felt like. It was a very soulful, very important experience for me, and it was an absolute delight.

In the studio, we didn't really think much. We were led by our hearts and instincts. We played around and had a lot of fun. There were very few words spoken, and when they were, Tom would be fascinated by things I'd say, using new words or different ways of speaking. It was kind of like puking, only in a nice way.

I was there for a week initially, and I came back one more time once he had wrapped his head around all of the ideas we'd planted. He had let them grow into small plants and I came back later to water them and help them grow into really strong, steady plants. The second time I went, I had forgotten to sort anywhere to sleep, which was kind of silly, so Tom put me up in a spare room in his attic. I slept there and ended up crashing his daughter's eleventh birthday. I'd flown over without a plan. I can be quite whimsical like that; it's not new for me to not know what I'm doing because I haven't planned ahead. The future doesn't exist yet, you know? I wanted to give them some space, so I went for a walk in their garden, and just kept going. I was away for many hours and it got dark. I walked into some woods and had to cross a river, then I ended up on a road, found a bar, had a beer, talked to some people, crossed many different people's gardens and got back quite late. They had been really worried about me but because there's no phone connection they couldn't get hold of me. I ended up becoming more trouble than I'd intended, but I did have a lovely adventure.

Working with Tom felt very free. It's one of the first collaborations I've done with another artist in the studio. The whole thing felt like I'd been freed from restraints of beauty. We didn't have to make something beautiful, and that felt very liberating. I love the contrast between the beautiful and the ugly and the hopeful and the menacing. I think those contrasts in art help tickle the brain, and I think we all need to experience that feeling. It felt wonderful to explore the ugliness within the beauty. There's a lot of rawness, and otherness, a lot of freedom and instinct in the music we made. We are very similar in the studio, quite messy and all over the place, jumping from idea to idea, then going back to

Paused in Cosmic Reflection 283

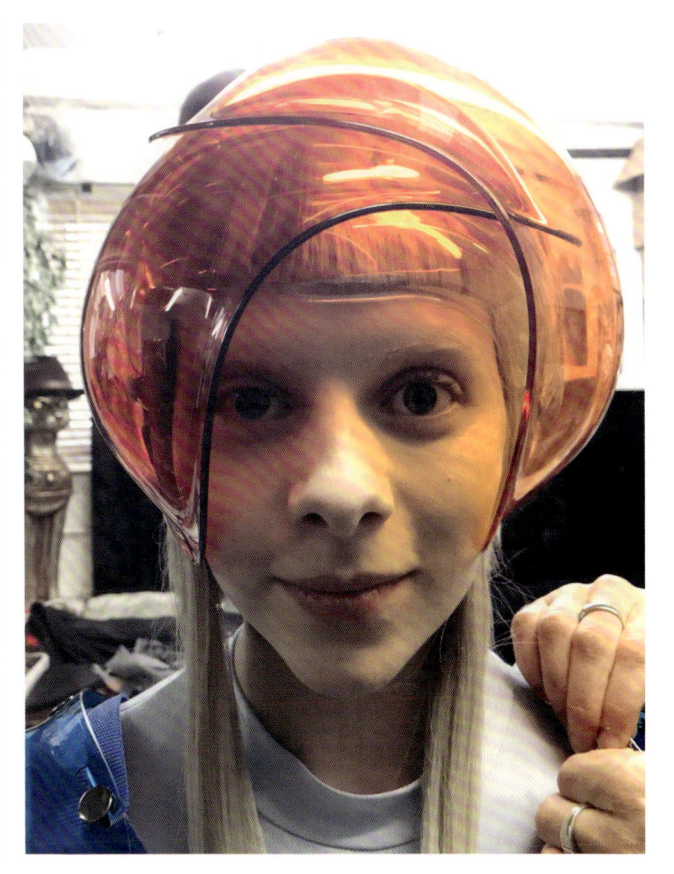

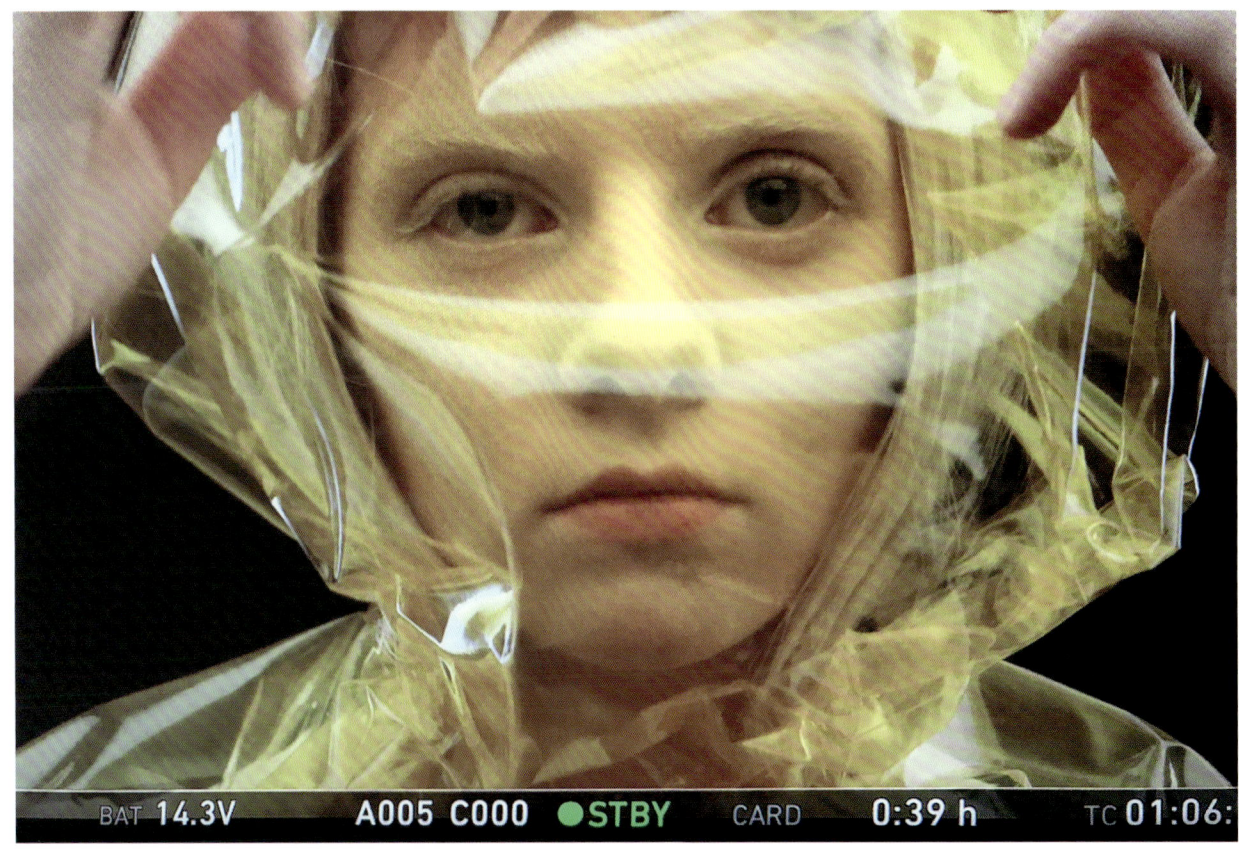

earlier ideas. We moved a lot like two rivers when we worked, each taking our distinct path before ending up merged together into some kind of beautiful glimmering puddle.

When we made the film for 'Eve of Destruction', it felt very correct to become that manga character. I'm very into sci-fi and fantasy so anything that plays into that makes me feel like a very true version of myself. Lots of different versions of yourself can feel true, and that one definitely did. It was a very fun thing to explore. It helped my love of the whole thing, that everyone involved in The Chemical Brothers project seemed like such genuine, artistic and beautiful people. And it was a lot of fun. I tried to bring out multiple personalities within me.

After the shoot, I got to keep the costume. It's in my apartment, and I wear it sometimes when I cook. I love making food but I hate the patience that cooking sometimes requires, all the focus. Wearing the costume makes the whole thing a lot more fun.

Adam Smith

The 'Eve of Destruction' film was originally created as part of the visual backdrop for the *No Geography* tour. Filming Aurora was an incredible amount of fun. She got really into it. She loved the costumes and was really excited about getting deeply involved. One of the lovely things about making the visuals for the live shows is that you've got a bit of time to create. If you're making a video, the clock's ticking away and you can't really play with performance, you need to get things locked so quickly. With this, we had more time and she was absolutely up for using it and trying things out in different ways. During the process of making the film, she came up with lots of ideas about who this character was and what her motivations were.

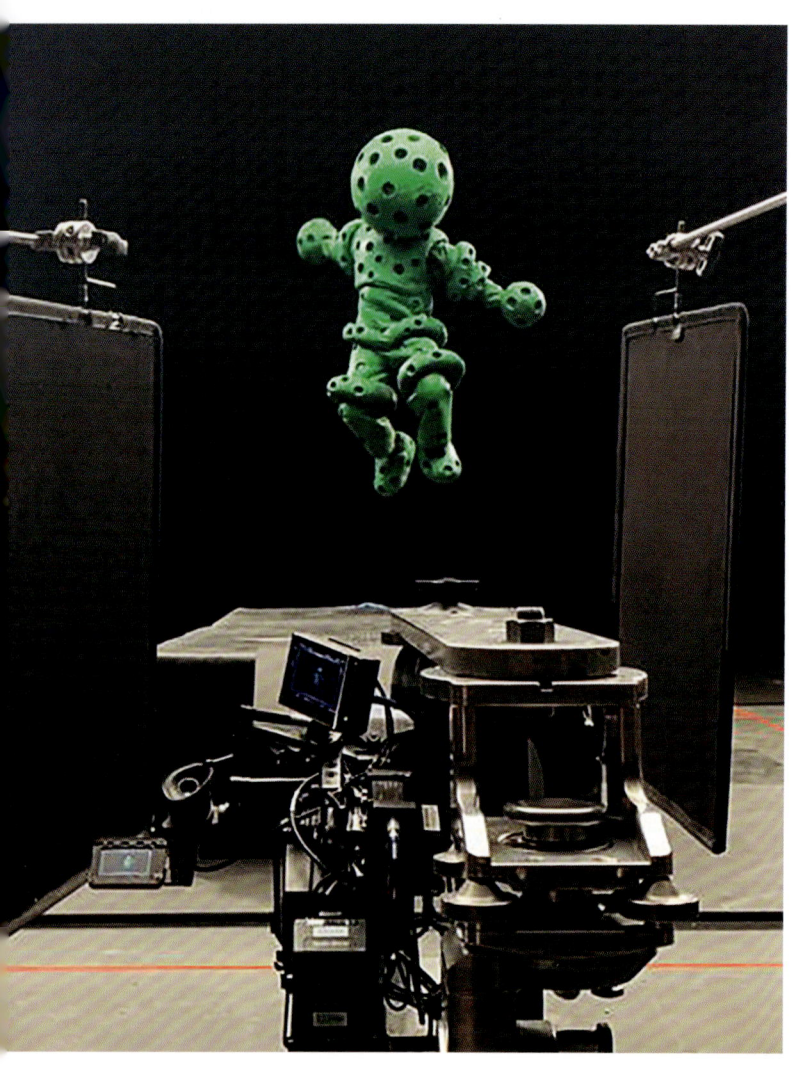

On set for 'Eve of Destruction' live visuals.

Paused in Cosmic Reflection   285

286   The Chemical Brothers

Paused in Cosmic Reflection   287

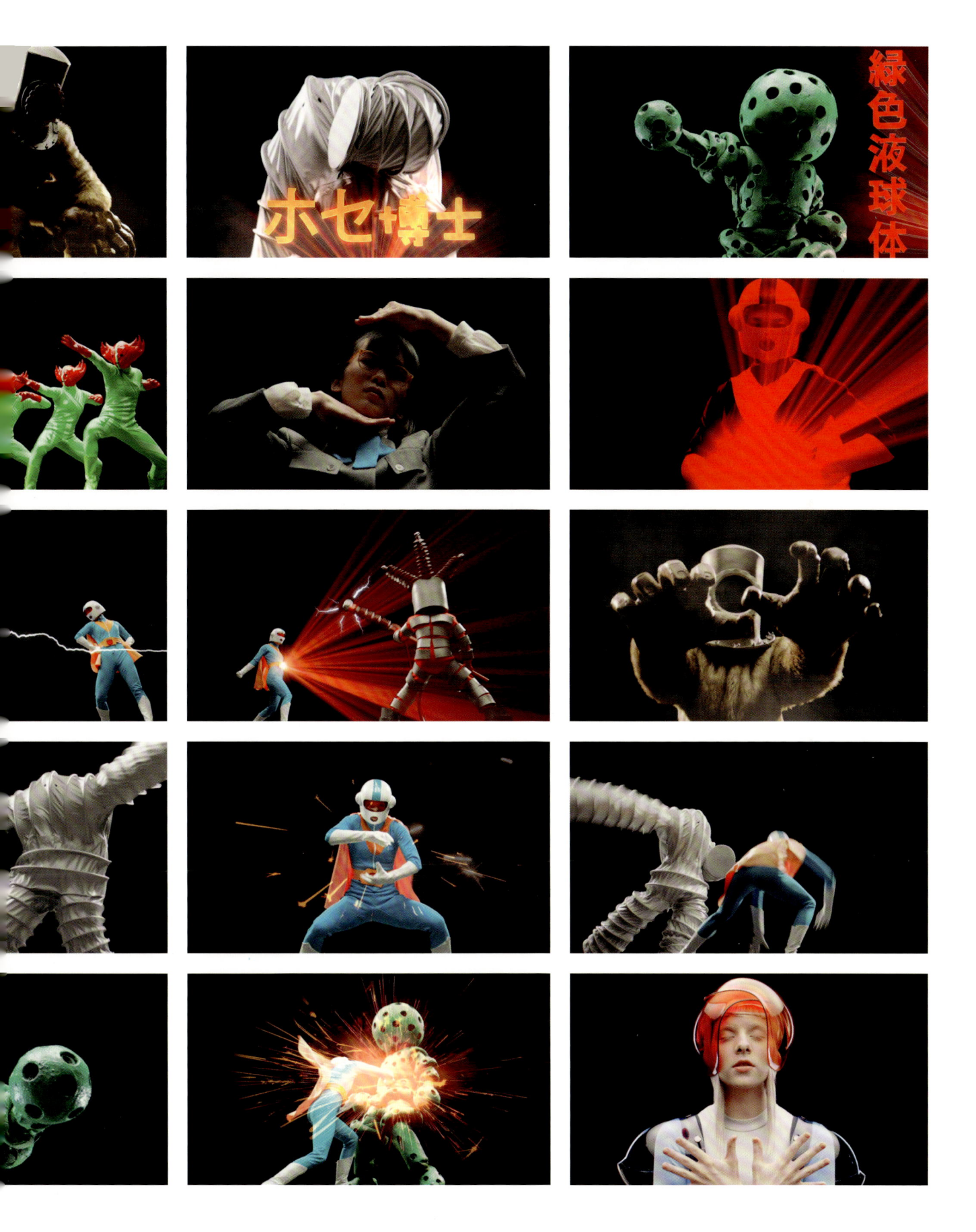

288　**The Chemical Brothers**

Paused in Cosmic Reflection 289

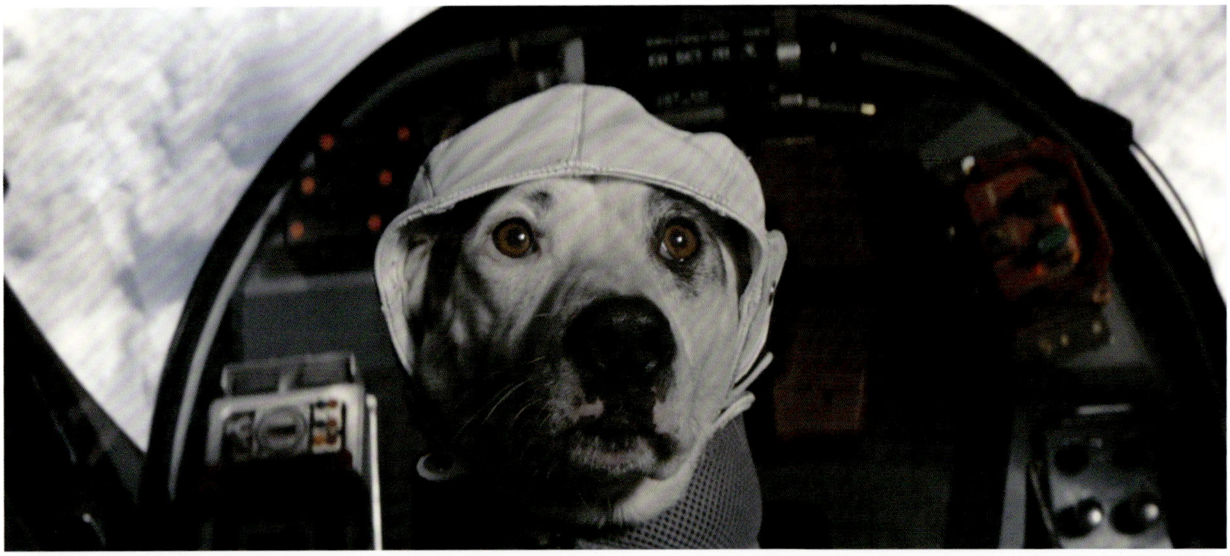

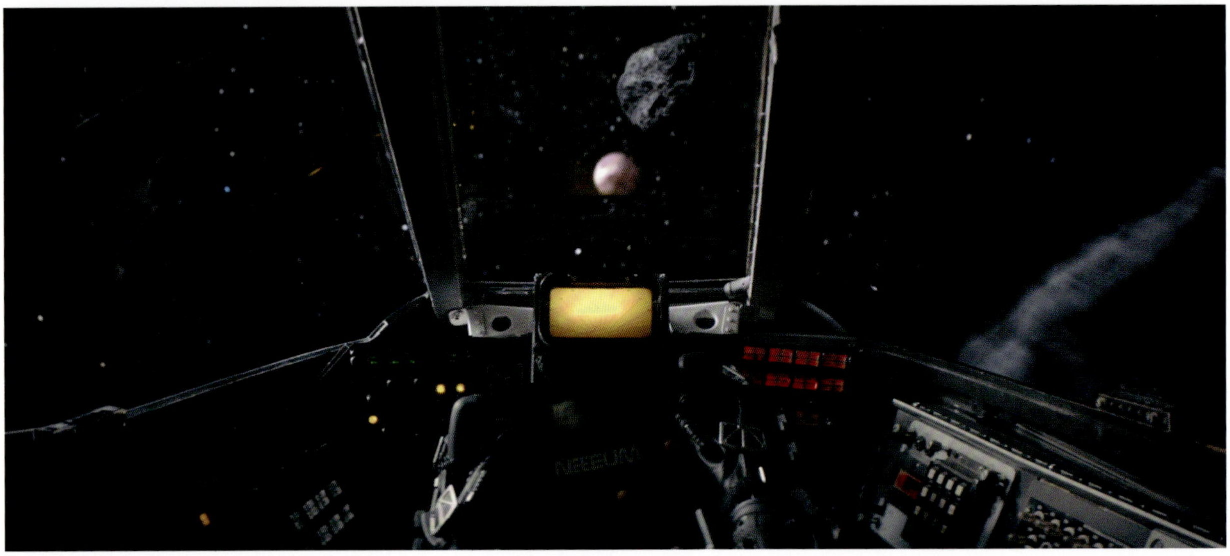

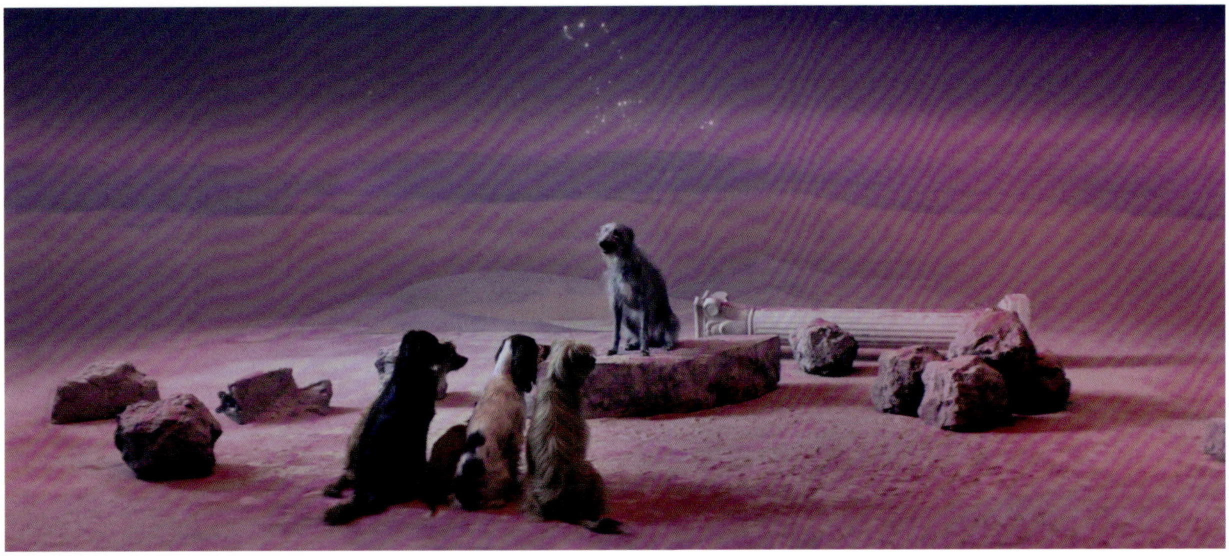

We've Got to Try

Opposite and next page: Stills from the 'We've Got to Try' music video, directed by Ninian Doff.

Next page left: Storyboards for the 'We've Got to Try' music video drawn by Ninian Doff.

On 3 November 1957, Soviet scientists launched Sputnik 2 into Earth's orbit. The craft's sole occupant was Laika, a stray dog found on the streets of Moscow. Laika's fate was preordained as technology did not yet exist to bring Sputnik 2 back to Earth. She died in orbit. Back on Earth, a canine legend was born.

Sixty-two years later, the video for The Chemical Brothers track 'We've Got to Try' tells the story of a space-bound mongrel partly inspired by Laika. It adds a Formula 1 racing car, a touch of subterfuge and the wild prospect of some far-flung planet populated by the kind of fearless space dogs the Soviets launched all those years ago.

'We've Got to Try' was released ahead of *No Geography* in March 2019. The release was accompanied by the 'WGTT15000BPM F1 NEEEUM' remix, which celebrated the start of the 2019 Formula 1 season. That mix saw the original track 'broken down, re-engineered and accelerated to 15,000 beats per minute in order to reflect the 15,000 beats per minute that today's hyper-complex F1 cars are capable of reaching'. Pushing the track to that speed means the mix lasts for all of three seconds, and the entirety of the track whooshes past in barely a blink.

Ninian Doff (director, 'We've Got to Try' music video)

The video began with the car. Through an F1 collaboration the band was working on, they had access to this insane car and a day on the track just outside Bedford. The brief was basically 'What's a Chemical Brothers video that takes advantage of this mad chance to include a zillion-pound car?' The best thing was that there was no catch. It absolutely wasn't to be an advert. The car came with no strings attached.

I was a huge fan of The Chemical Brothers before working with them. It's wild that they just don't date, which seems especially rare in dance music. In the same way that a good Beatles song just doesn't feel fifty years old, The Chemical Brothers' songs just seem to work outside of fashion, trends, time. Songs from twenty years ago could easily be released today and still feel like the best new thing.

The formative years where I daydreamed about one day maybe being a director coincided exactly with the Spike Jonze/Michel Gondry glory years. Their *Director's Bureau* DVDs were as important to my desire to be a director as any Kurosawa or Scorsese film. And The Chemical Brothers are music video royalty to me. I always saw The Chemical Brothers as the pinnacle of music videos, like the very highest honour you could reach. My favourite would have to be a classic Gondry, though I'm unable to choose between 'Let Forever Be' and 'Star Guitar' as they're both pretty much as good as it gets. Making two videos for The Chemical Brothers is still one of the things I'm most proud of.

The only rule I set myself when brainstorming was to think of ideas that didn't involve actual motor racing. How could I take this mad opportunity, go an unexpected route and warp it into the world of Chemical Brothers videos? I love all the old space-race stories. The story of Laika was an inspiration here. However, the real Laika story often ignores how horrendously tragic the story really is (spoiler: they flew a dog into space, but not back to Earth). I really liked the idea of retelling the story so that the dog gets the upper hand and the happy ending she deserved.

Before working on 'We've Got to Try', we shared a few emails. They had full approval of the edit, but there really was incredible faith and support in what I wanted to do, which is amazing and unique for such a big artist. They were absolutely trusting of what I was doing.

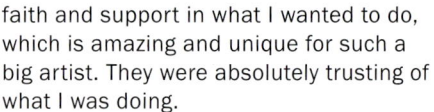

I'd previously actually done an advert with real cats genuinely playing music instruments and through that met this incredible animal trainer, Charlotte Wilde. She told me she'd trained a rescue dog to fly an aeroplane for a TV show. An actual plane, for real. I think as a director you're always mentally logging interesting locations, actors, facts for future use and that titbit went straight into the file. So when it came to it, everyone kept asking how on earth we're going to fake a dog doing all this stuff and I kept saying 'Don't worry about it, I know a dog . . .' No one believed me. In fact, I think some people thought I was fully deluded in pre-production, until he arrived on set and was an absolute legend, doing everything perfectly. The dog is called Shadow, a total pro and very special dog.

Ailsa Robertson (The Chemical Brothers' video commissioner)

Commissioning The Chemical Brothers' videos is an incredibly simple process. I'm very lucky because they were so well established in terms of their videos when I started working with them. The legacy they've built up over three decades is so great, you can just ask, 'Can I have a Chemical Brothers video please?' and you don't need to say anything else. Everybody in the music video community knows exactly what the DNA of a Chemical Brothers video is, there's no need to explain what will or won't work.

Over the years, they've worked with the best of the best in terms of directors. And they attract that kind of talent consistently. When we look for scripts, generally there's an open brief and everybody brings their best game. Directors are given freedom to explore areas they might not look at with other artists. That means you end up with incredible, fantastical ideas. When scripts are submitted you have a stack of brilliant ideas from different directors, and you cry for the ones you can't make.

It helps that Tom and Ed know what they want. They trust directors. There's no need to have a zillion conversations to discuss the minute details; the band trust the judgement of the people they're working with. At the end of the day, all the brilliance comes from them. That's why they attract such incredible talent and why the whole process is a joy.

Paused in Cosmic Reflection 293

And then the rain comes down
Like tears, like tears

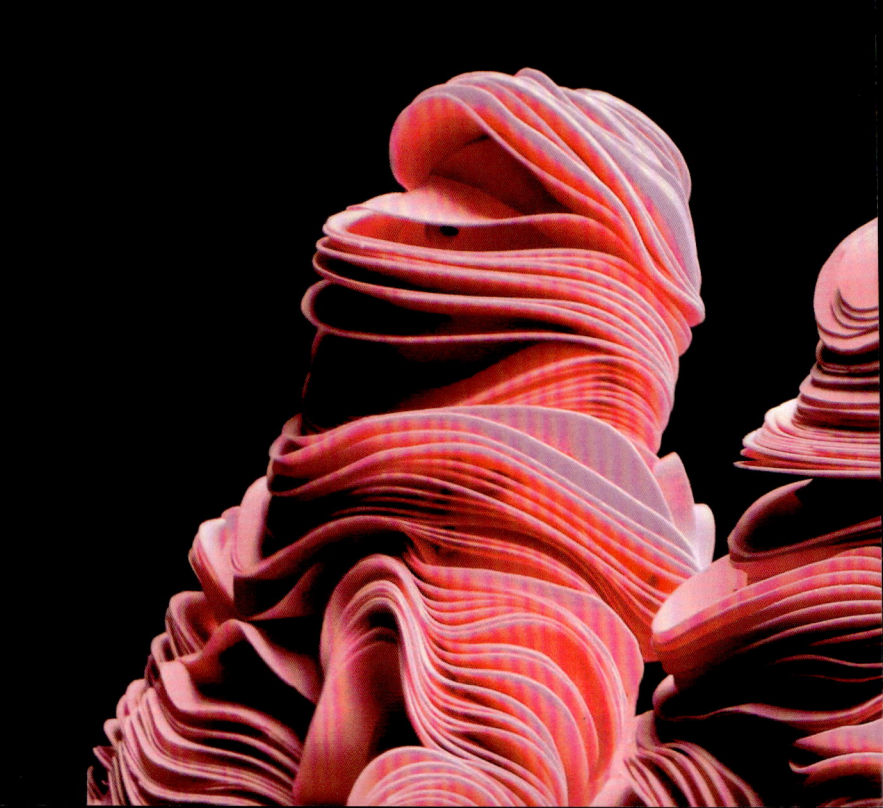

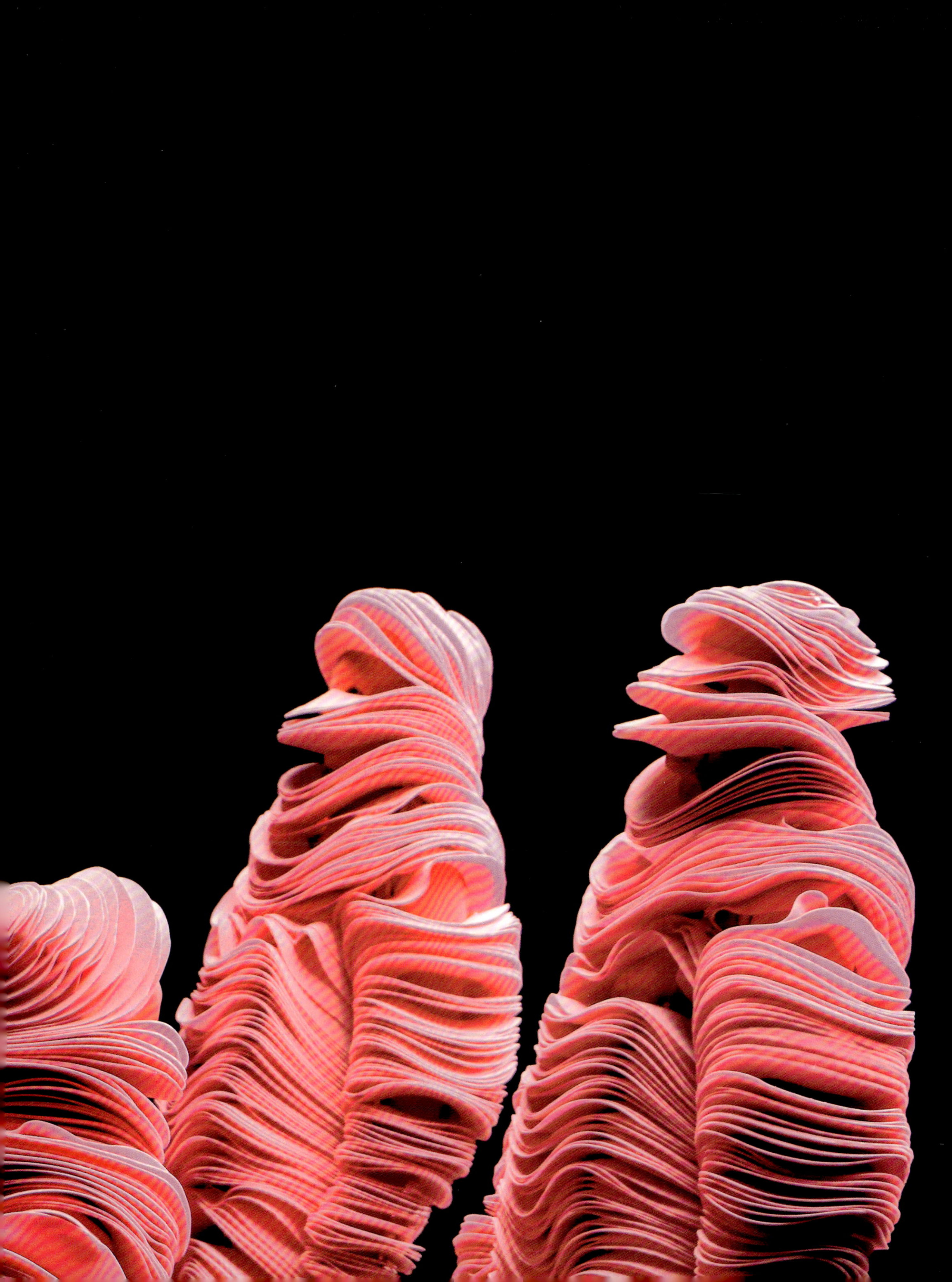

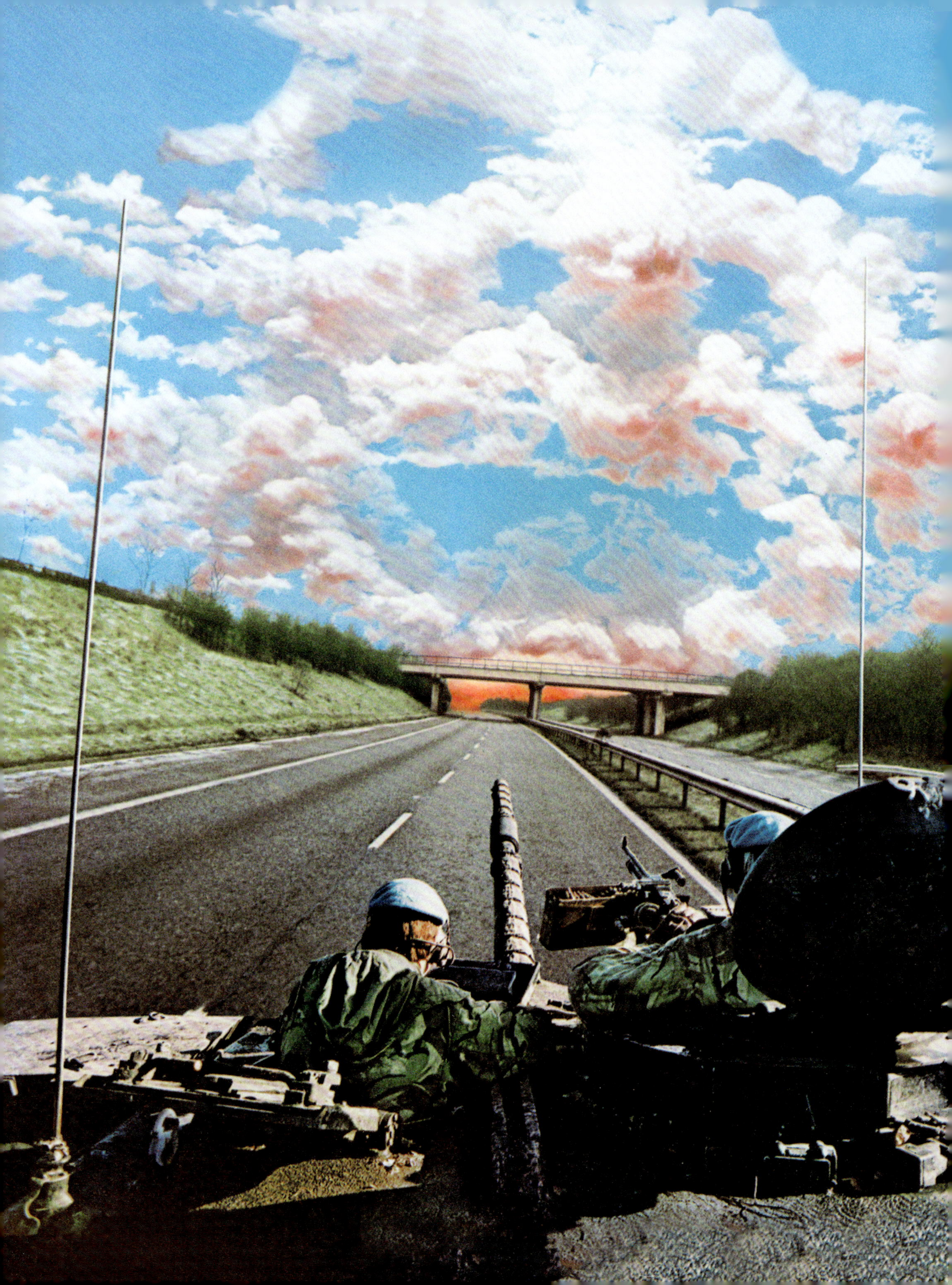

No Geography

'It's 1969, the phone is the medium and the poem is the message. Dial-A-Poem is brand new. You pick up your phone, dial (212)628-0400 and hear one of a dozen recorded poems by William S. Burroughs, Allen Ginsberg, Joe Brainard, Anne Waldman, John Cage or who knows who. The next day there's a fresh dozen. Some are dirty. Some are radical. A lot are about guns. Some really aren't poems at all but songs or rants or sermons.'

'Millions called. "The busiest time was 9 a.m. to 5 p.m., so one figured that all those people sitting at desks in New York office buildings spend a lot of time on the telephone," wrote John Giorno, the founder of Dial-A-Poem. "The second busiest time was 8:30 p.m. to 11:30 p.m. then the California calls and those tripping on acid or couldn't sleep, 2 a.m. to 6 a.m."' [Sarah Boxer, New York Times, 2005]

The record sleeve is old and battered, its spine cracked and roughed up from five and a half decades of wear and tear. The cover does look promising though. Peace and love personified on the front with a picture of a man and a woman straight out of beatnik Central Casting. On the back, a sit-down protest surrounded by tooled-up police officers. The record's strap line completes the picture. 'At this point, with the war and the repression and everything, we thought this was a good way for the Movement to reach people.'

The names featured on the back are a rollcall of beats, Black Panthers, poets from the New York and the West Coast schools, and assorted dissident voices of the late sixties. Drop the needle. You'll hear Allen Ginsberg, Diane di Prima, Bobby Seale, Bernadette Mayer, Jim Carroll, John Sinclair. All those voices, caught at their prime. Flip this record over in your hands, it's the counterculture writ large. And it's crate-digger's catnip. Discogs rating: sleeve fair (F), vinyl good (G) to good plus (G+).

The Dial-A-Poem Poets album was released on New York poet John Giorno's Giorno Poetry Systems Records in 1972. Giorno saw the project as part of the great divide between the late-sixties youth movement and the Establishment. As he states in the sleeve notes, 'We used the telephone for poetry. They used it to spy on you.'

Over the years, Giorno's label would release compilations that captured nascent US music scenes with all of their fizzing energy and brilliant chaotic naivety, bands as they bust out of the garage alongside poets who embodied a permanent punk-rock ethos. *A Diamond Hidden in the Mouth of a Corpse* from 1985 featured the likes of Hüsker Dü, Sonic Youth and Cabaret Voltaire in a sleeve designed by Keith Haring, while 1987's *Smack My Crack* took in Butthole Surfers, Swans and Einstürzende Neubauten. Both albums feature a grizzled William S. Burroughs in full flow.

Let's go back to that Dial-A-Poem album, back to side C track 7 and a six-and-a-half-minute piece by New York poet Michael Brownstein written under the influence of speed that forms the basis of the title track of 2019's *No Geography*.

Tom Rowlands

One of the things that really influenced the album was finding that resource of poets. In the late sixties in the States, there was a phone line where you could dial up and listen to a live recording of a poem for free. The Diane di Prima poem that 'Free Yourself' is built around was one of those poems ['Free Yourself' features an extract from di Prima's poem 'Revolutionary Letter #49'].

Sometimes you choose samples and you don't really know what's guiding your hand. 'Geography' just felt really timely. It's about a

The Dial-a-Poem Poets LP cover, 1972.

Page 302–3: Stills from the 'The Darkness That You Fear' music video, directed by Ruffmercy.

relationship between two people and the idea that the distance between them can't really affect the way they love and feel for each other. It also plays into the idea of geography not being a barrier between collaboration and that arbitrary divisions between people aren't really the way to go.

When choosing samples, it's interesting which things you choose to get a message across. They aren't just random things. There's a reason why the 'No Geography' sample resonated when we were making the record; you can't really help but be influenced by feelings about the world around you. Sometimes you want the record you're making to mean everything, to represent everything you like about music. *Surrender* did that – it was everything we wanted to say about music at that point. 'No Geography' wasn't like that. It was more focused on one feeling. It's more singular. It doesn't matter that it's not everything you like about music – it's got a feeling and it runs with it.

There's a whole hinterland of music around the track; it could have been a lot longer but I kept listening to it thinking, 'What do I want this track to say?' Everything it needed to say was there in those three minutes. Brevity made it stronger.

Michael Brownstein

The poet John Giorno asked me to read something that he could put onto his Dial-A-Poem service in the late sixties. I read a poem called 'Geography'. How that poem came about, I'll be honest with you: my girlfriend and I were staying out in the country in the middle of the winter and a friend came over with some hardcore amphetamine. I got ripped out of my head, the friend left and after he left I wrote 'Geography'.

Up until the mid-1960s in America, everything was still like the fifties. It was very straight and tight. Although New York wasn't a hippie place like San Francisco, there was this huge opening, and it was fabulous. In the late sixties, early seventies, people were escaping from small-town USA on every level, be it sexually, politically, whatever. The whole of the straight world was one of contraction. This was an expansion.

Later on, young people had this whole idea that the sixties were a failure, full of drug casualties and maybe politically it didn't achieve what it set out to do. That's all baloney. It's ignorant about what the whole sixties movement had to deal with. The weight of the thing that was holding people down was gone, all because of that movement. And that's what the poem is about. The openness in the sixties is in the openness in that poem.

'Geography' allowed me to communicate that expansion in an immediate way. A nice hit of speed, I was sailing. I had something to say, I wasn't just writing gibberish. I'm tracking my state of mind. It's almost like it came out of my body, like it was releasing a lifeforce.

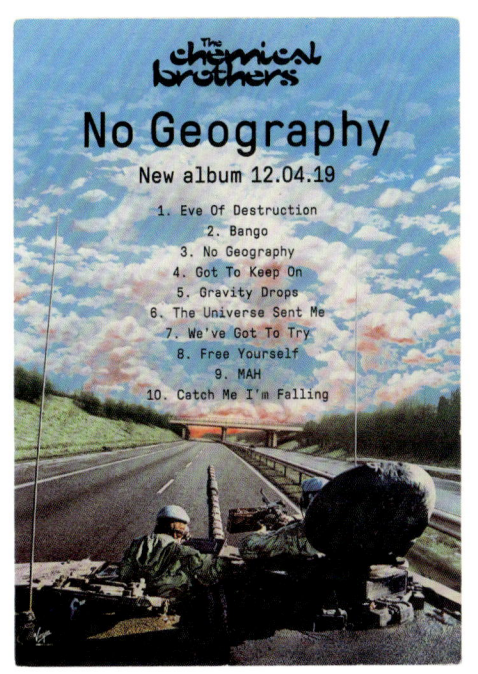

Many years later, I got this email from the manager of The Chemical Brothers. He said the band were making a new album and they wanted to use something from one of my poems. They'd obviously listened to the whole of the Dial-A-Poem record that had come out after the service ended. They chose a piece by Diane di Prima and they chose that one section from 'Geography'.

They were psyched about the poem but afraid that I was going to say no, nervous that I'd be precious and say, 'No, you can't touch my work for some kind of *pop music*.' I said, 'Please go ahead. I think it's great and I'm interested to see what you'll do.' I think they'd already decided that it was going to be the title of the album.

I knew The Chemical Brothers' name. I knew they were big and I understood exactly where they were coming from because I was going to raves in the early nineties in New York City. I was a little older than a lot of the people on the scene but I thought ecstasy was really interesting. There's plus and minus sides to it but it made people drop all their defence mechanisms. People of both sexes, walking up to you, looking you in the eye, coming from the heart. Big smiles in New York City where everyone was guarded. Those raves continued a spirit that started in the sixties and continued through the whole psychedelic movement. It continues today with The Chemical Brothers.

What The Chemical Brothers took was a small sample of this longer poem. They heard the section 'If you ever change your mind about leaving it all behind, remember, remember, no geography', and that's what they took. You could make a point of saying what I'd written was political, but it kind of transcends that. It has an activist tone to it.

I really wanted to meet the Brothers after they'd done the track. They had a concert at Forest Hills, this huge tennis stadium outside New York City. There were thousands of people there. I went backstage and got talking to them and they were talking about how when they put the record together, they were thinking a lot about changing social and political climates. Things were separating people. One of the big themes in my work has been about how nationalism separates people, as 'Geography' was. The Chemical Brothers were pissed about what was coming; they were thinking in a similar way years later. It's why they'd been attracted to those words.

I think they were nervous when they reached out – what's this poet going to say, we're this music band, is he going to be OK with what we want to do to his poem? And I was happy. I like what they did. They ran my voice through a gizmo and I thought the whole thing was great. If someone is inventive and has a great imagination, a driving force and a musical ability . . . if they want to make use of what I wrote, go for it. The poem that I'd written decades earlier, flipped out of my mind, was just sitting there on the page. Go for it.

Paused in Cosmic Reflection

Nick Dewey (The Chemical Brothers' co-manager)

The Chemical Brothers have slowly morphed from an incredibly visceral, heavy sound that sledgehammered its way into pop culture to something altogether more melodic and often beautiful, but still psychedelic and vital. And sometimes even more visceral and heavy. I think their secret is a rare combination of sonic innovation and killer pop instinct. And drive. They put so much work into making their music – the detail, the craft, the layers beneath the layers – creating these moments that feel so startling and original, and hit you with such immediacy, but have been orchestrated in the studio over weeks and months, sometimes years. They've made so much music over the years but somehow you always know it's The Chemical Brothers, whether it's 'Song to the Siren' or a track like 'No Geography'. It's one of the most emotional things that they have made, a career highlight after so many years of highlights. It mixes poetry and noise and music into some kind of ecstatic symphony. The whole thing is not so much a sound as an aesthetic.

Making records has always been simply about the music and the art and bringing people or ideas together. The Chemical Brothers don't crave celebrity and have chosen a path outside of that. Right from the start they have made life difficult for themselves in some ways, in terms of selling stuff. They've never really done TV performances outside of the odd festival, they never really do meet-and-greets and all that glad-handing, they rarely do interviews and have no interest in becoming 'personalities', yet somehow they've created all these pieces of music that have really touched people around the world. And they've never compromised. But they have kept this wonderful friendship all the way through. It's magic. I feel very lucky to have been along for the ride.

Paused in Cosmic Reflection

302 The Chemical Brothers

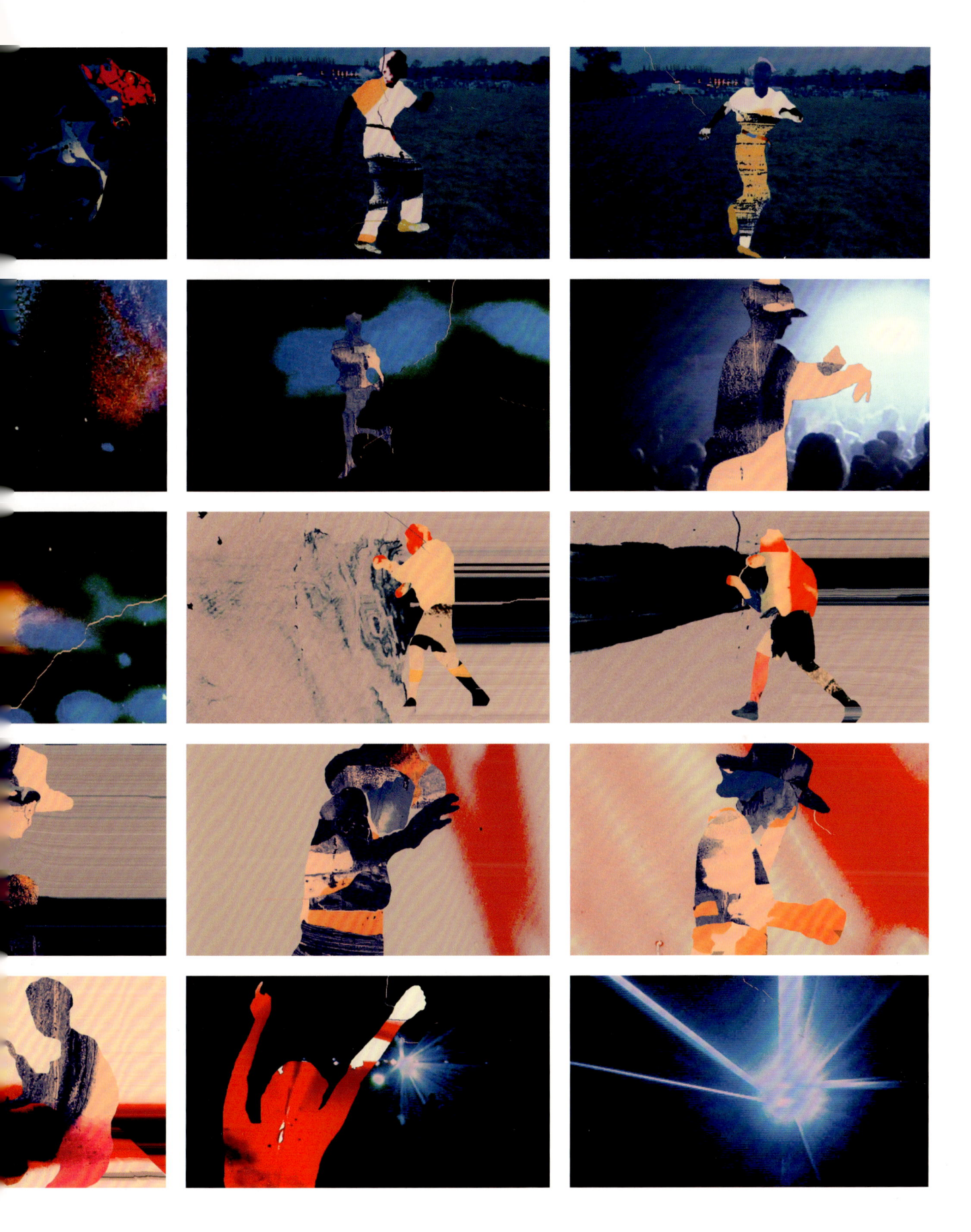

Paused in Cosmic Reflection 303

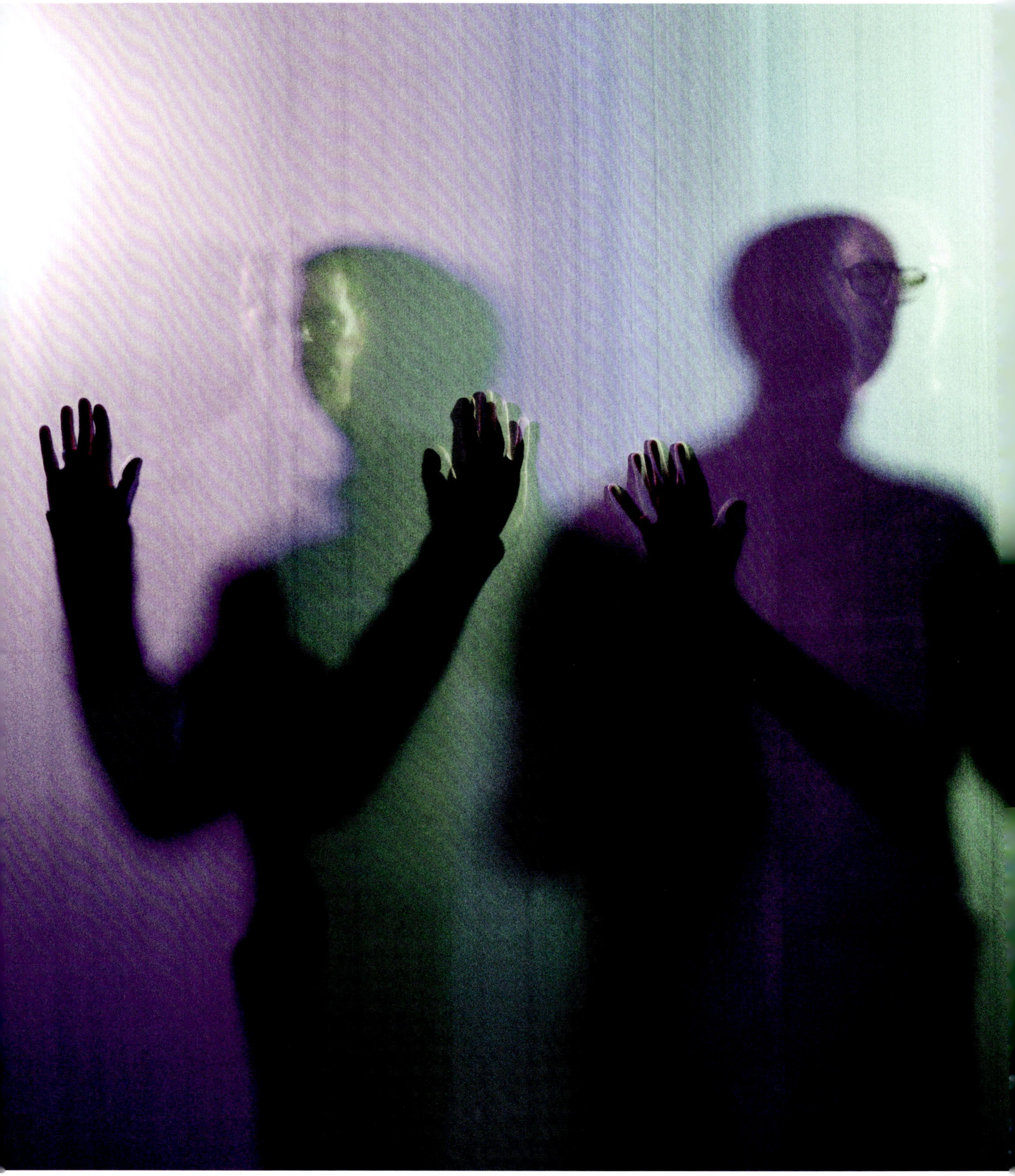

A Modern Midnight Conversation

Paused in Cosmic Reflection came together after a year of mainly separate conversations. We met at gigs, in the studio and on computer screens (multiple times). Towards the end of the process, we met in the living room of Ed's house in west London. Outside, spring was trying to break through.

Robin: *I talked to a lot of people who've brought their uniqueness to The Chemical Brothers' records, people that have been part of your story and become honorary Chemical Brothers or Sisters over the last thirty years. All of their stories got me wondering about collaborations that didn't happen or didn't work out.*

Tom: We've always sidestepped that question when it's been asked in the past. There's nothing that interesting in the ones that didn't work, and you can hear all the ones that do work on the records. I can't think of anyone we really wanted to work with that never worked out . . .

Ed: Well, you did have that phone call with Kate Bush.

Tom: Oh God, I did, didn't I? It was around *Come with Us*. I had to phone her up. She was living somewhere near where my parents so I used that as my ice-breaker. I remember she was in the kitchen when I rang.

Ed: Her voice on one of our records would have been amazing.

Tom: The working title of the track we sent her was 'Rev Intro'. I'm not sure what it became in the end; it might have ended up becoming 'Denmark'. She'd heard the music, and someone told us to 'give Kate a call'. She was lovely on the phone, but she said, 'I think you'll be OK as you are, it's a great song.' Thinking about it, it would have been amazing if she'd done it.

Robin: *Wasn't there a move to get Bob Dylan to sing on a record?*

Ed: I can't remember what happened with Dylan. He's been influential since the start though. Both of us have always loved Bob Dylan, he's quoted on our records as far back as *Fourteenth Century Sky* ['One Too Many Mornings'].

Tom: We've always loved a stolen title. We left one for all the Huggy Bear heads out there on that EP too ['Her Jazz'].

Ed: Dylan requested we send a letter explaining what we intended to do. I'm not sure whether we ever got round to writing it.

Tom: We did get sent a bottle of bourbon by Bob Dylan's manager. Bob's own bourbon [Dylan's Heaven's Door brand]. That's as close as we got to collaborating with him.

Robin: *We talked a lot about live shows and the impact they have on the audience. I was wondering about rituals that you've adopted over the years and their effects on you as performers. I know there's the painting that travels with you.*

Tom: In 2015, we were playing in Vilnius in Lithuania. Before the gig we were given an oil painting on canvas by the local promoter. After the show, our monitor engineer, Barts – one of the greats – packaged it up and put it with all the outgoing gear. After that, it just started appearing in the dressing room before every gig as if by magic, wherever we were. In the years since adopting it as a kind of lucky charm, it's been christened 'A Rainy Night in Tokyo'.

Ed: Our pre-gig behaviour has changed a bit over the years. We used to drink quite a bit before shows because we weren't natural performers.

A Rainy Night in Tokyo *backstage, somewhere in Britain.*

Tom: Before gigs, we always used to play a cassette of warm-up music that was labelled 'Scum Busters'.

Ed: It had tracks like 'This Must Be the Place', 'Boops (Here to Go)', 'Know the Ledge' and 'Thank You (Falettinme Be Mice Elf Agin)'. The music got more joyous as the show got closer. We can generate a frenetic atmosphere from the stage, but sometimes in the hours before a show you can end up getting a little morose. You're away from loved ones, sat in a Portakabin somewhere, not connecting with the outside world. You have to remember what it is that you're about to do, how important it is. We'll always play 'Enjoy Yourself (It's Later Than You Think)' by The Specials. Our tour manager comes in to give us a five-minute warning, that track goes on and we have a little dance about. It works as a prompt to put you in the right headspace. From then on, it's all about the ninety minutes on stage.

Tom: 'Enjoy Yourself' is a really good setup track. And it's incredibly poignant, saying however you feel, make the most of this moment because no one knows how many more times you've got left doing it. It sets the mood.

Robin: *Thinking about when you started out – about Manchester and how things started to snowball – I wondered when it all started to feel 'real' for you. When did it feel like things had escalated beyond those first steps?*

Ed: The time I thought something was going on was when I pulled up in a minicab outside The Albany on the third week of the Heavenly Sunday Social. The queue was round the block. It had come out of nowhere. Before that, I knew 'Chemical Beats' was an amazing tune and hearing other people play it out was a head-turner, but the moment of really thinking, 'This is connecting,' was stopping in that taxi and seeing that queue. Pre-internet, I've no idea how everyone switched on and turned up to the same place at the same time.

Tom: I've always been consumed by making music, so it's always felt real to me. I'd spend all my time making music. There was no certainty that there was a way of making money out of making music, but I was going to do it anyway because it was what I loved doing and was obsessed with. When Steve Hall gave us an advance to make an album, which allowed us the space to explore ideas, that felt very real. With Ariel, there was never the feeling that it was the right place to express all of the things I want to say. *Exit Planet Dust* definitely was that place. All those ideas running through your head, finally being able to channel them. And having people around you who are excited about what you're doing and believe in it and want to champion it. Being able to realise it. You can have the idea but realising it isn't an easy thing. To be able to stand your own album next to some of the records that you love ... that was a really big thing.

Ed: We didn't meet until we were eighteen, but you can hear all of those things that got under our skin when we were growing up in our early records. We grew up in a period where hip hop exploded, then indie music, then acid house. Combining all of those elements in our early music felt natural. There was no conscious intent to marry rock and dance. We both loved lots of music; you can hear all of those things that inspired us in our early records and remixes. The two years that led up to *Exit Planet Dust* – 1992 to '94 – they were really the essence of us just *doing things*. We were playing out all the time and doing remixes every weekend if the offer was there. Ariel was still going but we'd be hanging out, going to clubs like Merry England (at the Café de Paris). It was also a period where I was working for a management company that looked after bands like Incognito and Urban Species, as well as Orbital. I'd shipped out to my more natural habitat among the gods of acid jazz. We'd have Gilles Peterson on the phone every day.

Tom: You really were at the forefront of a global jazz fusion scene back then.

Ed: So, while I was doing that and Tom was vaguely thinking of training to become a sound designer at the National Theatre, we both had a dream of being able to be in a recording studio for a prolonged period of time. I'd be in work answering phones on behalf of these acid jazz bands, while thinking about the mixes we were doing for Saint Etienne or The Charlatans or Primal Scream – that initial run of remixes we'd worked on after we'd left Manchester. And we'd be getting calls from labels like Virgin, who were chasing us. I think there was a sense of 'How is that fucking kid who's answering the phones and making the coffee getting all these calls from labels?'

Tom: 'You can stick your franking machine right up your arse, I'm out of here!'

Ed: The slew of remixes we did after we started working with our manager, Robert – The Charlatans, Primal Scream, Saint Etienne, The Prodigy, the Manics – was something else. I was working during the week and we'd be in the studio at the weekends. And we'd have such a laugh. Whatever was going to get delivered had to be on the DAT by Sunday night. Whatever worked at 3 a.m. in the morning was what was going to come out. We had this really intense period, just me, Tom and Dubby in a

Paused in Cosmic Reflection

studio seemingly every weekend. We'd go to Orinoco, which was near Elephant and Castle in south London. It would be completely deserted round there. The three of us would be doing these remixes against a ticking clock; there was such an intensity to it. I think it's among our best work.

Tom: When Primal Scream decided to play our 'Jailbird' remix in their headline set at Reading Festival in 1994 with Mick Jones from The Clash on guitar . . . that was a pretty incredible moment.

Ed: They loved that remix. We brought something really different to the track. All of those remixes seemed to really connect that year.

Tom: And 'Open Up' was a great remix. The record was obviously huge. And that's when we met Dubby. We did an arrangement on 'Open Up' where the big moment was the bassline coming in. And Leftfield sent it back and said it needed an edit; they chopped out the bit we were most excited about. We got back in touch saying, 'You have to keep that bit.' They seemed a bit baffled by our insistence. To us, that bit was the point of the remix. At the time, I remember someone saying how ballsy we'd been. For us, it was the release point of the record, and it was us knowing early on what we wanted our records to be. That remix was the first time we went in the studio with Dubby and we found that the ideas we had had were achievable. He'd make things sound the way you wanted them to sound. He was amazing, and it was fun. He was so into it, too. He'd show you tricks rather than be secretive about process. We'd be doing these sessions way into the night and all three of us would be so into it. We'd come from a world of writing music rather than creating it from scratch. Dubby was really enthusiastic about making things work.

Ed: The Leftfield/Lydon mix was quite different. It takes the track in a different direction from the original. This would have been 1993. Tom and I would have known each other for four years by that point, which really seems like an eternity when you're young. Dubby very quickly became part of our world; he'd take the piss out of us and he'd help us work things out. Everything improved. In the summer of 1994, we ended up in the studio for four weeks to make a record. Steve Hall from Junior Boy's Own was instrumental in that process. He was releasing our singles and EPs, and he encouraged us to go in the studio to make an album. Even at that time, you could still see a version of the future where Tom was that sound guy in theatre and I maybe retrain as a solicitor, or get higher up the acid jazz pecking order. We were enjoying making music and DJing, but there wasn't a clear path to us being able to do it full time. I do think first meeting Dubby and working with him gave us an idea of what was possible.

Tom: It was such a big thing to be given the keys, to be given the go-ahead to make an album, which is what Steve Hall gave us. 'Woah, you mean we can go into the same studio every day for four weeks and work on an album?' That didn't happen with Ariel. When it did for us, it just felt awesome.

Robin: *One of the things that's been constant with The Chemical Brothers' records is the visual aesthetic. It's something that's been there since the start (special mention for Ed's BBC Micro-generated green diamond logo on the original 'Song to the Siren' 12-inch). Apart from* Surrender, *we haven't really gone into the sleeves in detail.*

Tom: We've always taken a lot of care over the sleeve images. It's a massive part of how the records are initially perceived. So much work has gone into the music, and the sleeve needs to reflect that. I think the cover of *Exit Planet Dust* was so important in setting the tone of what we were doing. It made it feel so different to other records. It felt like a natural thing that symbolised the album. I couldn't really tell you why that image spoke to us, but there was something about the feeling that the image evokes, how it connected with the sensibility of the record at a time when electronic records and dance records looked completely different. Back then, we'd go to a commercial image library in Soho called Barnaby's Picture Library. We'd always head straight for the reject box. All the shots on the sleeves of the first two albums and all of the singles were taken from advertising campaigns that had been rejected. It was the equivalent of crate-digging for records, but we'd be there trawling through boxes and boxes of images.

Ed: Both of us would go to the library together and then scurry off to different corners to find things we liked.

Tom: I still really want to know what they were trying to advertise with the picture we used for the 'Elektrobank' cover. It was a girl, sat on a lemon, underwater, smoking a pipe.

Robin: *People you work with refer to a strong familial bond that's always present around the band. A lot of the people around you have been there since the early years, whether that's studio partners or crew. Do you think that's one of the reasons why it's worked for so long?*

Tom: There are few other bands out there where you can get a job for life. Work with The Chemical Brothers, you'll be alright. There are quite a few people in the crew who've been constant in our team since the start. I like that aspect of what we do and who we are. We really trust the people around us; our crew have all been with us a long time. When you think about Adam, that relationship has been there since the very start of us touring.

Ed: Steve Dub has mixed everything. He has made the music sound as good as it does. Adam and Marcus have been determined to realise a fantastic show. The guy who's now the production manager for our entire live show started when he was seventeen as an assistant, putting the lights back into their boxes after gigs.

We've been lucky with the people we've been friends with all the way through, right back as far as Manchester. Our friend Phil South finding people who could fill a room and turn it into a party. The people at Heavenly when we moved to London. A track like 'Leave Home', it's still a massive part of our live set, but its first contact with people would have been in a tiny pub basement near Regent's Park. The most consistent relationship outside of us two has been with our manager, Robert. He's retained an air of mystery over the years though. I remember when *Muzik* magazine did a piece on the most important people in dance music, they had Robert in there and they just put a silhouette on the page.

Tom: Brilliant! Did that actually happen?

Ed: That's really the ultimate answer to why this all works. That silhouette. No other words needed.

310 The Chemical Brothers

For That Beautiful Feeling

For That Beautiful Feeling *album design by Hingston Studio with artwork by US abstract painter Nicholas Krushenick.*

Back at Rowlands Audio Research, it's already dark outside. You must have been here for hours, maybe even days. No one's keeping count.

What started as a curious, low-profile tour of the corners of the studio has ended up a blissed-out reverie. Lost in stories. Suspended in sound.

Snap out of your daze and gather your bearings. This feels a little like coming round on the dance floor when the lights go up and you're caught in that mini-rapture moment where it's way past time to go home.

All around you, the machines are still radiating heat, humming contentedly, their jobs done for the day. While this place never switches off, it does power down and breathe a little more softly.

The building might be empty but there's still resonance in the air. Echoes of the day are audible, though the distance between them grows as they fade away like the space between concentric rings. The whole place is bathed in an audio glow, and it's beautiful.

Those blinking lights look heavy-lidded now. Their internal rhythms dance at half speed, scattering and flickering like fireflies in the middle distance, just out of reach. Squint hard enough and you're in a slowed-down version of 'Escape Velocity''s dot world.

In the building's main room, an SSL desk stretches from wall to wall. Although it's been left alone, it's still lit up like the bridge of a movie starship, faders caught mid-flight. Either side of the desk is flanked by colossal speakers that would shake foundations along any carnival route.

As you take a few tentative steps into this mothership, the studio's main computer wakes from sleep. Moving closer, you see there's a series of files bundled together on the screen. 'Chem Ten Album'.

Pull up a seat, press Play.

Seconds in, there's an almost overwhelming rush of sound as a swirl of distortion forms into a woozy, descending riff. Two interlocking vocals fly directly through the heart of the noise, each contrasting perfectly with the other. One is tightly edited to the point of wordlessness, the other keeps time with a single thought: *Yeah, we live again*.

Driven by a clipped, forceful rhythm track, it's as thrilling as the first climb and drop of a rollercoaster ride. Repeated, that hook line starts to feel like a statement of hope for an age of uncertainty.

This is the kind of territory The Chemical Brothers have made their own – so definitively – for thirty years since their first recordings back in the early nineties. This is psychedelia as a positive force. Eyes forward to a brighter future.

––––––––

The recording and mixing of the tenth Chemical Brothers album happened concurrently with the writing of this book.

When I talked to Tom and Ed over the course of fifteen months, each interview was bookended with off-the-record conversations about how the new album was coming along and how it might sound. Although I've worked with the band since 1994, I still approach their music as a fan. I want to know what their new music sounds like because I want to play it. Repeatedly, and at volume.

Like this book, the record fully formed itself in the editing stages as initial ideas warped themselves into new shapes. I was lucky enough to talk to a few interviewees (Beck Hansen, Steve Dub) as they were in the process of working on new music with Tom and Ed. Their excitement was unmistakable. They too talked like fans.

The first music I heard from the record wasn't in the studio, but in a field in Bristol on a Sunday night at the start of September. I'd taken my daughters to see The Chemical Brothers for the first time. This was after having taken my seventy-eight-year-old father to see them the last time they toured, months before the pandemic put a stop to all live shows. If the two years of on-off lockdowns between those gigs had taught me anything, it was that if you've got a chance to do something, do it, as tomorrow's events are not a certainty. *Enjoy yourself, it's later than you think*.

From the vantage point of the sound desk, I watched The Chemical Brothers with my nine-year-old, ear defenders clamped tight to her head (my elder daughter had run straight into the melee at the front with her friends and was not seen again until the venue cleared out).

For ninety minutes, the band saw out the summer with a juggernaut live set that flipped early on from that first Diamond-labelled 12-inch single to a deeply cathartic call and response for 'Mad As Hell'. Then, a few tracks in, a rattling snare roll shifted the direction of the music as a Day-Glo marching band appeared on screen, undertaking a synchronised stomp in garish greens and purples.

That track – 'No Reason' – was set to Adam and Marcus's stunning and berserk new visuals. It was met with a roar of the kind of intense, frantic enthusiasm you'd expect to greet one of the band's many instantly recognisable singles, not a brand-new piece of music being heard by pretty much everyone in the field for the first time.

Shortly afterwards, the discombobulated voice of Wolf Alice singer Ellie Rowsell blasted out, repeating a single line: *. . . and I feel like I am dreaming*, over a pummelling drum track that eventually gave way to a full-on analogue synth freak-out. The screen was projecting a film that seemed to be equal parts psychedelic kabuki theatre production and an up-close and claustrophobic Bollywood horror epic. Again, the crowd welcomed it the only way they knew how – with crazed fervour.

Throughout all of this, I kept looking back to my daughter's face. Lit up by the heavily saturated colours of the screen, it was a portrait of pure joy. And how could it not be? Surrounded by thousands and thousands of like-minded souls all experiencing this band at the height of their powers, she was now a part of a community, part of the great big family of Chemical Brothers and Sisters all around the world who meet in fields and in arenas to *hold tight* wherever they are and share in the collective experience.

It's a family I've been part of since first hearing Tom and Ed play at the Job Club in Soho. And it's one that I've watched grow ever since, as each new generation discovers the band and surrenders to their music.

You're in the studio chair, the album has nearly finished playing.

The last sounds ripple from the speakers like cool, cool water. The album's title track has a gorgeous melancholy and a dazed wonder running all the way through it. Hearing it is like witnessing The Beach Boys surfing the shores of the Sea of Tranquility, or watching as Eno's 'The Big Ship' sails west into a never-ending sunset. As with previous Chemical Brothers tracks like 'Asleep From Day' or 'Radiate', it seems to melt around you like the edges of a daydream.

Close your eyes, spin the chair around, contemplate leaving.

But then again, no one knows you're here. Or if they do, they don't seem to mind that you're sat alone, paused and reflecting for another minute or two.

Maybe you should press play again, run back through the record, sat right in the heart of this mighty orchestra of analogue synths stacked up all around you, machines that glide and grind across every track.

Just once more. Maybe turn up the volume this time.

Here we go.

Paused in Cosmic Reflection   313

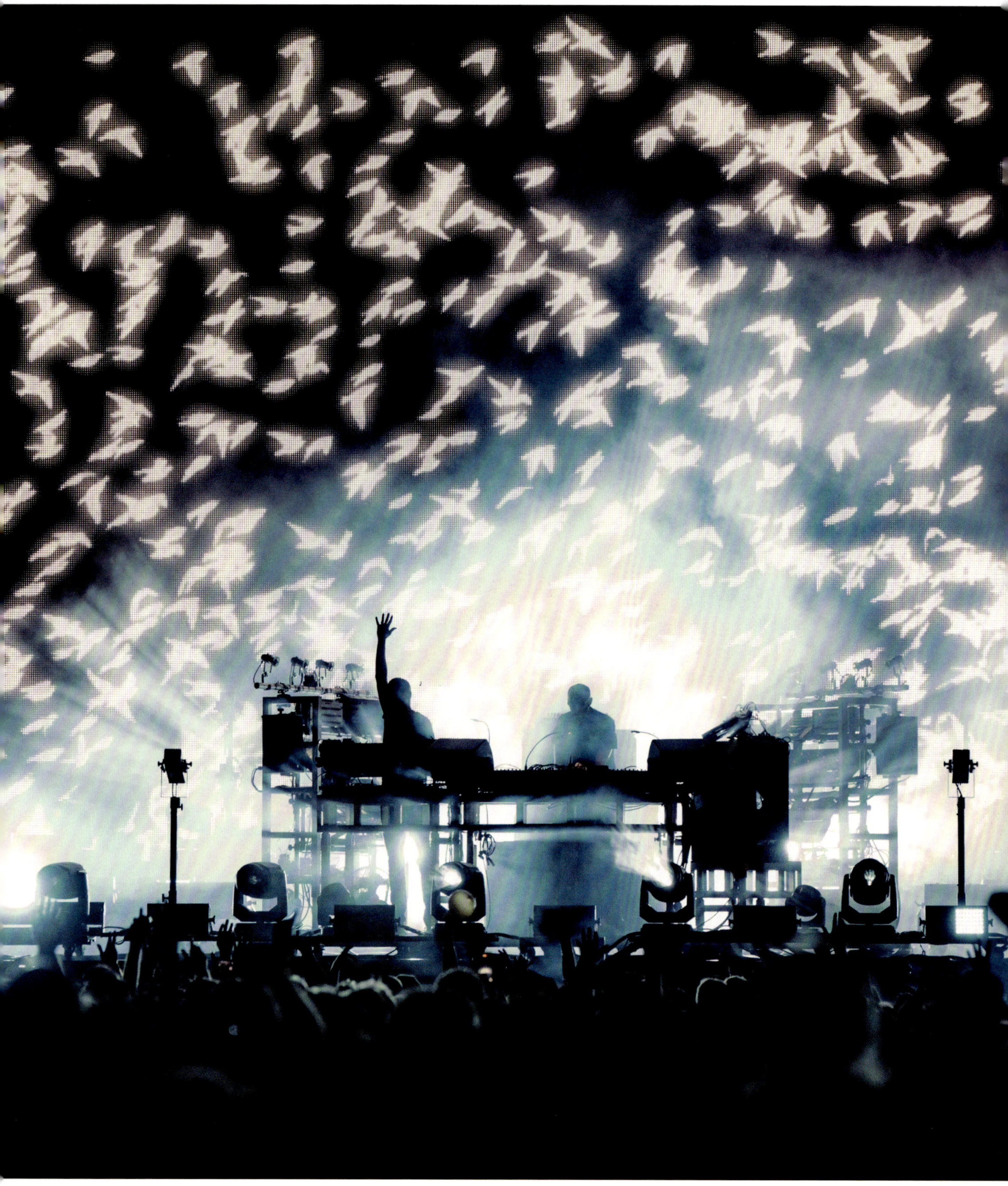

Paused in Cosmic Reflection   315

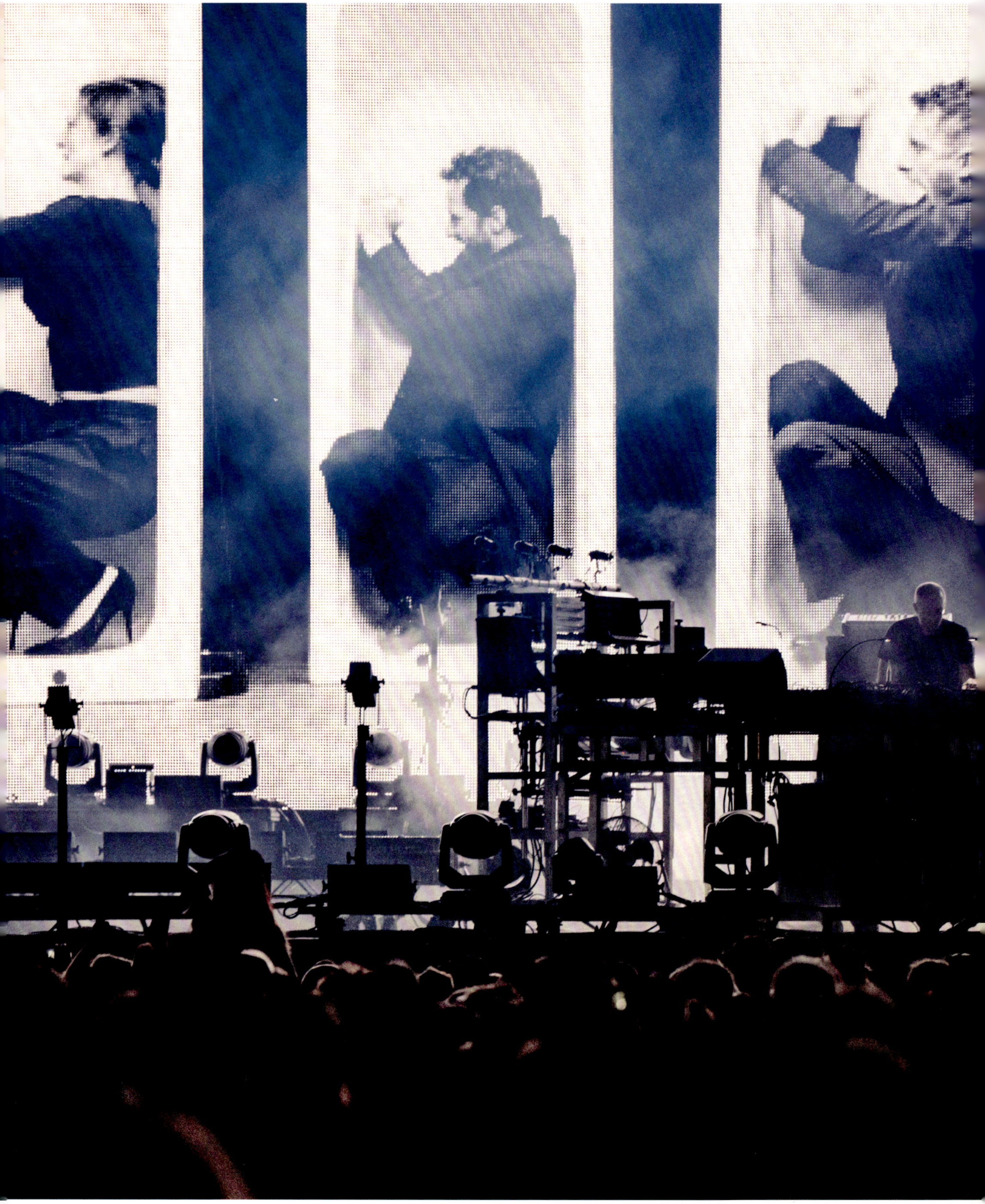

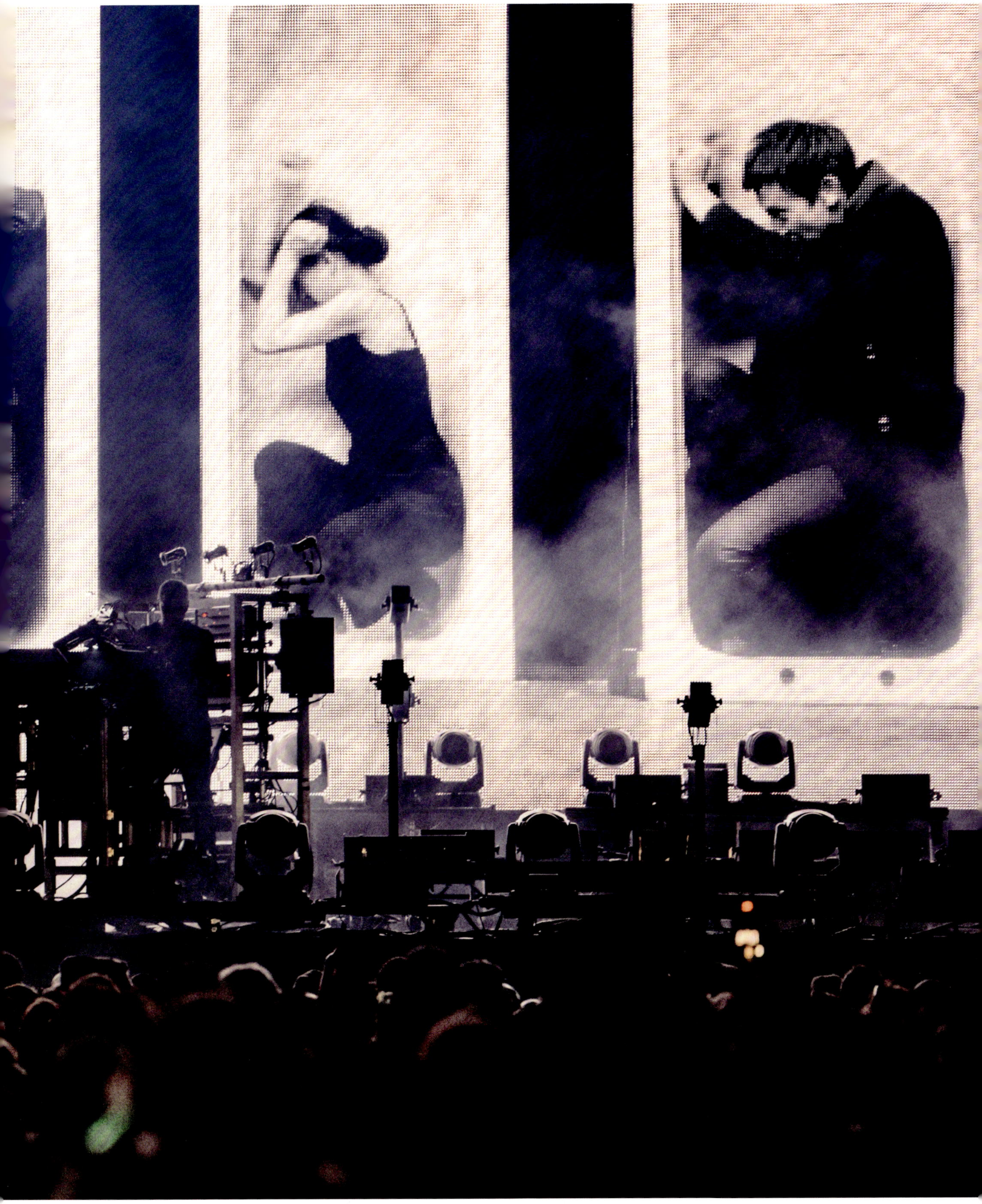

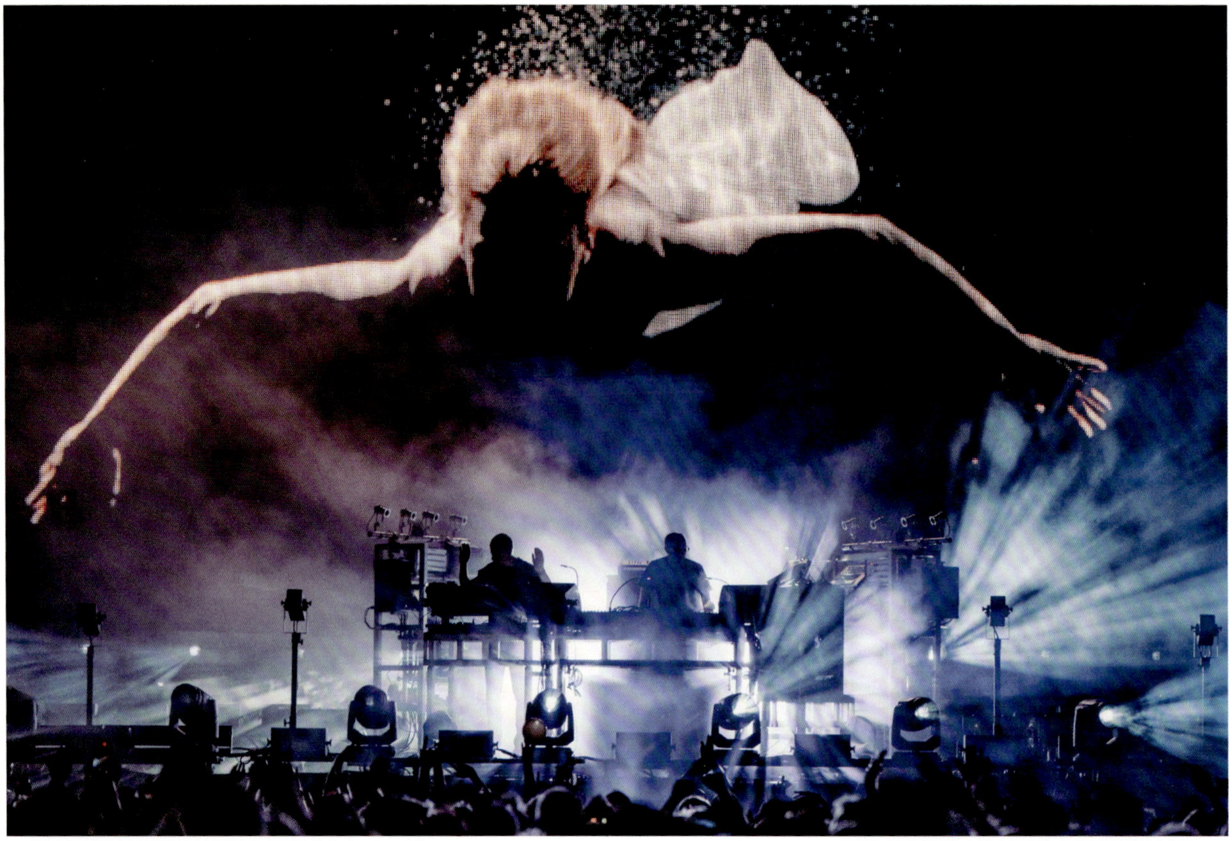

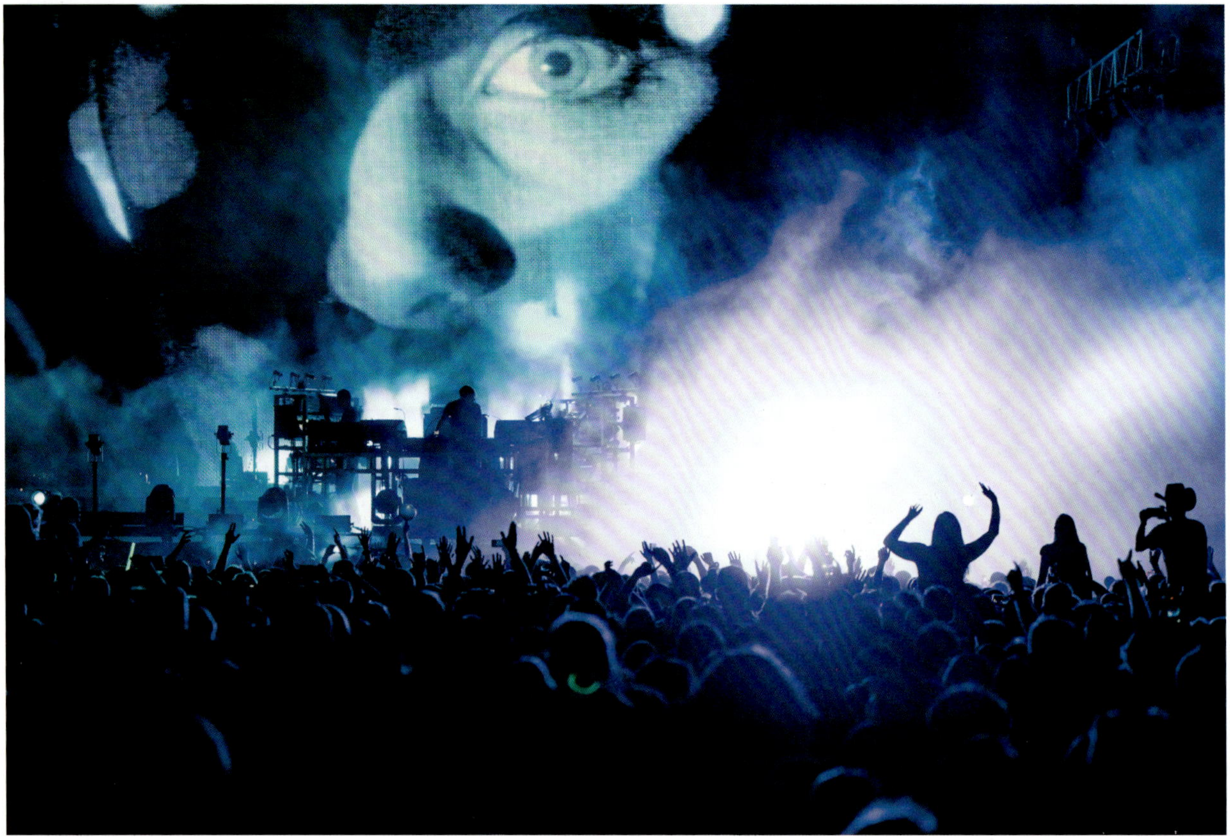

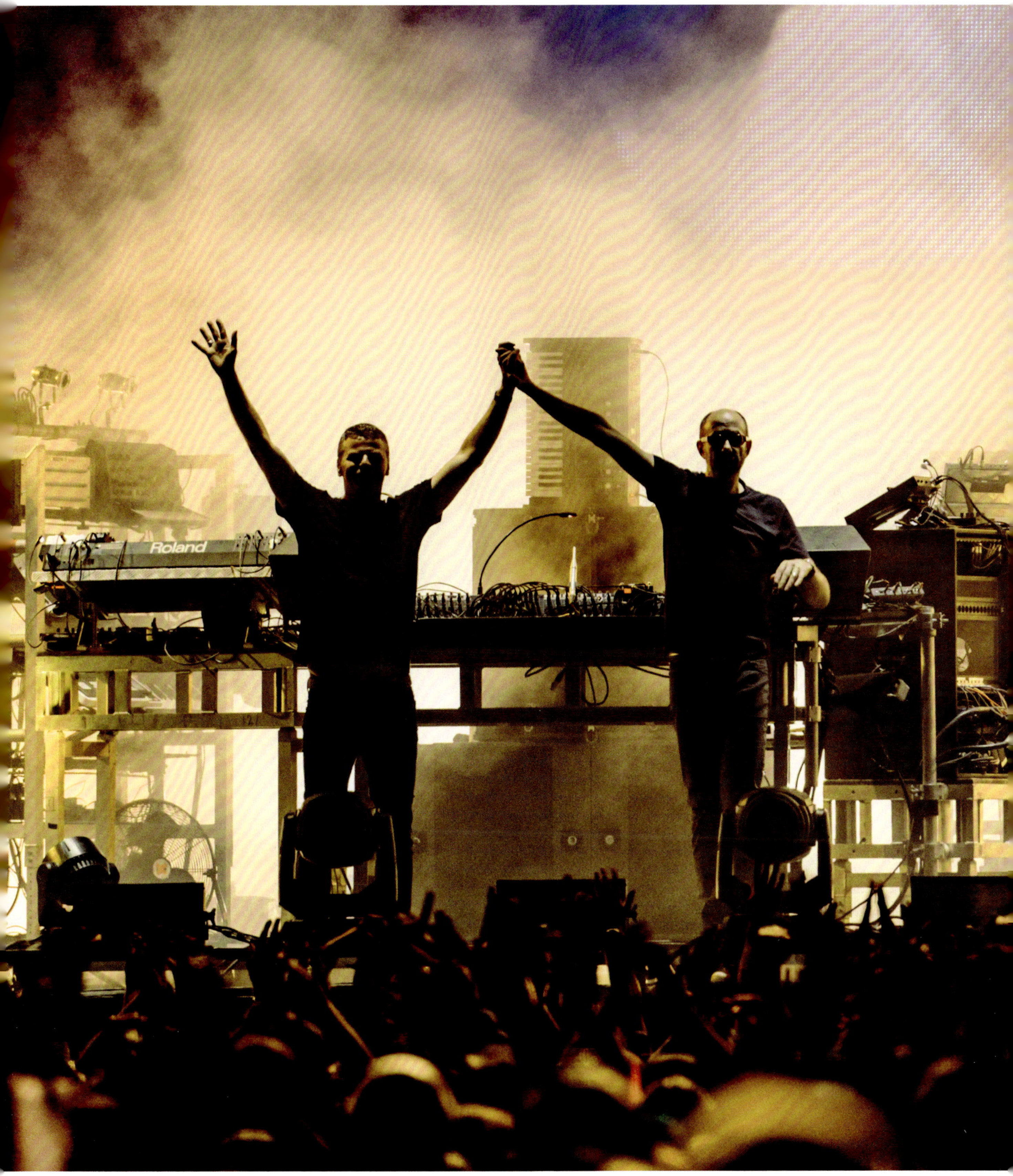
Roland

320 The Chemical Brothers

Paused in Cosmic Reflection 321

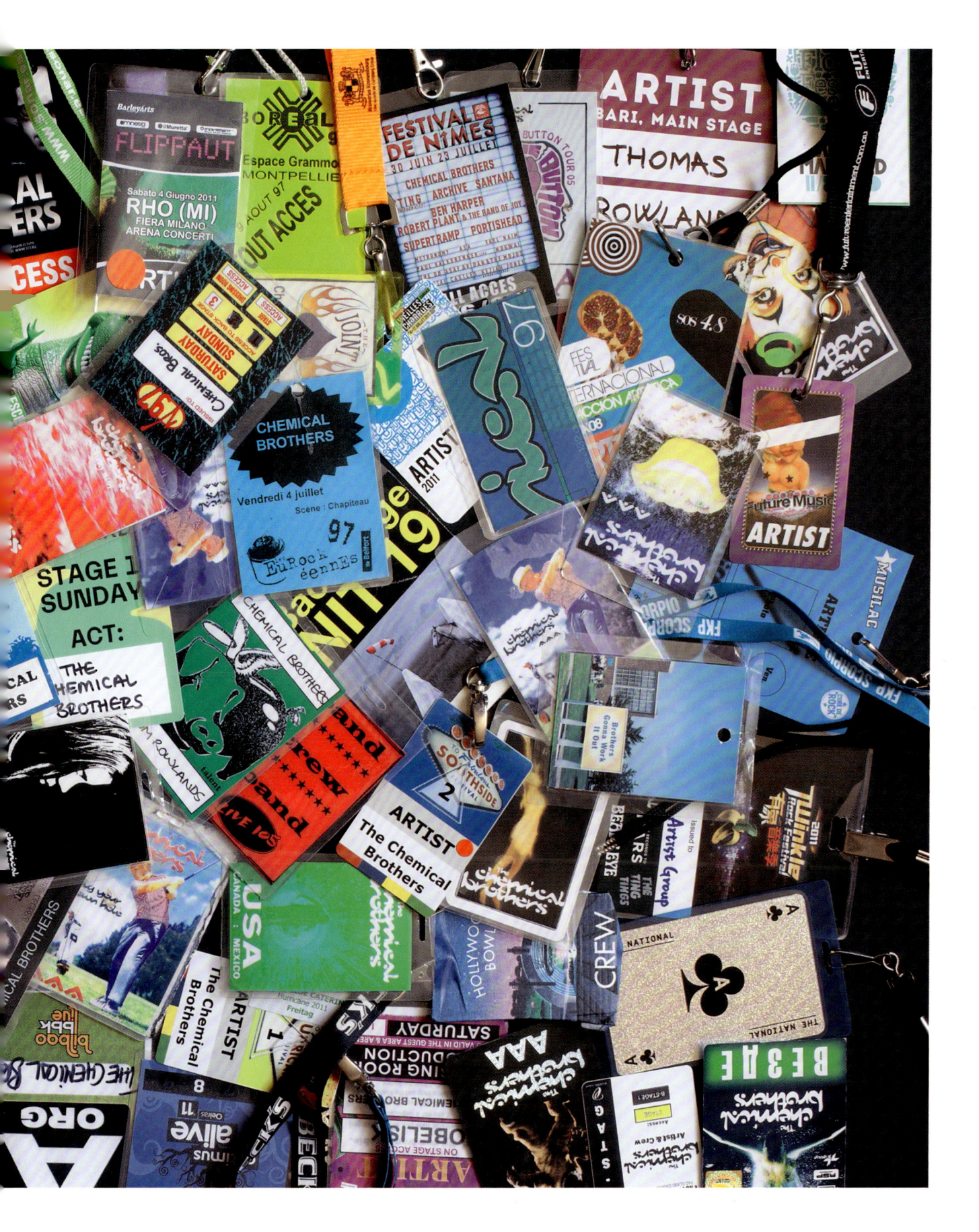

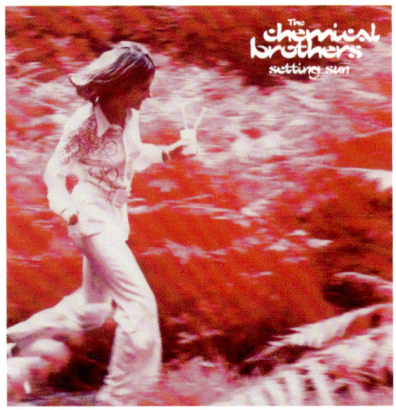

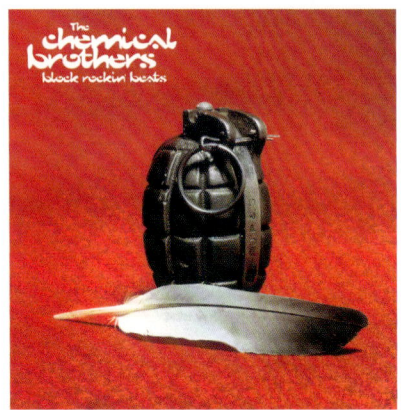

322   The Chemical Brothers

Paused in Cosmic Reflection 323

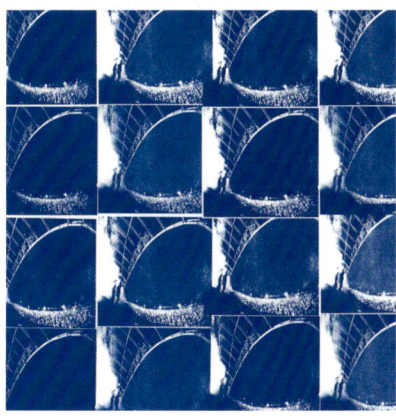

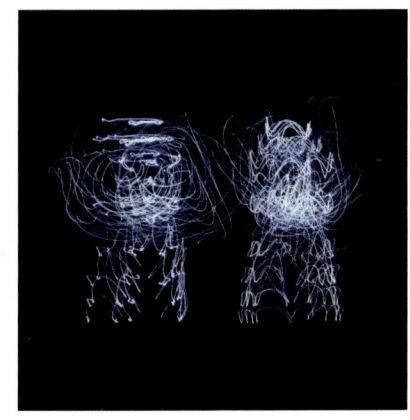

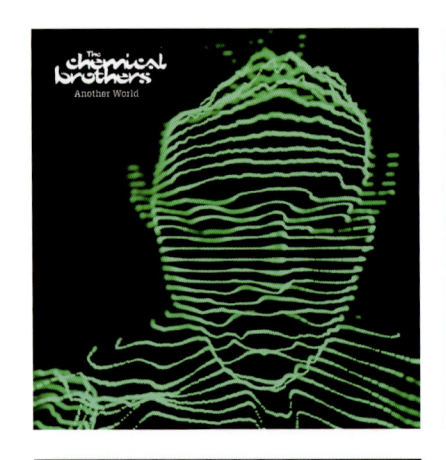

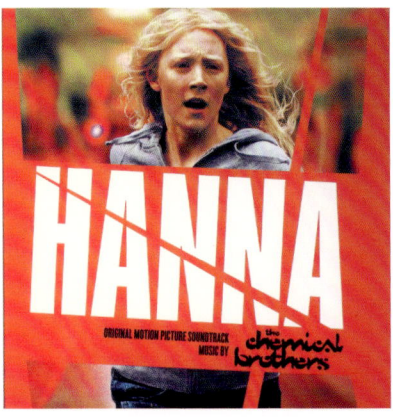

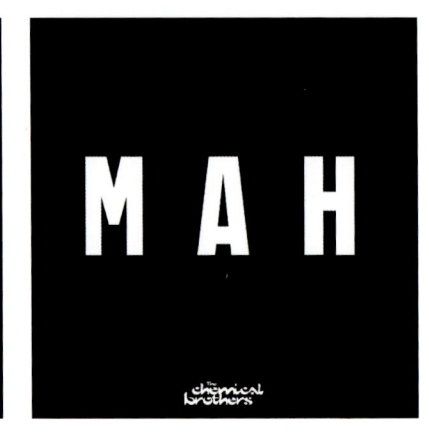

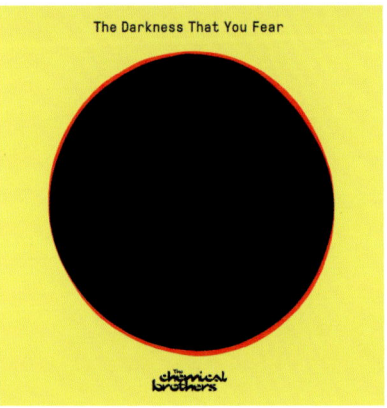

324   **The Chemical Brothers**

Singles 1995–2023

Leave Home 1995
Life Is Sweet 1995 Featuring Tim Burgess
Loops of Fury 1996
Setting Sun 1996 Featuring Noel Gallagher
Block Rockin' Beats 1997
Elektrobank 1997
The Private Psychedelic Reel 1997
Hey Boy Hey Girl 1999
Let Forever Be 1999 Featuring Noel Gallagher
Out of Control 1999 Featuring Bernard Sumner
Music: Response 2000
It Began in Afrika 2001
Star Guitar 2002
Come with Us / The Test 2002 Featuring Richard Ashcroft
The Golden Path 2003 Featuring The Flaming Lips
Get Yourself High 2003 Featuring k-os
Galvanize 2005 Featuring Q-Tip
Believe 2005
The Boxer 2005
Do It Again 2007
The Salmon Dance 2007 Featuring Fatlip
Midnight Madness 2008
Escape Velocity 2010
Swoon 2010
Another World 2010
Container Park 2011
Velodrome 2012
Go 2015 Featuring Q-Tip
Under Neon Lights 2015 Featuring St. Vincent
C-H-E-M-I-C-A-L 2016
Free Yourself 2018
MAH 2019
Got to Keep On 2019
We've Got to Try 2019
The Darkness That You Fear 2021
Work Energy Principle 2021
No Reason 2023
Live Again 2023

326 The Chemical Brothers

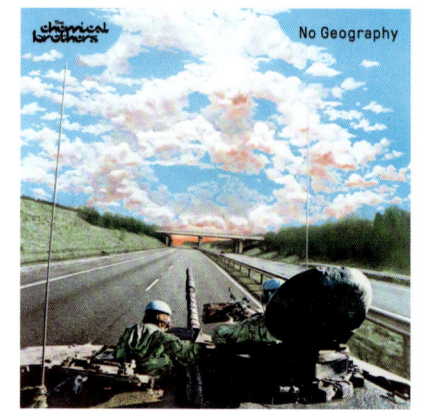

Albums 1995–2023

Exit Planet Dust 1995
Dig Your Own Hole 1997
Brothers Gonna Work It Out 1997 (Mix Album)
Surrender 1999
Come with Us 2002
Singles 93–03 2003
Push the Button 2005
We Are the Night 2007
Brotherhood 2008
Further 2010
Born in the Echoes 2015
No Geography 2019
For That Beautiful Feeling 2023

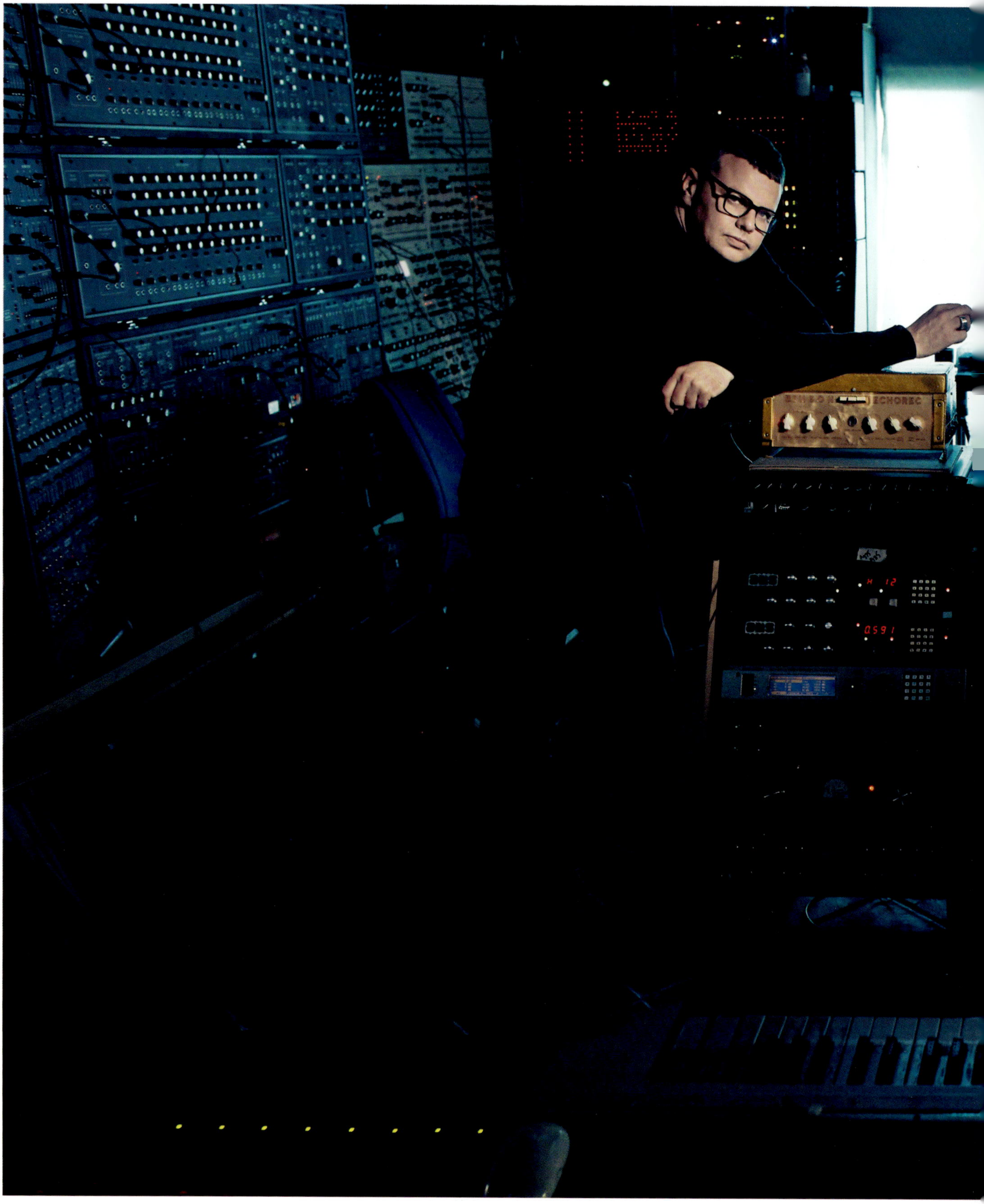
ECHOREC

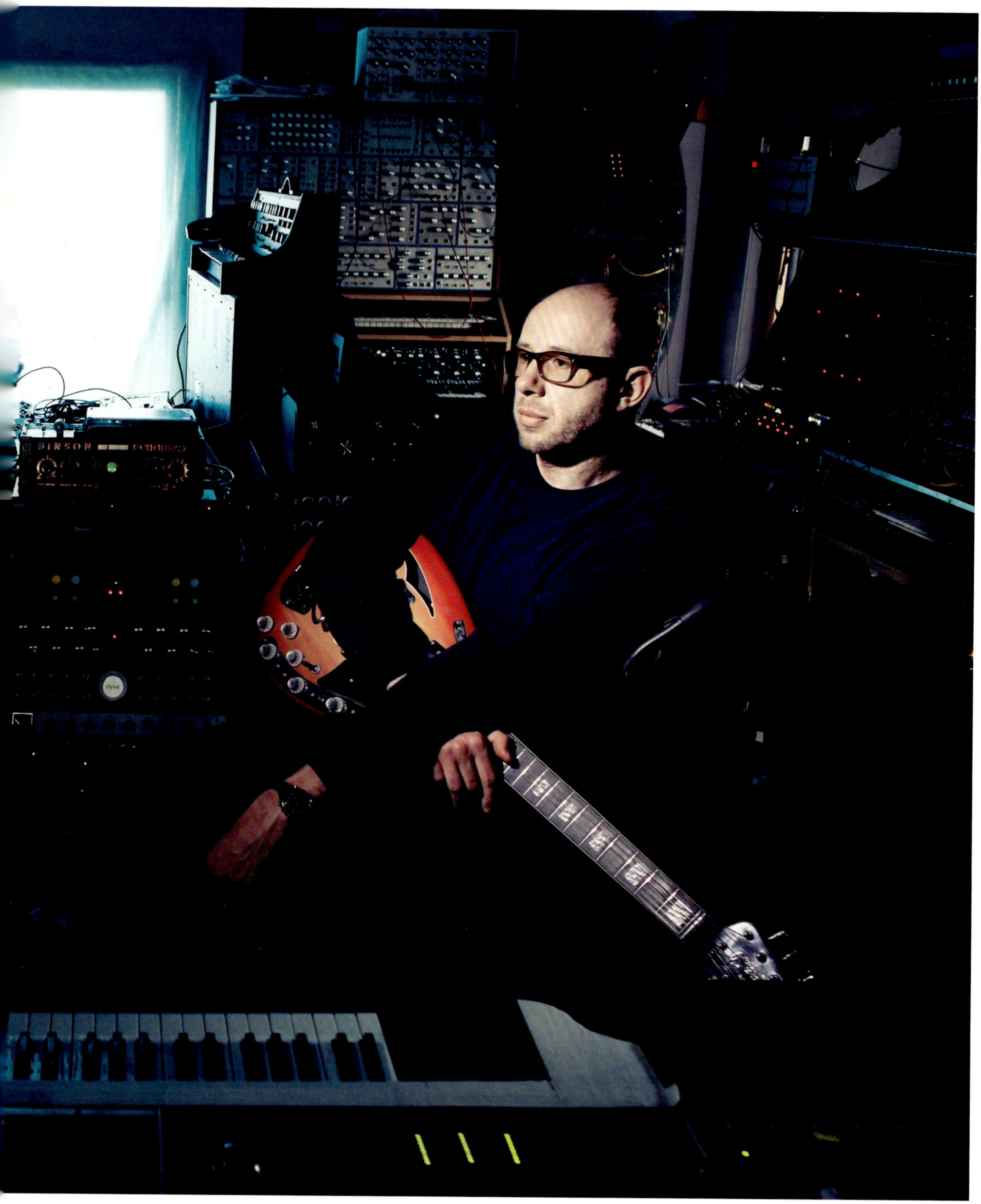

Endnotes and Credits

Endnotes

p.104 'Anything that gives Chris...' Taylor, Sam, *The Observer* (27 October 1996).

p.120 'electronic country, a kind...' Kaye, Lenny, 'Presenting... Lothar & The Hand People'. *Rolling Stone* (3 May 1969).

p.179 'Every new lie of...' Debord, Guy, *The Society of the Spectacle*. (London: Rebel Press) 1994.

p.273 'The exhibition culminates in...' Lynskey, Dorian, 'Electronic at the Design Museum review – a sweaty rave paradise lost'. *The Guardian*, 28 July 2020. [available at: www.theguardian.com/artanddesign/2020/jul/28/electronic-at-the-design-museum-review-kraftwerk-chemical-brothers]

p.297 'It's 1969, the phone...' Boxer, Sarah, 'Dial-A-Poem Enters the Internet Age'. *The New York Times*, 30 April 2005. [available at: www.nytimes.com/2005/04/30/arts/dialapoem-enters-the-internet-age.html]

p.297 'At this point, with...' Giorno, John, *The Dial-A-Poem Poets* album sleeve notes. (Giorno Poetry Systems) 1972.

Image Credits

Khali Ackford 272, 314–15, 316–17, 318, 319, band photo used in front cover collage. **The Age/Getty** 212–13. **Ray Baseley** 78 (top right), 80, 81, 82–3, 85 (top), 141, 280, 291, 300–1, 312, 313 (left), 332, 334. **Mark Benney** 24–5, 30, 33, 51, 57. **Hamish Brown** 2, 118, 220–1, 225, 239, 304, 328–9. **Ray Burmiston** 48. **Andrew Catlin** 98–9, 100 (bottom left), 119 (top right). **Jake Chessum** 103, 105, 106–7. **Noah Clark** 61 (top left). **Errol Colosine/Astralwerks** 159. **Joseph Cultace** 151, 186–7. **Neil Davies** 263 (bottom). **Jake Davis** 196–7. **Daniel Daza** 179. **Nick Dutfield** 28, 29, 34, 35 (left and centre), 65, 116, 121 (top). **Luke Dyson** 86–7. **Fleet River** 190. **Kate Gibb** 175. **Paul Grover/Shutterstock** 84 (right). **Sarah Hughes** 236, 237. **Paul Kelly** 8, 11, 13, 13, 14–15, 21, 40, 42, 90, 91, 124–5 (main) 146–7, 162, 171, 185, 195, 198, 244, 245 (top), 268, 320–1. **Mark McNulty** 38. **Tony Pletts** 249 (top right), 277 (left top and bottom), 294–5. **Ripley** 123, 125 (bottom), 128. **Stephen Roberts** 84 (left). **Tom Rowlands** 16, 19, 121 (bottom), 306–7. **Rufus** 26. **Adam Smith** 35 (top right), 61 (top right and main), 70, 71, 72, 73, 76, 77, 78 (bottom left), 85 (bottom), 283, 284, 285, 276, 277 (left top, middle & bottom). **Steen Sundland** 133. **Brian Sweeney** 135. **Tara Stift** 263 (top). **Dave Tonge** 143, 145. **Robin Turner** 313 (right) (Peggy at Bristol Forwards Festival 2022). **Laure Vasconti** 172. **Vegetable Vision** 66, 67, 68, 69. **Bruno Vincent/Getty** 206–7. **Peter J. Walsh** (www.peterjwalsh.com) 62, 74. **Kevin Westernberg** 154. **Joe Wright** 92.

Live Visuals

Flat Nose George 72. **Robots designed by Adam Smith & Marcus Lyall** 80. **Show directors Adam Smith & Marcus Lyall** 78, 83, 85, 141, 249, 251, 272, 280, 283, 289, 301, 314, 315, 316–7, 318, 319. **Vegetable Vision** 61, 71.

Video Stills

'Life Is Sweet' dir. Walter A. Stern 96–7. 'Setting Sun' dir. Dom & Nic 112–13. 'Block Rockin' Beats' dir. Dom & Nic 126–7. 'Elektrobank' dir. Spike Jonze 138–9. 'Hey Boy Hey Girl' dir. Dom & Nic 156–7. 'Let Forever Be' dir. Michel Gondry 160–1. 'Out of Control' dir. WIZ 180–3. 'Out of Control (The Avalanches Surrender to Love Mix)' dir. Jimmy Turrell & Kate Gibb 188–9. 'Star Guitar' dir. Michel Gondry & Olivier Gondry 200–1. 'Galvanize' dir. Adam Smith 217, 219. 'Midnight Madness' dir. Dom & Nic 222–3. 'The Salmon Dance' dir. Dom & Nic 226–7. 'Escape Velocity' dir. Adam Smith & Marcus Lyall 235. 'Swoon' dir. Adam Smith & Marcus Lyall 240–3. 'Another World' dir. Adam Smith & Marcus Lyall 254–5. 'Go' dir. Michel Gondry 258–9. 'Wide Open' dir. Dom & Nic 260, 264, 265. 'Free Yourself' dir. Dom & Nic 270–1. 'Got to Keep On' dir. Michel Gondry & Olivier Gondry 279–80. 'Eve of Destruction' dir. Adam Smith & Marcus Lyall 286–7. 'We've Got to Try' dir. Ninian Doff 290, 292, 293. 'The Darkness That You Fear' dir. Ruffmercy 302–3.

Magazine Covers

Jockey Slut cover by **Mark Benney** 56. *Muzik* cover by **Vincent McDonald** 100. *NME* cover by **Steve Double** 109. *POP* magazine poster designed by **Stefania Malmsten** and **Lars Sundh**, photograph by **Andrew Catlin** 119. *Option* cover by **Joseph Cultace** 125. *Select* cover by **Ripley** 125. *Jockey Slut* cover by **Ripley** 128. *Raygun* cover by **Guy Aroch** 133. *CMJ* cover by **Joseph Cultace** 133. *Jockey Slut* cover by **Simon King** 170. *Time Out* cover by **Tom Dunkley** 170. *The Big Issue* cover by **Andy Cotterill** 245. *Muzik* cover by **Jason Bell** 245.

Additional Credits

Brotherhood artwork 7. Deconstruction Records sleeve artwork 23, 46. *Exit Planet Dust* artwork 89. *Dig Your Own Hole* artwork 114–5. *Come With Us* artwork 204–5. *Singles 93–03* artwork 210, 211. 'Galvanize' inner sleeve artwork 216. *Further* inner sleeve artwork 229, 230. *Further* artwork 234. *Don't Think* artwork 246–253. Bear featuring *Born in the Echoes* artwork 268. *No Geography* artwork 296. *For That Beautiful Feeling* artwork 310. Poster design: Adam Smith & Marcus Lyall 269. 'Electronic: From Kraftwerk to The Chemical Brothers' poster, London Design Museum 275. 02 poster: creative direction by Smith & Marcus Lyall; design/layout Hingston Studio 288. 'No Reason' visual sketches by Adam Smith & Marcus Lyall 78, 79. 'Dissolve' visuals: creative direction by Smith & Marcus Lyall, design/layout Hingston Studio 229, 230. 'Got to Keep On' visuals by Adam Smith & Marcus Lyall 294–5. Flyers and memorabilia courtesy of Tom Rowlands, Ed Simons, Fleet River Management and Nick Dutfield 16, 35, 39, 40, 41, 55, 130–1, 134, 136, 148-9, 155, 193, 299. Bugged Out! and Drum flyers courtesy of Johnno Burgess 132, 137. Kate Gibb artwork 152, 162, 164–5, 166, 167 168, 169, 202, 203 204–5, 210, 210, 228. 'Out of Control' storyboards by Mark Bristol courtesy of WIZ 176, 177. *Hanna* poster courtesy of Alamy/ PictureLux / The Hollywood Archive 258. 'We've Got to Try' storyboards courtesy of Ninian Doff 292. *The Dial-A-Poem Poets* LP Cover (1972) courtesy of the John Giorno Foundation 298.

Use of lyrics courtesy of BMG Rights Management (UK) Limited.

Singles

'Leave Home', 'Life Is Sweet',
'Loops of Fury', 'Setting Sun',
'Block Rockin' Beats', 'Elektrobank'
Design by Negativespace

'Hey Boy Hey Girl', 'Let Forever Be',
'Out of Control', 'Music: Response',
'It Began in Afrika', 'Star Guitar',
'Come with Us'/'The Test'
Design by Big Active
Artwork by Kate Gibb

'The Golden Path', 'Get Yourself High'
Design by Blue Source

'Galvanize', 'Believe', 'The Boxer'
Art direction by Tappin Gofton
Design by Kim Tang, Big Active

'Do It Again', 'The Salmon Dance',
'Midnight Madness'
Art direction by Tappin Gofton, Big Active
Artwork by Kate Gibb

'Escape Velocity', 'Swoon'
Creative direction by Smith & Lyall
Design: Hingston Studio
Stills photography: Jez Tozer

'Another World'
Image by Smith & Lyall
Sleeve design: Hingston Studio

'Go'
Design and art direction: Hingston Studio
Cover art: Fabric design 1843.
The National Archives, Kew

'C-H-E-M-I-C-A-L'
Design and art direction: Hingston Studio
Original photograph: © Magnum Photos

'Free Yourself', 'MAH'
Design: Hingston Studio

'Got to Keep On'
Image by Smith & Lyall
Photo credit: Tony Pletts
Sleeve design: Hingston Studio

'The Darkness That You Fear'
Cover art: Sir Terry Frost RA (Black Sun, 1978)
© Estate of Sir Terry Frost RA
Sleeve design: Hingston Studio

'No Reason'
Image by Smith & Lyall
Sleeve design: Hingston Studio

Albums

Exit Planet Dust (1995)
Design by Anthony Sweeny and Mark Bown
Negativespace

Dig Your Own Hole (1997)
Design by Anthony Sweeny and Mark Bown
Negativespace

Surrender (1999)
Design by Big Active
Artwork by Kate Gibb

Come with Us (2002)
Design by Big Active
Artwork by Kate Gibb

Push the Button (2005)
Art direction by Tappin Gofton
Design by Kim Tang, Big Active

We Are the Night (2007)
Art direction by Tappin Gofton, Big Active
Kate Gibb (Screen Print)

Brotherhood (2008)
Art direction by Tappin Gofton, Big Active
Kate Gibb (Screen Print)

Further (2010)
Creative direction: Smith & Lyall
Design: Hingston Studio
Stills photography: Jez Tozer

Don't Think (2012)
Creative direction: Smith & Lyall
Design: Hingston Studio
Stills photography: Tony Pletts

Born in the Echoes (2015)
Design and art direction: Hingston Studio
Cover art: Fabric design 1843.
The National Archives, Kew

No Geography (2019)
Design: Hingston Studio
Original cover concept: Kevin Godley

For That Beautiful Feeling (2023)
Design and art direction: Hingston Studio
Cover art: Nicholas Krushenick, courtesy of the estate of
Nicholas Krushenick and Garth Greenan Gallery, New York

Robin Turner is the author of *Believe in Magic: 30 Years of Heavenly Recordings*. He is one of the people behind the Heavenly Sunday Social and the Social bar in London and was one of the original editors of the Caught by the River website.

Paul Kelly is a film-maker, photographer and designer. Other books he has designed include *Believe in Magic: 30 Years of Heavenly Recordings* and *Fender: The Golden Age 1946–1970*.

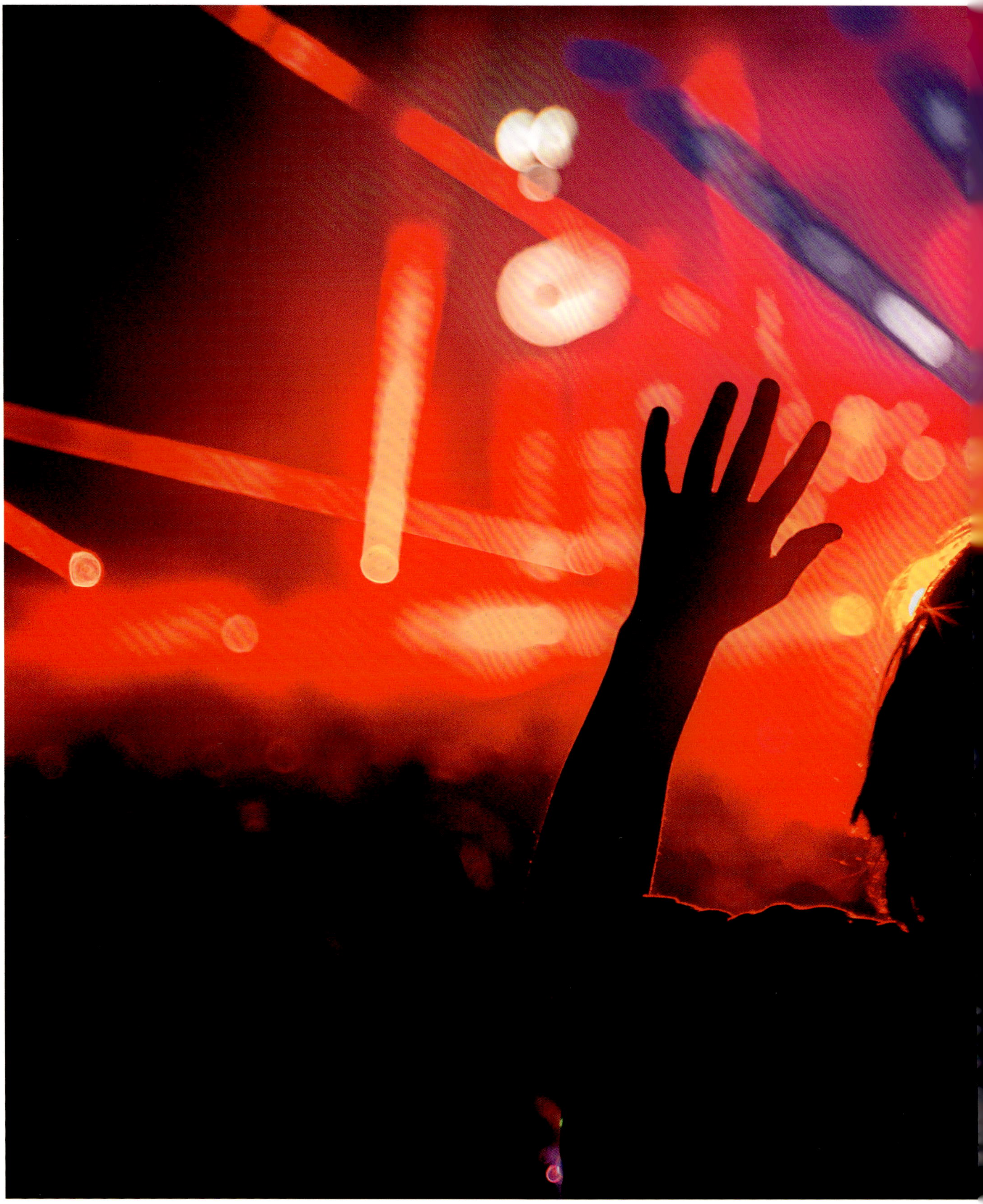

Paused in Cosmic Reflection

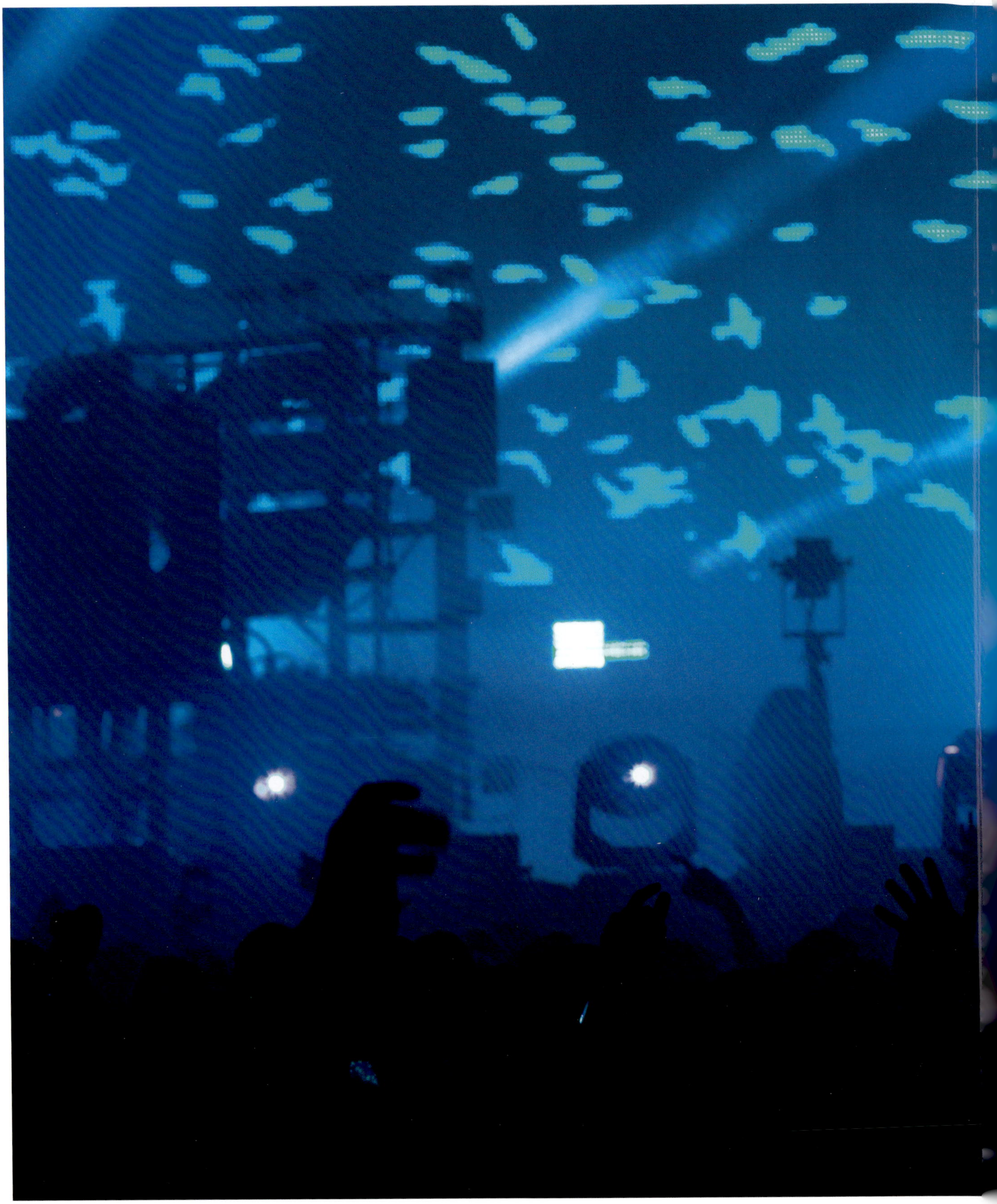

Paused in Cosmic Reflection 335